Mark Hollingsworth

The Press and Political Dissent

Pluto Press

First published in 1986 by Pluto Press Limited,
The Works, 105a Torriano Avenue, London NW5 2RX
and Pluto Press Australia Limited, PO Box 199, Leichhardt,
New South Wales 2040, Australia. Also Pluto Press,
27 South Main Street, Wolfeboro, 894-2069 USA

7 6 5 4 3 2 1

90 89 88 87 86

Set by Boldface Typesetters, London EC1
Printed in Great Britain by Cox & Wyman Ltd.
Reading, Berks.

British Library Cataloguing in Publication Data

Hollingsworth, Mark
   The press and political dissent: a
   question of censorship.
   1.   Press and politics – Great Britain
   I.   Title
   070.4′49320941   PN5124.P6

ISBN 0 7453 0139 8

Contents

Acknowledgements

This book is an attack neither on the profession of journalism nor on the abilities of individual reporters. Far from it. It is, however, a critical investigation of many newspapers and their editorial management. I have been pleasantly surprised, in fact, that concern about the lack of political diversity, the power of the press barons and their disregard for editorial independence, is shared by many, many journalists. Unfortunately, given the attitude of management, most of the journalists and subeditors I interviewed would do so only on the condition of anonymity.

However, there are a number of people whom I can thank by name. I am particularly grateful to Philip Braithwaite from Birmingham CND. His help was invaluable in uncovering the truth about the press coverage of the demonstration by Greenham peace women against Michael Heseltine in Newbury in February 1983. Without his highly meticulous and diligent checking and letter writing, my analysis of this scandal would have lacked much of its substance. I am also grateful to Daphne Francis for her help regarding the Heseltine protest, particularly concerning the Press Council hearings. In addition, Carola Addington and many Greenham peace women were kind enough to lend me their personal cuttings and papers.

I would also like to thank Peter Court for allowing me to publish his remarkable *Sun* diary which I used for the chapter on racism. Tony Benn was particularly generous and hospitable in permitting me access to his personal cuttings and other files.

The staff at Holborn, Westminster and Colindale reference libraries certainly deserve a vote of thanks for putting up with my persistent requests for back copies of newspapers. As does the staff of the Commission for Racial Equality Library and the Press Council. I am also indebted to Davy Jones and Lesley Wood from the Campaign for Press and Broadcasting Freedom for their help and encouragement.

I would like to thank the following for agreeing to be interviewed: Joe Ashton, Tom Baistow, Francis Beckett, Tony Benn, Anthony Bevins, Bernard Brook-Partridge, Paul Brown, Paul Burnell, Nita

Clarke, Veronica Crichton, David Dubow, Oliver Duke, Michael Foot, Monica Foot, Jonathan Fryer, Rodney Gent, Geoffrey Goodman, Peter Grimsditch, Joe Haines, Keith Harper, Margaret van Hattam, Pat Healy, Eric Heffer, Christopher Hird, Jim Innes, Derek Jameson, Helen John, Peter Kellner, Michael Kemp, Martin Kettle, Louis Kirby, Martin Linton, John Lloyd, Suzanne Lowry, Andrew Lumsden, Donald Macintyre, Sir Tom McCaffrey, Chris McLaughlin, Michael Meacher, Jim Mortimer, Nell Myers, Andrew Neil, Terry Pattinson, Tully Potter, Mike Power, Peter Robinson, David Rose, Paul Routledge, Tony Sheldon, Joan Smith, Pat Smith, Jean Stead, Peter Tatchell, Walter Terry, John Torode, George Tremlett, Lloyd Turner, John Warwicker, Aidan White, Arthur Williamson and Malcolm Withers.

In addition, I received help from: Frank Allaun; Steve Boulton, Laurie Flynn, Tricia Lawton and Jan Elson (Granada Television); John Brown (*Sun* NGA), Duncan Campbell (*City Limits*), Harold Evans, Paul Foot, Alan Jones (North Wales NUM), Nicholas Jones, Denis MacShane, Chris Mullin, John Pilger and Caroline Rees.

But I owe my greatest debt to the countless journalists, subeditors, printworkers and executives who provided crucial information and leads during my research. I cannot name them for obvious reasons but their help was indispensable.

Finally, I would like to thank Paul Crane for commissioning this book. Also my editor Neil Middleton. When I first had the idea for this book in the autumn of 1983 he generously provided me with invaluable advice despite the fact that he was not, at that time, working for Pluto Press. Lastly, my parents who put up with me over Christmas and the New Year while I wrote this book and whose encouragement and advice I have always valued.

Mark Hollingsworth

For Theresa

'Not the violent conflict between parts of the truth, but the quiet suppression of half of it, is the formidable evil. There is always hope when people are forced to listen to both sides.'

John Stuart Mill, 'On Liberty'

Introduction: Fleet Street—The Pursuit of Power

'I believe that the suggestion of editorial independence is a romantic myth dreamed up by editors. There is no doubt in my mind at all that proprietors who, having spent a great deal of money on a newspaper, at the very least will not allow it to express views consistently with which which they strongly disagree. Editors would rapidly find that if they wanted to do otherwise, they would be looking for a new job.' Lord Richard Marsh of Mannington, Chairman of the Newspaper Publishers Association since 1975, *The Press Barons*, BBC World Service, 23 December 1984.

'You can just take my word for it. There are no poor in this country.' Lord Victor Matthews, then Deputy Chairman of Trafalgar House and Chairman of Express Group Newspapers, owners of the *Daily Express*, *London Evening Standard*, *Daily Star* and *Sunday Express*, during telephone conversation with Peter Grimsditch, editor of the *Daily Star*, 12 June 1979.

Between 1945 and 1979 the language of political debate in Britain was relatively restricted within what became known as the Butskellite consensus. The political and economic institutions remained largely intact, despite the rotation of governments. There may have been occasional attempts at redistributions of wealth and ministerial asides about the unacceptable face of capitalism, but the foundations of the free market economy and the liberal democratic state were well preserved. Class divisions were said to be 'out of date' (*Daily Express* [1]) and a diversion from what Britain's national newspapers saw as 'the national interest' [2] Society was like a giant locomotive engine. It required regular repair and continuous supervision in the interests of efficiency, but its basic overall design was regarded as quite satisfactory. As agents of this machine, the national newspapers became its mechanics.

Differences of opinion and dissent were not allowed to escalate and endanger the smooth running of the engine and hence the stability of the political consensus was maintained. As a *Daily Express* editorial declared in December 1973: 'It is clear that the "them" and "us" attitude in Britain today is wholly, permanently and dangerously out of date . . . It is Mr Heath's job to spell out the national objectives. These objectives would be the same whichever party holds power: to pretend otherwise is to play a silly political game'.[3] The *Daily Mail* agreed: 'We want a nationally minded government which puts the national interest first every time'.[4]

However, by the late 1970s it was becoming clear that the old establishment engine was not only gathering rust but in danger of breaking down completely. A quick service of the machine was no longer good enough. It was unable to cope with the problems of high unemployment, rising inflation, lack of capital investment and industrial disruption. The consensus had broken down.

The undermining of the political, economic and cultural establishment had in fact been simmering since 1968 – the year of student unrest. New forms of protest and radical ideas had sprung to the surface. The traditional style of machine party politics was being swept away. Instead, tension replaced stagnation, conflict was substituted for compromise. Confrontation was seen as the only way of achieving real political and social change. The subsequent protest came from the voices of the unheard. Many people felt that there was an enormous gap between the politicians' interpretation of the crisis and what they could actually feel and see for themselves.

People were angry. After the smoke and fire of the spirit of 1968 had cleared, new political and social forces emerged. Black people were campaigning against job discrimination, racial attacks and harassment – but using much more militant methods. Women were reacting after decades of being portrayed as purely sexual objects and childbearers, devoid of professional independence and social identity. The peace movement was reborn after the government's decision to allow American cruise missiles on British soil. But instead of violent protest, feminist and anti-nuclear campaigners turned to peaceful, direct action which became personified by the Greenham Common peace camp. The cultural backlash also involved gay men and lesbians protesting more vigorously against harassment and discrimination. The issue of gay rights was never more prominent than during the controversy surrounding Peter Tatchell's candidature for the Bermondsey parliamentary by-election.

The late 1970s also saw more militant forms of industrial action by trade unionists, with the collapse of the Social Contract and the 'Winter of Discontent'. By the early 1980s the erosion of Britain's manufacturing industrial base had led to large-scale redundancies and closures. The 1984–5 miners' strike was seen by many as the trade union movement's 'Waterloo' in the struggle against mass unemployment.

By the early 1980s this 'Rainbow Coalition' of peace activists, women, blacks, gay people and trade unionists were venting their anger inside the Labour Party. They felt betrayed by past Labour governments and they wanted radical change. For many of these disgruntled and disenfranchized people, Ken Livingstone's GLC administration was providing a blueprint at local government level for their aspirations. At parliamentary level, Tony Benn was undoubtedly their representative and articulated their ideas, and the 1983 general election was seen as the great opportunity to secure a mandate for those policies.

Like any radical movement in a democracy, the 'Rainbow Coalition' needed their voices to be heard by the mass of the population if they were to have any real impact. However, in recent years their voices have been effectively muzzled. Britain's national newspapers have simply refused to accept that anyone with views to the left of James Callaghan or Harold Wilson is politically legitimate. And so Fleet Street's response to the radical 'Rainbow Coalition' has been to suppress, distort or ridicule their ideas and policies. The press's violent reaction against the Rainbow Coalition has not been merely to restore the old centre of British politics – stretching from the Left of the Tory Party to Labour's Rightwing. Most of Fleet Street – *Daily Express*, *Sun*, *Daily Mail* and their Sunday sister papers – have actually attacked the Left from a rightwing ideological view. As Hugo Young, the award-winning columnist and former political editor and joint deputy editor of the *Sunday Times*, concluded in March 1984:

Taken as a whole, the press is massively biased in one direction. In the last three years, it has become distinctly more so. Not only has detachment been devalued and politicization increased, but the process is all one way – with strange results, both politically and commercially.

At the very time when politics is becoming more open, fissiparous and diverse, the press becomes more narrow, monolithic and doctrinaire. There are invaluable exceptions, but they are becoming fewer. While political life, from the far Left to the middle of the Tory Party, teems with uncertainty and debate, it is to the remaining fragment of the spectrum, on the heavy Right, that most papers of all qualities are now unflinchingly committed ... It fails to reflect and assist in the debate about the future of the British Left – that is anything to the left of Mrs Thatcher. It is generally so preoccupied with reinforcing everything the government is trying to do that all activity is assessed by its helpfulness to that enterprise. Most press criticism of Mrs Thatcher, indeed, comes from the right not the left of her.[5]

And while the Right's critique of the post-consensus crisis has been given a free ride by Fleet Street, the Left's solutions have been given rather different scrutiny. The 'Rainbow Coalition' has not even been attacked as a genuine set of proposals. Instead, their challenge to the establishment has been portrayed as a sinister, subversive conspiracy of the consensus. For the press, they have ventured outside the traditional structures of society, left the 'normal' arena of politics and entered an almost criminal world of disruption and anarchy. In effect, Fleet Street have decided that the Left's analysis and prescriptions are not legitimate.

In the Soviet Union such critics of the existing state and ideology are dismissed as irrational eccentrics and intellectual misfits. Their beliefs are portrayed as symptoms of a 'mania for subversion' and 'reformist delusions'. Leading Soviet psychiatrists call it 'schitzo-dissent'.[6]

Is this so different from press coverage of Britain's dissenters? The aim of this book is to provide factual evidence that the broad perception of this country's radicals and dissenters by our national newspapers is very similar indeed. After all, they are stigmatized as irrational and unrepresentative, and their motives are questioned. Their alternative explanations of political and social realities are reported in terms of the personal quirks of a few individuals rather than a reasoned critique. Their views are presented as 'extreme' or 'Red' or 'hard-line', somehow dangerous. Such an aura of sceptical denigration has led almost inevitably to Britain's radicals being marginalized on the political agenda. They are seen, in effect, as being beyond the pale.

However, this marginalization has also enabled the press to use groups in society as a way of deflecting responsibility for social and economic problems. In other words, blame the crisis on the enemy within. This is the notion of the rotating scapegoat: Crime? Blame the blacks. Unemployment? Blame the scroungers. Inflation? Blame the unions. Permissive society? Blame the teachers. Miners' strike? Blame Arthur Scargill. Division in the Labour Party? Blame Tony

~ high degree of personalization which has little to do
~ccessible, readable or factually accurate. By
~ns of people, the press can sidestep

the problem of overt political bias. The papers don't say, for example, that it's ludicrous to have workers' control in factories. They declare it is dictatorial for Benn or Scargill to suggest such a policy. This has ensured that the political debate is curtailed within a presupposed framework of what is acceptable. The agenda is largely confined to a parliamentary beauty contest over which group of individuals is best capable of managing and maintaining the current socio-economic system. In effect, sources of knowledge are being hijacked.

Attacks on individuals for political aims are, of course, not a new phenomenon. As Neal Ascherson, the *Observer*'s chief foreign correspondent, has pointed out

Northcliffe and his like ran vicious slander campaigns against individuals, but their victims were much of their own weight: generals, Cabinet ministers, party chieftains. Press bullying today is different. It arises from the dogma of 'consensus', which in its turn is another aspect of the whole system's loss of self-confidence . . . Scargill, Benn, Ken Livingstone, even the pathetic Peter Tatchell, are harassed and hounded with a venom and persistence which have no justification and no precedent. Well, perhaps one precedent. When the rightwing press launched the New Bullying some ten years ago by encouraging citizens to take private vengeance against the power workers, they were acting in the tradition of Horatio Bottomley's call in the First World War for the persecution of those with German names – 'The fabric of our society is under threat'.[7]

The significance given to personalities is certainly not reflected in the way the electorate view politics. Take the 1945 general election. Labour's leader, Clement Attlee, had the personal charisma of an average tax collector, while the Tory Party's Winston Churchill had Hollywood-style popularity throughout the country. Yet the Labour Party won the election with a massive majority of 145 seats. More recently, Harold (now Lord) Wilson and James Callaghan were both more popular than their Conservative counterparts, Edward Heath and Margaret Thatcher, in the 1970 and 1979 elections. Yet Labour lost both polls. And for years the Liberal Party leader, David Steel, has had the highest personal ratings but the Liberals have never even come close to winning a general election. The reason for this apparent paradox is that, while leadership is obviously important, people vote largely on the issues, the incumbent government's record and traditional party loyalties. They don't vote on the basis of personalities. This was confirmed after the 1983 general election when a March poll revealed that 66 per cent of the sample said they were most influenced by party policies.[8] As Lord Beaverbrook once remarked: 'The truth is that people do not care very much who sits in the Cabinet room so long as success presides over the battlefield.'[9]

Some political journalists freely admit that they are not concerned about policies. The former *Observer* political columnist, Hugh Massingham, stated openly that he was not interested in the issues. When negotiations for Britain to enter the Common Market began in 1961, Massingham told a friend: 'I can't possibly write about that sort of thing.'[10] Alan Watkins, the current *Observer* columnist, takes a similar line: 'Nor is there any need to apologize for thinking that image is more important than policy ... When you hear a politician say, "Let's concentrate on policies," you may be fairly sure he is up to no good.'[8]

Nevertheless, it would be quite wrong and misleading to suggest that personalities and individuals don't matter in the coverage of politics. 'You can't discuss political issues without personalities,' said Geoffrey Goodman, former industrial editor of Mirror Group papers, 'I don't think it's possible.' Strictly speaking, he is correct. The Cabinet system of government, for example, relies heavily on the patronage of the Prime Minister, and so clearly he or she has enormous power to shape an administration in their own image.

There is also the fact that in the popular press it is much easier to portray political events, issues and ideas in terms of the leading protagonists than discuss them in purely abstract terms. The average reader can identify with unemployment much more easily if he reads about an individual's experiences rather than having to interpret a stream of statistics or economic dogma. In addition, there are the professional criteria for what constitutes a news story. According to Harold Evans, former editor of the *Times* and *Sunday Times*, 'News is people. It is people talking and planning decisions. They are only news because they affect people.'[12] And in their basic training, journalists are encouraged by their editors to look for five basic ingredients when writing a news story – conflict, hardship and danger to the community, novelty, scandal and individualism.[13] Consequently, to some extent at ···t reporters will tend to look upon personalities rather than broader ···he substance of a news story.

···annot be argued that character assassination of leading ···bour Party activists is born out of misplaced pro-···rnalistic ignorance, as some maintain. ···cept of the rotating scapegoat again. ···ement or organization can be reduced to 'Bennery' or 'Scargillism', then the public can perhaps be persuaded into thinking that only Benn or Scargill believe in such policy. Hence, they are unrepresentative and illegitimate, and their views are not to be taken seriously.

But why have Britain's national newspapers gone to so much trouble to gag and discredit the leading figures of many radical political movements, particularly when they lose readers by doing so? It cannot be for commercial reasons. After all, in 11 out of the 12 general elections since 1945, the number of Labour voters was far more than the editorial support the Labour Party received from Fleet Street. And despite the fact that the Conservative vote has fallen since 1959, press support for the Tories has steadily increased. In the 1983 general election, the Conservative Party received 44 per cent of the vote and yet they were given 74 per cent of the national daily circulation support by the press. On specific issues, not one national newspaper has called for the withdrawal of American cruise missiles from Britain. And yet every opinion poll since 1983 has confirmed that the majority of British people, usually between 55 and 65 per cent, oppose the siting of US cruise missiles in the UK.

Since the press clearly do not reflect and represent public opinion and many of the political views of the British people, today's proprietors must surely be concerned with other issues beyond the circulation war and the pursuit of profit. There must be other motives. The answer, I believe, lies in the ownership of Fleet Street. It is no coincidence that as the concentration of ownership has contracted, so the range of political views expressed in the press has narrowed.

Conflicts of interest

When Rupert Murdoch was asked in November 1977 whether newspaper companies should own outside commercial concerns, he replied: 'I don't think that a newspaper should own outside interests . . . By owning something outside journalism you lay yourself open to attack. And newspapers should be above that.'[14] Two years later, the proprietor of four British national papers with a circulation of 11.2 million had bought a 50 per cent (controlling) shareholding in Ansett Transport Industries. Murdoch now also has substantial interests in offshore oil and gas, warehousing, cable television, ranching and the cinema industry. He maintains that he doesn't use his papers to support his more lucrative commercial enterprises. 'Just look at the papers,' he said. 'I don't use influence like that.'[15]

However, there is growing evidence that in recent years some proprietors and their corporate management have, on occasions, used their newspapers to promote and protect their commercial activities. As the *Guardian* commented in September 1984: 'One of the traditions of British journalism is that the editorial content of a newspaper is independent of the activities of the groups which own them ... now it has been shattered.' But Robert Maxwell, publisher of Mirror Group papers, denies there are possible conflicts of interest between his commercial investments and the editorial content of his papers: 'Well, I haven't noticed the danger and neither has anybody else. If it has happened it would have been pointed out. There are a lot of busybodies around. They don't know what they're talking about ... We are the guarantees of the freedom of the press.'[16]

Maxwell and Murdoch will always deny the potential conflict of interests, but journalists argue that their proprietors' divergent business investments do result in self-censorship. As one senior *Standard* executive admitted: 'There's not a lot of point in sending a reporter to cover a story about the proprietor's building company knocking down a listed building in London when you know it's not going to get into the paper ... News editors and journalists will censor themselves.'[17] This was clearly a reference to the demolition in November 1985 of the Firestone building in West London by the construction company Trafalgar House. The *Standard* was then jointly owned by Trafalgar House and Associated Newspapers Ltd.

On other occasions editors or journalists are initially not aware of their owner's interests. In September 1974, the *Daily Mail* was in the midst of a campaign against the Labour government's nationalization policies, particularly North Sea oil – 'Harold's Plan To Grab North Sea Oil' ran one headline. A *Mail* executive decided to send a reporter, disguised as an ordinary labourer, on board a North Sea oil rig to expose the alleged bad and dangerous working conditions. However, the project was swiftly cancelled when it was pointed out to the editorial executive that the rig was owned by Blackfriars Oil, a subsidiary of the Associated News Group Ltd, owners and publishers of the *Daily Mail*. More important, in its first year of production Blackfriars made over £25 million profit.[18]

Perhaps the most graphic, and certainly the most publicized, example of a proprietor intervening in order to protect his investments came in April 1984. Tiny Rowland, Chairman of the *Observer* board, openly rebuked the paper's editor, Donald Trelford, for publishing a full-page report of alleged widespread assaults and murders by Robert Mugabe's Fifth Brigade in Matabeleland, the southern province of Zimbabwe. Rowland attacked the article – 'Agony of a Lost People' –

as 'discourteous, disingenuous and wrong'. He threatened to either close down the paper, sell it or sack Trelford. Rowland's company, Lonrho International, earns £15 million of its annual profits in Zimbabwe. The *Observer*'s proprietor is also the largest private employer of black labour in the country: Lonrho owns ten companies in Zimbabwe, with interests ranging from gold and copper mining, transport and textiles to wattle growing and processing.

Before Lonrho bought the *Observer* in 1981, their bid was referred to the Monopolies Commission. In his submission, Trelford said that nothing in Rowland's record suggested that he was capable of restraint when his interests were at stake. He referred to a previous *Observer* article on Zimbabwe and asked, 'Could Rowland have kept out of that dispute, with so much at stake for himself and his company?' His answer was, 'It seems unlikely.' Trelford concluded: 'For Rowland to grant the *Observer* editorial independence would be to give one of his own companies carte blanche to damage the whole business to which he has devoted his life. It is as illogical as it is unbelievable.'[19] Rowland was asked by the Monopolies Commission whether there was not a risk that Lonrho might occasionally have to choose between restraining the *Observer* or endangering their commercial interests in parts of Africa. He assured the Commission 'on behalf of Lonrho that it would not impose any limits on the *Observer* whatever the cost'.

When the paper was eventually bought by Lonrho, the government imposed a series of guarantees to safeguard its editorial independence. One of the conditions, incorporated in the controlling company's articles of association, was the following clause: 'The editor of the *Observer* shall retain control over any political comment published in the newspaper, and shall not be subject to any restraint or inhibition in expressing opinion or in reporting news that might directly or indirectly conflict with the opinion or interest of any of the newspaper proprietors of the *Observer*.'

However, an early warning that Lonrho's guarantees were far from watertight came when the *Observer*'s staff met Rowland for the first time in November 1981. The paper's proprietor became involved in an argument about Tanzania and asked them: 'I want to know to what extent I could ask for support from the *Observer* . . . In these particular circumstances could I have counted on your support?' One reporter replied: 'Surely the point about editorial independence is that you – the owners – can't count on anything at all.'[20]

In less than two years Rowland's promises and Lonrho's guarantees were put to the test. In July 1983, without consulting Trelford, Rowland hired Godwin Matatu, a Zimbabwean journalist and political editor of *Africa* magazine, as the *Observer*'s roving Africa correspondent. However, Matatu is more than just a journalist. He is a relation of Dr Eddison Zvobgo, Zimbabwe Minister of Legal Affairs, and also employs Dr Zvobgo's son in his office. Matatu is also employed by Lonrho as a political consultant and mediator to smooth relations between Rowland and Robert Mugabe (Rowland had backed Joshua Nkomo during the Zimbabwe elections). When Rowland appointed Matatu as Africa correspondent, with his wages paid by Lonrho, the *Observer* staff were furious. The foreign editor resigned and the editorial staff blacked Matatu's copy. Eventually a compromise was negotiated by Trelford that avoided a full-scale conflict. But Matatu was still hired as Africa correspondent despite the objections of Richard Hall, the paper's highly experienced Africa and Commonwealth correspondent. Ironically, Hall had been one of Rowland's strongest supporters when he gave evidence to the Monopolies and Mergers Commission. 'I can't deny being disappointed with Tiny Rowland over the incident,' said Hall. 'I feel it personally after having been a leading supporter [of Rowland] in front of the Monopolies Commission . . . I think we're all a bit wiser now and a bit sadder.'[21]

But the real showdown came six months later when Trelford published his article on 15 April 1984 concerning atrocities in Zimbabwe. Early on the Saturday afternoon, the day before publication, Rowland telephoned Trelford. According to the *Observer*'s editor, his proprietor threatened to close down the newspaper in an attempt to prevent publication of the report. This is Trelford's account of their telephone conversation:

> Rowland: I hear you're trying to destroy my business in Zimbabwe.
> Trelford: The last thing I want to do is cause any embarrassment to you or your company, but the story I found in Matabeleland seems to me to be one that should be reported.
> Rowland: If you damage my Zimbabwe interest, I may have to sell my newspapers because I won't be able to afford to keep them. You should think about the consequences.
> Trelford: I have my job to do – to tell the truth as I see it.
> Rowland: You have your job and I have mine. You must expect me to protect myself.

Rowland denies that he referred to Lonrho's business interests during their conversation: 'I have never once mentioned our commercial interests to him in the two-and-a-half years we have owned the paper.' Rowland also said that Trelford told him: 'My story won't do Lonrho any good. On the other hand, it won't do any harm because it

will confirm that the *Observer* has complete editorial independence.'
Rowland said that he replied: 'I'm not worried about your story
harming us in Africa because we've been trading there for many years.
We're at home in Africa. I'm only worried about the *Observer*'.[22]

The following morning (Sunday), Rowland cabled a letter to Robert
Mugabe apologizing for the article and describing his editor's conduct
as 'discourteous, disingenuous and wrong'. Later that evening, 15
April, Paul Spicer, a Lonrho director, said that the *Observer* was 'a
monster out of control, being paid for by us and our shareholders. It
costs money to keep the *Observer* going and the people down there
think they can do whatever they like'.[23] On 18 April, Rowland wrote to
Trelford and told him that his position 'doesn't mean that you could,
or should, have licence to lead the paper where you like, or change its
balanced character as if you were the owner-editor.' He added that the
article was 'based on unsubstantiated, unresearched material' and that
Trelford had been 'in repeated collusion with a very junior *Sunday
Times* reporter Peter Godwin.' Trelford replied that it was ludicrous
to suggest that his story had come from the *Sunday Times*: 'Our
sources were totally independent.' This was backed up by Godwin
himself: 'I felt I had a fairly hard story and I wasn't anxious to give him
too much help, even background information, at that stage ... It would
be quite wrong to say that we exchanged information. The suggestion
that I fixed up Donald Trelford's meetings is utter rubbish. Why on
earth would I do that for my direct rival?'[24] Rowland then withdrew all
Lonrho advertising from the *Observer*, worth about £20,000 a week,
and had a working breakfast with Robert Maxwell at the Claridges
Hotel on 23 April to discuss the possible sale of the paper.

The *Observer*'s journalists, meanwhile, unanimously backed Trelford and called for a meeting with the five independent directors.[25]
They urged the independent directors to consider whether Rowland's
remarks constituted proprietorial interference in breach of the articles
of association which were drawn up when Lonrho bought the paper.
The five independent directors talked with both sides and then issued a
stinging rebuke to Rowland for 'improper proprietorial interference' in
editorial freedom. They also said that Trelford had their 'full support
in vigorously maintaining his editorial freedom and defending his
professional integrity'.[26] Some of the directors also acted as mediators
between Rowland and Trelford and eventually a truce was resolved.
On 28 April 1984, Trelford wrote to Rowland offering to resign and
added: 'I accept that you acted as you did, not out of a crude concern
for your commercial interests, as I originally suggested, but out of a
genuine personal conviction that the truth about Zimbabwe is more

complex than I presented it.' Rowland had also changed his mind and replied: 'I support your editorship and I refuse to accept your resignation. The arm's-length arrangement made three years ago, when five national directors were appointed to the board, left me the only option of expressing my indignation publicly ... It seems to me an absolute demonstration of your integrity and care for the paper that, although there is no need for you to offer your resignation, you have done so.' There has always been a potential for conflict between a newspaper and its owner's business interests. But as the power of proprietors has increased, so their commercial investments have expanded. And so a conflict is increasingly likely. But what is more disturbing is that there is evidence that the press barons are using their newspapers actively to promote these interests. Never was this more apparent than the press coverage of the BBC during 1985.

The attacks on the BBC began in January 1985, during the corporation's negotiations for an increased licence fee, and were sustained throughout the year. On 14 January 1985, the *Times* published the first of three successive leading articles extolling the virtues of advertising and the need for deregulation of the BBC: 'The BBC is today accused of inefficiency, unaccountability, self-aggrandisement and feather-bedding its employees ... Are the critics justified? In their main principles: yes.' The next day Labour MP Joe Ashton launched his private member's bill calling for advertising on the BBC. That morning the *Times'* editorial was headlined – 'Wither The BBC' – and called for the breaking-up of the corporation: 'Advertisers can clearly pay some part in generating the revenue to pay for many programmes ... We need a more open, less monolithic system of broadcasting in which customers can choose what qualities they want from their TV screens.' The next day the *Times* thundered again at its 1,300,000 readers: 'Lord Annan's Committee recommended a break-up of the BBC into its radio, TV and local radio components. The government should now prepare to go further than this. It should consider quickly the establishment of a new broadcasting commission to auction franchises that are currently operated by the BBC.'

Now, what the *Times* fails to tell its readers is who will directly benefit if these franchises are auctioned. At the front of the queue will be a certain R. Murdoch, proprietor of the *Times*, who will benefit commercially if the BBC is broken up. Murdoch's company, News International, owns Sky Channel – a cable and satellite operation which transmits 73 hours a week of alternative television and has three million subscribers in 11 countries. In 1983 Murdoch also took control of Satellite TV, Sky's parent company, at a cost of £5 million and has a 75.5 per cent shareholding. Satellite began transmitting in 1982, beaming English-language programmes to Norway and Finland for two hours a night. In 1985 the *Times'* owner acquired the biggest stake in 20th Century Fox to provide films for his satellite Sky channel to beam across Europe. Clearly, if even parts of the BBC are privatized, these Murdoch-owned companies will make a lot of money.

Murdoch's views on the BBC are quite clear. 'I would like to see it privatized,' he said in November 1985. But this was not just his private opinion. According to the *Mirror*'s Paul Foot, Murdoch 'has personally ordered a sustained attack on the BBC and all its people'.[27] Alastair Hetherington, former editor of the *Guardian* added weight to this assertion when he accused the *Times* of conducting 'a vendetta against the BBC in its leaders, news stories and features'.[28] This is certainly borne out by the evidence. The *Times* published at least eight anti-BBC editorials throughout 1985. The paper also published a series of news reports, often based on the thinnest material, which suggested extravagance and incompetence among BBC management. 'BBC Condemned As Licence Fee Monster' was the headline for one story which was merely a report of an article by an obscure ex-BBC employee in a trade journal.

Moreover, when angry readers have written to complain about the coverage or offer an alternative point of view, the *Times* have refused to publish their letters. This was revealed by Paul Fox, Managing Director of Yorkshire Television. On 2 November 1985, the *Times* published another leader attacking the BBC, the IBA and ITV companies and misquoted comments that Fox had made about public service broadcasting. Fox wrote to the paper to set the record straight about his misrepresented remarks, but his letter was not published. Three days later, on 5 November 1985, David Plowright, the Managing Director of Granada TV and Chairman of the ITV Companies Association, also wrote to the *Times* to complain about a front-page news report of a MORI opinion poll on advertising on the BBC. In his letter, Plowright pointed out that the *Times* opinion poll showed that more people were either 'very' or 'fairly' satisfied with the quality of TV in Britain than those who took the opposite view. How curious, wrote Plowright, that the paper's news story had failed to include these facts. The letter was not published and the issue was not corrected.[29]

The *Times* was not the only Murdoch paper to attack the BBC. His tabloids have joined in the fun. Here's the *Sun* on 23 January 1985: 'Oh, what superior people they are at the BBC. Here is the Director-General, Alastair Milne, raising his hands in horror at the idea of accepting adverts ... Just where is the BBC superior to the commercial channels ... There is only one area where the Beeb shines. No-one could possibly match its overbearing, totally unjustified smugness.' And again on 2 September 1985: 'The BBC should compete in the market so it ceases to be such a burden on the public.' The *Sun*'s sister paper, the *News of the World*, began its campaign a trifle later than most but soon made up for lost ground. Every week throughout April 1985 there was a news story about the expenses of BBC staff which were reaching 'scandal' proportions. The next month *News of the World* journalists were instructed to file detailed reports of the eating and drinking habits of fellow reporters on the BBC during a royal tour. One brave woman journalist refused, because she said this was not her job. A *News of the World* executive then telephoned from London to accuse her of being disloyal. However, halfway through his lecture, the editorial executive was much dismayed to find that he had been put through by mistake to Kate Adey – a BBC television news reporter.[30]

Another press baron to benefit from any privatization of the BBC is Robert Maxwell, publisher of Mirror Group newspapers. In 1984 he bought control of Rediffusion Cablevision for a reported £9 million. In its first year of operation the company has expanded from 14 to 40 towns and has 100,000 subscribers who are offered more than 330 hours a week on the five channels. Maxwell is also the major shareholder in Mirrorvision, another cable TV company, and has bought into one of the pioneers of pay-television, Select-TV. He now owns the biggest existing cable system and its technical research division, plus a 13 per cent share in Central Independent TV.

Given this context, the *Mirror*'s reporting is revealing. This is how a *Daily Mirror* leader concluded on 4 March 1985: 'The government is right to be thinking very hard whether the BBC should continue to be financed at the expense of the viewing and listening public.' The following week, on 16 March 1985, the centre pages of the *Mirror* were devoted to a feature headlined – 'The World At The Touch of a Button'. Its subject? Cable television, particularly the benefits available to subscribers of a company called Rediffusion Cablevision. To be fair to Maxwell and the *Mirror*, the paper did, unlike the *Times*, declare its interest in the article. But it was still using the pages of a once-great and independent newspaper to crudely promote the business investments of its owner.

Perhaps the intrusion of commercial interests over editorial interests is the inevitable price of the power of Fleet Street proprietorship. Maybe it's a temporary phase, though I doubt it. As the American journalist Herbert Brucker once said: 'Self-government will be the more secure if the editorial page recovers the vigor and stature it had before the businessman took over from the editor as the top man in journalism.'

The advertisers – sanctions and boycotts

While a few newspapers like the *Guardian* are not influenced by the commercial interests or political ambitions of their proprietors, there are other financial pressures on editorial policy. One of these is the indirect, and occasionally direct, power and influence of advertisers. Tom Baistow, former *Daily Herald* and *News Chronicle* journalist, believes that 'The average Tory-supporting British industrialist would advertise in *Pravda* if they thought they could sell more goods.'[31] However, there is evidence that this is a much-exaggerated analysis, and that some advertisers will boycott radical publications for political and commercial reasons.

Discrimination by advertisers was far more prevalent during the 1940s and 1950s against papers like the pro-Liberal *Reynolds News* and pro-Labour *Daily Herald*. But in 1975 a potential advertiser told the *Scottish Daily News* (a radical paper run as a co-operative): 'I'm not going to support a newspaper which, the first time I get a strike, it will back the strike.' In 1978 Cunard, the shipping company, wrote to Sir William Rees-Mogg, then editor of the *Times*, and Harold Evans, then editor of the *Sunday Times*, complaining that they had offended 'the special relationship' between newspapers and advertisers. The two papers had published articles criticizing cruises on luxury liners which were owned by Cunard. When the critical articles continued, Cunard proceeded to withdraw £18,000 worth of advertising from the two papers. In addition, advertising agencies told the Royal Commissions on the Press in 1948 and 1978 that leftwing publications had sometimes been blacked for political reasons.

Advertising boycotts should come as no surprise. Private advertisers depend on and are heavily involved in the market economy and the free flow of capital. They are hardly likely to invest in and support any newspaper which actively campaigns to dismantle that economic system. The serious papers are particularly reliant on advertising revenue to cover their heavy production costs, because of relatively low circulations. As advertising revenue is also tax deductible, because many of the newspaper companies get tax allowances, this money is absolutely crucial to the papers' existence.

The loss of advertising revenue would be especially damaging to a paper like the *Guardian* which cannot make up the losses by subsidies from other profitable parts of its company. It can also be a factor in influencing the paper's political policy. On 10 August 1979, the *Guardian* published a statement in *Campaign*, the weekly magazine of the advertising industry, which declared that the paper is read by: 'The Thinking Rich . . . 85 per cent of them are ABC1 (social class) which is a better percentage than the *Financial Times* or *Daily Telegraph* can offer.' The statement also stressed that its readers 'were not down-at-heel extremists without a penny to bless themselves with . . . They have bank accounts full of lovely money.' Nearly two years later, in April 1981, the *Guardian*'s marketing strategy appeared not to have changed. Another *Campaign* message, under the name of Gerry Taylor, *Guardian*'s Managing Director, ran: 'To assume that the *Guardian* is only for leftwing trendies and drop-outs is as outdated a view as the dinosaur . . . If the newly constituted SDP really takes off, then the *Guardian* is ideally suited to champion the new party's cause as the centre-party voice in the 1980s.' The advertisement was taken from an article by a London advertising director, but it had clearly been sanctioned at the highest level by the *Guardian* management.

The press barons and editorial independence – promises, promises . . .

In a remarkably candid interview on the BBC World Service, Lord Marsh, Chairman of the Newspaper Publishers (Proprietors) Association, told how one Fleet Street proprietor had confided in him that the purchase of a newspaper 'was an expenditure on his public relations department and useful to have'.[32]

However, the evidence is that today's press barons are seeking a far more influential role for their products. According to Harold Evans, former editor of the *Times* and the *Sunday Times*: 'It's just like the 1930s again . . . and the political reality is that the press barons are seeking to use newspapers not simply for money-making but for exercizing personal power.'[33]

Evans' analysis has been proved correct by two acquisitions in Fleet Street in recent years. In January 1981 Rupert Murdoch bought the *Times* and *Sunday Times*, and in July 1984 Robert Maxwell paid £113 million for Mirror Group newspapers. If Murdoch was so cash-conscious he would never have bought the *Times* which has been losing millions of pounds for several years. And if Maxwell was so driven by the profit motive, why did he pay such an enormous amount for the Mirror Group, far more than the papers were worth? The answer lies in their pursuit of personal and political power, although allied with a strong will to protect and preserve their wide-ranging business investments.

The ownership of Fleet Street has become increasingly concentrated in fewer proprietorial hands. Five multimillionaires (Robert Maxwell, Rupert Murdoch, Tiny Rowland, David Stevens and Viscount Rothermere) control 84 per cent of the daily and 96 per cent of the Sunday newspaper circulation in Britain. According to 1983 ABC figures, Maxwell, Stevens and Murdoch have secured two-thirds of total daily and Sunday circulation. In 1948 the three biggest groups commanded only 48 per cent of the total circulation.[34]

Combined with this concentration of ownership, has been the buying up by proprietors of holdings and companies outside the newspaper business. They include extensive interests in oil, transport, mining and other media like cable TV, publishing and the cinema industry (see Appendix 1 for details). Newspapers are thus now part of huge multinational conglomerates. The traditional image of corporate management is often bland, profit-conscious and even cautious. Their political inclinations tend to be conservative rather than rightwing in the ideological sense. They would prefer not to 'rock the boat' politically, but will always be hostile to unofficial strikes and support management's 'right to manage'. However, Fleet Street's proprietors now operate in a political atmosphere where government decisions do affect their commercial interests. Politics do matter for the press barons.

The primary source of editorial and hence political power for the proprietor is through the appointment of the editor by the Chairman of the company's Board of Directors (the only exceptions being the *Observer* and the *Guardian* where there are wider consultations). The most lucid example of how this system operates was the appointment of Andrew Neil as editor of the *Sunday Times* by Murdoch in June 1983 after the retirement of Frank Giles. When Murdoch bought Times Newspapers two years earlier, he signed a number of editorial guarantees to reassure the staff who were concerned about his reputation for hiring and firing editors at will. One of these written commitments was that Murdoch should 'sound out' the views of his staff so they could have some influence over the choice of a new editor. The arrangement was that a journalist of 'independence and distinction' would join the board to represent his colleagues' point of view. Murdoch appointed Peter Roberts, the *Sunday Times* managing editor, who, though popular with the staff, was essentially a management man. However, when Giles announced his decision to retire as editor the scheduled 'consultation' never took place. Roberts later admitted that the paper's staff were not consulted because they would have preferred an internal candidate like Hugo Young, the joint deputy editor and political editor, who had been on the paper since 1966. This conflicted with Murdoch's choice of Andrew Neil, home affairs editor of the *Economist*, who was subsequently appointed. Most of the journalists had never even heard of Neil, let alone been consulted. Clearly, Roberts' powers were cosmetic. But this breach of the signed editorial guarantees was hardly surprising, given Murdoch's view that 'they're not worth the paper they're written on'.[35]

Neil's appointment was significant. He had had no previous experience on national newspapers and at 34 was the youngest editor in Fleet Street. But Murdoch knew that by giving someone like Neil the job he could ensure that his editorial line would be followed because the editor depended on his proprietor for his position. And he has been proved correct. Since Neil took over the *Sunday Times* editorship the paper has moved significantly to the right in its news and editorial columns.

As Neil himself told some of his staff at the Gay Hussar restaurant, Soho, in November 1983: 'Since I've become editor I've definitely taken the paper to the Right politically ... I've no interest in the *Sunday Times* becoming a pluralist paper.' Neil was more explicit in February 1985 when he said:

> There is an editorial college but I have placed a strong imprint on that college and the change in direction is almost entirely down to my own view of how things should be. Our paper is radical and anti-establishment, that sums up who we are. What that means in practice is that on microeconomic policy – we're in favour of competition, trust-busting, deregulation, privatization – we're on the radical Right. On macroeconomic policy – on the overall governing of economic policy – we take a view that is much closer to David Owen's.[36]

With such an editor at the helm, Murdoch could relax and look forward to every Sunday morning when his view of the world would be read in millions of households throughout the country.

However, when Murdoch was faced with an editor who didn't share his political views and wanted a semblance of independence, the situation changed dramatically. When he took over the *News of the World* in 1969, Murdoch told the incumbent editor, Stafford Somerfield: 'I didn't come all this way not to interfere.' According to Somerfield, the new proprietor 'wanted to read proofs, write a leader if he felt like it, change the paper about and give instructions to the staff'.[37] As the paper's long-serving editor, Somerfield was used to a fair amount of independence and he tried to resist Murdoch's interference. In 1970 Somerfield was dismissed by Murdoch.

A similar fate befell another *News of the World* editor a decade later. Barry Askew had been appointed by Murdoch in April 1981 after a successful career as the crusading editor of the *Lancashire Evening Post* during which he published a series of stories about corruption among local public officials and institutions. However, when Askew and the *News of the World* declined, like the *Times* under Harold Evans during the same period, to give the Conservative government unequivocal support, Murdoch took action. 'He [Murdoch] would come into the office,' said Askew, 'and literally rewrite leaders which were not supporting the hard Thatcher monetarist line. That were not, in fact, supporting – slavishly supporting – the Tory government'.[38]

Askew believes the big clash came over an exclusive story about John DeLorean, the car tycoon. A freelance journalist, John Lisners, had persuaded DeLorean's former secretary, Marian Gibson, to reveal details about her boss's business practices and alleged irregularities. It was a superb story, backed up by other sources and also cleared by Gibson's lawyer – Clarence Jones.

However, just after noon on Saturday 3 October 1981, Murdoch telephoned Askew, as he invariably did every week, to discuss the main stories. Askew told him about the DeLorean scoop and Murdoch appeared initially to be enthusiastic. Later that afternoon Murdoch arrived at the office in Bouverie Street and went straight to the 'backbench' to read the DeLorean material. One of the key sources was William Haddad, who had worked for Murdoch on the *New York Post*. On learning of Haddad's involvement, Murdoch said: 'He's a leftwing trouble-maker', although he later denied saying this. 'I may have referred to Bill's love of conspiracy theories.'[39]

Murdoch then consulted his legal advisers and they decided the story was legally unsafe. The story was killed. The next day the *Daily Mirror* published the same story on its front page and the rest of the media followed it up. Interestingly, according to Ivan Fallon and James Srodes' book *DeLorean*, it was Murdoch who arranged for Lord Goodman to act as DeLorean's lawyer to discourage the rest of Fleet Street from pursuing the story.[40] Within a year DeLorean's car firm was bankrupt. Within two months, in December 1981, Askew was dismissed and he returned to Lancashire a bitter man: 'I don't think Fleet Street gives a damn about ethics, morality or anything else. It gives a damn about attracting a readership that will attract an advertising situation which will make a profit which will make the press barons powerful politically.'[41]

But by far the most revealing example of Murdoch's desire to set the political line of his papers also came during 1981, when the Conservative government was very unpopular because of high unemployment. When Harold Evans was appointed editor of the *Times* in March 1981, he was given official guarantees by Murdoch about editorial freedom. On 23 January 1981, the new owner of Times Newspapers had given formal undertakings that 'In accordance with the traditions of the papers, their editors will not be subject to instruction from either the proprietor or the management on the selection and balance of news and opinion.'

Within a year, however, Evans had been dismissed, claiming he had been forced to resign over constant pressure by Murdoch to move the paper to the Right. Evans added: 'The *Times* was not notably hostile to the [Conservative] government but it wanted to be independent. But that was not good enough for Rupert Murdoch. He wanted it to be a cheerleader for monetarism and Mrs Thatcher.'[42] Murdoch denied the charge: 'Rubbish! Harry used to come and see me and say, "Rupert, it's wonderful to have you in town. What do you want me to say, what do you want me to do, just let me know."'[43] On this crucial point, Evans told me: 'Lie plus macho sneer with a useful ambiguity. It is a lie that I *ever* asked him what to say ... It is true that I asked his view from time to time on developments of the paper. The truth is that far from asking Murdoch "what to say", I followed an editorial policy often in opinion at variance with his own Thatcher-right-or-wrong view.'

The evidence certainly gives credence to Evans' interpretation of events, although he also fell out with some of the staff. According to leader writer Bernard Donoghue, features editor Anthony Holden and executive editor Brian Macarthur, there was political pressure on Evans because of what Mrs Thatcher called 'the *Times* centrist drift'.[44] When unemployment had reached three million in the summer of 1981 Murdoch and Gerald Long, Managing Director of Times Newspapers, wanted the *Times* to emphasize the number of people in work. Evans declined and Murdoch snapped at him: 'You're always getting at her [Mrs Thatcher].'[45] The *Times* editor and his proprietor continually argued over economic policy and on one occasion Evans received an extraordinary memorandum from Gerald Long: 'The Chancellor of the Exchequer says the recession has ended. Why are you having the effrontery in the *Times* to say that it has not.'

Evans believed the *Times* was simply taking a more detached, independent editorial position. But by early 1982, Murdoch was clearly losing patience. According to Bernard (now Lord) Donoghue, a leader writer and now a stockbroker at Grieveson & Grant, Murdoch had promised Mrs Thatcher that the *Times* would be back in the Conservative camp by the Easter of that year. But the editor refused to submit to what he later called 'political intimidation and harassment'. On 12 March 1982, Evans wrote the following editorial: 'Unemployment is a social scandal . . . We favour a more competitive society as against one which is subject to the monopoly powers of capital or the trade unions.' Three days later Evans was dismissed.

Such lack of sovereignty and independence for the editor has been prevalent throughout the Murdoch empire. 'I give instructions to my editors all round the world, why shouldn't I in London,' he told Fred Emery, home affairs editor of the *Times*, on 4 March 1982.[46] However, since 1983 all four of Murdoch's London papers have taken a consistently pro-Conservative government line and so there has been no need to interfere. According to a reporter on the *Sunday Times*' 'Insight' team, this is how the system works: 'Murdoch appoints people who he knows are sympathetic and Neil [the Editor], in turn, appoints people who are sympathetic to him. Thus most of the senior staff like Hugo Young have left or been completely emasculated or replaced . . . To survive you have to self-censor. You approach a story in a different way than if you'd run it in the way you wanted to.'[47]

It is true that Murdoch rarely interferes editorially at the *Sun*, because he has been able to rely on two trusted cohorts as editors in recent years. Sir Larry Lamb, knighted by Mrs Thatcher in 1980, was instrumental in moving the *Sun* to the right of the Conservative Party. In 1981 Kelvin McKenzie became editor and has retained the same political policy.

The other Fleet Street press baron to impede editorial independence has been Robert Maxwell, publisher of the *Daily Mirror*, *Sunday People* and *Sunday Mirror*. During the miners' strike he constantly interfered in the *Mirror*'s coverage (see Chapter 8). This is how one of the *Mirror*'s star columnists summed up the situation:

The general position is that *he* runs the Daily Maxwell – which is exactly what it is. He dictates the whole of the paper – and the point to make is that the effect has been disastrous. He is in a position to do what he likes with what he owns – and that's the philosophy which governs most of us . . . He may say he's Labour, but he's pro big business. And it soon became clear that if you went out to get big business, you ran against him.[48]

A graphic example of how Maxwell perceives his role came in late April 1984 when he tried to buy the *Observer* from Tiny Rowland. Maxwell was asked his view of the *Observer*'s revelations concerning Mark Thatcher's business activities in Oman and his role in securing a contract for Cementation. 'Make no mistake,' the *Mirror*'s publisher replied, 'if Mr Trelford [the *Observer*'s editor] had published that story and I had been the proprietor then he would no longer be the editor.' Maxwell added: 'I thought it [the story] was appalling, and I would have been very quick to stop that kind of nonsense.' But what he declined to mention was that one of his companies – Hollis Bros, an educational equipment manufacturer and subsidiary of Pergamon Press – was at the time negotiating to act as a subcontractor in Oman.[49]

Other proprietors are less inclined to take such a robust role in the editorial affairs of their papers. The *Daily Mail* and *Mail on Sunday*'s owner, Lord Rothermere, is a tax exile in Paris and rarely intervenes, although he keeps a watchful eye on leading articles. 'I see myself as the King,' he remarked in a rare interview, 'mapping out the overall strategy my papers will take. My editors are the generals who carry them out.' He added: 'I tell him [the editor] the kind of things that the paper, so to speak, belongs to. I don't tell him what to say in the paper, because it's the way he says it which is important . . . I tell him what ought not to be in the newspaper if I see it in the newspaper and that's about all.'[50]

The *Daily Mail*'s editorial structure is very hierarchical and, according to the paper's journalists, under the strict control of the editor, Sir David English. On one occasion in 1980 Mike Power, father of the *Mail*'s NGA Imperial Chapel, was making up the front page. He found, as is often the case, that he had a surplus of editorial copy and so he told a nearby subeditor:

'I'm just going to leave out these quotes because there's not enough space.'

'Oh no, you can't do that,' said the subeditor.

'Why not?' asked Power.

'We've had a memo from the editor. It says that anything said by Frank Chapple must be given prominence,' the anxious-looking subeditor replied. Frank (now Lord) Chapple was the rightwing leader of the electricians union, the Electrical, Electronic, Telecommunication and Plumbers Union (EETPU). He now has a regular column in the *Daily Mail*.

The overall reality of the situation is that an editor has complete editorial control as long as he adheres broadly to his owner's political line. As Lord Matthews remarked in July 1977 after being appointed Chairman of Express Group newspapers, then owned by Trafalgar House: 'By and large my editors will have complete editorial freedom as long as they agree with the policy I have laid down.'[51] This means that when a senior journalist with different views to his proprietor becomes editor, he has to either censor his own politics or delegate responsibility. Most resort to the latter ploy. In the autumn of 1977, Lord Matthews offered the editorship of the pro-Conservative *Daily Express* to Derek Jameson, a life-long Labour voter. At first Jameson demurred:

'I'm delighted and flattered that you should offer me a job but I'm afraid you've got the wrong man. I'm a *Mirror* Executive and I support the Labour Party'.

'That doesn't matter, replied Matthews. 'You wouldn't be stupid enough to try to turn a Tory paper into a Labour newspaper.'

Jameson was soon persuaded and accepted the *Express* job where he rarely wrote leading articles and took a low profile on the political policy of the paper. He later became editor of the *Daily Star* and *News of the World*. Jameson believes it's a difficult and even unfair dilemma for Labour supporters in Fleet Street, but that they don't really have a choice. 'What's a socialist to do? If you've dedicated all your life to Fleet Street popular newspapers and you've got to the point of your career where you have the necessary ingredients to be an editor, do you turn it down on the basis that the paper happens to be Tory?'

One of Jameson's proprietors, Lord Matthews, rarely interfered with the day-to-day political coverage of his papers, particularly the *Daily* and *Sunday Express*. He didn't need to. Instead he appointed editors who he knew would follow a certain political line, namely rightwing Conservative. It's done by proxy.

Only on the *Guardian* and the *Observer* does the editor have the freedom and autonomy to resist proprietorial pressures, although for different reasons. Peter Preston, the *Guardian*'s editor since 1975, is accountable to the Guardian Trust and there is little doubt he has complete independence (see Appendix 1 for details). However, not everyone on the *Guardian* staff is completely happy about the situation. 'The ordinary reporters are not consulted [about editorial policy],' said Aidan White, the Guardian's NUJ FoC, 'and they have absolutely no representation.'

The *Observer*'s editor, Donald Trelford, has managed to retain some form of editorial integrity and survived despite several trials of strength with proprietors. One reason for this is that Trelford is the only Fleet Street editor to have been elected by his own staff. The other, according to Trelford, is that the system of independent directors has been made to work. When Lonrho, the multinational conglomerate with interests from mining to newspapers, launched their bid for the *Observer* in 1981, Trelford and his staff lobbied the Department of Trade to have the sale referred to the Monopolies Commission. As in Murdoch's acquisition of the *Times*, the Monopolies Commission ruled that the sale should not go ahead unless built-in guarantees of editorial independence were met. Among these was that five independent directors would sit on the *Observer* board. Their role is to deal with any problems that arise between the editor and the proprietor. They're also responsible for appointing or dismissing the editor.

Trelford says this system of independent directors has been successful: 'They are there to ensure the control of the paper's staffing and policy ... The system does work because the people who are the independent directors are jointly chosen. They're acceptable both to Lonhro and to us. They have a vested interest in seeing it work.'[52] The *Observer*'s editor could well point to his notorious row with his proprietor Tiny Rowland in April 1984 as evidence of the safeguards provided by the independent directors.

However, the independent directors system didn't work at the *Times* where Murdoch effectively ignored them. Former *Times* editor, Sir William Rees-Mogg, believes their influence is limited: 'Independent directors are useful, but I don't think they stand up to extreme pressures ... They can offer some restraint and influence on the proprietor. The idea is a good one but not totally safe.'[53] Robert Maxwell is more dismissive: 'Somebody has got to be in charge. There's a lot of nonsense about independent directors. They are a complete waste of time ... It doesn't work on the *Observer* and it doesn't work anywhere. Newspapers, if they are to be well run, have to be a dictatorship.'[54]

Perhaps the most revealing comment on the power of the press barons has come from Lord Marsh, Chairman of the Newspaper Publishers Association.

> I believe that the suggestion of editorial independence is a romantic myth dreamed up by editors. There is no doubt in my mind at all that proprietors who, having spent a great deal of money on a newspaper, at the very least will not allow it to express views consistently with which they strongly disagree. Editors would rapidly find that if they wanted to do otherwise, they would be looking for a new job ... If you buy a company and if the executives, that you hire and pay, pursue a policy to which you are strongly opposed, you will fire them before you accept someone else using your money and organisation to do something which you are opposed to.[55]

The journalists and editorial independence – responsibilities and dilemmas

In July 1984, the editor of the *Times*, the late Charles Douglas-Home, issued a memorandum to all his staff, outlining his 'editorial prerogative': 'Nobody except the editor and his editors make decisions on what goes into the paper. Neither management, Mr Murdoch or the NGA, and I don't think the NUJ should make that decision.'[56]

By and large ordinary journalists in Fleet Street have accepted the editor as having the ultimate power to control the tone and content of their paper's political coverage. British journalists have rarely, if ever, taken any kind of industrial action to protest at political bias and distortion in their papers' news columns. The nearest came during the 1983 general election when the *Daily Mail*'s NUJ chapel passed a motion expressing their concern at the one-sided coverage of the campaign. Sir David English, the editor since 1970, replied that the content of the paper was the sole responsibility of the editor and of no concern to the National Union of Journalists (see Chapter 7 for details).

American and Australian journalists are, however, made of sterner stuff. In the early 1970s Rupert Murdoch launched a campaign in his *New York Post* to support Edward Koch against Mario Cuomo for Mayor of New York City, because, as Murdoch said at the time, 'It's very simple. There are 2½ million Jews in New York and one million Italians.'[57]

However, the bias became so blatant that 80 *New York Post* reporters signed a petition, strongly protesting against the distortions in the news columns (confirmed by a survey in *More* magazine). Barbara Yuncker, an official of the paper's Newspaper Guild, was summoned by Murdoch to discuss the petition which said: 'Political stories should be written by the best intelligence good reporters can bring to the facts – and not homogenized to fit an editorial position ... We are dismayed to be manipulated into becoming mere pamphleteers.' When questioned on this point, Yuncker told Murdoch defiantly, 'It's our newspaper too.' 'Oh no it's not,' said Murdoch. 'When you pay the losses you can say it's your paper. It's my newspaper. You just work here and don't you forget it.'[58]

Murdoch's attitude to his own journalists was equally dismissive in his home country of Australia. His flagship paper, the *Australian*, has had a turbulent history with 13 editors in 16 years – one departed after just 48 hours on the job. Another, Adrian Deamer, was sacked in 1971 because the paper was becoming too liberal. Although the

Australian supported the Labour Party in 1972, within two years the paper was calling for the government's resignation.

During the 1975 general election campaign the *Australian*'s editorial management, according to the paper's own journalists in a signed statement, suppressed stories, rewrote headlines and slanted the news against the Labour Party. On 2 November 1975, 75 staff journalists signed a letter complaining that the *Australian* was becoming 'a laughing stock' and that its staff were being treated with 'derision'. One leader writer, Robert Duffield, even confirmed that he had been ordered to write anti-Labour editorials. The signatories of the letter said they did not dispute Murdoch's prerogative in deciding the editorial policy of the paper. However, the letter continued:

It is not so much the policy itself but the blind, biased, tunnel-visioned, ad hoc and confused way in which so many people are now conceiving it to be carried out, both in the editorial and news columns . . . We cannot be loyal to a propaganda sheet. We are loyal to the best traditions of journalism and must remain so to retain our sanity. We cannot be loyal to those traditions, or to ourselves, if we accept the deliberate or careless slanting of headlines, seemingly blatant imbalance in news presentation and political censorship. Also on occasion the distortion of copy from senior, specialist journalists, the political management of news and features and the stifling of dissident and even unpalatable impartial opinion in the paper's columns.[59]

There was no response from Murdoch, and his editors continued to distort the news against the Australian Labour Party. However, on 6 December 1975, a crowd of demonstrators burnt hundreds of copies of the *Australian* as they came off the presses outside the Holt Street offices in Sydney. Editions of the *Sunday Mirror* and *Sunday Telegraph*, also owned by Murdoch, suffered a similar fate. Two days later, the journalists on the three papers, no doubt inspired by the public concern, voted to strike for two days in protest at the 'slanted headlines, distortions and suppressions of dissent'.

It seems highly unlikely that British journalists would resort to such industrial action over biased political coverage. Fleet Street reporters react in a different way. They argue that, particularly on the popular papers, the responsibility for bias lies elsewhere – usually with the 'back-bench'.

The night desk, or 'back-bench', as it's more commonly known, is the power base of a Fleet Street newspaper. In an average office this consists of about five assistant editors, a night editor and the chief subeditor. Once a news story has been typed by the reporter, a subeditor usually issues the printing instructions and on popular papers will often rewrite the story. In theory, the subeditors are supposed to check with the journalist but usually there is no time. The stories are then collated at the 'back-bench' where a small group of executives, the editor and his deputy decide what is to be published and how it's to be presented. The page is then designed and set out by a stone-sub who works closely with the printers.

Hence the published news story is manufactured through a series of different processes. This formal division of labour and production means copy can be substantially altered – often without the knowledge of the journalist. This was revealed to me by Jad Adams, an experienced former Fleet Street journalist who worked on popular papers from the *Daily Mail* to the *Mirror*. On Tuesday 31 July 1979, Adams wrote a story for the *London Evening Standard* about how the Lambeth, Southwark and Lewisham Area Health Authority had been dismissed from office because they refused to impose spending cuts in their services. According to Adams, 'there was no way the facts could be presented as sympathetic to the government'. When his news story appeared on the front page as 'Health Rebels Face Axe' the whole premise of the report had been changed. 'When I saw my story in print,' recalls Adams, 'it was under a joint by-line because, unknown to me, the executives had drafted in their political editor Arthur Hawkey to write in some pro-Conservative comment for the first two sentences . . . What really disturbed me was that a story that was about underfunding of the health service had been turned into a story about overspending by the council.'

Such experiences explain why so many journalists blame either subeditors or management when they are accused of political bias. They see themselves as mere individual cogs in a complex machine. They say it's a fraudulent scenario that they are the willing accomplices in a sinister conspiracy, conducted daily by their Draconian press barons to destroy the labour movement. Donald Trelford, the *Observer*'s editor since 1975, argues:

It is an insult to many good journalists to say that they are unwilling to fight to preserve their independence under fire. In my experience, there are plenty of journalists with guts and convictions who are prepared to stand up and be counted. Not all proprietors seek to impose their opinions . . . Even on those papers where there are heavy-handed proprietors, only a small number of journalists are likely to be involved.[60]

It is true that some journalists do fight back. Quite often he or she will discuss the story with the editor. If they cannot agree the reporter then has two choices. He can either resign or take his by-line off the story. The latter course is, understandably, nearly always taken.

However, the system also ensures that there is no need to order a journalist to slant a particular story. Instead, it's done by a process of selection and delegation. Ideas for stories are either ignored or belittled by the news editor and in some cases suppressed. In December 1983, Paul Routledge, then labour editor of the *Times*, approached David Blake, the paper's home affairs editor, to ask him to publish a piece by his colleague Barrie Clement. It concerned Sir John Donaldson, Master of the Rolls, who presided over an injunction against the National Graphical Association in their dispute with Eddie Shah's Stockport Messenger Group. The story, revealed by *Time Out*, showed how Donaldson had been involved in secret talks with government ministers the previous year about the possibility of making strikes illegal and other anti-union measures. Three times Routledge tried to persuade the home editor to publish the story. He was refused on every occasion. I asked Routledge whether he thought the editorial decision was politically motivated. 'I can't think of any other reason,' he replied.

In recent years, however, some journalists and particularly print-workers have become impatient at what they see as reporters abdicating their responsibility. 'I believe some journalists are guilty of hiding behind their editors far too often,' said Geoffrey Goodman, former industrial editor of Mirror Group Papers. 'It's an easy excuse.' And only on the popular papers like the *Sun* and the *Mirror* is news copy substantially rewritten. On the *Times* and the *Guardian* very little is changed and so, in theory, the political and labour correspondents have complete editorial freedom and cannot blame the subeditors. In addition, a journalist can never completely absolve him or herself from responsibility (especially if their name is above the story) because only he or she can be held answerable for the information in the article.

A *Daily Telegraph* subeditor, who has worked in the paper's Manchester office since 1980, believes that the notion of objective copy being rewritten for political purposes is much exaggerated. 'I have never been asked to bias a story – only ''debias'' them,' he told me.

I have found that the bias often comes directly from the reporter and that the extent to which that bias is 'diluted' depends on the political sympathies, or simply the conscientiousness, of the subeditor handling the copy . . . The more hysterical adjectives peppering the Manchester reporters' stories on the miners' strike, for example, are eloquent proof of this . . . I have very little idea of the position in London, but I do know that the 'real' bias of the paper comes from the very top – a small clique of leader and feature writers, protected fiercely by the editor and management, whose copy is 'untouchable'.

Jad Adams, who has worked on the *Daily Star*, *News of the World* and *Daily Mirror*, rejects the view that the journalists are to blame: 'Reporters are interchangeable between papers because they are not the source of bias. The public sees it as a sign of apostasy when left-wing journalists work on rightwing papers. The public does not understand that the reporter does the job to the best of his or her ability, regardless of the political character of the paper'.[61]

Victims of press bias, however, see this attitude as a cover-up. Print-workers are particularly angry and in recent years have secured a number of right-of-replies and disclaimers for people and groups who have been misrepresented or unfairly attacked. They have received only tacit support from the journalists. There is little love lost between the production unions (NGA and SOGAT) and the NUJ.

Few journalists are prepared to align themselves with the print unions and make a public stand. Oliver Duke, a former editorial lay-out artist on the *Sun* and an NUJ member, was, however, concerned about the contents of his newspaper. He was one of only two *Sun* employees willing to speak to me 'on the record'. Duke, a member of the Socialist Workers' Party, was virtually the only NUJ member to attempt to discuss editorial issues during chapel meetings. He also regularly and vocally attacked the paper's editorial content on the art desk which is adjacent to the back-bench. This made him very unpopular with the *Sun*'s editorial management and he was warned, more than once, that he could be dismissed. One such occasion was on 29 March 1985 when Duke wrote an article in *Socialist Worker* criticizing the *Sun* over its handling of a dispute with the paper's print unions. That same day he received a letter from the editor Kelvin McKenzie:

> I am advised that, in publishing this vicious and hysterical article, you are in clear breach of the duty of loyalty, mutual trust and confidence between employer and employee. The Company would be entitled to dismiss you without compensation or warning. We do not propose to take so drastic a step on this occasion. However, I must ask you to accept this as a formal written warning that if there is any repetition by you of conduct which would entitle the Company to dismiss you, we will not hesitate to terminate your employment here forthwith.

Malcolm Withers, the *Sun*'s NUJ father of chapel, replied on 3 April 1985:

> I have now seen the offending article in *Socialist Worker* and, quite frankly, apart from the rhetoric, the facts seem the same as reported in the *Financial Times* . . . To claim that 'loyalty, mutual trust and confidence between employer and employee' can be used to silence political criticism is quite ridiculous. If management sincerely believe that the article is 'tendentious, inaccurate and damaging', then I suggest there is a straightforward case for action to be taken in the courts, the Press Council or even using the NUJ Code of Conduct.

But McKenzie was insistent: 'I am astonished at your attitude,' he replied on 9 April 1985.

> There is hardly a company in the country that would not have dismissed on the spot any employee who behaved as Mr Duke has done in this matter. Please make clear to your chapel members that . . . such leniency should not be taken as a precedent for any repetition, whether by Mr Duke or any other journalist. In fact, if Mr Duke were foolish enough to write a similar article for *Socialist Worker* – or any other periodical – I can assure you he would be sacked at once.

Such intimidation of NUJ members perhaps indicates why so few journalists are prepared to take a stand on editorial issues. However, Duke has little time for many of the *Sun* reporters:

> I once tried to do a collection amongst the journalists for the hospital workers who were on strike. Out of a chapel of over 200 people, I managed to collect the grand sum of £52 – and a lot of abuse. . . . When it comes to taking a bite out of Murdoch's huge cake, they begin to salivate and become quite excited. But when it comes to helping other groups of workers – well, that poses a bit of a problem, what with the editorial content of the paper. And when it comes to freedom of the press, almost all of them agree. Yes, the editor can publish any union-bashing, racist, sexist filth he can conjure up with a totally free hand – and a lot of help from the journalists.[62]

News management – knighthoods, secrecy and the courts

On 16 December 1983, Sir John Donaldson, Master of the Rolls, said: 'The responsibility for deciding what should or should not be published is that of the government of the day, and not that of individual civil servants or editors.' He was referring, specifically, to the leaking of documents by civil servants to the press – namely the Michael Heseltine memorandum sent by Sarah Tisdall to the *Guardian*. But that remark did reveal the judiciary's attitude towards newspapers that publish information which embarrasses the establishment (after all, the Heseltine memo had nothing to do with 'national security').

Donaldson's comment also focuses on another key factor that has restricted and contracted the range of political debate and dissent in Britain – news management by the government, the courts and the police. Obsessive secrecy by government ministries and Draconian official secrets legislation has obstructed the many journalists who *do* try to investigate the rich and powerful. However, as *Observer* journalist David Leigh pointed out in his book *The Frontiers of Secrecy*, 'the British media are not strong-willed' and have never accepted 'that knowledge about public affairs should be a right and not a privilege'. He adds that the press are generally willing to rely on officially provided information and so 'are often channels for official or political propaganda'.[63]

News management is neither new nor confined to Conservative governments (although given the papers' editorial allegiances, Tory MPs are naturally more successful). Lloyd George, Liberal Prime Minister between 1916 and 1922, literally sold peerages and knighthoods to the press barons in exchange for political support, collecting over £3 million. For the Conservatives, Neville Chamberlain was their news manipulator and regularly lied to the press in order to create a favourable image for his appeasement policies in the 1930s. But it was Labour's Harold (now Lord) Wilson who became the most enthusiastic exponent of news management. According to the late James Margach, former political correspondent of the *Sunday Times*, Wilson demanded the dismissal of lobby correspondents David Wood (*Times*) and Noyes Thomas (*News of the World*) and even had Nora Beloff of the *Observer* shadowed by his private staff.[64]

Little has changed. According to David Basnett, former General Secretary of the General and Municipal Boilermakers Union, Downing Street hosted a meeting of Fleet Street editors to help co-ordinate the coverage of the TUC Day of Action in May 1980. The relationship between some newspapers and governments is often so close that the proprietor will simply censor his own paper, as Lord Matthews admitted in 1979: 'I would find myself in a dilemma about whether to report a British Watergate affair because of the national harm. I believe in batting for Britain.'[65]

It would be dishonest to suggest that the Labour Party is not as keen as the Conservatives to control the flow and tone of press coverage of politics. But the simple reality of the situation is that the balance of editorial allegiance is so slanted in favour of the Tory Party that they have a much easier task.

The management of news has been particularly successful since 1975 when Sir Gordon Reece became Mrs Thatcher's personal media advisor. He has regular meetings with the editors and senior executives of the *Sun*, *Daily Mail* and *Daily Express*. This has proved a most fruitful relationship for both sides. Indeed, to such an extent that Reece has deliberately been given a low profile in the popular press. On 9 April 1985, a *Sun* news story was rewritten by a subeditor under the orders of the editor Kelvin McKenzie, because the report mentioned Reece's name. The original news copy, filed by political correspondent Chris Potter, reads: 'The "image-builder" advisor Gordon Reece has told her [Mrs Thatcher] it is vital to present the nation with a new-look top team well before the party conferences get underway.' This was changed to: 'Advisors have told her it is vital to present . . .'. According to Tony Sheldon, a former *Sun* proof-reader who saw what happened: 'McKenzie picked up the copy and instructed the subeditor to cross out Reece's name. He told him that Reece was not to be mentioned in the *Sun*, ever.'

Within six years of Reece's appointment, the following editors were given knighthoods on Mrs Thatcher's recommendation – David English (*Daily Mail*), Larry Lamb (*Sun*, now editor of the *Daily Express*) and John Junor (*Sunday Express*). In addition, Victor Matthews, former Chairman of Express Group Newspapers, received a life peerage. According to Jocelyn Stevens, former Managing Director and Deputy Chairman of Express Newspapers, Matthews received his peerage in June 1980 on Mrs Thatcher's recommendation because of John Junor's influence, who is a close friend and admirer of the prime minister. A year later, in June 1981, Junor received his knighthood. Stevens, now Rector of the Royal College of Art, says that Matthews was so grateful for his title that he said Junor could remain editor of the *Sunday Express* for as long as he liked.[66]

In return for these ennoblements, the popular press have given Mrs Thatcher a remarkably free and uncritical ride. This is even the view of many Conservatives. Tory MP and former deputy Foreign Secretary Sir Ian Gilmour, said: 'To put the blame for present ills [in the Conservative Party] on failure of presentation is bizarre. The broadcasting services are cowed, if still independent, and large sections of the press are obsequiously anxious to print Downing Street's bidding.

No government has been given an easier ride by the media.'[67] For Lord Alport, the ex-Tory MP and former Director of the Conservative Political Centre, the national press has 'for the most part gone to extraordinary lengths to support the government's policies and flatter the Prime Minister'.[68]

Conservative Central Office are particularly adept at exploiting their Fleet Street friends. In April 1979, Sir Angus Maude, then head of the Tory Research Department and the Party Vice-Chairman, compiled a list of what he called 'Labour's 12 Big Lies' in their 1979 general election manifesto. On 25 April 1979 the *Daily Mail* reproduced the document virtually in full on their front page under the banner headline – 'Labour's Dirty Dozen'.[69]

Another technique is to simply plant stories. This was revealed in early 1984 when Maurice Romilly, a former *Daily Telegraph* journalist then working for Tory Central Office, telephoned Labour's Deputy Leader Roy Hattersley by mistake. Assuming he was talking to a Conservative MP, Romilly said: 'I have been asked to telephone you by Anthony Shrimsley [Director of Tory Publicity and ex-*Daily Mail* political editor] to discuss a very good story we've got and which we want to plant in a newspaper sympathetic to our cause.'

Perhaps the cosiest relationship has been with the property and shipping multinational corporation, Trafalgar House. Until December 1982, the company owned the *Daily Express*, *Daily Star*, and *Sunday Express* through its subsidiary, Fleet Holdings. Lord Matthews is a friend of Mrs Thatcher and a strong supporter of her economic and industrial policies. For the 1979 general election, Trafalgar House contributed over £40,000 to Tory Party funds and then campaigned enthusiastically in their papers – 'Maggie's The One'[70] and 'The Red Face of Labour'[71] were some of the *Daily Express* headlines. The day after Mrs Thatcher's election victory, on Friday 4 May, a celebration lunch was hosted by Lord Matthews and his deputy Jocelyn Stevens at the Ritz Hotel, also owned by Trafalgar House. Among the guests were Lord Carrington (Foreign Secretary in Mrs Thatcher's first Cabinet), Lord Grade, Alistair McAlpine (Treasurer of the Conservative Party), Lord Marsh, Gordon Reece, Rupert Murdoch and Lord George-Brown.[72] Within a year Matthews had received a life peerage and on 13 November 1980 Trafalgar House resigned along with Sir James Goldsmith from the Confederation of British Industry (CBI). The reason? The CBI had criticized the Conservative government's monetarist economic policies.

The few newspapers who have taken a sagacious and critical view of the Conservative government are given rather different treatment.

The *Observer* is one such paper. According to its editor Donald Trelford:

> We have a government that rewards the journalists it favours as never before – arise Sir Larry, Sir John, Sir David, Sir Alastair (Burnett) – but takes its hostility towards papers that oppose its policies, or leak embarrassing information, to spiteful and vindictive lengths. When the *Observer* wrote about Mark Thatcher's business connections, for example, the Prime Minister's press secretary, Bernard Ingham, went so far as to threaten 'dirty tricks' against us. Mrs Thatcher clearly sees the press's task as to reflect faithfully her own vision of the world. Anyone who doesn't do that is seen as ill-intentioned and irresponsible.[73]

It is no coincidence that Trelford is the only Fleet Street editor not to be invited to dinner at No. 10 Downing Street by Mrs Thatcher.

Trelford also believes that such a political climate gives encouragement, and even some legitimacy, to the agents of the establishment – the police, civil servants and the judges – who prefer Britain to remain a secretive society. Trelford said:

> The law doesn't touch papers who libel poor people, make up interviews, invade privacy, and engage in general muck-raking. But it makes life impossible for papers who want to investigate the rich and the powerful, to probe the waste in government departments and to find out about the financial connections of politicians or their families. It does this through refusal to reform the laws on official secrets and libel, and by refusing to reform properly the law on contempt.[74]

The British establishment's obsession with secrecy is contrasted sharply with the United States where there is far greater freedom of information. *Observer* journalist David Leigh gives a graphic example of this in his book *The Frontiers of Secrecy*: 'We apparently live in a country where a subcommittee of MPs is required to say in 1976 that the range of the Tow anti-tank missile is "xxx" and the Dragon missile is "only xx". (The US military announced to Congress at about the same time that the range of Tow was about 3,000 metres and the Dragon was medium-range, 60-1,000 metres).'[75]

The issue of freedom of information enters the political arena because secrecy is, of course, at the core of power and authority. To keep secrets implies status. As Elias Canetti, the Nobel-prize-winning writer, once said: 'It is the privilege of Kings to keep their secrets from father, mother, brother and friends.' And so to let the people know is almost a sign of weakness – a sharing of power.

Journalists and editors like Leigh and Trelford are clearly right to point out that Britain's laws on contempt of court, confidence and official secrets prevent them from investigating the rich and powerful. The political crimes of Watergate, for example, would almost certainly not have been revealed if they had occurred in this country, because of the restraints on freedom of expression. But that is only part of the truth. Much more important is whether the press would have actually investigated such corruption in high places. Lord Matthews, until recently owner of four national newspapers, openly admitted that he would 'find himself in a dilemma' about reporting Watergate. And so, of course, secrecy and lack of freedom of information is a very serious issue but it's only part of a much wider political landscape.

The real issue, if Britain wants to become a truly informed and pluralist democracy, is whether the voices of people and groups who have genuine radical views are allowed to be heard. At the moment the river of democratic political debate is far from clear. Indeed, it is polluted. Ideas and policies on boats chartered by the radical Left, trade unions or the peace movement are rarely allowed a trip downstream without sabotage. More than often, they are sunk without trace. They are rarely given a free ride. Instead, their advocates' speeches are described as 'belligerent' and their oratory as 'ranting'. If they are elected to a political position, they 'grabbed' or 'seized' the job, and their names are prefixed by 'extreme' or 'Red'.

For the purposes of this book 'they' are Tony Benn and the Labour Left, Ken Livingstone and the GLC Labour Group, Peter Tatchell, the Greenham Common peace women, black people and the miners during the 1984-5 dispute. These are Britain's dissidents for the early 1980s and have been treated as such by Fleet Street.

In contrast, rightwing philosophies and policies are given rather different receptions on the river of democracy. Most newspapers have instead fastened themselves to the rightwing mast. This is Hugo Young, the award-winning former political editor of the *Sunday Times*, on Fleet Street's response to the first six years of Mrs Thatcher's Conservative administration:

> The Thatcher government has had the least critical press of any government since the war. The vast bulk of it has done exactly what the government wanted it to do. On the two occasions when the government's very life was at stake, the Falklands War and the miners' strike, most newspapers fought the Tories' battles for them. No sustained critique was marshalled at any stage of either event.[76]

Meanwhile, the editors and the owners of our national newspapers maintain that their coverage of the Labour Party, strikes, the peace movement and general elections is, by and large, justified and fair. They argue that it's the oldest trick in the book to blame bad news on the messenger or the thermometer for the fever. Readers of this book will have to judge for themselves whether or not the messenger has been kidnapped or the thermometer doctored.

2. Tony Benn—the Socialist Threat

'It is because Tony Benn believes you can't change the nation without rocking the boat that he has been turned into an ogre by a right-wing press, devoted to defending the status quo.' Philip Andrews, political correspondent of the *Sheffield Star*, 20 January 1984.

'Bent on the destruction of Britain as we know it.' – the *Sun* on Tony Benn, 7 June 1983.

It was October 1980 during the Labour Party conference. Jill Tweedie, the *Guardian* columnist, met her neighbour who was out jogging.

'Isn't it awful about Benn?' said her neighbour. 'I mean, he's quite mad.'

'But you spent eight years marching for CND and Benn wants nuclear disarmament,' replied Tweedie.

'That's as may be,' said the lady jogger, thin-lipped.

'You're anti-Market and Benn wants out.'

'I dare say,' said her neighbour, frowning.

'And the other day you said you'd give anything to see Ulster vanish in a puff of smoke. Benn only wants to withdraw our troops.'

'Possibly so,' said the lady jogger, 'but the man is mad. Good heavens, don't you read the papers?' and she ran off crossly.[1]

Such a paradoxical reaction to the standard-bearer of Labour's left-wing has not been uncommon in recent years. For since he began to adopt a more radical political position in the early 1970s, Tony Benn's views have been consistently reported by Fleet Street as an insidious threat to British public life. He has been depicted as a sinister bogeyman, preparing to pounce on the hapless electorate. His name carries more political health warnings ('Führer'[2], 'extreme'[3], 'dictator'[4]) than perhaps any other radical politician. His speeches provoke paroxysms of rage and indignation among *Sun* and *Mirror* leader writers alike.

This was despite the fact that Benn was little more than a parliamentary tribune for a whole range of different political movements and ideas which were absorbed into the Labour Party in the mid-1970s.

Some were radical Liberals and disillusioned Trotskyists, others were socialist feminists and peace activists. They were frustrated by the impotence of revolutionary and fringe politics. And their joining of the Labour Party in the mid-1970s coincided with the rise of mass unemployment, social inequality and the apparent failure of the mixed economy. This was highlighted by the Labour government's dependence on foreign bankers and markets, culminating in 1976 with the humiliating IMF loan. And then the government's incomes policy was wrecked during the 'Winter of Discontent' in 1978-9 by industrial disruption.

The virtual collapse of the British economy inevitably resulted in the demise of the political and ideological consensus. Stimulated by the Conservative Party's move to the radical Right, Labour embraced more leftwing policies. This was intensified by the failure of Party leaders Harold (now Lord) Wilson and James Callaghan to adopt the radical proposals agreed by the National Executive Committee and conference.

Tony Benn undoubtedly became the parliamentary voice of Labour's resurrected radicalism. But he was unable to be more than that in a party with so many political factions and often conflicting ideas. Yet policies such as extensive nationalization were reduced by the press to 'Benn's Great Grab Plan' (*Daily Mail*[5]), and reform of Labour's constitution to 'Benn's Missing Link' by the *Sunday Mirror*.[6]

Clearly, Benn was seen as a real threat.

From Saint Wedgie to Fleet Street Satan

For many years Benn was neither a 'wild-eyed political looney'[7] (*Daily Mail*) nor the 'monster' (*Sun*[8]) he is today for the popular press. In the 1950s and 1960s, though always a radical, he was advocating 'more efficient management' and the need to make 'the mixed economy work, make it successful and competitive'.[9] And so he was adopted as Fleet Street's favourite son. 'A brilliant Minister of Technology', enthused the *Daily Mirror*[11], 'lots of talent', agreed the *London Evening Standard*.[11]

In October 1969, Benn was given responsibility for both private and public-sector industry. He continued to support a managerial role for the state and a corporatist alliance between industry and government. The liberal press were enthusiastic. The *Sunday Times* saw him as 'often right and far ahead of his time' and 'the only possible contender for the party leadership a decade from now'.[12] The *Observer* published a favourable profile commenting that Benn 'had a reputation for being bright and forward-looking'.[13]

Such adulation deserted Benn during the occupation of the Upper Clyde Shipbuilders' yards in 1971. After two of the three UCS yards had been sold off by the Conservative government, 400 workers were made redundant. Benn fully supported the subsequent occupation by the workforce and called for the shipyards to be nationalized. This time the press support was not forthcoming. For the *Daily Mirror* his 'support for a state-takeover does more credit to his heart than his head'.[14] And now the *Sunday Times* was commenting on 'the superficiality of Mr Benn's thinking ... He resembles nothing more than an erratic and power-hungry butterfly'.[15] The *Observer* had also changed its tune. Just after the UCS dispute, Mary Holland, the experienced Irish journalist and broadcaster, was commissioned to write a lengthy profile of Benn for the paper's colour magazine. The article was read by the then editor David Astor and other editorial executives but rejected. It was considered politically 'too favourable'. A few months earlier Holland had produced a profile of Shirley Williams, the prominent rightwing Labour MP and now President of the SDP. That was published by the *Observer*.

Nationalization, workers' control and 'Bennery'

During a meeting of Labour's National Executive Committee on 28 February 1975, a prominent member suggested that if Tony Benn were to save a child from drowning, the headlines the next day would read 'Benn's Latest Grab'. He was exaggerating, of course, but not by much. For between May 1973 and June 1975 Labour's industrial policies were consistently portrayed as the pipedream of one politician.

The press campaign began with the advent of 'Labour's Programme for 1973' – a radical nationalization document. Benn fully backed its proposals

> What we have in mind goes far beyond the window dressing of some European schemes. We are thinking of say 50 per cent of workers, elected through their trade union membership onto supervisory boards with real power. And we mean to carry through this sort of reform in the public sector as well as in the private sector. We shall carry through a real redistribution of income and wealth by radical changes in the tax system.[16]

Fleet Street was horrified. Suddenly Benn was part of 'the wild Left',[17] 'trying to attract the support of the extreme left militants'.[18]

The *Sun*, at that time loosely pro-Labour, stated: 'If Mr Benn is to be believed, Britain may shortly become a Marxist state',[19] while the *Sunday Telegraph* preferred 'Bolshevik Benn'.[20]

In September 1973, Labour's National Executive proposed that 25 leading companies be taken into public ownership. The *Daily Express* interpreted this plan as Benn toeing the Moscow line: 'Marx, Engels, Lenin and Stalin – those four grim, grey spectres from the past who started it all – might not have been displeased with the former Lord Stansgate.'[21]

But the press's hostility to nationalization was for reasons much closer to home, according to Charles Wintour, then editor of the *London Evening Standard* and now a member of the SDP: 'They're planning this socialization of the 25 firms,' said Wintour at the time.

> Well, in the long run, if this process continues indefinitely, they will start brooding on state control of the newspapers. I mean, nationalization means a production – the newspapers are produced. In the long run, this must be part of their policy. That's logical. They believe in it. And consequently I think that the newspapers have a right to be particularly suspicious of the Labour Party in its extension of nationalization and state control.[22]

Wintour's analysis turned out to be correct. The press was deeply hostile to nationalization. But this political opposition was concealed in the form of linking the policy with Benn's political ambition. This is how Noyes Thomas reported the issue for the *News of the World*: 'In his thirst for power he has seemed recently to be prepared to see even his party out of office for a further term provided it brings Wilson and his moderate colleagues to the end of the political road. It was Benn who bludgeoned through the party's policy document – the threat to nationalize Britain's top 25 companies.'[23]

When Benn was appointed Minister for Industry in February 1974, and began to implement Labour's nationalization and industrial democracy policies, the press reacted sharply. 'I'll reveal state grab plan', were Benn's words according to the *Daily Mail*. In fact, the words came from a subeditor but the scare campaign had started. 'Don't go too close to the spider's web', warned the *Daily Mail*. 'He [Benn] sits like a spider, waiting patiently – yet ravenously – for feeble firms to flutter too close to his web.'[24]

This image was one of several caricatures which became a dominant feature of Fleet Street's coverage of Labour's industrial policies. For the *Sun* and *Daily Mail* Benn had a number of disguises – 'Dracula',[25] 'Mad Mullah'[26] or 'Kamikaze pilot'.[27] For the *Guardian*'s Peter

Jenkins, now a member of the SDP, 'popular worries about Mr Anthony Wedgwood Benn appear to be less that he is a leftie than he may be a loony'.[28]

But the consistent portrayal was Benn as the 'state grabber'. 'Benn Out To Grab The Lot', said a *Sun* headline[29] when the Industry Minister outlined plans for the government to nationalize some private companies. The idea was clearly to present public ownership as the whim of a power-crazed individual – 'Benn Set on ''Dictator'' Road. The ''megalomaniac'' Mr Benn planned to give firms orders', reported the *Daily Telegraph*.[30]

Such proposals were, of course, already agreed by the National Executive and Cabinet and so the personalization angered many MPs. 'If Tony Benn were to disappear into thin air this afternoon,' Ian Mikardo told a Labour Regional Council, 'those policies would still be there as the keystone of the government's industrial policy.' Even Sir Edward du Cann, then Chairman of the influential 1922 Committee of Conservative Party backbenchers, agreed that the press were way off course: 'The task is not to attack Benn alone. It is to attack the whole socialist movement . . . Calling Anthony Wedgwood Benn an ignorant bully is not the way. There is nothing that he is proposing which has not been approved by every Labour Minister.'[31]

Yet the nationalization issue was constantly reported as Benn 'out to grab as much for the state as he can' (*Daily Mail*[32]). This was revealed on 7 June 1974 when Benn announced at a Nottinghamshire miners' gala that Department of Industry officials were analyzing the accounts of Britain's 20 largest companies and their 4,000 subsidiaries. The government wanted to disclose the extent of the public funding of private industry. This was later reported by the *Daily Express* as 'Benn Widens His Grab Net: Ready to Pounce on 4,000 Little Firms'.[33] In fact, there was never any intention to bring all of them into public ownership.

But it was the *Daily Mail* that was leading the scare campaign in the summer of 1974 – 'It's your money that Mr Benn is after'.[34] On 18 July 1974, the paper's political editor, the late Anthony Shrimsley, a former Labour supporter[35] who later became Director of Publicity and Communications for the Conservative Party, entered the fray. Under the headline of 'The Unacceptable Face of Citizen Benn', he wrote: 'The true menace of Citizen Benn is that he has far greater ambitions than merely to take over everything that contributes to the industrial and commercial strengths of these islands. Mr Benn's aim is to obliterate democracy as we know it and replace it with something else under the same name.' For the *Mail*, Labour's industrial policies were

Benn 'using his advocacy of ''open government'' to force his plans into Labour's policy statements and then into grudging acquiescence by colleagues too scared of the Left to make a public counterattack.'

This was not the view of the management who negotiated with the Labour Industry Minister. Lord Kearton, a cross-bench peer who was Chairman of the British National Oil Corporation and Courtaulds in the 1970s, did not find Benn authoritarian. 'I've never found that in any sense was he autocratic. In fact, I would say he went to enormous pains to sound out all possible sources before he made up his mind,' Lord Kearton said.[36]

Nor was it the view of *Daily Mirror* columnist Keith Waterhouse. On 5 August 1974, he analysed just what lay behind Fleet Street's campaign against Benn. He argued that the press technique was not to dispute whether workers should have seats on the boards of companies or that there should be more investment in industry. It was to say, instead, that it was absurd for *Mr Benn* to make such suggestions. He wrote

> How much easier it is to ridicule Mr Benn than to put up a coherent argument against the ideas he propagates ... A recent quip by Mr Peter Walker on the possibility of a state takeover of banks and building societies: 'The thought of one's savings being managed by Mr Wedgwood Benn is a pretty frightening prospect.' Is it? WHY is it? And in what way – what REAL way, not the kind of fantasy dreamed up in a *Daily Express* cartoon, would Mr Benn be managing our savings anyway? Examine a statement like that for a while and you can see how contemptible it is. But the contempt is not really for Mr Benn, it is for the voters of this country. A quip, a sneer, a cartoon, a headline – is that the level on which we're asked to make up our political minds?

Labour's publication of *The Regeneration of British Industry* in August 1974 brought down more wrath upon Benn's head, particularly over plans to nationalize the major shipyards. 'Fight to Stop Benn's Grab,' announced the *Daily Mail*[37] and tried to accuse Labour of acting against the wishes of the workers – 'He's scuppered us, say the shipyard workers.' The 'workers' the paper quoted was one storeman and a Clifford Bayliss, Director of Shipbuilders and Repairers National Association. The *Sunday Times* did in fact analyse Labour's planning agreements and investment plans. Their conclusion, after lengthy examination, was 'All Power to Benn's Soviets'[38] which was on a par with 'Commissar Wedgie' from the *Sun*.[39] Ironically the Left press were also critical – 'a retreat from Socialism', remarked the

Communist *Morning Star*, 'propping up capitalism', said the Trotskyist *Socialist Worker*.

It was also true, however, that in some cases Fleet Street was merely
responding to and reflecting the hostility to Labour's industrial policies from very powerful interests. The plan to set up a workers' co-
operative at the Triumph motorcycle factory at Meriden, for example,
was strongly opposed by civil servants, some members of the Cabinet
and the Treasury. There is some evidence that these interests were
briefing the press in order to undermine the Industry Ministry's plans.
'We were sharing the isolation that the Official Secrets Act imposes
on a minister,' said Frances Morrell, Benn's political advisor. 'Tony
was being vilified in the press, briefed I'm afraid by some of his own
colleagues, in a really appalling way.'⁴⁰ In addition, pressure groups
like Aims of Industry openly lobbied political journalists and spent
over £600,000 in an advertising and promotional campaign against
nationalization. Indeed Michael Ivens, Director of Aims of Industry,
invented the term 'Bennery' during a telephone conversation with a
Fleet Street political correspondent.

The 1975 Industry Act precipitated a new wave of hostility among
the establishment. Treasury ministers reported to Harold Wilson that
the City of London was unhappy with the bill. The press reflected this
opposition. 'Benn's Great Grab Plan', proclaimed the *Daily Mail*.
'The Benn plan to control industry was denounced last night by
employers as damaging and dangerous.'⁴¹ Many Labour MPs and
junior industry ministers were furious at such coverage. They argued
that the Industry Act was based on a green paper, drawn up by a
National Executive subcommittee which included rightwingers like
Tony Crosland. The subsequent white paper was then drafted by an
internal Industry Committee of at least 20 people, mainly civil servants. 'The Industry Bill is a Labour bill, not just Tony Benn's,' Eric
Heffer told the House of Commons.

But by this stage almost every economic or industrial Labour policy
was being portrayed as Benn 'grabbing, forcing or dictating'. On
10 February 1975 the Party's Home Policy Committee met to consider
a document on the Burmah Oil Company. At 5.50 pm Benn vacated the
chair and left the meeting for another appointment before the Burmah
Oil item was discussed. He was replaced by Ian Mikardo. After the
meeting the committee issued a statement and it was not thought
important enough to report that Benn had left the chair early. The following morning the *Daily Mirror* reported: 'Benn: Let's Take Over
Oil Giants . . . It was seen in some quarters as Mr Benn's answer to a
bid by Premier Harold Wilson to take him down a peg by saying last

Friday that a Cabinet committee would decide on major takeovers.' The *Daily Mail* declared: 'Benn's Shock Demand On Oil. Industry Secretary Mr Tony Wedgwood Benn ripped into the heart of business confidence about Labour's nationalization plans last night. At a meeting of the Party's Home Policy Committee, he led the most audacious demand yet – the takeover of Britain's two biggest oil firms, BP and Burmah'.

Ron Hayward, then Labour's General Secretary, immediately wrote to all the offending papers to complain about such political personalization and demanded a retraction from the five papers concerned. Only the *Sun* published a correction. Hayward then submitted a complaint to the Press Council but eventually withdrew it after the Council's Chairman, Lord Shawcross, made a speech describing Benn as among those who wanted to destroy 'Britain's civilized and democratic way of life'.[42]

What was significant about the coverage of the Labour government in early 1975 was the way comment had invaded the news pages. On 6 January 1975 Benn was elected Chairman of the Home Policy Committee (not particularly influential when Labour was in power) after the retirement of Bill Simpson. Four other members had turned down the nomination for the post – Tom Bradley, Sidney Weir, John Cartwright and Bryan Stanley – before Benn was nominated by Ian Mikardo. The next morning the *Daily Mail* headlined their story as 'Benn's New Power Grab', while the *Daily Telegraph* preferred 'Benn Seizes Key Post'. The distinguished critic Kenneth Tynan particularly resented such reporting:

> If a Tory became chairman of a party committee, we would read that he'd been 'appointed' to the post. When someone like Mr Benn is elected to a similar position, the headline says 'Benn Seizes New Job' – as if he had done it by force. . . . The attitudes expressed in this kind of writing get absorbed into our intellectual bloodstream although they simply reflect the convictions of the small group of people who own and control our press. So whenever we find in a news item a word that implies a value judgement, we are in the presence of corrupt journalism.[43]

But it was the portrayal of Labour's industrial policies that most clearly ignored the distinction between news and opinion. ' "Dictatorship under Führer Benn" was the first reaction from the Tories as they studied Labour's revolutionary proposals', reported the *Daily Express* on 1 February 1975. The paper added the following month: 'The creeping and doctrinaire philosophies of Anthony Wedgwood

Benn continue to find fat targets. It was announced last night that the government intends to nationalize 43 firms. Many people see this policy as nationalize-for-nationalization's sake or sheer craziness.'[44]

In April 1975, the Labour Party announced a plan to redirect some of the banks and insurance companies' funds and invest in British manufacturing industry. 'Mr Benn dips in your pocket,' declared the *Daily Express*,[45] while the *Sun* reported: 'Benn Plan to Grab Cash From City'.[46] After this disclosure City financiers and investors began to lobby the Treasury in order to undermine the government's new industrial proposals. They said that a run on the pound was a strong possibility 'as international confidence in Britain diminishes'. Much of this criticism was reflected in the *Daily Telegraph*: 'In every way Mr Benn seeks to pander to the most bloody-minded and irrational elements in our industrial life. Had his philosophy been applied during the nineteenth century, it is hard to believe that Britain would ever have become a great industrial power in the first place. The question now is whether we are to have any sort of industrial future.'[47]

The *Telegraph* performed a more useful political function for Harold Wilson the following month. The Prime Minister wanted to reassure the City and the International Monetary Fund that Benn would eventually be dismissed as Industry Minister. However, according to Wilson, it would have been 'very difficult, provocative indeed'[48] to sack Benn before the Common Market referendum. This was because Ministers were given a free role during the campaign. And so on Tuesday 6 May 1975 at a garden reception at the High Commissioner's house during the Commonwealth Premiers' Conference in Jamaica, Wilson summoned Harry Boyne, the *Daily Telegraph*'s political correspondent, to a specially reserved room. The Prime Minister told him he was going to 'clip Benn's wings' and demote him from Industry Secretary. 'Of course, I won't put any byline on this story. I think I'll just send it as "*Daily Telegraph reporter*",' said Boyne. 'Well, no,' replied Wilson, 'you can make it "by our political staff".'[49]

The story was published as a front-page lead the next day with Wilson's suggested byline. 'Wilson To Clip Benn's Wings – Cabinet Will Be Shown Who's Boss, ran the headline. Later in the story Boyne added:

From a strictly political point of view the obvious purpose of Mr Wilson's exercise of his authority is to persuade the electorate that Mr Benn is not the dictator of Labour policy . . . By his own utterances Mr Benn has made himself the favourite target of the media, and Mr Wilson evidently realizes that the point has been reached at which he has been scaring voters off the Labour Party. Hence the decision to diminish, it is hoped, the ogre of Bennery without sacking Mr Benn.

Within six months Harry Boyne received a knighthood on Wilson's recommendation in the New Year's Honours List. Two years later, in July 1978, Boyne became Press Secretary to the Conservative Party leader Mrs Thatcher.

The Common Market press match: pro-EEC 15, anti-EEC 0

Before Britain officially entered the European Economic Community (EEC) on 1 January 1973, the Conservative government had faced a serious problem. A substantial proportion of the British people were strongly opposed to the Common Market. In order to counteract this situation a secret media strategy was implemented by powerful pro-EEC interests.

Throughout 1972 the European Movement, a pro-Common Market organization funded by the EEC and the Foreign Office, co-ordinated a special public relations plan. They set up a Campaign Group and arranged weekly 'media breakfasts' for City editors, businessmen, civil servants, TV and radio executives and ministers at the luxury Connaught Hotel in central London. About 12 people usually attended these meetings, where newspaper executives advised the government on their public relations plan to persuade the wary anti-Common Market masses. The senior Fleet Street editors also agreed to inform the European Movement when there was a forthcoming anti-EEC speech or statement so they could counter it swiftly. These media breakfasts were masterminded by public relations consultant Geoffrey Tucker, a former Tory member of the European Parliament. He was also Director of Publicity for the Conservative Party during the 1970 general election.[50]

Tucker's public relations operation was in effect dismantled after Britain's entry into the EEC in January 1973. But when Labour became increasingly hostile to the Common Market and committed itself to a referendum, the pro-EEC lobby again became concerned about public opinion. And so in the spring of 1974 Tucker's media machine was again cranked into action under the cover of the European League for Economic Co-operation (ELEC). In July 1974, John Harris (now Lord Harris of Greenwich) and a close advisor of Roy Jenkins, was appointed Chairman of ELEC. An elite group known as 'the principals' was also set up which included Tucker, Harris, Douglas Hurd, Bill Rodgers, Geoffrey Rippon, John Sainsbury and Lord Harlech. Once again secret meetings were arranged to co-ordinate the pro-EEC campaign. They were usually held over breakfast at the Dorchester Hotel or over dinner at the Rank Organization's headquarters in South Street, Mayfair.[51]

By early 1975 Harris and Tucker were working under the auspices of a group called Britain in Europe which was actually part of the European Movement. As joint chairmen of both the Media Policy Group and the Publicity Committee, Harris and Tucker were the key figures in this strategy. Indeed, Tucker's own company, Tucker, Nicholls & Robinson, prepared most of the PR copy and material. In all, Britain in Europe spent £600,000 on the campaign to keep Britain in the Common Market.

What effect such news management had on the final result of the EEC referendum in June 1975 is unclear. But what is undoubtedly true is that by the time of the referendum campaign itself the press were singing in entire harmony on Europe.

Unfortunately the debate that should have taken place – about British sovereignty, trade, jobs and taxation on food – never happened. Halfway through the campaign, on 22 May, the *Daily Telegraph* even complained that the debate had turned into 'a row about jobs, prices and percentages'. And so the press focused instead on the alleged political ambitions of Tony Benn and the divisions in the Labour Party. 'The real reason for the referendum was to cover up a split in the Labour Party,' said the *Guardian* on 5 June. The *London Evening News*, the *Daily Mail*'s sister paper, was more direct. Labour's Industry Secretary was a 'fully-fledged fanatic' who 'is out for total power'.[52] Three weeks later the *Evening News*' analysis of the referendum was that 'Benn has gone too far to be treated as a joke ... now he is seen in some quarters as a vampire, a fanatic and a bully'.[53]

This was not the opinion of businessmen who worked with the Industry Minister. John Shore, Chief Executive of the Bristol Chamber of Commerce, dealt with Benn as a local MP for 14 years: 'I certainly never found him bonkers. He always presented in all his dealings with us a well-reasoned response to anything that we put to him.'[54] However, it was Benn The Threat that became the central issue for Fleet Street during the EEC referendum campaign. On 5 May 1975 the *Sun* introduced the Industry Minister as 'Danger-Man ... Wedgie has the qualities – good and bad – of some of the great fanatics who have brought nations to the edge of ruin and rejoiced in it'. The same day the *Mail* had an identical theme – 'The Most Dangerous Man in

Britain Today'. Four days later, on 9 May, the *Mail* repeated its slogan – 'Will no-one rid us of this dangerous man?' But it was the *Daily Express* that caught the eye that morning. The paper published a photograph of Benn with the addition of a Hitler moustache and the headline – 'Frightening Sketch of Wedgie'. It was the work of artist Terence Cuneo who managed to 'see a considerable likeness between Tony Benn and another of fanatical disposition'. The *Express* diarist found it most amusing – 'Is the Commissar taking on new and more sinister characteristics?'

For the *Express* Sunday edition Benn, who had volunteered and served as an RAF pilot against Nazi Germany during World War Two, was a traitor: 'In 1940 we knew we had no enemies within our own shores, that we were all united against Hitler. Can we say the same thing now? Could you, for example, be absolutely positively sure on whose side you would find people like Anthony Wedgwood Benn?'[55]

The personalization of the Common Market referendum was so intense that a 'Yes' or 'No' vote really meant whether you were 'for' or 'against' Tony Benn as an individual politician. This was revealed by an anonymous *Daily Telegraph* reporter on 20 May 1975 – 'Benn Factor Now Dominant Issue In Campaign'. The journalist declined to say how the Industry Secretary had become the 'dominant factor'. Nor did the journalist say who had made him the 'dominant factor'. Instead he or she disclosed that Benn had 'dominated yesterday's press conference *without actually being there*'.

Such coverage infuriated the many prominent anti-marketeers who were campaigning with equal vigour against the EEC. Other Labour MPs like Peter Shore, Barbara Castle and Michael Foot were unable to get their views across, because of press diversions like 'Can anyone stop this man before he turns the entire country into a poverty-stricken museum?'[56] Censorship was also a key factor. Three weeks before the referendum vote the *Times* asked Benn to write a feature on the Common Market. Then, without asking or informing him beforehand, the subeditors rewrote sentences and inserted extra words.[57] Benn wrote that being in the EEC would lead to 'a confrontation with organized labour in Britain, for our workers will not accept the suffering caused by this destructive and mechanized industrial philosophy'. The *Times* subeditor inserted 'we had in Britain last year' after 'confrontation with organized labour'. The article was also illustrated by a cartoon depicting Benn with wild staring eyes, clutching parliament and kicking away the continent of Europe with his boot.

Readers of the *Scotsman* were also not entitled to a balanced debate about the EEC during the 1975 referendum, according to former leader writer Colin Bell. 'I was not allowed to write anything that was critical of the Common Market. It was the one thing, apart from Concorde, that we were not allowed to be against,' recalls Bell, now a producer at BBC Scotland. 'It was the only time in 25 years of journalism that I have been stopped from writing something.' The editor, Eric MacKay, strongly denies that journalists were not allowed to write critical articles on the EEC: 'The policy of this paper has been that Britain should stay in the Common Market, but we have written hundreds of leaders critical of the EEC.' When asked whether a *Scotsman* leader writer could have advocated withdrawal from the Common Market during the 1975 referendum, he replied: 'Under no circumstances. Support for the Common Market has been the policy of this paper for many, many years.' I then asked Mr MacKay who decides that policy. 'I do,' he said.

The *Scotsman*'s editorial attitude would not have been a problem if there had been other papers to put the case against membership of the EEC. But, as David Butler revealed in his book on the referendum, there was 'grossly unequal treatment of the two sides as far as sympathetic column inches were concerned'.[55] The mean balance turned out to be 54 per cent for the EEC and 21 per cent against which didn't even reflect public opinion or the final result. Only the *Guardian* and *Times* provided any kind of balance. And those final days before the poll consisted almost entirely of the press quoting pro-marketeers who accused Benn of lying about the effect of EEC membership on employment. 'We have probably lost half a million jobs as a result of our trade deficit with the Nine countries,' said Benn. 'When we were taken into the EEC three years ago, we were told by Mr Heath and his ministers that membership would mean we would sell more goods in the Market than we bought, and create jobs in Britain. The opposite has happened.'[59] The *Sun* described this as 'Citizen Benn's wild claim'[60] while the *Mirror* talked of 'Lies, More Lies and Those Damned Statistics'[61] in a front-page editorial. The *Mirror* accused Benn of playing on people's fear of unemployment. But the paper's own banner headline – 'The Minister of Fear'[62] – was hardly likely to reassure the voters.

On 19 May 1975, the day after Benn's comments on unemployment, it was clear that the agenda had been set for the rest of the campaign. At a press conference that morning a journalist asked William (now Viscount) Whitelaw, Deputy Leader of the Tory Party: 'Do you think Mr Benn is a liar?' The issue of the Industry Secretary's honesty was sustained for the next ten days with large banner headlines –

'Fantasy and Myth – Denis Lashes Benn',[63] 'Heath Lashes Benn's "Big Lie"'.[64] On 4 June, the *Daily Mail* reported Denis Healey's rejection of the jobs claim as his 'magisterial pronouncement' together with the front-page banner headline – 'The Debunking of Tony Benn'.

But as the vote drew near more sinister interpretations were being drawn by the popular press. Sir John Junor, editor of the *Sunday Express* and close personal friend of Mrs Thatcher,[65] remarked: 'How do you fancy Citizen Anthony Wedgwood Benn as the next Commissar of an Iron Curtain Britain. I wouldn't laugh at the idea. If next Thursday's vote is against staying in the EEC there is a chance that sooner or later we will be having him as just that.'[66] The day before the final poll the *Sun* commented: 'What have Citizen Benn and Brigadier Powell and the Communist Party and the racist National Front got in common? The answer is simple. And sad. They are frustrated. They are bitter. They are demagogues. They rant and rave while better men reason. Benn rants that the Market has cost us 500,000 jobs.'[67]

The direct effects of press coverage of the EEC referendum campaign on the actual vote are almost impossible to assess and quantify. However, in May 1974 all the opinion polls showed a substantial majority against the Common Market. There is also some evidence that portraying Benn as representing the whole of the anti-EEC movement and then attacking him had a detrimental influence. The Industry Minister received press photos of himself daubed as Hitler – a clear reference to the *Daily Express* picture. One individual attached the *Daily Mirror*'s 'Minister of Fear' to a postcard and wrote – 'You're a Communist Liar'. These are, of course, not necessarily typical of the average voter's reaction. But there can be no doubt that the referendum was not about the merits or defects of the EEC. It was about Benn. Alfred Browne, weekend editor of the Press Association, bears this out to some extent:

> What the referendum did reveal was the power of the press when linked with the big battalions of politics. It is probably true that newspapers do not shape people's opinions, at least not directly. Readers read the news columns and do not automatically adopt the opinions of the leader columns. But when the news is opinion, as it was during the campaign . . . with no facts to go on, and the emphasis is in one direction then readers are swayed in that direction.[68]

Private health, the *Daily Mail* and the 1978 election

One morning in January 1975, the *Daily Mail* sent a reporter to see Mrs Caroline Benn at her Holland Park home in West London. He told her that her that her youngest son Joshua was in hospital after a car accident. As she knew this was not true, she told the journalist he was mistaken and thought no more of it. However, over the next two days the Benn family received a series of telephone calls from the *Daily Mirror*, *Daily Telegraph* and *Daily Express*. Benn's mother Margaret, who was nearly 80 at the time, was told that her eldest grandson Stephen was in hospital. Then Benn's other son, Hilary, was told by his college tutor at Oxford University that the *Daily Mail* had called to say his brother Joshua had been seriously injured. The same stories were then repeated to relatives and close friends during the next three days despite the strong denials.

The Benn family then met together one evening to consider the possible meaning of these calls. Tony Benn telephoned Sir David English, editor of the *Daily Mail*, to ask him about his paper's inquiries. English refused to talk to him.

After that the calls ceased temporarily, but then the political heat of the Common Market referendum, in which Benn played a leading role, fuelled a new wave of harassment. In May 1975, family friends and teachers at Holland Park Comprehensive were being told, again by the *Daily Mail*, that members of the Benn family were injured or ill. In one day alone there were nine calls. At no time had any of them been ill or injured.

The autumn period revealed what lay behind this press campaign. On 23 October 1975, Jamie Morris, a National Union of Public Employees shop steward at Westminster hospital, confirmed that journalists had been making regular enquiries about whether Joshua or Hilary Benn were being treated privately. Morris was asked to monitor the hospital records by checking all possible names – Milton, Stansgate and De Camp – and then contact Fleet Street. The shop steward was then asked to bring out his NUPE members on strike in protest. When Morris angrily refused the reporter replied: 'I'm sure you would do so if one of your own people used private medicine.'

By this stage it was clear that this was no hoax and the phone calls persisted for the next 18 months. The summer of 1977 saw a new chorus of alleged stories about the Benn family when the Common Market again became a topical issue. The campaign had now moved to the Radcliffe Infirmary in Oxford where a NUPE official informed Benn that national papers, notably the *Daily Telegraph*, were making extensive inquiries. On 2 August 1977, the story was finally published. The *Times* reported: 'A member of Anthony Wedgwood Benn's family has been receiving medical treatment in the private wing of the Radcliffe Infirmary at Oxford. We all know Comrade Benn's views about private medicine. We are interested to learn, therefore, that when his son indulges in it, he does so under his maiden name of De Camp.'

The *Times* diarist had not checked the story with either the Benn family or the hospital. It was entirely untrue. The editor of the *Times*, Sir William Rees-Mogg, a Conservative Party candidate in the 1959 general election, removed the story after the first edition. An editorial executive had noticed the diary piece and knew it to be false. But by then it was too late. The *London Evening Standard* and *Daily Express* had already started to follow up the story.

The next day the *Times* published Benn's denial and their own disclaimer – 'We apologize unreservedly for the report'. But that was not the end of the matter. Although the *Times*' first edition is only available at night in Fleet Street, someone had bought a number of copies and cut out the Benn story. He or she then pasted them on to postcards and sent them to about 20 newspapers, magazines and individuals in London. Although they were posted anonymously, the cards were all sent through an office franking machine with the same number – PBT982W. This was the mark of the British European Movement, based at 1a Whitehall Place, London SW1.

An all-party organization, the European Movement is funded by the Common Market to promote information in favour of the EEC. Until 1976 it also received grants from the Foreign Office. When asked about the *Times* story and the use of his franking machine, Ernest Wistrich, Director of the European Movement, said he was 'quite appalled' and would launch a full investigation. He strongly denied any member of his staff being involved. However, he added: 'As a political organization, we are dependent on many voluntary workers who have access to our offices and it is very difficult to have proper control over their work.'[69]

Moreover, according to Labour MP Brian Sedgemore, the press inquiries into Benn's personal life for political purposes did not end there. On the morning of 14 April 1978, Sedgemore, then Parliamentary Private Secretary to Benn in the Energy Ministry, was approached in the lobby of the House of Commons by a *Daily Mail* political journalist. The reporter warned him that his paper was 'searching for dirt' about Benn's private life in order to damage him and the Labour Party in the run-up to the widely assumed general election in October 1978. The *Mail* political correspondent told Sedgemore that a random search was taking place in Britain and America. There was also a specific story which a *Mail* reporter was checking out. He then gave details of the alleged story which, according to Sedgemore, turned out to be 'a tissue of lies'.

A general election was never called for the autumn of 1978 and the 'story' never appeared in the *Mail*. The paper's editor, Sir David English, a former Labour activist, Party official and Gaitskell supporter in the late 1950s, rarely gives interviews. But the previous year he did reveal the *Mail*'s general editorial stance towards the labour movement: 'If there is a story that is accurate and damaging to the Labour Party we will certainly print it . . . I suppose you could say that reporters know that if they get that sort of story it's likely to get a good show in the paper. I don't disguise that we are opposed to the Labour government and I think it's a disastrous government. The sooner we get rid of it the better.'[70]

Power plots, reselection and the road to 1984

The week after Labour's general election defeat in May 1979, Tony Benn issued a statement to the press. He had decided not to stand for the Shadow Cabinet. He wanted to have a free role in the ensuing debate about the relationship between the parliamentary Party and the wider labour movement, as well as policy issues. This is how the *Sun*'s political editor Walter Terry reported Benn's press release. Under the front-page banner headline of 'Benn's Bid For Power', Terry wrote:

> Former Energy Minister Tony Benn yesterday made a desperate bid for the leadership of the Labour Party. Less than a week after the Tory election triumph, he said publicly what he has thought in secret for years. And his message was that he is: *Fed Up* with ex-Premier Jim Callaghan. *Wants* Labour to swing to the Left – and fast. *Has* his sights on being Prime Minister one day.[71]

Benn had made no other statements that day, nor did he give any radio or TV interviews. The 'message', attributed to Benn, was not in his statement and nor were any of the three points. On the day of publication, 11 May 1979, Benn wrote to Malcolm Withers, father of the *Sun*'s NUJ chapel, and to Sir Larry Lamb, the then editor: 'I believe the article is a breach of the Code of Conduct of the NUJ of which I have been a member since 1949 . . . Would you agree to report this to your chapel and ask them if they would allow me to discuss the matter with Walter Terry present.'

Sir Larry Lamb, soon to be knighted in the 1980 New Year's Honours List, replied: 'Since you have chosen such an eccentric way of seeking satisfaction, I feel no comment from me is called for.'[72] Malcolm Withers said that the NUJ's scope for investigation was severely limited, and any Code of Conduct procedure had to go through Benn's own NUJ branch. However, the *Sun*'s chapel did discuss the matter. Withers put Benn's request to discuss the article to a chapel meeting but it was defeated by 60 votes to three. Instead they recommended Benn to seek redress through the courts or the Press Council. One *Sun* journalist said at the meeting: 'We can't have any old ex-Cabinet minister wandering in and attacking one of our members.'

When I asked Walter Terry about his news story, he was unrepentant: 'Well, it turned out to be true, didn't it . . . I stand by the story. I took the view that Benn was a menace and a number of people in the Labour Party would agree with me.'

The *Sun* was not the only paper to 'take a view' about the debates and arguments inside the Labour Party in the summer of 1979. On 4 July the National Executive passed three motions. Firstly, that Labour leaders should never again nominate life peers to the Honours List. Secondly, that the Party conference should consider a new system of electing the leadership. Thirdly, that conference should decide on whether sitting Labour MPs should face reselection tests by their local parties. The *Daily Mail*'s front-page headline ran – 'Wedgie Puts The Boot In – Three Major Defeats For Sunny Jim By the Left'. Under the byline of '*Daily Mail* Reporter', the news report stated

> Leader of the Opposition James Callaghan was yesterday dealt three humiliating blows by Labour's National Executive Committee . . . Led by Tony Benn, the Left mounted a ferocious assault on Mr Callaghan and his supporters on the NEC . . . This time the battle will be over a scarcely concealed attempt to seize the Party by Tony Benn and commit it irreversibly to extreme leftwing policies.

That same evening the *Mail*'s sister paper, *London Evening News*, echoed those sentiments: 'He [Benn] has set out his strategy for becoming leader, and for assuming virtually dictatorial powers . . . and to discipline, even dismiss, any Labour MP who failed to toe his line.'

The next NEC meeting, on 26 July 1979, provoked more uproar in the popular press. After the Committee had passed a motion giving the National Executive the power to draft the Party manifesto, Callaghan was quick to brief Fleet Street. 'Red Britain', declared the *Daily Express*. The *Daily Mail*'s front-page headline was 'Benn's Commissars', followed by 'This Sort of Move is More Like Eastern Europe'. At the same NEC meeting, a resolution condemning Czechoslovakian repression of the Charter 77 dissidents was unanimously passed. It was moved by Eric Heffer, a close political ally of Benn. The *Mail* declined to mention this motion in their news report.

It was now quite clear that Benn was no longer simply a prominent figure in the Labour Party, he was a political adjective to be used in place of addressing the issues. Labour's National Executive, the 28-member committee elected by the annual Party conference, was said to be Benn's power base. The press claimed that he controlled the NEC single-handedly – 'Anthony Wedgwood Benn's NEC'[73] – and manipulated its business by 'forcing through another motion'.[74] Many trade union delegates and NEC members, who also supported the constitutional reforms, found such coverage offensive. And by September 1979 they had had enough. Just prior to the Labour Party conference Neil Kinnock, Renee Short and Judith Hart issued a joint statement condemning the press reports and confirming that no single individual controlled the National Executive.

Four months later that joint statement appeared to have had a dramatic impact on the personalized coverage. On 11 February 1980, the *Daily Express* announced that 'Mr Benn must be fought . . . not on the question of power and who wields it, but on policy and what Labour stands for.' Unfortunately such fair-mindedness did not last long. On 10 June 1980, the *Express* had returned to personal attacks: 'Though his tongue speaks with sweet reason, he has the mind of a ranter and the eyes of a fanatic.'

But it was the spectre of George Orwell's 'Big Brother' that began to dominate Fleet Street's coverage of Labour's policies from 1980. On 10 July, the Party's NEC produced their draft manifesto. Under the byline of '*Daily Mail* Reporters', the paper's front page reported the NEC draft as 'Big Brother Blockbuster' under the sub-headlines of 'Benn Reveals His Master Plan' and 'The Road to 1984'. The *Mail* interpreted Labour's nationalization plans in their news story as 'far-reaching Big Brother powers for the state over private companies which refused to follow Ministerial directives'. This seemed at odds with the actual proposals – 'Workers to have 50 per cent representation on boards of major companies, participation in management decisions'.[75]

The NEC document contained at least 20 detailed policy proposals from abolition of the House of Lords to job training to nuclear disarmament. The *Sun* told its four million readers a rather different story that morning. In his weekly column, the paper's political editor Walter Terry wrote:

Ayatollah Benn has injected so much poison into the party machine that Iran-style madness is taking over. His local Mullahs babble slogans inciting mob thinking against bewildered Labour MPs. The dottier the idea the better . . . Mr Benn is the hypnotic inflated monster that so many are afraid to puncture.[76]

I asked Walter Terry whether he genuinely believed Benn was 'mad'. He said 'Yes, I think Benn is mad and a lot of Labour people would agree with me . . . I don't regret writing that story, but in any case my weekly column was supposed to be purely my own opinion and meant to be entertaining.'

By the 1980 Party conference many of the NEC's initiatives were on the agenda and Benn's speech was a clear sign that Labour was moving to the Left. He advocated large-scale nationalization, the transfer of EEC powers from the Commission in Brussels to Parliament and the creation of 1,000 Labour peers to abolish the House of Lords. Benn sat down to a thunderous standing ovation, but the press were unimpressed. For the *Daily Star*: 'Benn is training a suicide squad to put him into power.'[77] For the *Daily Express* he was a 'wolf in sheep's clothing, unleashing a terrifying vision of socialism on the rampage in 1984.'[78] Fred Emery, the *Times* political editor, claimed that Labour MPs were 'unprintably angry that through his demagogy he had nullified the Party's earnest attempt to open proceedings by trying to get itself taken seriously.'[79]

The Party conference went on to vote for withdrawal from the EEC by three million votes. Abolition of the House of Lords has been official Labour policy since 1918. In 1977 the Party conference called for Labour to 'take every possible step open to them to secure the total abolition of the House of Lords.'

Fleet Street's reaction to the next day's proceedings at the 1980 conference was equally apocalyptic. 'Labour In Chaos – Fury As Benn and The Left Take Charge', reported the *Daily Mirror*.[80] 'Triumph for Lunacy', the paper's editorial added. The *Daily Express* declared: 'Labour In Anarchy – Party In Ruins After Shock Vote For Benn'.[81] The *Mail* was more precise – 'In an incredible and electrifying display of manipulating rank-and-file power, Mr Benn turned the tables.'[82]

Conference had passed a motion making MPs accountable to their local parties by reselection tests with a majority of nearly 500,000 votes. Delegates also supported the setting up of an electoral college by a majority of 100,000 votes. The 'chaos', cited by the *Express*, was due to the procedural problem that a formula had not yet been decided for the electoral college which would conduct future leadership elections. These constitutional reforms had been on Labour's conference agenda since 1975. Indeed, in 1978 mandatory reselection of MPs was only defeated because Hugh (now Lord) Scanlon, General Secretary of the Amalgamated Union of Engineering Workers, had apparently misinterpreted the motion.

And yet the 1980 conference was portrayed as though 'Benn's Bandits' (*Daily Express*[83]) were taking over the party. For the *Sun* this could only lead to one thing: 'We know now what the dominant left-wing would do if it ever achieved office . . . The Marxist extremists are committed to leading Britain along the road to the corporate Marxist state.'[84]

The deputy leadership campaign

The day after Tony Benn announced his candidature for the Labour Party deputy leadership on 2 April 1981, the *Sun* commented: 'Nothing really surprising about Tony Benn announcing at 4 a.m. that he will try to become Labour's deputy leader. That is the time the police state always swoops.'

Such language and imagery of totalitarianism and dictatorship proved to be the dominant theme of the popular press's coverage over the six-month campaign. For Benn was to be portrayed as a ruthless power-crazed tyrant who would lead the Labour Party into 'a valley of darkness and ultimate extinction'.[85] The personal attacks on Benn, comparable to Cicero's oration against Cataline in ancient Rome, became more bitter as the campaign wore on: 'Why Labour Leaders Tremble at the Relentless Advance of Benn's Army. Torn Apart by the Politics of Fear', warned the *Daily Express*.[86]

But why did most of Fleet Street react in such a Pavlovian way to an internal Party election? Michael Foot had stood for the deputy leadership in 1970, 1971 and 1972. The *Times* did not accuse him, as they did Benn, of being 'divisive, ambitious, jockeying for position and fratricidal'.[87] And when Benn himself stood for the deputy leadership in 1971 and the leadership in 1976, the press hardly raised an eyebrow. In 1981 there was a difference. The Left candidate was within striking distance of winning the election.

It was perhaps rather naive of Benn's supporters to believe that the 1981 deputy leadership campaign could have been conducted on the basis of policies rather than personalities. For as Labour MP Joe Ashton pointed out at the time: 'There are two and a half million people who don't give a damn about Tony or Denis or Michael. They just want to get back to work. If Benn runs, the arguments for the next six months won't be about these issues. They will be about Benn . . . It will be Benn does this or Denis moves in or Foot speaks out'.[88]

This was a valid point. There were glaring political differences between Denis Healey and Benn on the EEC, nuclear disarmament and the economy. Yet Fleet Street simply refused to report the issues. The *Daily Mirror* provided a good example of this on 10 September. Benn said in a radio interview: 'Those who want to shackle the unions with a discredited wages policy, keep Britain in the EEC and allow US nuclear bases to remain in Britain are now losing the arguments.' The *Mirror*'s headline for this story was 'Now Benn Attacks Foot'. This was despite the fact that Michael Foot agrees with Benn on all three issues.

It is, of course, misleading and even dishonest to discount the role of personalities in politics. Personal qualities are obviously important for any candidate in a leadership election. And it is also difficult to see how a person's values can be separated from his or her character. But when political differences are almost completely ignored, as they were during the deputy leadership campaign, then other forces are at work.

This was revealed in the press reaction to Benn's candidature. 'Stop Benn', cried the *Sun*,[89] but it was the *Mirror* which set the tone for the next six months – 'Power-Bid Benn'.[90] The *Guardian*, usually sympathetic to Labour in its features and letters pages, accused Benn of being 'recklessly divisive' in its editorial.[91] Some of the paper's staff became angry at the subsequent coverage. They were mainly concerned that the senior staff, three of whom were prospective parliamentary candidates for the SDP, were using their position to push the Alliance ticket in the leader columns. There was never a serious row as there wasn't even a meeting held to discuss the issue. But news reports like the following didn't help: 'Tony Benn and his leftwing supporters yesterday succeeded in marginally tightening the garotte around the throats of Labour MPs.'[92]

Fleet Street's explanation for the prominence of the radical Left in the Labour Party in recent years has been to portray the official Opposition as a product of irrational and authoritarian elements subverting its true vocation. Hence, during the deputy leadership campaign, the *Daily Mail* proclaimed: 'Order of the Bennite Loon. For devotees of crazy political ideas'.[93] The *Sun* was more direct on 22 May 1981: 'Mr Benn – Is He Mad or a Killer?'

Six days later the *Daily Express* was even more explicit. On 28 May, its front-page headline ran 'Benn The Dictator' together with 'He Puts 200 MPs At Risk'. The paper's political editor reported that Benn had 'bulldozed his way to another Labour coup yesterday – forcing moderate MPs to run the gauntlet of leftwing rivals for their seats'. It was based on the National Executive's decision that a one-name short list for mandatory reselection of MPs was 'not normal practice'.

Jack Doherty lives at Hornby Road, Blackpool, and a copy of the *Daily Express* has been delivered to his home every day for over 40 years. When he saw the 'Benn The Dictator' headline, he was furious. Doherty immediately wrote to the Press Council and described the article as 'an unsavoury hotch-potch of cowardice, lies, and wanton negligence bordering upon the libellous'. He added:

> The *Express* gives the lie to its own headline by conceding, some six column inches further down in the main text, that all Mr Benn had in effect achieved was to win support for a motion by persuading 15 elected members of the NEC of the Labour Party to support his motion, with only nine voting against. Nothing is made of the fact that Mr Benn's victory would appear to be the very essence of democracy in action.

Gerald Ellis, from North London, also complained: 'A dictator is someone who has achieved political power by force. Mr Benn has not done so. If the *Daily Express* ill-informs me, I cannot form the right opinion and am unable to vote for the party that serves me best.'[95]

On 9 June 1981, Morris Bennett, personal assistant to the then editor of the *Express*, Arthur Firth, replied to Doherty's complaint:

> MPs are elected by the whole country, whereas NEC members are chosen by a few hundred Labour Party zealots. These zealots are not responsible to the electorate, and do not even represent the trade unions whose views they purport to reflect — because they are not elected by a full ballot of trade union members. In these circumstances, Mr Benn's use of the NEC to subvert the position of sitting MPs is a clear and dangerous manipulation of the democratic process. For the above reasons, it is felt that the use of the word 'Dictator' was justified.

On 25 October 1981, James McMillan, the *Express*'s policy advisor and political columnist said:

> It is my opinion that the state of debate within the Labour Party at the time in question fully justified the use of the headline about Mr Benn ... Mr Ellis appears to be under the impression that a newspaper has a duty to help him make up his mind on politics. The *Daily Express* is not a consensus newspaper. Its view of Mr Benn was clearly expressed in the headline.

The author of the story was political editor John Warden. This was his statement to the Press Council

> By late May 1981, the debate in the Labour Party had reached a crescendo, and was being conducted in language which left no doubt as to what the issue was – 'party democracy' versus 'party dictatorship'. For months the argument had been summed up in these actual terms by Labour MPs and others involved. And for both sides, mandatory reselection of MPs was the touchstone of how they saw 'democracy' or 'dictatorship' in practice. By May 28, only a visitor from Mars could have been so ignorant of events as to be surprised either by the prominence given to our story or the headline above it. One should also recall the formation of the SDP, the steady defection of Labour MPs, and Mr Benn's initial reaction, which was to demand from those remaining in the party an oath of loyalty. This evoked a comparison with the Thought Police of 1984.[96]

As 'evidence' he reproduced 14 quotations by prominent Labour politicians, four of which came from Denis Healey. None of them subsequently voted for Benn in the deputy leadership election.

The Press Council's verdict was that 'The headline ''Benn The Dictator'' was unjustified, inaccurate and not supported by the text of the article. It reflected an editorial opinion rather than the substance of a news item.' The *Daily Express* published the Council's adjudication on 24 April 1982 on the bottom left-hand corner of page 9 – nearly a year after they had published the original story.

Nevertheless, Warden's use of comments by Benn's political opponents was significant. For leading members of the labour movement did use the press to make highly personalized attacks. Here is a tiny sample. Frank (now Lord) Chapple described Benn as 'a little Stalin' who wanted to set up a 'Socialist horror camp in Britain'.[97] Labour MP John Golding declared that 'The bully boys of the Left who support Benn are acting like Hitler Youth'.[98] Denis Healey accused Benn of encouraging a 'sort of People's Democracy the Russians set up in Eastern Europe after the war, against which the Polish workers are now rebelling'.[99]

Such eye-catching, temperate language was naturally lapped up by Fleet Street news editors, but for professional as well as political reasons. As Michael Foot once remarked: 'You go to Marble Arch and try to make a speech about goodness and love. You won't have a soul to listen to you. Try good, juicy hatred and you'll get an audience of hundreds.'[100]

On a political level, the personal attacks by shadow cabinet members also gave credibility to the press accusations of extremism in Labour's ranks. This took the form of portraying Benn as a Communist sympathizer – 'Benn's Red Army'.[101] The *Sun* was quite open about alleging that his first loyalty was to the Warsaw Pact: 'An end to the sham. A cross on the ballot for a party which has Benn waiting in the wings for its top job is a cross for the bleak and cold regimes of Eastern Europe and for a government on their model. A government like the one that runs East Germany. A Klan like that lot in the Kremlin.'[102] Britain's biggest-selling paper, *News of the World*, whistled a similar tune: 'Citizen Benn who shouts from the rooftops the debt we owe to a man called Joseph Stalin.'[103] This was despite the fact that Benn had been a vociferous critic of the Soviet Union for many years. In 1956 he wrote a letter to *Pravda*, along with five other Labour MPs, protesting about the Russian invasion of Hungary. In 1968 he denounced the occupation of Czechoslovakia. In 1980 he condemned the repression of Afghanistan and Solidarity in Poland.

As Benn's chances of becoming Labour's Deputy Leader increased in the autumn of 1981, so Fleet Street's language became more desperate. 'Benn's Britain – What It Would Be Like Under Wedgie's Boot in 1984', asserted the *Sun* during the TUC Conference.[104] The *Mirror* claimed: 'Benn's supporters are now sneering, hate-filled creatures'.[105] Two days before the final poll the *London Standard* gave prominence to an interview with Mrs Peggy Jay, mother of Peter Jay. 'When I close my eyes and hear the voice of Benn saying our people,' she told Max Hastings, 'it could be Hitler in the 1930s.'[106]

However, the extent of the threat posed by Benn's candidature was only really exposed on the weekend before the vote. On Saturday 19 September 1981, an unemployment rally was held in Birmingham. At the end of the demonstration Denis Healey was unable to finish his speech because of loud heckling by a group of people who positioned themselves in front of the cameras near the platform. The press automatically assumed that they were Benn supporters. 'Healey Gagged By Benn Mob', said the *Sunday Mirror* front-page headline the next morning. 'An angry mob forced Labour moderate Denis Healey to abandon his speech at a party rally yesterday. Uproar broke out when about 50 militant supporters of Tony Benn tried to storm the platform in a "gag Healey move"'. The *Sunday Times* political staff came to the same conclusion: 'Healey was shouted down by Benn's supporters when he tried to speak to a Labour rally . . . Healey angrily denounced his jeering opponents who have now tried to deny him a hearing at three party rallies.'

The next day, Monday 21 September, Healey accused Jon Lans-man, Benn's campaign organizer, of orchestrating the heckling at the demonstration and at a previous rally in Cardiff. That same morning Nigel Stanley, secretary of the pro-Benn Labour Co-ordinating Committee, had been at his desk no more than 30 minutes when two *Times* journalists and a photographer burst into his office in Poland Street, central London. They immediately accused him of secretly organizing the hecklers. Unhappily for the *Times*, Stanley's only subversive activity that Saturday afternoon was shopping in Brixton High Street.

So what really happened? Firstly, Lansman was on holiday in Sicily during the Birmingham meeting. At the time of the Cardiff rally in July, he was driving from London to Aberystwyth. Secondly, the *Sunday Mirror*'s 'Benn Mob' at Birmingham turn out to be members of the Revolutionary Communist Party (RCP). They are strongly opposed to the Labour Left and have publicly admitted heckling *Benn's* speeches. 'We make no secret of the fact that we intervene on the Irish issue at Labour Movement meetings,' said RCP member Anne Dillon, 'or that we were present at the Birmingham rally.'[107] Fellow RCP member Fran Eden confirmed her party's hostility to the Labour Left: 'We are asking people not to support Healey or Benn. We think Benn represents a real danger because active workers will get sucked into the Left of the Labour Party.'[108] A more graphic description of what happened came from Alan Clarke, a National Union of Public Employees area organizer, who said: 'There were two people, pissed, shouting at everything, and a group of H-Block protesters. And there was general booing of Healey, but there was nothing co-ordinated about this.'[109]

Within two days a new 'scandal' had erupted and Fleet Street was unanimous in its condemnation. The Transport and General Workers Union's Executive had voted to recommend that their delegation should vote for Benn because his policies were more in line with the union than Healey's views. This was despite an apparent majority in branches for Healey where the members were consulted. 'A fraud, farce and fiasco', commented the *Guardian*,[110] 'Benn Votes Hijack', said the *Sun* headline.[111] However, it transpired later that only 20 per cent of the TGWU branches had been consulted. In truth, the whole process was badly organized and an indecisive shambles.

But if the press were partly correct to attack the TGWU decision, there can be little excuse as to why they ignored the way other unions 'consulted' their members for the deputy leadership ballot. The Iron and Steel Trades Confederation (ISTC), National Union of Railwaymen (NUR) and the Electricians Union (EETPU) all voted for Healey with virtually no vote at either branch or executive level. Bill Sirs, the ISTC's General Secretary, simply announced they were going to vote for Healey and 'that was that'. Several ISTC executive members didn't recall discussing the issue and so they asked to see the minutes or the cassette tape of the relevant meeting. They were told that 'political decisions were not recorded in the minutes' and that the tape recorder had not been working on that particular day. None of this was reported in the national press.

Rather more prominence was given by the *Times* in that final week of campaigning to Benn's alleged financial wealth. On Friday 25 September 1981, two days before delegates casted their votes, the *Times* published a feature purporting to list the financial assets of the three candidates. The author of the article, City journalist Philip Robinson, managed to dispose of the considerable business and property interests of John Silkin and Denis Healey in one sentence each.

Benn's personal finances were given rather more scrutiny. He was said to own a 'large house in Holland Park and farm in Essex'. Also that 'city sources confirm the existence of a Stansgate trust in the tax haven of the Bank of Bermuda'. In fact, Benn does not and never has has owned a farm in Essex. The 'farm' is a house built on two acres of land near the ruins of Stansgate Abbey. The residence had previously belonged to Benn's mother, Margaret, who bought it in the 1930s for £1,500. The 'Stansgate trust' was confirmed as nonexistent by the Bank of Bermuda itself who wrote to their London representative, Mr H.J. Witheridge: 'I confirm that a search of our records does not reveal that a trust in the name of Stansgate has ever been maintained or managed by this bank.'[12] Nevertheless, Philip Robinson claimed that, while he had no proof, he believed that a trust might exist and the Benn family could be its beneficiaries. The *Times*' then editor, Harold Evans, said the paper had received telephone calls making similar allegations but he also had no evidence.[113]

The *Times* report also claimed that 'most of the Benn family wealth comes from legacies and trusts connected with his American-born wife Caroline. The estimated total is several million dollars'. The facts paint a rather different picture of the 'Benn wealth'. The Benns own their house in Holland Park which they bought in 1952 for £4,700. The Register of Members' Interests reveals that Benn owns about one per cent of the total number of shares in the family publishing firm Benn Brothers Ltd. He is not a director of the company and his links are very small. James Benn, Managing Director of Benn Bros, said that his holding was 'a family inheritance from his mother'. He added: 'I don't think it's very large. In fact, I'm sure it isn't. No, Tony Benn has played no role in this business as far as I can remember, and I've been here 15 years.'[114]

Apart from his parliamentary salary, Benn's only other income comes from writing and broadcasting. A financial legacy does exist in the form of a bequest by Caroline Benn's mother, Mrs Anne Hamill. Mrs Benn has officially disowned the money, but her mother has left it in a trust to be shared between her four grandchildren. The actual amount is £172,000 – or £43,000 each. This was hardly the 'several million dollars' as claimed by the *Times*.

The idea of checking the candidates' financial assets was discussed during a *Times* daily editorial conference. It was suggested by Peter Stothard, the paper's deputy features editor who is now a senior executive. The information about Benn was then provided by Philip Robinson and a freelance journalist. The story was not checked with either the Bank of Bermuda or Benn. When asked by *Tribune* journalist Chris Mullin why this did not happen, Harold Evans replied: 'That was a professional error for which two people have been rebuked. I was livid when I found out.'[115] In fact, Robinson only telephoned Benn the day *after* publication of the article and proceeded to argue about the existence of the 'Stansgate Trust'.

The day after this short story was published, the *Times* printed Benn's letter of denial with a modest nine-word apology. Many readers wrote to Benn angry that a more substantial redress was not allowed. Evans wrote to Benn the same day: 'I am very sorry indeed that wrong statements appear to have been published. It is unfortunate that we had an exceedingly bad night's production at the *Times* last night. This page would, of course, have been changed after I saw the first edition.'[116]

Benn then replied with three requests as a way of dispelling any future rumours. He asked for one, the source of the story. The *Times* could not claim to be obliged to protect the source as it had given false information; two, a right of reply in a prominent part of the paper; three, personal damages. Evans refused on all three counts on the basis that 'the letters page was the most read part of the *Times*. I utterly reject your accusation that we have a campaign against you.'[117]

In later correspondence with Benn, Evans said: 'The error which we corrected was due to a misunderstanding in the office and to information supplied by two outside sources. It was thought that it had been put to you by Mr Haviland. In fact, Julian Haviland, the *Times*' political editor, had telephoned Benn three days before publication of the article. However, at no time did he question Benn about the 'farm' or 'trust in Bermuda'.

To be fair to Evans, he did take full responsibility for the story. 'It was not a sinister event at all and had nothing to do with the proprietor,' he later told me. 'It is true, of course, that Rupert Murdoch rejoiced in anything to Benn's discredit. But if there is anybody to criticize over this incident it should, at the end of the day, be me since I was editor of the paper and have to take full responsibility.'[118]

However, like many smears, this one stuck. The *Daily Mail* reproduced the story the next day – 'Angry Benn Denies That Family Trust Funds Are Locked Away in Bermuda Tax-Haven'. Benn received dozens of letters from Labour voters who had not noticed the two-line apology in the *Times*. Many of them expressed disgust that 'you have a tax haven' and would no longer support him because of his 'wealth'. The story was quoted with wild accusations about Benn 'having stocks and shares in the City of London'. Yeovil Liberal Party quoted from the *Times* in the November edition of their newsletter *Counterpoint*: 'The Stansgate Trust ... is safely tucked away in the Bank of Bermuda, one of the world's largest tax havens.' The newsletter was distributed to all the Labour strongholds of the town.

Not everyone, however, was taken in by the *Times* story. Jeffrey Cox, Assistant Professor of History at Iowa University, wrote to Harold Evans complaining that the paper wrongly depicted Benn as a threat to democracy. Evans replied: 'The tradition of the *Times* has always been to be tough and fair and I am proud to continue that tradition. You are right that we have been tough on Mr Benn – though no tougher than our treatment of some aspects of Mrs Thatcher's Tory government.' The paper's editor went on to discuss Labour's constitutional reforms and said that Benn had 'lobbied to increase the power of the party activists (who are not elected) and reduce the power of Labour's elected representatives in Parliament ... We oppose Mr Benn's plans because we prefer parliamentary democracy to Party democracy.'

How much effect the *Times* feature, two days before the deputy leadership election, had on the final result it is difficult to say. Although Benn lost by less than one per cent, it is unlikely that backbench Labour MPs would have been swayed by one *Times* story. However, there is some evidence that the wider coverage of the deputy leadership campaign had some bearing on the political views of the electorate. Research into media coverage and public images of the Labour Party throughout 1981 revealed that 73.1 per cent of the sample felt that Benn was not to be trusted because of 'his dictatorial ambitions'; 62.3 per cent believed that he was 'a Communist' whose main political aim was to make us 'just like Russia'. Of those intending to vote Labour at the next general election, 27.7 per cent said they would reconsider their decision if Benn became deputy leader.[119]

The Chesterfield by-election

The 1983 general election defeat was a crushing blow to Labour's left-wing. For the Party's manifesto was largely a product of their making. An additional catastrophe for the Labour Left was Tony Benn's defeat in the marginal constituency of Bristol East. This meant he was unable to be a candidate in the inevitable leadership contest which took place in the autumn of 1983. However, when Eric Varley resigned his Chesterfield seat in November 1983, Benn was a front-runner as the subsequent by-election candidate.

The issue for the press was whether Neil Kinnock, Labour's new leader, wanted Benn as the candidate. Several Party backbenchers had told Lobby correspondents that Kinnock 'didn't want Benn back in Parliament'. On 17 November 1983, Kinnock told the lobby this was completely untrue. The following morning the *Times* headlined their story – 'Labour Unites Against Benn The Bogeyman'. The *Sun* insisted that 'the Kinnock camp has already tried a discreet ''Stop Benn'' campaign'. Other papers persisted with the story the following week by quoting anonymous Labour MPs who 'knew the leadership's views'. At the next National Executive meeting Kinnock denounced the press reports as 'absolute nonsense', said they were personally offensive and would be damaging to the Party's chances in the by-election.

Benn's eventual selection as the by-election candidate for Chesterfield on 15 January 1984 was received with almost apocalyptic warnings from Fleet Street. 'His wild-eyed fanaticism is a constant warning to any voters temped to support the Tories' opponents,' advised the *Sun*.[120] The *Daily Mail*'s Paul Johnson wrote that

he [Benn] is a certain vote-loser ... The spectre of Bennery has haunted Labour in the last two elections, and frustrated the efforts of three successive leaders, Wilson, Callaghan and Foot. But now, like Frankenstein's, the Bennite monster has been reactivated to smash through the fragile structure of compromise and moderation which a fourth leader, Kinnock himself, had just begun to build and to turn Labour once again into an unpredictable comic-horror story.[121]

Such sentiments strike a hollow chord coming from the pen of Johnson. For on 27 May 1977, he wrote an open letter to Tony Benn in the *New Statesman*:

In my judgement you are by far the ablest and most valuable politician in the Labour Party ... What I like about you best of all, you have absolute faith in democracy ... Now, it is precisely because you possess this wide range of qualities, and because I want to see you leader of the Labour Party – possibly in the quite near future – that I am anxious you should withdraw your support from the hideous shambles of the Callaghan government.

However, apart from the polemics of the *Mail*'s Paul Johnson, the initial coverage of the Chesterfield by-election campaign was relatively fair and balanced. Indeed, at the beginning of the campaign the *Daily Star*'s editorial management even sent a memorandum to its political staff ordering them to treat the Labour candidate fairly. And within ten days Benn's press officer, Monica Foot, remarked: 'The local papers have been smashing and the nationals have given the party a fair crack of the whip.'[122] Foot's comment was borne out by much of the coverage by the *Daily Telegraph*, *Derbyshire Times*, *Sheffield Star* and *Sheffield Morning Telegraph*.

This was partly due to a new strategy of dealing with the press. The Labour camp had decided in mid-January to try and prevent Fleet Street from setting the political agenda. 'If we don't allow coverage of politics to return to what is said, what people feel, and what happens', said Benn, 'then we shall actually undermine the confidence in the democratic system.'[123] And so the national press were bypassed. Traditional press conferences were largely abandoned – there were only six in three weeks, mainly on specific policy issues. This angered some reporters like the *Daily Express*' Geoffrey Levy who said this 'cheated voters out of hearing Benn's responses to questions put by journalists'.[124] However, Labour, as the *Daily Telegraph* observed, 'has successfully reimposed the primacy of direct communication with the citizens who have votes to cast'.[125]

In many ways it was a very old-fashioned campaign. Benn himself went out to meet nearly 50 per cent of the electorate and about 13,000 people attended his 25 public meetings – indoors and in the Market Square. He took part in six forums and 14 Labour Party evenings. Benn did, in fact, give press conferences – outside factories, unemployment benefit offices, hospitals and pensioners' flats. Journalists were allowed to ask him questions there. Many correspondents preferred this system, but others were frustrated. 'Benn has been on his best behaviour. He's not putting a foot wrong. The campaign is phoney,' said the *Guardian*'s Dennis Johnson.[126] The *Mirror*'s Terence Stringer maintained that the Labour candidate himself was the issue: 'It has been a Labour seat for 50 years. The majority at the general election was nearly 8,000. If Benn was not here, there would be little interest from the nationals and TV. The issue *is* Benn.'[127]

For the ordinary voters of Chesterfield the issue was not Benn. A week before the by-election a Harris opinion poll, commissioned by the *Observer*, showed that for 50 per cent of the sample unemployment was the most important issue; 25 per cent said the National Health Service, 20 per cent defence, 19 per cent inflation. Only 13 per cent replied that the individual candidate was the crucial influence on their vote.[128] A BBC2 *Newsnight* poll of 600 voters produced a similar result. A clear majority said that issues like the National Health Service and unemployment were more important than the identity of the individual candidates.

For the first two weeks of the campaign the Labour camp managed to overcome the problems of personalization and the expected onslaught from Fleet Street never bore fruit. However, some journalists tried hard. When Denis Healey, an old political adversary of Benn, came to Chesterfield they went to a local pub and sang a couple of songs for the locals. The next morning Peter Hitchens, the *Daily Express* political correspondent, and the *Sun*'s Chris Potter compared notes: 'Do you know if they argued over what song to sing?' asked Hitchens. 'No, they were being urged to sing "My Old Man's a Dustman,"' replied Potter. 'Geoff might have it on tape, actually, which is a thought, isn't it.'[129]

Hitchens' desire to find stories about splits in the Labour Party did not extend to the Conservative Party. When the Tory candidate, Nicholas Bourne, said that he didn't support the government's decision to ban unions at Cheltenham GCHQ, the *Express* correspondent hardly took a note. A fellow journalist asked him, 'Don't you think that's a good story?' Hitchens, a former full-time organizer for the International Socialists, replied: 'Not really.' He seemed more concerned that he had missed out on a rumour that the Labour candidate had had a half pint of bitter (Benn is a teetotaller). Hitchens did in fact give the story about Bourne's opposition to the union ban at GCHQ three paragraphs. However, when Benn condemned the decision as a threat to democracy itself, Hitchens reported: 'This sort of gigantic mental leap is what makes people call him an extremist.'[130]

The sign of the changing mood in Fleet Street was revealed in an incident involving the *Daily Telegraph*'s correspondent, R. Barry O'Brien. Throughout the campaign his reporting had received much praise from Labour Party workers and Benn himself for its balance and fairness. But as the Tory candidate Nicholas Bourne faltered, O'Brien came under pressure from the *Telegraph* editorial management to give the Conservatives more prominence. He was also receiving barbed comments from the paper's copytakers that the campaign was 'as exciting as *Coronation Street*'. On the evening of Friday 24 February 1984, O'Brien phoned through his copy. Later that night he received a message at his hotel ordering him to rewrite his news story. At first O'Brien was angry and refused to do so. He was then told by the *Daily Telegraph* subeditors that it 'would be in your own interests to do so'. Faced with this implied threat, he rearranged the story to give the Tories more prominence – ' ' ' 'Benn Doesn't Scare Me'' Tebbit Tells Voters'. O'Brien's original report was introduced by the latest opinion polls which gave Labour 48 per cent and 49 per cent of the vote. This level of support was relegated eight paragraphs down the page.

More evidence of editorial management trying to set the political agenda and damage Labour's campaign appeared in the press the next day. The front pages of both the *Sunday Express* and *Sunday Times* associated Benn with 'a looming crisis of violence'. The story originated from both the Tory and Liberal press conferences the previous morning. After the Conservative press conference, Glyn Matthias, the ITN's political editor, had an informal conversation with the Environment Minister, Patrick Jenkin. At the end of their talk, Jenkin mentioned that some Liverpool Labour councillors had threatened a demonstration outside his home over the government's refusal to increase grants to the City Council. As the minister had already gone on record about alleged threats of civil disobedience, Matthias, an experienced political correspondent, didn't follow up the story and thought no more of it. However, freelance journalist Graham Hind had tape-recorded the conversation and sold the story to the *Sunday Express* and the *News of the World*. The *Sunday Express* portrayed the report as: 'One of the most chilling insights ever into the violent nature of leftwing extremism.' Chesterfield, the paper added, was 'the focus of a looming crisis'.[131]

The *Sunday Times* also managed to link the by-election with a 'chain of violence'. For the paper this involved the demonstration against Jenkin in Liverpool, the alleged mobbing of MacGregor by some miners and a Labour MP's refusal to describe the IRA as terrorists. Their story was based on some remarks by the Liberal Party leader David Steel at the Saturday morning press conference. Steel had claimed that these incidents 'represented the true face of Labour'. Martin Kettle, the *Sunday Times* correspondent, asked him: 'Are you saying that Mr Benn condones or is associated with any individual cases that you've cited?' Steel replied: 'Well, he's very careful not to disassociate himself when asked'. Kettle didn't think it was a story but filed his copy along with a denial of the 'violence' charge by Labour MP Michael Meacher. At about 2 p.m. he rang Hugo Young, the *Sunday Times* political editor, who told him: 'I should tell you that the story is being rewritten to hype it up.'

Later that Saturday afternoon Andrew Neil, the editor, authorized the copy to be rewritten by the back-bench, despite objections from Hugo Young. The original headline – 'Benn Set To Win As Politics Turn Nasty' – was changed to 'Benn Set To Win As Politics Turn Rough', after protests from Young who had been political editor since 1973. When the three *Sunday Times* journalists were told about the editorial management's action, they were so angry that they removed their by-lines from the story before the first edition. One said: 'The paper was more interested in smearing Mr Benn than in fair reporting.'[132]

Based on Steel's comments, the *Sunday Times* front-page report began:

> Threats of violence and extra-parliamentary action faced the That-cher government on several fronts this weekend. Speaking in the Chesterfield by-election yesterday, David Steel, the Liberal leader, accused Tony Benn, Labour's candidate, of being linked with left-wing forces which threatened street violence, supported last week's 'mobbing' of Ian MacGregor and refused to describe the IRA as 'terrorists'.

After this first edition appeared there were much stronger complaints from some of the paper's executives, particularly over the headline. Faced with such objections from their own senior staff, Neil and the back-bench produced a limited rewrite of the story to soften the abrasive tone for the later editions. Two weeks later, on 14 March 1984, Hugo Young, who was also joint deputy editor, resigned from the paper. One of the main reasons for his departure was that the editor declined to take his judgement and advice on the political coverage of the *Sunday Times*.

Neil denies rewriting the story. He said that the news copy the paper received was not in a coherent form and needed to be restruc-tured by the 'back-bench' for 'stylistic reasons'. He added: 'We were faced with a week without an obvious splash story. There were four events and not one of them merited a lead story by themselves, so we had to bring them together. The problem was finding a headline that would fit the various stories.' However, Neil did regret the published headline and said that in a similar situation he would probably use a different form of words.

But it was the *Sun*'s coverage that would cause the most controversy during the by-election. The paper's subeditors had continually described the Labour candidate as 'Bogeyman Benn' — as if this was an established fact. According to the *Sun*'s former political editor Roger Carroll, the aim of the paper was 'to diminish Tony Benn'.

On 22 February 1984, the *Sun* tried to associate Labour MP Joan Maynard's views on the IRA with the Chesterfield by-election. Under the headline of 'The Sick Voice of Bennism', their editorial said: 'Anyone who can invest with glamour the skulking, cowardly butchers of the innocent and helpless is worthy more of the psychiatrist's couch than serious analysis.' The Ulster problem was clearly never an issue in Chesterfield, although the by-election correspondents *were* told by their news editors that morning to question Benn on Maynard's remarks. However, as Roger Carroll, now a *Sunday Telegraph* feature writer, explains, the *Sun* editorial 'very blatantly tried to associate Tony Benn with very unpopular views on the IRA and maybe even with the IRA itself . . . Nobody who really knows the man assumes he supports violence.'[133]

On the day of the by-election poll itself, the *Sun* presented to their 15,000 readers in Chesterfield what the paper saw as the most pressing issue of the day — Benn's mental health. The *Sun* had paid a Dallas psychiatrist, Dr David Hubbard, $350 to examine three and a half pages of facts about Benn's personal life and political career. The result was a telephone interview with the paper's New York correspondent Martin Dunn and a page-long feature — 'Benn On The Couch — A Top Psychiatrist's View of Britain's Leading Leftie'.[134] The *Sun*'s aim was clear from the first line — 'some say Tony Benn is raving bonkers'. The paper's former political editor Roger Carroll, an ex-SDP press officer, had no doubts about the *Sun*'s intentions: 'Benn the lunatic, this is the impression they're trying to get across . . . that this man is mad. You can certainly bet that if there were 20 psychiatrists who said he was perfectly normal, and one who said maybe he's disturbed, it would be *that one* who would be selected as the *Sun* psychiatrist.'

The article itself began: 'He is a Messiah figure hiding behind the mask of a common man. He is greedy for power and will do anything to satisfy his hunger. He is Tony Benn.' The *Sun* then quoted Dr Hubbard as saying:

People with these character disorders do not age well. Their peculiarities get worse rather than better. It sometimes scares the hell out of these sorts of people when they just suddenly say to themselves —

'Could I be crazy?' ... Mr Nobody-type characters are prone to
great periods of fantasy in which they try to change everything.

This analysis was based on a document written by Rosalind Grose, a
Sun feature writer, and contained what the paper described as 'every
known fact about Labour's candidate'. For a politician who is the subject of four biographies and whose collected works fill three volumes,
the *Sun*'s fact sheet makes remarkable reading. Benn was said to be
'convinced he alone was always right', 'claims the press are out to get
him' and that 'many of his detractors call him bonkers'. The paper's
fact sheet added:

As a boss, he always made sure all his juniors were called into meetings to decide on a course of action – yet his mind was already made
up ... He made sure he was boss – and seen to be so. Personally
took credit for all his department's successes. Even to the degree of
calling a press conference to launch a policy worked out by a junior
minister – while that minister was on holiday.

These are not facts.

An insight into the *Sun* correspondent's view of the Labour candidate for Chesterfield comes from the transcript of the interview, when
Martin Dunn says: 'He's absolutely committed 100 per cent to
nationalizing the country and controlling it himself.'

Dr Hubbard's role in this little saga was a trifle ambivalent. When
tracked down by Granada TV's *World in Action*, he claimed: 'I'm
disgusted. I've been lied to and misquoted. The trusting relationship
one should be able to have working with the media has just been
blown to hell.' When told of the conclusions he was supposed to have
reached, Dr Hubbard replied: 'I think they are markedly inaccurate – and in almost every case they are one side of a comparative
statement.' Judging from the transcript, Dr Hubbard has rather over-
reacted.

Whatever the exact inaccuracies or accuracies of Dr Hubbard's
comments, the real issue was the *Sun*'s motive in producing the
article at such a time. The paper's editor, Kelvin McKenzie, argued:
'Surely the *Sun*, like other newspapers and broadcasters, is entitled to
analyse the background and mind of one of the country's leading and
most controversial politicians.'[135] On 15 March 1984, two weeks
after the article was published, the *Sun* virtually accused Dr Hubbard
of lying and added: 'We believed that the venture was entirely proper
in the the public interest and justified by the wide range of opinions
held on Mr Benn's character, ranging from eccentric onwards.' But

Labour MPs Michael Foot, Tony Banks, Eric Heffer and Merlyn Rees strongly disagreed and submitted a complaint to the Press Council: 'that the [*Sun*] newspaper misled readers about the extent of a psychiatric analysis of Mr Tony Benn in an improper attempt to influence the result of the Chesterfield by-election'.

Ordinary voters were also angry about the *Sun*'s coverage of Labour's campaign. Tony Benn and Granada TV received several letters of complaint. Roger Carter, a long-standing Conservative voter from Havant, Hampshire, said of the *Sun*:

> That publication has done nothing to enhance or advance the cause of Conservatism and undoubtedly you [Benn] have suffered a most ungracious, banal and barely literate campaign of vilification through its paper. That such a standard of puerile, almost hysterical journalism consistently sets out to influence 4 million people is frankly alarming.

As it turned out, Labour won the by-election, with a reduced majority, despite the press campaign in the final week. Some argue that this shows that the coverage had no effect on the voters of Chesterfield. This is the perennial, often unprovable, issue concerning the power of the press. However, one must surely wonder why the *Sun* planned to publish their 'Benn On The Couch' feature on the day before the final poll – if it wasn't to try and influence the result.

The socialist threat – have the books been burnt?

In August 1980, Tony Benn's biographer Robert Jenkins, a Conservative voter and merchant banker, remarked that the Labour MP for Chesterfield wanted 'to become one soldier in a great army so that there is no place for the individual'. The next day the *Daily Mail* columnist Lynda Lee-Potter replied: 'Rubbish. Wedgwood Benn wants to be Field-Marshal, not a poor bloody infantryman. It's the rest of us he wants marching behind him in unison, in one faceless, mindless, silent subservient army.'[136]

Such an appraisal of Benn's long-term political philosophy has been the dominant feature of Fleet Street's coverage of Labour's Leftwing in the past ten years. Hundreds of thousands of people have thus, by implication, been portrayed as unthinking appendages of Benn's unrelenting political ambition. But, as *Observer* journalist Simon Hoggart argued in 1980

> If Mr Benn is so obsessed by power, as so many newspapers seem to

think, then he has a funny way of going about getting it. Had he decided to pursue a quiet, centrist line within the Labour Party there is little doubt that his intelligence, diligence, oratorical skills and charm would have made him by now the leading candidate for Jim Callaghan's job.[137]

The *Daily Star*'s political editor David Buchan put it better during the Chesterfield by-election: 'Had he been a trimmer he would be leader by now.'

So, if the press's judgement of Benn's motives has been so manifestly wrong, why has the mere mention of his name reduced Fleet Street to paroxysms of rage and indignation? In 1975 Paul Johnson, now a *Daily Mail* columnist, believed he had the answer

Mr Benn aims to rob us of our illusions . . . He knocks at the door and warns us that things cannot go on as they have. He challenges the old relationships between classes. He shows a rational contempt for established institutions . . . Wherever he goes he is followed by icy draughts and the unwelcome whiff of carbolic soap. We like the old dirt and disorder: how easy then, to dismiss him as an eccentric, a crank, a tinkerer – indeed, a public menace.[138]

Lord Kearton, former Chairman of the British National Oil Corporation, agrees

He [Benn] obviously attracts a devoted following from a certain political opinion and therefore to all sorts of people he can appear to be a threat. And therefore the one way of defusing a threat is to make your opponent out to be either a dangerous man or foolish or silly. I think to some extent Mr Benn has suffered quite a lot from that approach.[139]

But the roots of Fleet Street's political attacks on Benn go much deeper. Representing Benn as opportunistic and irrational are not merely smear tactics. Instead, for many editors and executives they seem convincing, because they provide an explanation for Benn's radicalism and his gradual conversion to the Left. Portraying radical ideas as the product of 'loony lefties' or the pipedream of one eccentric Labour MP (usually Benn) has little to do with journalistic idleness or sloppy professionalism. They are surely political acts. Indeed, the press's motives are most vividly exposed by the complete absence of such reporting of the radical wings of the Conservative Party.

There can be little doubt that the marginalized coverage of Tony Benn's views and political activities in the past ten years has had serious consequences. Labour's radical Left is now perceived as unrepresentative and politically illegitimate, largely the product of a few militant activists. The overall image is one of small groups of 'zealots', as the *Daily Express* likes to refer to them, manipulating committee and conference procedures in order to force through their policies. Such a Machiavellian scenario bears little resemblance to reality, particularly with issues like nuclear disarmament which has a lot of public support. But it has served its purpose. Labour's Leftwing is now effectively isolated and powerless.

How much of the apparent demise of the radical Labour Left can be attributed to the press attacks? Some journalists like Derek Jameson believe the power of Fleet Street is grossly exaggerated. Other press defendants argue that radical politicians like Benn and Ken Livingstone, the ex-GLC leader, revel in being vilified by the popular press, because they can present it as a sign of their socialist purity and goodness. The more Fleet Street attacks, so the argument goes, the more the Left can see themselves as ideologically sound.

A more feasible argument in defence of the press is that the Labour Left, like all political factions and groups, use and manipulate the media to their advantage and so cannot complain about adverse coverage. There is some evidence for this. When Benn was Energy Secretary in James Callaghan's Cabinet in the late 1970s, the government was receiving hostile coverage of its nuclear energy policy. At that time the Energy Ministry's head of information was Bernard Ingham, now Mrs Thatcher's Press Secretary. During one briefing, Fleet Street's energy correspondents were pleasantly surprised to be told by Benn: 'There can be few groups of correspondents who are so well informed as to what is going on as you.' Two days earlier Ingham had sent Benn a memorandum saying – 'Subject: the problem over Drax B proposed power station. I would see some merit in the Secretary of State going out of his way to make the point that there can be few groups of correspondents covering a particular area of government responsibility who are so well informed as to what is going on.'[40]

But perhaps a more important issue is whether the press campaigns against the Left through Benn in recent years have had any real effect on the electorate. Benn himself has no doubts: 'Everybody is waking up to the fact,' he said in 1980, 'that the mass media in this country are engaged in conditioning and brainwashing the people in order to get them to accept policies that are not in their interests.' This is strong stuff. And in an interview with *Socialist Challenge* journalist Alan Freeman, Benn went further: 'The problem is that many British working-class people are not yet aware of their condition and don't understand what's happening because the media prevents them from doing so.'[141]

There is little evidence fully to support this view. However, a National Opinion Poll (NOP) taken in November 1980 of 2,000 voters on policy and the influence of politicians did provide some insight. A majority of the sample believed that Benn, then a back-bench MP, was as powerful as Sir Geoffrey Howe, at that time Chancellor of the Exchequer. Benn's postbag also reveals that political hostility can be derived from adverse press coverage.

But Benn's argument is flawed in one important respect. The idea that working people in Britain are being 'brainwashed' implies that they are intellectually gullible. It also assumes that docility prevents them from working out social realities for themselves, because their world view comes from popular newspapers. Obviously the popular press did have some influence on people's political perspective of Labour's Left, notably during the deputy leadership campaign. The press can set the political agenda. But Fleet Street certainly can't tell people what and how to think. They can only control what we think *about*. This can undoubtedly be done by manipulating the flow and access of ideas and information. Perhaps that's why the radical Left have always been marginalized on the political page.

3. Ken Livingstone and the GLC—Sedition at County Hall

'It's not people out there who see him threatening their life, it's the people in Fleet Street. Fleet Street is populated by middle-class people who are trying to better their standard of living and they see Ken threatening that life ... It's just tough luck for him that he's got enemies as powerful as that. (Nigel Dempster, *Daily Mail* diarist, on Ken Livingstone and the GLC).[1]

'The IRA-loving, poof-loving, Marxist leader of the GLC Mr Ken Livingstone' *Sunday Express*, 27 September 1981.

During an interview with Terry Coleman, the former *Daily Mail* columnist who writes for the *Guardian*, Ken Livingstone remarked that he believed every factory should be run by its workers and each school by the parents and teachers.

'Chaos,' replied Coleman.

'No, no, no,' said the GLC leader. 'Concentrations of power produce chaos.'

'But surely few people could run anything,' responded Coleman. Livingstone then said that everyone was capable, given a chance, and that there was, for instance, nothing special about him.

'Rot,' replied Coleman.

'No, seriously,' said Livingstone, 'that potential is there in everybody.'[2]

That conversation revealed as much about Fleet Street as it did about the politics of Livingstone and the Labour group he led on the Greater London Council. It showed that one of the key factors behind the press hostility to the labour movement was their intense opposition to syndicalism – whether political, industrial or cultural. That in the eyes of editorial management, groups of ordinary people were incapable of running their own affairs. And it was neither practical nor desirable.

This attitude came into direct conflict with what the Labour group of GLC councillors were trying to do between 1981 and 1985. Their view was that people did have the potential for self-management – from tenants' associations on council estates to workers in factories. Also that the GLC would be a political and financial peg on which a whole range of groups in London – blacks, workers, Irish, women, gays – could hang their grievances, fulfill their capabilities and combat discrimination.

This may sound highly utopian and idealistic, but it was what the GLC administration tried to do on a local government level. 'Social-ism,' said Livingstone in December 1981, 'means people having day-to-day control over their own lives.'[3]

The response of most of the national press was to employ a familiar tactic, much used against the radical Left. It was to isolate the leader from the pack and then go for the jugular. According to John Carvel, the *Guardian*'s local government correspondent, 'The attack on him [Livingstone] by sections of the popular press was perhaps the most sustained example of vindictively biased reporting in recent British history.'[4]

Carvel also believes that the press campaign was counterproductive, because of its violent nature. In addition, there is some evidence that the tide of the onslaught was later stemmed. But for at least the first two and a half years, Livingstone and his Labour colleagues were under siege from Fleet Street. And, as we shall see, even some Conser-vative councillors began to complain about the coverage of their politi-cal opponents.

The emergence of Red Ken

When the Labour group of councillors won control of County Hall on 7 May 1981, the last thing they expected was a hostile press cam-paign. Most of them had spent their political careers trying in vain to persuade news editors that local government was a viable source for stories. Now exactly the opposite had happened: 'I'd spent the first ten years of my time on the council trying to get anyone from the press or television interested in anything we were doing, and all of a sudden this wave of interest just knocked us back,' Livingstone later reflected.[5]

The first tidal wave hit County Hall the day after Livingstone was elected leader of the Labour group by 30 votes to 20. Despite the fact that only two-thirds of his support could be described as leftwing, Liv-ingstone's victory was reported as a secretly planned Leninist putsch. 'Extremist Voted In As London's New Boss', said the *Daily Mail* headline on 8 May. The story continued

A leftwing extremist was installed as leader of the Greater London Council yesterday, less than 24 hours after Labour won control...

Mr Livingstone's election came as Mrs Thatcher was warning in a speech at Perth that extremists were busy manipulating Labour's membership to gain power. She said they had one purpose: 'To impose upon this nation a tyranny which the peoples of Eastern Europe yearn to cast aside'.[6]

The *Sun* ran a similar story[6] – 'Red Ken Crowned King Of London' – and added: 'Red Ken ousted moderate Andrew McIntosh, 46, in a private poll by the 50 newly elected councillors. His victory means full-steam-ahead red-blooded Socialism for London.'[7] A *London Standard* editorial argued that the election was more ruthless: 'The worst nightmares about the GLC and its new masters on the far left seemed to be coming true even faster than we had feared. Mr Ken Livingstone and his fellows have steamrollered their more moderate (and experienced) colleagues out of the way in record time.'[8]

It was a charge that would be repeated regularly for the next four years by all sections of the press. This was despite the fact that the possibility of Livingstone becoming leader was well publicized during the election campaign. Indeed, it was one of the main thrusts of the Conservative Party's strategy. The press were even publishing articles about it. Here's a *Daily Telegraph* leader on 30 April 1981, just seven days *before* the GLC elections:

If Labour is put in control at County Hall next week, it will almost certainly be led by Mr Ken Livingstone, whose leftwing supporters will outnumber those backing the present Labour leader, Mr Andrew McIntosh. The triumph of the Left in London, already substantially accomplished in the boroughs and constituencies, will then be crowned with glory'.

And yet the same paper published a rather different editorial just *after* Labour won the election:

Describing Mr Livingstone as a fool is like calling Mr Wedgwood Benn barmy – the truth, certainly, but not the whole truth . . . Using the cover of the moderate appearance of the previous GLC Labour leadership of Mr Andrew McIntosh, Mr Livingstone waited for the voters to return the sheep's clothing before he, the wolf, popped out and arranged the top job for himself.[9]

This accusation sparked off a wave of interest from Fleet Street. In the early months of the Labour administration, County Hall seemed full of journalists. This was partly due to the new policy of 'open house' which gave the public free access to the corridors and committee rooms of the building. Reporters took advantage of this and at first Livingstone was happy to oblige. 'At one time,' said a local government correspondent, 'you could go straight on to his [telephone] extension and get rentaquote.'[10] Some journalists would turn up for an interview, go back to their office and then return the same day for another session. The GLC leadership thought the papers were interested in their politics. But as Livingstone later explained: 'We did these bloody long interviews with the *Sun* discussing our policies and not a word would appear.'[11]

The published articles were of a rather different flavour. There was very little analysis, critical or complementary, about what the council was trying to do for Londoners regarding cheap transport fares or help for the voluntary sector. Instead there were personalized attacks on the GLC leader. 'Commissar Of County Hall – Around Him At County Hall An Inner Circle Of The Elite', ran the *Daily Mail* headline to a feature on 30 May 1981. On the surface, wrote David Norris, the GLC leader is quite normal and easy-going, but then:

> Underneath the real Mr Livingstone is as elusive as the disappearing natterjack toad – a threatened species which the 35-year-old part-time conservationist is fighting to protect . . . It is only when he goes on to offer his own socialist solution to the problem that the mask of reason and moderation begins to slip and the face of a dogmatic zealot peers through.

There then followed a period of sustained editorial abuse. 'The kind of loony for whom the silly season was invented', said a *Telegraph* leader, while the *Sun* concluded that 'Josef Goebbels, Hitler's lying specialist, could not have done worse than the leader of the GLC.' On 24 July 1981, the *Mail* leader reproduced some of Livingstone's comments during that week and concluded: 'Mr Livingstone is a doctrinaire clown. But there is little laughing now at the Rake's Progress on which he is leading the Kingdom's capital city. It is a grotesque portent of things to come; of what could happen to all of us if we let the New Left misrule Britain tomorrow as they are misruling London today.' Later that day a *Standard* editorial joined in: 'Surely no-one – but no-one – deserves Mr Ken Livingstone. His rule at the GLC goes straight into the cruel-and-unnatural-punishment class.'

Much of this coverage was derived from Livingstone's comments on a range of issues – from racism in the police to the H-Block hunger strikers. But some Labour councillors, including leftwing allies Valerie Wise and John McDonnell, believed that while they were legitimate issues, they were also diversions from the GLC's mainstream policies.

This point was made at a meeting on 27 July 1981 of the Labour group, as the minutes show under 'Public Relations': 'the group had a responsibility to the party to show that the programme on which all are agreed can be put into practice and be made to work'. In addition, Veronica Crichton was seconded from the Labour Party's national press office to act as Livingstone's press advisor. A series of meetings were then held with senior councillors to discuss how to set the political agenda.

But still the press kept coming. On 20 August 1981, the *Daily Mail* tried to show that the GLC leader's political views on a wide range of issues were due to psychological defects in his character. The paper had asked three psychologists to draw their conclusions from a series of reported comments made by Livingstone. The result, according to the *Mail*, was 'What A Shocker!' above this story: 'GLC leader Ken Livingstone displays all the traits of someone who needs to shock to gain attention, according to three leading psychologists. They gave their opinions yesterday on what makes Mr Livingstone tick, based on his actions and sayings since he took power.' 'When he makes his extreme, iconoclastic comments on bisexuality or politics, it is his way of saying, "I am not like my mother or father or my teacher"', said one of them, Dr Robert Shields. He added: 'There is a tendency for people who feel they have not made their mark competitively in adolescence to become aggressive in attitude and become extremist.' An anonymous woman psychologist gave her version: 'He may well be aware that simply by running the GLC – whether he does a good job or a bad one – would not be sufficient to attract bold headlines. Therefore he opens his mouth and gets the attention he thrives on ... He certainly appears to have all the determination to be a fanatic. In his mind everything is black and white.' The third psychologist, Dr Dougal MacKay, was quoted:

> This sort of person says – 'Like or hate what I say, it doesn't matter to me because you can't ignore me'. The desperate need for attention is the hallmark of the hysteric. Mr Livingstone is in the same category as a punk rocker who wears outlandish clothes – he is really saying, 'I don't care what you think'.

The British Psychological Society (BPS) strongly protested about the article. Its President, Professor D.E. Blackman, told the *Daily Mail* that the article 'falsely brought the profession of psychology into public disrepute, apparently on the basis of irregular behaviour on the part of your staff'.[12]

On 19 August 1981, the day before the article was published, Dr

Frank McPherson, Chairman of the BPS, received a phone call from a *Daily Mail* journalist asking for his co-operation to 'participate in a light-hearted character analysis of Ken Livingstone'. Dr McPherson refused point-blank and told him that no reputable psychologist would wish to be associated with such a project. He also told the *Mail* reporter that a character analysis of a named individual for publication without interviewing that person directly would be 'an abuse of psychological knowledge'.[13] Dr MacPherson strongly advised against the project and wrote to Sir David English, the *Mail*'s editor, the same day to repeat those sentiments.

The *Daily Mail*'s reporters, Richard Holliday and Howard Foster, ignored their advice and published. But one of the psychologists, Dr Dougal MacKay, district psychologist at St Mary's Hospital, is adamant that he was not talking about Livingstone. He later described the article 'as a personal vicious attack on a prominent public figure'. He added:

> When I was approached by the reporter concerned I made it clear that, although I was prepared to discuss a particular type of personality phenomenon with him, I was not willing to comment on any one individual. When the article appeared, however, the quotations attributed to me were cleverly woven into the text to suggest that I was referring directly to the subject of the piece.[14]

In another letter to the British Psychological Society, MacKay acknowledged: 'I did make some rather lightweight comments about people who tend to figure prominently in the media but I made it clear to the reporter that I would not discuss any particular individual. In fact, I have to confess that I had no idea who Mr Livingstone was until the article appeared.'[15]

The *Daily Mail*'s managing editor, Christopher Rees, denied this: '*All* the people quoted in our story were fully aware that the person under discussion was Ken Livingstone.'[16] Rees also maintained: 'I can find no evidence to support your allegation of irregular behaviour on the part of any of our staff'.[17]

Dr MacKay was not the only person angry about the *Mail* article. Michael Nicholson, a freelance journalist, wrote to the Press Council to complain:

> I wish to protest about this scandalous piece of character assassination and possibly false reporting which is reminiscent of Soviet methods of declaring those the establishment dislikes as insane . . . I would also like you to broaden out your investigation into looking

at the campaign launched against Mr Livingstone by the *Mail* and *Sun*. It seems to me that this is the most violently worded, vicious and misleading campaign I have ever come across.[18]

In his Press Council evidence, Nicholson also alleged that the GLC's political opponents used the *Mail* article as a weapon to attack the Labour group. The *Mail*'s managing editor, Christopher Rees, gave this reply:

The fact is that Mr Livingstone is part of that political element frequently referred to as the lunatic Left. Although it suits Mr Nicholson to make a contrary claim, the probability is that the one short article under discussion – which did not contain the words lunatic, insanity or mental instability – had no connection with what political adversaries were saying.[19]

On 9 August 1982, nearly a year after the original article was published, the Press Council rejected Nicholson's complaint against the *Daily Mail*.

By the autumn of 1981, the spectre of '*Red* Ken', courtesy of *Sun*, *Mirror*, *Mail*, *Standard* headline writers, had arrived on the political scene. I have yet to receive a logical justification from senior editors for the use of the word 'Red'. In the context of Livingstone, here's one explanation from Peter Cox, editor of the Oxford-based *Sunday Journal*: 'Mr Livingstone has at one time been a self-confessed Communist. He is certainly at least to the left of the Labour Party and in newspaper parlance this makes the use of the word ''red'' acceptable.'[20] The use of the word 'Red' implies, of course, sympathy for Soviet-style Communism and hence Marxism. So was Livingstone a Marxist? The press were certain. 'The IRA-loving, poof-loving, Marxist leader of the GLC Mr Ken Livingstone,' said the *Sunday Express*.[21] The paper would often repeat the theme: 'Livingstone's GLC is carrying on as if London were the independent Marxist republic he would no doubt like it to become.'[22] The *Sun* agreed: 'Livingstone and his grubby pack of Marxists.'[23]

And yet there is virtually no evidence either in his public speeches, articles, interviews or political actions that he is a Trotskyist or Marxist. Even his political opponents acknowledge this. Roy Shaw, who as Labour leader of Camden council was often under political attack from Livingstone and the Left, said: 'He embraces Marxism if he thinks it will be of advantage to him. But he is certainly not a Marxist. He plays along with them and uses a lot of their methods, but he certainly is not one of them'.[24]

Even the GLC's political enemies were unhappy about newspaper's coverage. 'Certain sections of the Tory Press have waged a steady hate campaign of distortion and exaggeration against the man [Livingstone],' wrote Bob Quaif in a published letter to the *Standard*. 'As a Liberal/SDP voter I am by no means in sympathy with Mr Livingstone's political outlook, but I've been impressed by the largely pluralistic and democratic terms in which he expresses his opinions.'[25]

The press obsession with Livingstone was not only seen as a diversion by Labour councillors. The reporting of the council's policy decisions or plans as 'Red Ken has...' or 'Ken Livingstone's GLC has...' was also deemed to be inaccurate. For after the 1981 election victory the Labour group removed some of the powers of patronage from the leader and delegated them to elected committees. Although clearly the leader's office controlled the direction of policy, the Fleet Street tag of 'Red Ken's GLC' was far from true. Real power lay within the Labour group which met every Monday. According to Livingstone:

> I act more like a chief whip, co-ordinator and publicist of the group. I go out and try to sell the message and to hold the group together ...People really only come to me when there is a problem. I never know anything that's going right, I only get involved in all the things that are going wrong. Committees run into problems with the bureaucracy and I come along and stamp on it.[26]

In addition, it would not be unreasonable to argue that if Livingstone had suddenly lost the leadership of the group in the autumn of 1981 – a possibility at one stage – the council's policies would have been broadly the same under John McDonnell or Andy Harris.

And yet the press continued to pull together all the wide range of policies – on ethnic minorities, women's rights, cheap fares and grants – and present them as the creatures of Livingstone's personality. And it *was* deliberate. This was revealed to me by a senior journalist on the *London Standard* who has worked in Fleet Street for seven years. He said:

> I wrote some stories on the GLC which would begin 'The GLC decided yesterday...' or whatever. Then when the paper came out I would see that the intro had been changed by the subs to 'Ken Livingstone's GLC decided' Livingstone was certainly a powerful figure at the GLC but he didn't run the place by himself.

The *Standard*'s editor, Louis Kirby, denied this accusation: 'I don't know of any cases of this sort ... In fact I was under pressure from the

Tories at the time to give Livingstone less publicity because he was being built up into a media figure.'

The reality of the situation was that instead of just talking about the evils of racism or sexual discrimination, the GLC was actually trying to do something about it. Judging by the press coverage of the council's grants policy, this was what Fleet Street resented more than anything else. 'The Livingstone ''Follies'' '[27] was how the *Daily Express* described the GLC's financial aid to a wide range of voluntary groups. The *Daily Mail* followed suit with – 'The Crazy Things They Do With Your Rates'. The article, cowritten by Freedom Association member Russell Lewis, continued: 'GLC leader Ken Livingstone was once again yesterday doing what he does best – giving London's rate-payers' money away to bizarre minority groups.'[28] Such reporting was sustained right through to 1984. 'Loony Lefties In £31 Million Hand-out', said the *Sun* on 23 February 1984.

> Loony lefties and fringe groups are grabbing millions of pounds a year from Labour-controlled council coffers. The rush to give away ratepayers' cash is led by Red Ken Livingstone's GLC which forked out £31 million in 1983 to bizarre organizations . . . Now disgusted rightwingers have hit back with a jokey 'scroungers guide'.

These 'bizarre' organizations included West Indian community groups.

But it was the GLC grants to gay rights organizations and groups like Women Against Rape that angered the press. This began after a speech by Livingstone to a Gay Unity group in Harrow, West London, on 18 August 1981 when he said: 'Public representatives have shown appalling ignorance of gays and the political parties have been riddled with bigotry. We must make it clear publicly where we stand on gay rights.' The *Sun* reported – 'Red Ken Speaks Up For The Gays – I'll Get Them Jobs and Homes, He Says'. There was also a picture caption of the GLC leader: 'Red Ken . . . would not talk about his private life last night'.[29] The *Express* commented: 'What is not so funny is his proposal to give ratepayers money to ''gay'' groups when the ''applications come in''. Is this what the people of London voted for when they gave Labour a majority? We doubt it.'[30]

The main published charge against the GLC was that they were wasting ratepayers' money. 'Red Ken Hands Out Cash With Gay Abandon', said the *News of the World*. 'Red Ken Livingstone was blasted last night for handing out cash to homosexuals, lesbians and prostitutes in a wave of ''squander-mania.'' '[31] But was this true in the context of the total GLC budget? Of the £850 million available to the council, only £17 million (less than 10 per cent), according to 1984 figures, goes to the Grants Committee which funds at least 1,000 of these 'controversial' groups. The grant for community relations is much lower at 1.4 per cent of the total GLC budget.

The grants attacked by virtually all the popular press – to ethnic minorities, homosexuals and lesbians – are also very small. Given the fact that black people in London make up 14 per cent of the population, even the GLC's policy is not representative. And the percentage for the gay community is even smaller. Since May 1981, grants totalling £292,548 and £751,000 were allocated to set up the London Lesbian and Gay Centres which opened in April 1985. This is 0.8 per cent of the GLC's grants budget and a minute fraction of the overall GLC budget.

The Irish come to town

It has been estimated that at least 300,000 people of direct or indirect Irish origin live in London. For councillors like Steve Bundred, Ken Livingstone and Andy Harris, that was reason enough to involve the GLC in the politics of Northern Ireland, particularly as many of the terrorist acts have occurred on the streets of London. But the GLC leadership's attempt to put the Northern Ireland issue on the political agenda provoked by far the most hostile response from Fleet Street.

On 21 July 1981, Harris, a member of the Labour Committee on Ireland, invited Mrs Alice McElwee, mother of the H-Block hunger striker Tom McElwee, to County Hall for a meeting. Livingstone welcomed the visit, backed the hunger strikers and called for British troops to be withdrawn from Northern Ireland. 'Left-Wing Plays Host To Terrorists' Mother', reported the *Daily Mail* the next day. 'Storm As Labour Boss Backs Maze Rebels', said the *Express*, and their leader added: 'Is Ken Livingstone a political clown? Or is he something worse? ... It is sickening and disgusting that the majority leader of Britain's capital city should be giving encouragement and publicity to the enemies of this country'. On 23 July the *Sun* commented:

Ken Livingstone, the pipsqueak leader of the GLC, opens his big mouth again. He accuses Britain of pursuing policies of murder and intimidation of the Roman Catholic population in Northern Ireland. This accusation is a breathtaking lie. ... In his brief spell on the stage, Mr Livingstone has proved himself a menace to stability in public life.

A month later, on 21 August 1981, Livingstone met the three sons of Mrs Yvonne Dunlop who had died in an IRA firebomb attack for which Tom McElwee had been convicted. 'Victims Face IRA's Backer', said the *Mail* and implied that he supported the IRA – 'Mr Livingstone said later that he still supported the IRA "fight for a free Ireland"'. This was to be a recurrent theme of the coverage of Ireland – the lack of distinction made between Livingstone's support for the *aims* and his rejection of their terrorist *methods*. In his statement on 21 August, the GLC leader said: 'I've never supported violence as a means to a political end ... I want all sides to sit round a table to bring about a united Ireland in which relatives of Mrs Dunlop and Mrs McElwee can grow up in peace together.'

An example of how this distinction was ignored by most of the press came two months after the visit of the Dunlop boys. On Saturday 10 October 1981, the IRA exploded a nail bomb outside the Irish guard barracks in Chelsea as a bus full of soldiers was passing. Two civilians were killed, 22 soldiers and 16 civilians were injured. Two days later Livingstone went to Cambridge to speak at a student meeting of the Tory Reform Group on the issue of rates. At the end of the meeting, he was asked about the bombing. The GLC leader replied that to try to crush the IRA as though they were simply criminals or lunatics would not work:

> It is the policy that has been tried for generations and still the killing persists. The IRA bombers and their supporters believe they have strong political motives. For this reason, if one is caught others come forward to take his place. This is not the case with individually motivated psychopaths; once arrested, the crimes cease.[32]

According to Livingstone, he 'answered an honest question honestly. No one at the time thought it was unusual ... There were no gasps of horror in the audience'.[33] However, there were two journalists at the meeting – Richard Holliday, the *Mail*'s full-time 'Red Ken watcher', and a Press Association reporter. The next morning, the day of a regular GLC council day, Fleet Street was in uproar. The whole of the *Sun*'s front page was devoted to a leader entitled 'This Damn Fool Says Bombers Aren't Criminals'. The paper continued:

> This morning the *Sun* presents the most odious man in Britain. Take a bow, Mr Livingstone, socialist leader of the Greater London Council. In just a few months since he appeared on the national scene, he has quickly become a joke. Now no-one can laugh at him any longer. The joke has turned sour, sick and obscene. For Mr

Livingstone steps forward as the defender and the apologist of the criminal, murderous activities of the IRA.[34]

Other papers took a similar line. 'As two men were being questioned by detectives yesterday about the IRA nail-bomb explosion in Chelsea, London, Mr Ken Livingstone, leader of the GLC, again took the side of the IRA', reported the *Times*.[35] 'IRA Bomb Gang Not Criminals, Says Livingstone', said the *Express* and added in an editorial: 'This is the behaviour of a man who through Marxist dogma has become an alien in his own country, blind to the IRA's bloodiest crimes even when committed on his own doorstep.'[36] The *Mail* agreed: 'London has endured fire, plague and the blitz. It should not have to endure Mr Livingstone at the head of its affairs for one more day.'[37]

Later that afternoon, Tuesday 13 October, the GLC leader called a press conference. He described the coverage of his remarks as 'ill-founded, utterly out of context and distorted ... I have no regrets, only that the press, particularly the *Sun*, totally distorted what I said.' Livingstone later said on BBC's *Nationwide*: 'I at no time said that people who set off a bomb aren't criminals ... Quite frankly, I wouldn't agree with what I was quoted as saying.'

Then a round-robin letter signed by 20 Labour GLC councillors was delivered to the party's Chief Whip, Harvey Hinds. It said that they were unhappy about the diversion and distraction the media row had caused, and suggested that Livingstone should concentrate on London affairs. The *Mail* reported this as – 'Red Ken Faces Revolt' and added: 'Red Ken Livingstone's support for the IRA left him facing a revolt last night from within his own leftwing group.' This was untrue. The letter was drafted by Alan Williams, a Labour rightwing councillor. He later explained that it was not a criticism of Livingstone's views but merely a warning about diverting attention away from their manifesto commitments: 'This is meant to be a genuine reminder to the leader – in no way is it anti-Livingstone. I am quite convinced that Ken was misquoted on his statements on the London bombings. The way he is treated in some parts of Fleet Street is quite outrageous,' said Williams.[38]

Steve Bundred was another Labour councillor to incur the wrath of Fleet Street over his views on Northern Ireland. In August 1982, he went to Belfast with a Troops Out Movement delegation. The *Sun* reported this action on its front page as 'Traitor – Leftie Police Boss Boosts The IRA'.[39] The following day the *Sun* headlined a picture of Bundred among Troops Out marchers as 'Traitor's March'. However, the issue of violence was given rather different coverage by the paper when it came to the SAS. In the same two issues, the *Sun* ran features on the SAS based on interviews with former members. 'Killing Men Never Bothered Me, But I Couldn't Hurt A Rabbit', ran the headline of the first article. There was no sign of condemnation from the paper for their violence. Instead, the next issue told of how another ex-SAS man danced in the street 'demonstrating how to remove a bayonet from a Japanese corpse'. The *Sun* added: 'He was taking a trip down memory lane which in his case is well stocked with corpses.'[40]

Four months later Steve Bundred was one of the key actors in perhaps the biggest press onslaught on the GLC. He had circulated a letter of invitation to Gerry Adams and Danny Morrison, newly elected Sinn Fein members of the Northern Ireland Assembly, to come to London on 14 December 1982. Apart from Bundred, 25 other Labour councillors signed the letter. On the morning of Sunday 5 December, the visit was announced on commercial radio and Clive Soley, Labour's Deputy Parliamentary Spokesperson on Northern Ireland, agreed to meet them. Bundred then released a press statement.

The next day, 6 December, all hell let loose. 'Fury At Ken's IRA Guests', reported the *Daily Star*, while the *Mirror* headlined their news story as 'An Insult To The Memory Of IRA Victims'. The popular press was unanimous – 'Fury Over Red Ken's Invitation To IRA's Two Henchmen' (*Express*) and 'IRA Men's Visit An Outrage' (*Mail*). The *Sun* news report headline was 'Backing For Terror' and continued: 'Fury erupted last night after two top IRA spokesmen were invited to London as official guests of ''Red Ken'' Livingstone.'

Later that Monday another GLC councillor, Gerry Ross, added his name to the invitation. The total was now 27 out of 50 – a clear majority of the Labour group. This fact was given little prominence by the press. The *Sun* managed to ignore it completely. Instead, one person was singled out for attack – Livingstone. 'It is typical of GLC leader Ken Livingstone, ''The Trotsky of County Hall'', to have invited Adams and Morrison', said an *Express* leader. 'Livingstone gorges himself on publicity. This time he must not get away with it to the deep hurt of the people of London who have lost relatives to the murderous IRA.'[41] This was quite untrue. The invitation was not issued by Livingstone. And the *Express* knew it.

However, the tension was heightened later that Monday night when a bomb exploded in a pub disco in Ballykelly, County Derry, killing 16 and injuring 66. It was planted by the Irish National Liberation Army (INLA) *not* the IRA, who were seeking electoral support at the time. However, on the Tuesday morning GLC councillors were awakened by journalists to get their immediate response *before* responsibility had been claimed. For the next two days the 27 signatories were under siege from journalists at County Hall, trying to get the councillors to change their minds. Few did.

The implication from Fleet Street was clear. To invite Sinn Fein leaders for private talks is to condone the killings and to support violence as a means to achieve political ends. This was the theme of a *Daily Mail* feature on the Tuesday (7 December) It was headlined – 'After That Astonishing Invitation To Sinn Fein – Why This Cynical Man Fills Me With Disgust' and written by Humphrey Atkins, the ex-Northern Ireland Secretary. He wrote:

> GLC leader Ken Livingstone is the fresh toast of the men of violence ... Let us be quite clear whom these men represent. Gerry Adams and Danny Morrison ... are the associates of the terrorists who have killed more than 2,500 people and injured another 25,483 since the troubles started 13 years ago.

Those figures, researched by a *Mail* subeditor, were quite untrue. The paper had attributed all the deaths in Ulster to the Republicans which was quite wrong. The Ulster Defence Association have even admitted killing 500 people. The true figure for the IRA up to December 1982 was about 1,300. To their credit, the *Mail* admitted their mistake and offered space for Donal Kennedy, a London-based Irishman, to rectify the error. His letter was not published but the mistake was corrected two months later on 9 February 1983.

The *Daily Star* refused to admit their mistake in a similar attack on Livingstone. The paper commented: 'Adams and Morrison represent men whose hands are bloody with the deaths of 2,260 people since 1969 and the wounding of 25,500 more.'[42] Despite being repudiated by the Press Council, the *Star*'s deputy editor Ray Mills stood by the following argument:

> It may be simplistic logic, but we believe it is admissible to say that if the Provisional IRA had not existed, or they had rejected violent means to achieve their aims, then 2,260-odd people would not have died in Ulster. Therefore we maintain that it is legitimate to say that the Provisional IRA bears the final responsibility for those deaths.[43]

Meanwhile, on that Tuesday 7 December, the GLC councillors reaffirmed their invitation to Sinn Fein. This is how the *Sun* reported the decision: 'GLC leader Red Ken Livingstone became the most hated man in Britain last night after he insisted: the IRA's spokesmen are still welcome in London.' An editorial added, inaccurately attributing the invitation to Livingstone: 'His friends tell us he is sincere.

So were Hitler and Stalin. To come nearer to home, so are the National Front.'[44]

The other papers on 8 March were equally apocalyptic. 'Horror Without End – The Visit Goes On, Insists Red Ken', said the front page of the *Daily Express*. 'No Mercy', proclaimed the *Daily Mail*'s front page. But it was the *Daily Star*'s coverage on that Wednesday morning that was particularly interesting. Two days earlier, on Monday 6 December, the *Star* had asked Gerry Adams for an article and that evening a 500-word feature was telexed back to Fleet Street from the Falls Road Republican Press Centre, Belfast. The paper's news editor had also telexed Adams to reassure him that, if published, his article would not be censored in any way.[45] On the Wednesday, the *Star*'s message to Adams was rather different – 'At Your Peril – Today's Message to Red Ken's Guests', declared the paper's front page. A leader added: 'Mr Livingstone's miserable bolt-hole, his ridiculous rationale, was that the massacre at Ballykelly was the work of the INLA and not the Provisional IRA whom Adams and Morrison represent . . . It is a rotten, stinking cowardly argument.'[46]

An interesting aspect of Fleet Street's abhorrence of the GLC councillors meeting the 'backers of terror' (*Sun*[47]) was revealed in a rather unexpected place – George Gale's column in the *Daily Express*. On 7 December, he wrote that it would be hypocritical for William Whitelaw, the Home Secretary, to ban Adams since he had met him in secret ten years ago. It was quite true, but very few papers mentioned that in July 1972 Whitelaw had met Adams in Chelsea along with six other Republicans, two of whom were armed. Very little prominence, if any, was given to another meeting with a Conservative minister. Just one week before the row over the London visit in December 1982, Northern Ireland Environment Minister, David Mitchell, met Adams and three other Assembly members at Stormont. Even more ironically, Adams received a letter from Mitchell thanking him for the meeting which arrived three hours after Whitelaw had banned him from visiting Britain.

Livingstone and his GLC colleagues were to provoke more hostility from Fleet Street over the Northern Ireland issue. The GLC leader went to Belfast in February 1983, and Adams visited County Hall in July 1983, and Livingstone received the usual abuse from most of the popular press. A month later, on 26 August 1983, the GLC leader said on Irish state radio that Britain's treatment of Ireland over 800 years was worse than what Hitler had done to the Jews in the Second World War. The *Sun* reported him as 'raving'[48] and accused him of being a lunatic. The *Express* suggested he emigrate to a Communist state in Eastern Europe.[49]

The climax of the GLC's turbulent relationship with Fleet Street over the Ireland issue came in November 1982 when the council voted to ban advertising in the *London Standard* because of what they saw as an offensive anti-Irish cartoon. On 29 October 1982, the paper had published a cartoon of a man walking past a cinema poster depicting a film entitled: 'The ultimate in psychopathic horror – The Irish – featuring the IRA, INLA, UDF, UFF, UDA, etc. etc.'. It was the use of the words 'The Irish', as if implying most Irish people were violent, that caused such resentment. The 'Irish in Britain Representation' group said that they had received 'a deluge of letters' complaining about the cartoon. At the full council debate on 24 November, Livingstone said the GLC had also received complaints. He described the cartoon as 'anti-Irish and likely to stir up racial hatred'. John Dobson, the Conservative spokesman on the ethnic minorities committee, admitted: 'The cartoon was offensive. But the fact is that the principle of free speech is more important. If they [the *Standard*] stepped over the line of the law then they will have to face legal charges in the normal way.'[50] But the GLC decided to ban advertising until the paper published an apology. Other councils like Hackney, Camden and Haringey also refused to advertise in London's only evening paper.

The ban has cost the *Standard* about £2 million in lost advertising revenue up to November 1985. However, the paper's editor, Louis Kirby, shows no sign of apologizing. When asked whether he thought the use of the words 'The Irish' implied associating all Irish people with terrorism and violence, he replied: 'I don't think it implies that at all. The GLC complained for political reasons. It was quite clearly a vendetta against us.'

At the Press Council hearing, Mortimer MacSweeney, an Irish reader of the paper, protested that it was a 'malicious and grossly insulting cartoon likely to inflame public hatred and bigotry against the Irish people'. Kirby replied that the cartoon was drawn when violence in Ulster reached a new peak of horror and a man's hand had been sawn off by terrorists. It was aimed at specific illegal organizations, not the London Irish community. The *Standard*'s editor added that if other Irishmen felt they had been included he was sorry but he would not erode his cartoonist's freedom. He said cartoonists had occupied a unique and independent place for 150 years. It was accepted, Kirby told the hearing, that the cartoonist making his point would often caricature people and events in the broadest strokes – which the innocent might feel included them.

Livingstone responded that the cartoon implied that the Irish were subhuman and enjoyed killing each other. It reinforced prejudice and did great damage he said. The Press Council rejected the GLC's complaint. And, in a later adjudication, also condemned the Council's ban on advertising as 'a blatant attempt by a local authority to use the power of its purse to influence the contents of a newspaper and coerce the editor'.

On the buses

Perhaps the most important manifesto commitment for the GLC Labour group when they were elected in May 1981 was the introduction of cheaper London transport fares to be financed by a supplementary rate. It was certainly well publicized during the campaign and even sections of the press admitted it was a popular policy. As the *Sun*'s Jon Akass acknowledged: 'I am not in the front rank of Mr Livingstone's admirers, but it happens that a majority of Londoners, perhaps inadvertently, voted for his cheap fares. They may have been misguided. But it is what they voted for.'[51]

But the proposal to cut bus and tube fares, financed by the ratepayers, was deeply unpopular in Fleet Street. On 21 August 1981, the day after the *Daily Mail* produced their psychoanalysis of Livingstone's character, the paper reported how London Transport, then controlled by the GLC, planned to pay their staff £50 bonuses to offset rising rates. This news story was headlined – 'And Now From The Red Leader . . . Cloud Cuckoo Land'. The paper explained: 'The increase was brought about in the first place by the leftwing council's decision to slash bus and tube fares by 25 per cent next month'.

Two months later began the intense legal battle when Bromley Borough Council from the South London suburbs went to the High Court to force the GLC to abandon their policy. 'Outlaw Livingstone's Cheap Fares', ran the *Standard*'s front-page banner headline. Their story continued: 'GLC leader Ken Livingstone was accused in the High Court today of blindly bringing in his "cheap fares" policy without counting the cost to Londoners. The extra cash ratepayers have to find was said to be "quite staggering"'.[52] The *Sun* followed suit the next day – 'Outlaw Red Ken's Fares' – and added: 'Council chief "Red" Ken Livingstone was blasted in the High Court yesterday for bringing in cheap bus and tube fares without counting the cost to ratepayers.'[53]

But it was Lord Denning's ruling that the GLC's policy of cheap fares subsidized by rate increases was illegal which won most applause from Fleet Street. 'Foolish! Unfair! Illegal' was the *Daily Mail*'s front-page headline in large print together with – 'Judges Order Livingstone To Unscramble His Fares Fiasco'. There was also a photograph of the GLC leader with this caption – 'Ken Livingstone: Accused of ''a crude abuse of power'' '.[54] The *Express* reported – 'Unfair Fares: It's A Fight Says Red Ken' – along with 'Judges Rule Foolish GLC Rates Policy Is Illegal'.[55] The *Sun* echoed this line – 'Red Ken Has Done It Again – ''Foolish'' Fare Cut Outlawed By Judges'.[56]

However, less than three months later, in February 1982, another form of cheap transport fares was given rather different coverage. On 5 February, Sir Freddie Laker's cheap air fares policy collapsed amidst massive debts and his company was declared bankrupt. 'We Love You Sir Freddie', ran the banner front-page headline of Rupert Murdoch's *News of the World* two days later. The article said: 'An incredible nationwide whip-round to get Sir Freddie Laker airborne again reached the £1 million mark last night. The message from housewives, workmen, schoolchildren and businessmen was: ''We love you, Sir Freddie – and we want you back'' '. The paper then quoted Ron Winter, an organizer of a 'Save Laker' fund in Sussex, who said: 'This country needs more men like Laker.' Other papers also launched 'Save Laker' collections. This was for a company with an overdraft of £250 million.

The following month, in March 1982, bus workers in London were condemned by the press for taking industrial action in protest at the doubling of fares because of Lord Denning's judgement. The *Sun* described the protest as 'Loony Day ... As if the public has not suffered enough from bludgeoning political strikes, we are now to have the most witless and futile of them all.'[57] On 2 March 1982, the *Standard* alleged that 'Drivers and conductors at a number of garages, mainly in South London, have voted to work normally. . . . The rebellion has centred on garages at Merton, Elmers End, Streatham south of the river, and Cricklewood in the north west'. Five days later the *News of the World* followed suit, claiming that bus crews at Stockwell, Clapham, Bromley and Merton were 'rebelling' against the strike call. The report was not attributed to any source. In fact, they were highly exaggerated. According to Geoff Whittaker, a member of the Transport and General Workers Union bus committee, Merton had voted unanimously the previous week to support the stoppage, as did Cricklewood. Elmers End and Streatham also voted, with smaller majorities, to support the strike.

There is also evidence that Livingstone's view of the busworkers' action was distorted by the press. On 5 March 1982, the *Standard*'s front-page headline ran – 'Livingstone Attack On Bus, Tube Protest – ''This Useless Strike'' '. The paper quoted him as saying: 'A one-day strike will have no impact at all. It will be a gesture . . . I am not going to lead people into what would certainly be defeat', and claimed that the GLC leader 'could not recommend either one-day or all-out strike action'.

In fact, Livingstone had taken a tape-recording of his speech which confirmed that he had never opposed the strike action, as suggested by the *Standard*. 'I would never have got out alive if I had made the remarks attributed to me,' said Livingstone who had been speaking at a fares protest meeting. He added

> Clearly, the *Standard* is developing an overt dirty tricks campaign to drive a wedge between the Labour Party and the trade unions . . . I said that I doubted if the government would back down and that we would have to commit ourselves as a Labour Party and trade unions to continuing the campaign right through to the defeat of the government at the next election.[58]

This was confirmed by Andrew Gregg who organized the meeting where Livingstone was alleged to have made his anti-strike comments: 'At no stage did Livingstone criticize the London Transport unions. In fact, he went out of his way to praise them for the campaigning work they have done in defending bus and tube services and the cheap fares policy.'

What was revealing about the opposition to cheap fares from large sections of Fleet Street was that this almost certainly contradicted the views of their own readers. As the *Observer* columnist, Clive James, commented: 'The most challenging act of insurrection we have yet been faced with is Ken Livingstone's unilateral lowering of public transport fares, and you will find few Londoners, beyond an insignificant minority inhabiting the upper offices of Fleet Street, who call him a dangerous radical for that.'[59] A senior *Standard* journalist agreed: 'The paper's greatest mistake was to attack the GLC's plans for cheap fares. It was crazy because most of our readers were commuters or tube travellers and so it must have lost us a lot of circulation.' The *Standard*'s editor, Lou Kirby, disagreed that cheap fares were popular with his readers: 'It was probably a 50/50 split, but the main reason we opposed the cheap fares policy was the way it was carried out. That was what we objected to.'

Plots by Tory Central Office, Downing Street and the abolition campaign

The decision to abolish the GLC had been discussed within the Conservative Party well before the general election in June 1983. Hostility towards the Labour group and particularly Livingstone ran very deep in the Tory Party – from the ordinary association members to Cabinet ministers. One Conservative GLC councillor told me how one of his colleagues would even get up earlier in the morning so that he could hate Livingstone for an hour longer each day! Their antagonism towards the GLC leader was due partly to the setting up of the Women's and Ethnic Minorities committees. But it was mainly because of Ken Livingstone's criticism of the police, particularly in March 1982 when he attacked the appointment of Sir Kenneth Newman as Commissioner of the Metropolitan Police and accused the force of being 'riddled with racists and bigots'.

The press echoed the Conservatives' resentment of such remarks – 'Mr Stupid' (*Sun*[60]) and 'Irresponsible' (*Express*[61]). But that was not enough. According to Rodney Gent, Conservative GLC member for Bexley and Sidcup, feelings were running very high in the branch meetings. 'I can't remember a single meeting during that time when the Tory members didn't want to talk about Livingstone,' said Gent, a former Tory Reform Group Chairman. 'There was definitely pressure building up through the party to do something about Livingstone.'

And so in November 1982, a special study committee was set up at Tory Central Office, in Smith Square, to prepare a series of options to give the GLC's powers to the local borough councils after abolition. Details of the plan were leaked to the *Daily Express* the next month – 'Maggie's Axe Hangs Over RED KEN – Tory Move To Abolish the GLC'.[62] That month, December, a series of meetings took place at Conservative Central Office where a pre-general election strategy was discussed by public relations advisors and senior party officials. They decided to use their political cohorts in Fleet Street to build up a 'Red scare' atmosphere leading up to the forthcoming general election. This would pave the way and prepare the political ground for the abolition of the GLC and the other Labour-led councils. The plan was to build up the theme of the 'Labour bogeymen' – Livingstone, Arthur Scargill and Tony Benn – as the 'enemy within'.

According to George Tremlett, then chair of the GLC Housing Committee, a Conservative councillor for 14 years and a lifelong member of the Tory Party:

> It is my view that the Conservative Party debased itself. The central plan was to smear Livingstone in the press by using Central Office officials. They believed that Livingstone was a central asset for votes ... I don't actually think people like Benn or Livingstone are the 'enemy within'. They may be misguided but they are genuine

radicals and should be treated as serious politicians. But the press coverage was way over the top and in some cases was quite disgraceful . . . I was horrified by the way in which the Conservative party press and some of our national leaders sought to build Mr Livingstone up into a hate-figure.

This broad strategy has been confirmed by other Tory councillors like Rodney Gent and Bernard Brook-Partridge who resented such tactics. But despite the protests of some of its own supporters, Central Office went into action. In January 1983, Tremlett received a telephone call from Arthur Williamson, Press Officer for the GLC Conservative group at County Hall. Williamson, a former Press Association political correspondent, asked Tremlett to come to his office in Room 114 to meet two journalists from the *Daily Mail* and *Daily Telegraph*. At the meeting Williamson said that Central Office was anxious for a censure debate to take place on Livingstone's leadership. The *Daily Telegraph* journalist then turned to Tremlett and said: 'I've come to get the dirt on Livingstone.'

The *Daily Mail* journalist at that meeting was Richard Holliday, now news editor of the *Mail on Sunday*, who said he was the paper's full-time 'Ken-watcher'.[63] That afternoon he took Tremlett out to lunch at the 'La Barca' restaurant, in Lower Marsh Street, near County Hall. During the meal, paid for by the *Daily Mail*, Holliday asked Tremlett: 'What we really want is something on his sex life. Is he queer? What about his women, who does he go out with?' Tremlett, a former journalist himself for four years, was rather taken aback. He said he didn't know and was not interested in Livingstone's private life. But Holliday persisted and said: 'Well, was he a Communist? Do you think he is a Marxist?' There the conversation ended and Tremlett refused to co-operate with what he regarded as underhand tactics.

Two months later, in March 1983, Tremlett received another call from Arthur Williamson. According to Williamson, Sir David English, the editor of the *Daily Mail*, had personally drafted a question for Tremlett to ask in the council chamber. English was convinced that Livingstone was anti-semitic. And so he wanted a Conservative councillor to request that Jewish groups like 'The Student and Academic Campaign For Soviet Jewry' and 'Women's Campaign For Soviet Jewry' be given facilities at County Hall. The *Mail*'s editor wanted it to be asked in Question Time because he was sure Livingstone would refuse, but Tremlett again refused to co-operate. However, the *Mail* persisted and the paper's home affairs correspondent, Anthony Doran, twice telephoned Tremlett to find out if he had asked the question. Unperturbed, the *Mail* launched their own campaign to champion these Jewish organizations – 'Jewish Group Accuses GLC: Why Can't We Hold Exhibitions?' reported Doran on 18 March 1983. The *Mail*'s campaign lasted nearly a year with the paper accusing the GLC of being 'The Politburo Beside The Thames'.[64]

Arthur Williamson denied that there was a Central Office plan to smear Livingstone: 'I was not aware of any plot.' But he did acknowledge the phone calls to Tremlett. 'There was nothing sinister about that,' he said. 'We would always ring up councillors to arrange meetings with the press.' However, Williamson did say: 'We did have the feeling that Livingstone was the front man for other political forces behind him.'

More evidence of news management came after the Conservatives' general election victory in June 1983. Tory MPs and many Cabinet ministers suddenly found themselves saddled with an unpopular manifesto commitment – abolition of the GLC. Patrick Jenkin, the Environment Minister, admitted this after he was sacked in September 1985. And at the time the Cabinet were far from happy with the abolition policy. 'How do we get out of this mess without appearing disloyal?' Tory councillor Rodney Gent was asked by a senior Cabinet minister.

The answer, according to some officials in the government's information departments, was to use their friends in the press. In November 1983, the Environment Secretary, Patrick Jenkin, suggested that the government should create a special information unit to counter the campaign being waged by the councils against abolition. Jenkin wanted this to include private public relations consultants and even some journalists. The idea was rejected by Mrs Thatcher. The following month a proposal by her chief press secretary, Bernard Ingham, was taken far more seriously. On 30 December 1983, Ingham had written a confidential seven-page memorandum proposing an official Whitehall committee to co-ordinate a public relations campaign defending the government's policies on abolition of the GLC and the metropolitan councils. The idea was endorsed by an inter-departmental committee of civil servants and was considered by Patrick Jenkin and other Cabinet ministers at a meeting on 18 January 1984.

Ingham put forward 20 ideas for public relations. Among them were 'remedial action with troublesome journals whether national, provincial or specialist'; 'special articles – e.g. *Sunday Express*, *News of the World*, regional press'. Within two weeks Ingham's idea had been taken up. On 15 January 1984 a long article by Jenkin appeared in the *Sunday Express*. The document also said that any successful plan should 'treat, as a matter of urgency, dissident elements among the government's own supporters, to ensure they are neutralized if not positively harnessed to the government's cause'.[65]

Within a month, in February 1984, the rightwing pressure group 'Aims of Industry' had launched their own propaganda campaign against the GLC. The group published a booklet, helped by Sir Alfred Sherman, Mrs Thatcher's former advisor and a *Daily Telegraph* leader writer, which alleged that the GLC had abused ratepayers money in their allocation of grants. Two months later, in April, another rightwing PR campaign was launched called 'Efficiency in London Ltd'. This was the brainchild of Lady Porter, leader of the Conservative-controlled Westminster City Council, who stressed at the time that their aim was to scrap the GLC and campaign for low rates.

The GLC, of course, also had their own propaganda machines – well-equipped with plenty of resources. But the difference was that the mighty engine of Fleet Street was in the enemy camp (although several newspapers strongly criticized the government for abolishing elections as well). Take this *Daily Express* article amidst the heat of the GLC debate. 'The Great Dictator – Proof That Citizen Ken Has No Time For Democracy', was the headline to this piece:

> As he fights to save the GLC, the hypocrisy of Red Ken Livingstone is hard to beat. 'If you want me out you should have the right to vote me out', is his slogan ... The trouble is that Londoners never had the chance to vote Red Ken in as their leader. He preaches democracy, but bears the hallmark of a Banana Republic dictator. He seized power in a squalid coup in 1981 after London's voters had elected a Labour moderate Andrew McIntosh ... ousted when Red Ken cooked up a caucus to organize the smashing of the unsuspecting McIntosh.[66]

Londoners knew very well of the possibility of Livingstone becoming leader after the election and McIntosh, of course, was not 'unsuspecting'. Such untruths were commonplace for the first three years of the Labour group's administration. But what had changed by the summer of 1984 was the absence of vituperative attacks on the GLC leadership, apart from the *Sun* and *Express*. Instead, as the abolition debate progressed and the government's action proved increasingly unpopular, the tone of the press changed to mild criticism of the banning of the elections. With even the House of Lords in open revolt against the government and backing the GLC, papers like the *Daily Mail* and *Standard* could no longer continue to attack the Labour group as a gang of political devil worshippers. The strength of feeling against abolition was too strong and too wide in its constituency.

However, the spectre of news management, according to the GLC leadership, re-emerged during the four by-elections called by the Labour group in the autumn of 1984. Throughout the campaign Ken Livingstone claimed that the popular press, after being persuaded by Downing Street, was deliberately refusing to cover the by-elections. 'The Tory government has organized a blackout on coverage of these by-elections,' said Livingstone on 16 September 1984. 'There has been a co-ordinated boycott. It's obvious – you only have to look at the coverage compared with every other by-election. There's been nothing in the popular press . . . Quite clearly, the line from Downing Street is to ignore the elections, play them down.'

The *Financial Times* almost appeared to agree when the paper reported a photo-call for a meeting between Livingstone and the Labour leader Neil Kinnock: 'But the press was thin on the ground, either demonstrating lack of national interest in an essentially local election or, as Mr Livingstone asserted, because the media had been told by the Tories to keep away.'[67]

Was there any evidence for such a serious allegation? There is some, but not very substantial. In the four months leading up to and including polling day for the by-elections, the daily tabloid papers managed a total of 14 articles. That's less than three each in 17 weeks. This was an incredibly small figure, particularly when the election involved a national political figure like Livingstone. It also contrasted strongly with the serious papers like the *Times* and *Guardian* which published 16 and 19 articles each respectively.

Nita Clarke, the GLC leader's political press officer, said: 'It was extremely difficult to get any press coverage at all. I've no doubt the word went out to play down the by-elections despite the fact that Ken was a national political figure and the press machine was going at full throttle.' In fact, the GLC press office was so desperate to get coverage that Clarke rang *TV-AM*, ITV's morning breakfast show. She asked if Livingstone could appear with 'Mad Lizzie' on her early morning exercise routine. *TV-AM* agreed and Livingstone's workout proved a great success. So much so that the SDP/Liberal Alliance asked for equal time!

Over a wider period of time during the fight to oppose abolition there was, according to one GLC Tory, Downing Street pressure on the press. 'There is no doubt the press were leaned on during that period,' said Bernard Brook-Partridge, Conservative GLC member for

Havering and a former GLC Chairman. 'There is no question about it
. . . Some editors were invited to Downing Street and urged to attack
the GLC dissidents who opposed abolition. I know because I had dinner with a Fleet Street editor and he told me himself.'

The other noticeable absence from the by-elections coverage was the
three other Labour councillors. After all, there were four by-elections.
A *Guardian* leader had other ideas: 'Ken Livingstone . . . has never
underestimated the value of the GLC as a platform for the prosecution
of political causes. Now, faced with the threat of abolition, *he has*
responded with a characteristic bid for the maximum propaganda
advantage . . . By refusing to contest *Mr Livingstone's by-elections* the
Conservatives can at least hope to prevent the size of these majorities
being measured.' The *Standard* took up a similar theme: 'The GLC
by-elections which *Mr Livingstone* is beginning to stage . . . ' (empha-
sis added).

It was Conservative Central Office, in the shape of the then Party
Chairman John Selwyn Gummer, who launched the counter-offensive
against the by-elections. Throughout the campaign he made repeated
and consistent allegations about the cost of the elections which were
reported uncritically by Fleet Street. On 20 July 1984 the *Daily Telegraph* quoted Gummer as saying that the price of the polls would be
£100,000. But, less than two weeks later, on 3 August (the first day
of the campaign), Gummer told the *Telegraph* that they would 'cost
London ratepayers £150,000'. Suddenly the cost had increased by
£50,000! And yet the London *Standard* repeated this figure three
days later without qualification and said of the by-elections campaign:
'It takes its place as just one more charade – with any luck the final
charade – to have been thought up in the corridors of County Hall,
and stages at a cost to the ratepayers of up to £150,000.'[68]

The GLC had organized the by-elections to try to draw attention to
the fact that the forthcoming May 1985 elections had been cancelled
by central government. In addition, the council wanted a chance to
show the public what the GLC actually did in London. And a by-
election campaign was that ideal opportunity. This was a forlorn hope.
Instead, a lot of prominence was given to the claim that the Labour
Party had put up 'stooge' or 'fake' Conservative Party candidates.
However, as the polls approached even the most partisan papers had to
admit the likelihood of a Labour victory, as a *Daily Express* editorial
put it:

What a laugh it will be if Ken Livingstone's mini-election turns out
to be the sham it has always looked. So dubious are the credentials

of his 'Tory' opponents that it is alleged they could be Labour supporters in disguise. Labour, of course, denies fielding any fake candidates... The election was a stunt anyway. Mr Livingstone and three others resigned their seats to fight by-elections they were bound to win... The Tories have shunned this mock campaign. Hence, the suspect Tory labels to ensure Red Ken gets his publicity campaign on the rates.[60]

As polling day approached, the press was keen to dismiss them as a stunt. This reflected Central Office attempts to delegitimize or belittle the by-elections. Hence the *Times* on 10 September 1984: 'A low turnout will enable ministers to claim that the voters share their contempt for the Labour Party's by-election tactic.' And the *Mail* joined in on polling day itself with – 'GLC Voters Go To The Polls In "Stunt" Elections... With the Tories boycotting the elections, many voters might regard the exercise as a farce or a political stunt.' This virtually repeated the government line as Environment Minister, Kenneth Baker, said on the same day: 'This was a sort of prank stunt election.'[70]

When the election results were announced on 20 September 1984, the popular press had no doubts about the quality of the Labour victories. 'Red Ken's Poll Is A Damp Squib', said the *Daily Mirror*. 'Ken's Poll Ploy Flops', agreed the *Daily Express*, while the *Sun* and the *Mail* were in unison: 'Red Ken's Poll Yawn' (*Sun*) and 'Red Ken Creeps Back As London Yawns' (*Mail*). Meanwhile the *Times* had returned to the Environment Ministry's theme – 'Livingstone Poll Win Denounced As "Stunt"'.

From Red Ken to Citizen Ken

On 21 July 1983, the *London Standard* published a harmless enough story about the GLC leader being upset after seeing some particularly violent horror films – 'Nasties Sickened Me – Livingstone'. However, a subeditor had inadvertently tried to insert a 'Red Ken' label in the headline which the *Standard* had occasionally used since May 1981. The next day the paper's subeditors received strict instructions from their editor Louis Kirby. They were not to use the phrase 'Red Ken' in either headlines, captions or in the text. Kirby says he had been trying to make the paper a 'Red Ken-free zone' for some time and that the decision was long overdue.

The *Standard* was not the only paper to have a mild editorial volte-face regarding coverage of the GLC. On 16 May 1984, the *Daily Mail*, according to Tory MP Julian Critchley 'our house magazine',[71] published a feature illustrated by Livingstone and Mrs Thatcher in running clothes. 'The Man Running Rings Round Maggie', ran the headline and added: 'When it comes to the propaganda war, Livingstone is much too fast for her.' This was from the paper that had labelled him 'The Commissar Of County Hall'[72] less than three years earlier. Even the *Sun* was capable of a mild change of mind: 'Friendly Ken', said an editorial. 'Wouldn't it be hilarious if Ken's memorial turned out to be "he was the ratepayers' friend"'.[73]

These papers had not suddenly become supporters of the Labour-led GLC. It was the issue of abolition itself which forced the press to take a step back in the propaganda war. This was particularly so for the *Standard*, despite being the *Daily Mail*'s sister paper. Throughout 1983, London's only evening paper had conducted its own opinion polls and found that the vast majority of Londoners opposed the GLC being abolished. Hence a leader on 27 March 1984: 'The *Standard*'s poll on what Londoners think of the GLC shows one thing beyond a doubt – the propaganda battle up to now has gone completely to those who want to save it from abolition.' Given the *Standard*'s falling circulation, an editorial rethink was clearly called for.

However, according to the GLC's press office and public information department, fear of losing readers was not the only reason for the toning down of the attacks on the GLC, particularly on Livingstone. They argue that it was also due to what the *Sunday Times* described in July 1984 as an 'inspired public relations campaign in defence of the GLC'.[74] Nita Clarke, a former press officer with the health union COHSE and Livingstone's chief press adviser since May 1983, believes that the improved press coverage was partly due to their ability to set the agenda rather than simply react to situations. 'I tried to set the agenda as far as that is possible,' she said.

> We had lots of press conferences, providing detailed information and briefings on how the different policies affected services and directly benefited Londoners ... Obviously you can't stop the press attacking the GLC all the time and there's not much we can do about the *Sun*. But at least we can make sure there are no own goals by presenting the facts in such a way that you can control the flow of information.

Clarke also used television and radio to bypass the popular press. She had been able to do this because, in effect, Fleet Street had bungled their assassination of the GLC leader. The popular press had attacked Livingstone with such venom and intensity that ITN and the BBC were forced to interview him because of all the public attention. The

GLC leader was then able to take advantage of the inevitable contrast between image and reality, especially on live television. As the *Guardian*'s John Carvel explained: 'They [the popular press] built up an image of a caricature revolutionary, part sinister, part raving lunatic, which it was all too easy to dispel when he gained the access to TV and radio which press hyperbole opened up.'[75]

In addition, the GLC launched their 'Public Awareness Campaign' which involved direct campaigning to 'Save the GLC' – leafletting, petitions, public meetings, etc. An advertising agency was hired, Boase, Massimi & Pollit, to co-ordinate the advertising campaign on large billboards and in national newspapers.

Judging by the abolition polls, this public relations venture was relatively successful. But even the GLC's own press officers would admit that the situation would have been very different if Livingstone had not been leader of the council and if abolition had not been so inherently unpopular. The GLC also had an abundance of resources – 42 press officers and a lot of cash to pay for advertising. This was an advantage which the Labour Party at national level and most trade unions cannot afford.

The GLC's campaign against abolition was also blessed by some remarkable political bonuses. Senior Conservative MPs like Edward Heath, several GLC Tories like George Tremlett and a whole range of politicians opposed the abolition bill. There were also the embarrassing defeats in the House of Lords. This all-party hostility to abolition gave the GLC the opportunity to hit back against the government without appearing merely partisan. The campaign had credibility. And so it was rather difficult for Fleet Street to attack the GLC Labour group while it had such wide-ranging support, although there was a press attempt to discredit the by-elections in September 1984.

It would also be wrong to equate a relatively improved press image for Ken Livingstone in the abolition campaign with a fairer coverage of the GLC as a whole. The council's policy of grants to the voluntary groups of London continued to be consistently attacked by Fleet Street. The activities of the Women's Committee, for example, was consistently pilloried, to such a degree that the press office sought the refuge of the women's magazines to promote the image of its chairperson Valerie Wise.

These noble, and partly successful, attempts by the GLC press machine to set the political agenda to offset and bypass the hostility of Fleet Street can, in my view, have only a limited effect. They are unable to combat the politically motivated campaigns and stories that emanate *from* the editorial management of certain newspapers. Nor can they stop the personalized muck-raking, which had nothing to do with genuine investigative journalism, from the *Daily Mail* as revealed by George Tremlett.

More importantly, the 'setting of the agenda' has more serious implications. This is because making judgements about what or should not be publicly debated is, of course, politically subjective. And so, particularly in a local government environment, the question of what should or should not be discussed is highly significant if a leader's press advisors are keen to 'set the agenda'. To what degree should a leading politician like Livingstone give opinions on matters that, at first glance, are not strictly relevant to his political vicinity? Or, for agenda-setters, should a local politician refuse to talk about 'controversial' issues which would potentially cause a media backlash against his council? This issue was raised by John Carvel, the *Guardian*'s local government correspondent and now on the political staff, in his book *Citizen Ken*.[76] Carvel pressed the GLC leader on this very point: why did he make *so many* public pronouncements in the early months of the Labour administration? Livingstone replied:

> If somebody who's asked me to speak on Ireland half a dozen times in the last ten years, comes to me after the election and says, will you say-and-so, I'm not going to behave differently. Because once you start down that route, immediately the whole of the activist wing of the party and beyond them the aware sections of the public are going to say: it's just the same old routine of getting into office, then changing and becoming establishment-minded.

'But why allow the media-provocative opportunities to keep coming?' asked Carvel.

'It's not a question of allowing them. They do keep coming. It's a question of how you respond to them,' replied Livingstone.

Carvel's premise is, in my view, almost censorial in its implications. In effect, he is saying that a leading GLC councillor should not speak publicly on a regular occasion about issues which the press deems controversial, i.e. Ireland, gay rights, police, etc. It seems that the logical conclusion to this argument is that if Livingstone believes that Fleet Street are going to attack him on a certain policy, then he should keep quiet because of the potential press backlash. It is far too expedient and, in the long term, politically self-defeating. It also restrains free speech.

4. Racism in Fleet Street: an Illness or a Disease?

'I'm not having pictures of darkies on the front page,' said Dave Shapland, the *Sun*'s assistant editor.

A night editor agreed, 'That's the last thing our readers want – pictures of blacks raking it in.' Conversation on the evening of 2 August 1985, from Peter Court's diary.

'The *Sun* has constantly championed the rights of the black communities in Britain.' *Sun*, 30 September 1985.

For the past three decades black people in Britain have been treated and portrayed as a problem, rather than fellow citizens with problems. In the 1950s they were said to be living off immoral earnings. In the 1960s the vocation of most black Britons was supposed to be in drug-pushing. By the 1970s and early 1980s the spectre of the black mugger and rioter became the standard stereotype.

The alternative view that some black Britons of Asian and Afro-Caribbean descent resort to crime because of social and environmental factors is given short shrift by most of Fleet Street. This is despite the fact that all the evidence, published in academic and government reports, shows that black people in Britain's inner cities suffer proportionately far more from unemployment and bad housing than do whites. The 1971 census revealed that unemployment among black men was only slightly higher than among the male population as a whole – 6.8 per cent compared with 4.9 per cent. But, as male unemployment rose through the late 1970s and early 1980s, the rate for male blacks rose faster. This is partly because they work in the most vulnerable sectors of the economy. However, even within particular skill and age groups, blacks are more likely to lose their jobs than whites. This was borne out by both the Scarman Report and an all-party Home Affairs select committee in 1981.[1] In addition, a 1981 Home Office Research Unit report revealed evidence of housing discrimination: 'Minorities may be at a disadvantage in having to pay more for the same housing as whites – a sort of "colour tax". There is also some evidence that they find it more difficult to get housing finance and thus pay for it when they do get it, and pay more for rented accommodation.' More recently, even the Conservative government have admitted that between 50,000 and 100,000 black youngsters were without a job because of their colour in November 1985.[2]

Faced with such conditions, many young blacks have become increasingly politically vociferous and organized. Their anger has been fuelled by the spiralling rise in racial attacks which has led to the establishment of numerous 'Defence Committees', particularly in east London.

The reaction of most of the press to the deprivation of Britain's ethnic minorities has been twofold. Firstly, that discrimination and violence against blacks is grossly exaggerated, and mostly propaganda from the 'race relations industry'. Secondly, that protest and rioting by Asians and Afro-Caribbeans is a purely criminal activity and has little to do with the circumstances in which they live. Instead, any attempt to explain and analyze violent protest by Britain's ethnic minorities is seen in almost genetic terms and as simple human greed. Hence Peregrine Worsthorne, now editor of the *Sunday Telegraph*:

> Good relations are only possible in basically law-abiding communities where most people are on the side of the police, in favour of orderly behaviour. That essential condition does not apply in Brixton – any more than it does in Jamaica – where criminal behaviour among the young is fast becoming more the norm than the exception …If there are families living in Railton Road in houses unfit for human habitation, should this not be seen as an indictment of the local youths who prefer to loll around on street corners smoking pot for the price of which they could buy a lot of paint and plaster? … Brixton is the iceberg tip of a crisis of ethnic criminality which is not Britain's fault – except in the sense that her rulers quite unnecessarily imported it – but the fault of the ethnic community itself, from whom the cure must come, as has the disease.[3]

Such a view may not be accepted by all of Fleet Street's editorial management but, judging by the coverage of most of the popular press, it is far from an isolated opinion.

The 1981 riots – the voices of the unheard

A week before the riots in Toxteth, Liverpool, in July 1981, Edward Heath, the former Conservative Prime Minister, told a business conference in London: 'If you have half a million young people hanging around on the streets all day you will have a massive increase in juvenile crime. Of course you will have racial tension when you have young blacks with less chance of getting jobs.'[4]

This analysis of the 1981 riots was given little credence by most of Fleet Street. The first inner-city district to explode was Brixton, in south London, and this is how the *Sunday Express* interpreted the events:

> Every do-gooder in the country has been spouting about the conditions in which south London's blacks have to live. And making excuses for the viciousness and violence which not only characterized last weekend's riots but which have been a way of life in the area for years and years. Does nobody, apart from the police, give a damn about what happens to south London's whites?[5]

This became the predominant view from the first night of rioting on Friday 10 April 1981. The next day the *Sun*'s front page was headlined: 'Battle Of Brixton – 100 Black Youths In Clash With The Cops'. The main news story began: 'A mob of 100 black youths battled with police in a London street last night', and inside the report concluded: 'Brixton, the heart of Britain's West Indian community, is known to its inhabitants as ''The Front Line''. It is notorious for muggings, assaults and murders.'

What had begun with a simple arrest early on Friday afternoon had turned into a vicious and prolonged riot, the worst for many years. What was the main cause? According to BBC journalist John Clare:

> Blacks I talked to were in no doubt what had caused it. Like this shopkeeper in Railton Road, they put it down to constant harassment by the police: 'We don't really want to have a row with the police, but if they are antagonizing us like that . . . If I left my shop now and walked down the street, there is a ten to one chance that five or six policemen will stop me, for nothing.'[6]

A rather different explanation was given on the Saturday afternoon by Sir David McNee, Commissioner of the Metropolitan Police, in a statement for the Sunday papers. He claimed: 'We have unconfirmed reports that what you have seen tonight was not spontaneous, but has been orchestrated and very well planned.' McNee added that there were 'trouble-makers from elsewhere' but didn't provide any evidence. Most of the Sunday papers gave this statement plenty of coverage. But the only newspaper which claimed to have proof of any secret plot was the *Daily Star*. The paper said that black youths 'had schemed to take to the streets over Easter weekend. But police involvement in a stabbing incident sparked off the violence early'. The *Star*'s journalists had talked to young people in squats, illegal drinking clubs, derelict houses, drug dens and illicit gambling clubs. However, their evidence was pretty flimsy.

The allegations of an 'orchestrated' conspiracy turned out to be quite untrue. The Scarman Report concluded that the Brixton riot was spontaneous and not premeditated.[7] And the only 'evidence' for a conspiracy was confined to one woman with an American accent who had asked the police to withdraw, and the allegation from a policeman that many of the black people opposing him were strangers.[8]

The best coverage of the Brixton riots came from the *Observer* who was one of the few papers to publish direct quotes from the rioters themselves about the causes of the trouble: ' "It's not a race riot", we were constantly told along a blazing Coldharbour Lane. "It's more of a police-community thing ... It's not against the white community, it's against the police." '[9]

But what was noticeable about the reporting was the absence of certain key issues. Firstly, the views of the rioters themselves. What were their motives? Why did they apparently hate the police? This was not necessarily the fault of the journalists. Some of the rioters distrusted the press and often abused reporters. There was also the physical danger involved in trying to interview rioters amidst the chaos and debris. That's one reason but not the whole story. Secondly, and more importantly, there was very little scrutiny of police actions in Brixton which, together with unemployment and bad housing, were later regarded as the chief causes of the riot. For example, there was little mention, certainly in the popular press, of Swamp '81'. This was the secret policing exercise by units of plain-clothes police which involved the stopping and searching of hundreds of local people in the Brixton area in the week before the riot. Nor was there space given in other papers to a report by London barrister David Turner whose working party produced an 88-page document after 18 months of research. The report was published on 30 January 1981 just ten weeks before the riot. It said: 'If you are black and live in Lambeth (the borough surrounding Brixton), you risk having your home busted for a police search for no apparent reason.'

However, in contrast to the coverage of the 1985 riots, there was some attempt by a few papers to examine the underlying causes. Here's a *Sunday Telegraph* leader: 'The trouble which flared in Brixton had been predicted by race workers in the area ... It is a poor area, houses dilapidated and unemployment high. Blacks complain of being harassed or attacked by police but Brixton is also a hotbed of leftwing politics.'[10]

After the Brixton violence Lord Scarman was appointed by the

Conservative government to conduct a public inquiry. His brief was, as the London *Standard* put it, 'to find out if the riots were a spontaneous reaction by the black community of Brixton protesting at police harassment or if they were deliberately started'.[11]

One of the local community groups to present evidence to Scarman was 'Concern', a Brixton residents group, whose barrister, Louis Blom-Cooper QC, is an expert in criminal statistics. Blom-Cooper argued that the high crime rate in Brixton before the riots could have been the result of a large police presence. He also accused the Metropolitan police of seriously misinterpreting the crime statistics in the Brixton area. Under the headline ' ' ' "More Police Mean More Crime" ' ', Lucy Hodges of the *Times* reported: 'Evidence to be presented to Lord Scarman today suggests that increasing the number of policemen in an area increases the crime rate and that Scotland Yard should stop mounting special operations until it has tested that thesis.'[12] The day that news story was published, Monday 8 September, the then editor of the *Times*, Harold Evans, was summoned by his proprietor Rupert Murdoch. 'Why do you use these Commies?' said Murdoch, who had been gouging his ballpoint pen through Hodges' report. Evans replied that it was a good story and it was absurd to call Hodges a Communist. 'It was in character,' Evans said later, 'that Murdoch should dislike carrying an immigrant community' s statement critical of the police.'[13] Indeed it was. During that same period Murdoch had also told Evans, regarding a march by black people, that there was nothing that couldn't be solved with a good crack on the head with a police baton.

Murdoch's belief that protesting blacks should be met with violent force was also reflected in the press coverage of the Toxteth riots during the first weekend of July 1981. Looting and rioting around the area of Upper Parliament Street had taken place on a large scale by both black and white people. However, on Monday 6 July, the *Daily Mail*'s front-page headline left no-one in any doubt about who was to blame – 'Black War On Police' it said in huge print. Underneath was a photograph of the police lines confronting the stone-throwing youths, with the caption: 'Facing the fury of the mob: Row upon row of police behind their riot shields at Toxteth'. Also prominent was a quotation from Kenneth (now Sir) Oxford, Chief Constable of Merseyside, who said: 'For 100 years we haven't had a problem – now they're hellbent on confrontation', and added that he blamed the trouble on 'young black hooligans'. It was only at the end of the story that the *Mail* acknowledged that the rioters were both black and white. The paper quoted a young woman's eye-witness account stating that 'more whites were looting our store than blacks'. So how did this fit in with their front-page banner headline of 'Black War On Police'? Many *Daily Mail* journalists and subeditors in the Manchester office didn't know and were also unhappy with the paper's general coverage of the 1981 riots. However, unlike the 1983 general election campaign, their dissent did not reach the NUJ chapel level.

And then suddenly, on the second day after the riot, just as in Brixton, came the news of the conspiracy. On Tuesday 7 July, the *Daily Mail*'s front page proclaimed: 'Search For The Masked Men – The Riots And Political Militants ... Special Branch Is Called In'. The news report began: 'The hunt is on for the hidden men who directed the riots in Toxteth, Liverpool, on Sunday night. Merseyside's Deputy Chief Constable, Mr Peter Wright, said yesterday that Special Branch detectives were investigating this aspect of the rioting.' What was the evidence for such an extraordinary claim? The *Mail* said that 'masked figures on motor cycles were seen issuing instructions to groups of rioters', but it didn't say who saw them. The paper also quoted a 'law and order campaigner' called Charles Oxley who said: 'There is no question that this was orchestrated from outside. I could hear Cockney and Scottish voices shouting in the middle of a mob in Lodge Lane.' This was hardly conclusive evidence for a national newspaper read by 6 million people.

Two days later, on 9 July, the *Mail* returned to the same theme – 'Looting "Was Organized"'. This time the proof was that a police chief '*believed* many of the stolen goods were taken to a central point where they were distributed'. The police chief added: 'It was too much of a coincidence that 500 youths gathered in ten minutes – we must look at the guiding hands.' The next day it was the turn of the *London Standard* with 'Riots: Four Men Hunted – Special Branch Work On Link Theory'.[14] Earlier that morning the *Mail* kept plugging away. Under the by-line of '*Daily Mail* reporter', their front-page headline was 'Extremists' Master Plan For Chaos'. The story continued: 'Political extemists are directing the riots that have ravaged Britain's cities. Police now know they are fighting a skilful group of agitators hellbent on bringing guerilla warfare to the streets'.[15] The conspiracy had now moved to Manchester's Moss Side and this time the *Mail* had more detail about 'mobile factories', 'CB radio squads' and 'rioters brought in by van'. But the whole story was based on allegations made by James Anderton, Chief Constable of Greater Manchester, and there was no corroboration. There was no actual evidence that young blacks were being duped by outside agitators. It was all circumstantial. But Ronald Butt, writing in the same issue of the *Mail*, had no doubts:

'Young blacks, instructed that they are discriminated against, oppressed and denied work by a racialist society, and are misused and abused by the police, stage further disturbances.'[16]

The conspiracy theory has been wheeled out by the establishment to divert attention for hundreds of years. During the 1780 Gordon riots, French and American agents were said to be slipping across the Channel to act as ringleaders. The 1830 and 1831 Captain Swing riots were attributed to 'Jew-looking fellows'. They never existed. Then in the 1919 Liverpool riots, the *Times* printed a story headlined 'Plot Financed From Abroad', claiming that 'the authorities' were convinced that the disorders were 'part of a definite conspiracy, which had its roots abroad, to subvert the present system of government in this country'.[17]

Clearly, in 1981 the revolutionary Left (Socialist Workers Party, Militant Tendency, Workers Revolutionary Party) would have liked to exploit the rioting. No doubt many of their activists did try, but it is well known they were also deeply unpopular with the local young blacks. And, more importantly, the youth in the inner cities are organized in a completely different way, built around informal gangs and unofficial leisure centres.

However, the search for the masked red raiders went on right through the summer. While the *Daily Telegraph* and *Mail* warned of the 'four hooded men', The *Times* blamed the 'wide range of race relations bodies' and 'mischief-makers and do-gooders'. This theme was taken up by the Police Federation in their submission to the Scarman inquiry. The real problem, they said, was 'well-educated activists' who are 'getting young blacks to believe they are victims of police oppression'. Such an analysis is, of course, deeply insulting to young black people. Ironically, it was the *Daily Mail* on 13 July 1981, just three days after their latest 'secret plot' story, that discounted their own theory of a conspiracy behind the riots: 'The idea of a large-scale racial or political conspiracy breeding on mass unemployment seems to have been largely discounted. Professional agitators have been seen on the streets, but it is thought they are riding on the backs of the uproar, rather than creating it.'

The cause of the riots was now switched to 'criminal hooligans' and 'immigration'. Everything from the 'permissive society' (Mrs Thatcher) to John McEnroe's behaviour at Wimbledon, to 'seditious socio-logical clap-trap' (Tory MP Ian Lloyd) in fact. Both the *Sun* and *Daily Mail* gave prominence on 10 July to Enoch Powell's view that mass immigration was the problem and that repatriation was the answer. The *Times*, under Harold Evans' editorship, hit back: 'Certain newspapers see only black hooligans,' ran a leader. 'These crude depictions of events have contributed to racial prejudice. Mr Enoch Powell promotes this fantasy . . . It is nonsense to suggest, as he does, an inescapable connection between colour and street rioting.'[18] The *Times*, the *Daily Star* and the *Guardian* were the few papers to look at other causes of the appalling violence and looting by both black and white youth. Hence the *Times* on 7 July – 'Liverpool: Why The Clue To Violence is Economic Not Racial'.

But most of the press continued to emphasize either the 'criminal element', the 'black mobs' or 'the outside conspiracy' as explanations of the riots. Here's a *Mirror* editorial: 'The latest night of mob violence in Liverpool had nothing to do with the city's problems of bad housing and unemployment. It was a spree of naked greed . . . It was not a protest on Monday night. It was a pillage.'[19] The paper's leader added that the riots were rooted in 'appalling housing, education, and unemployment', but it set the tone for the terms of reference. Other papers took a different route of analysis. After the Scarman report, the Salisbury Group, a small society of Conservatives, invited Charles Moore, then a *Daily Telegraph* journalist and now editor of the *Spectator*, to write a pamphlet based on his talks with elderly white people of Lambeth.

Much of his report was published in the *Daily Telegraph* in March 1982. The series of anonymous interviews gave vent to the old people's understandable fear of violent crime. But Moore's own comments reveal some of the racial prejudice which is often prominent in Fleet Street.

> The great problem for the old English people of Lambeth lies with West Indians who they think are threatening their own way of life . . . Deeper down, there is a feeling that white English life has a richness of civilization which West Indian life lacks. People told me how they had been taught dignity and discipline, for all their poverty . . . Added and connected to this is mass immigration, which arrived suddenly and unasked. The native population of Lambeth feels little natural sympathy with the West Indian arrivals, who they believe lack their respect for law and privacy.[20]

Crime statistics – 'Black = Crime'?

In an internal Scotland Yard memorandum on 24 May 1973, the then Commissioner of the Metropolitan Police, Sir Robert Mark, wrote: 'There is convincing evidence that, given the opportunity to do so, the press ... will give a great deal of support to the Force.' Two years later he was even more convinced of Fleet Street's co-operative role:

> We believe the press have such a high degree of trust in us that we expect them to believe us when we tell them the truth, and we are fully confident of a responsible attitude on their part ... There is such a degree of confidence and trust now between Fleet Street and the Metropolitan Police Force that you almost make a journalist uncomfortable if he disbelieves you.[21]

Nowhere was the uncritical attitude of the press more prominent than in their reporting of the Metropolitan Police's crime statistics between 1982 and 1984 when, for the first time, figures for some offences were broken down on the basis of race.

The figures for robbery and other violent thefts were released on 10 March 1982, shortly after policing methods in Brixton had been strongly criticized by the Scarman Report. The complaints about assertive police tactics in black communities and the advocacy by Scarman of more 'community policing' did not go down well at Scotland Yard.

And so the timing of the release of the crime statistics on the basis of race was particularly interesting. In fact, most of the popular press had been running a campaign for the previous six weeks about 'black muggers'. On 21 January 1982, the *Daily Mail*'s Peter Burden wrote a story headed 'More And More Muggings But The Yard Fights Back'. He reported that 'muggings' had broken all records in 1981 and that 'case files show that in some areas, most attacks are carried out by young blacks'. The next month, Burden was writing:

> Police chiefs are working on new battle plans to tackle the mounting crimes of violence on Britain's city streets. Home Secretary William Whitelaw, concerned at the alarming increase in mugging, is to make a personal tour when he will hear about the new plans ... It is known that he has the final 1981 figures which show an all-time high in serious crime nationwide ... a major drive is to be launched against muggers. Police say that in some areas the majority are black youths.

Later that month, on 25 February 1982, the *Mail* was again reporting: 'With street crimes, particularly muggings, at record levels, Scotland Yard is facing a crucial law and order problem.'

Five days before the figures for violent theft and robbery were released, the *Mail* ran a double-page story entitled 'Prisoners Behind

Net Curtains'.[22] It was based on an elderly widow's dramatic account of being robbed on a Brixton council estate. Three days later, on 8 March, it was the turn of the *Daily Express* to publish scare headlines. ' ''It Adds Up To A Mugging Every Half An Hour In London'' ', the paper reported, announcing that 'this will be revealed in Scotland Yard's worst-ever crime figures', and 'in some inner London suburbs muggings have hit record levels with more than 2,000 in Brixton alone last year'. The *Express* story also revealed just what lay behind this carefully orchestrated campaign: 'Publication of these grim statistics will certainly lead to renewed demands for a fresh look at the consequences of Lord Scarman's report on last year's Brixton riots ... Senior officers have already complained publicly of ''tied hands'' following the publication of the Scarman report.'

The following day, 9 March, the *Express* returned to this 'muggings' theme, based on unquestioned and unpublished crime statistics from the Metropolitan Police. The paper ran a two-page feature headlined 'On Britain's Most Brutal Streets'. Underneath was a large photograph of three black youths walking down Railton Road, Brixton, flanked by a picture of an elderly white woman sitting on a bench in the shopping precinct, captioned: 'A moment's peace ... But the old rarely venture out alone'. Another caption under the picture of the black youths ran: 'The Front Line ... a line of hatred dividing black from white'. The accompanying story set the theme perfectly: 'The new crime figures for this black arc of racial disharmony that sweeps south from the Thames through Brixton and Lewisham and Southall and north to Notting Hill Gate and Stoke Newington will be published this week and the police call them ''terrifying''. It adds up to a mugging every half-hour in London.'

The Scotland Yard Press Bureau must have been delighted with such coverage from most of the popular press. After all, the Metropolitan Police's press office had been the only source for these stories. Clearly, the whole news management operation had been designed to provoke an official encouragement to return to the aggressive policing methods which the Scarman Report had criticized. For their part there was little independent scrutiny or criticism from most of the press.

And so the popular press had set the scene for the Metropolitan Police's press conference on Wednesday 10 March 1982, when Assistant Commissioner Gilbert Kelland announced the much-heralded crime figures. For the first time the statistics for 'robbery and other violent thefts' had been broken down in terms of the race of the offenders.

The next day the *Daily Mail*'s front-page banner headline declared:

'Black Crime: The Alarming Figures – Violence Double That By Whites, Yard Reveal'. The story continued:

> Scotland Yard revealed for the first time yesterday the extent of black crime in London and immediately started political controversy. The figures were broken down from statistics showing an increase in 1981 over 1980 of 34 per cent in cases of 'robbery and other violent thefts' in the capital. Out of 18,763 crimes in that category 'the assailants were identified as coloured', according to the Yard, in 10,399 cases – or 55.42 per cent of the total. This compares with a 13.8 per cent non-white proportion of the population of Greater London. The assailants were said to be white in 4,967 cases, mixed gangs in 704, and their appearance was not known in 2,693. The figures do not mention mugging as such, but do categorize street robberies (41 per cent up at 5,889) and snatch thefts (19 per cent up at 7,330). There were also 2,684 robberies at business premises and 2,860 'other robberies'.

The *Sun*'s front page on 11 March took a similar theme – 'The Yard Blames Black Muggers – Huge Rise In Street Crime'. The news report added: 'Black gangs were blamed by Scotland Yard yesterday for a massive rise in muggings in London. Robberies and street crimes in the capital soared 34 per cent last year to a record 18,763. And 10,399 of them were carried out by blacks.' Inside the paper the whole of page five was taken up by five cases of 'muggings' The headline ran – 'The Victims' – and continued: 'Gangs of vicious, merciless, black muggers stand accused today of a crime wave that is threatening to turn London into New York.' The *Daily Express* whistled a similar, if less shrill, tune – 'Home Secretary William Whitelaw last night pledged that immigrants who commit crimes will be treated as severely as anyone else.' The paper also gave prominence to comments by Police Federation spokesman Jim Jardine – 'Police Blame ''Soft'' Tactics'.

What was the evidence for such coverage? Firstly, there is no such thing as 'mugging' in legal terms. Secondly, and more importantly, the 18,763 crimes of robbery and other violent theft includes offences which in no way could be regarded as 'mugging'. This includes 2,684 robberies at business premises, 7,330 'snatches', i.e. stealing a bag without using other violence and 2,860 'other robberies' which do not count as street robberies. That leaves only 5,889 robberies which could be accurately reported as 'mugging' in the popular sense of the term – 31 per cent of the original figure. And even that figure need not involve any significant violence.

The legitimacy of the figures was also undermined in terms of the colour issue. The press assumption that 'coloured' means black is not based on police statistics. There is also the problem of recognition. According to a Home Office survey in March 1982, 'Given the victims' restricted and uncertain descriptions of the muggers, we must treat with caution statements as to the race or colour of the attackers. In many cases, judgements were based on a quick glimpse in the dark.' The survey also found that 59 per cent of robbery involved no injury and that the largest number of victims was male and between 21 and 30 years of age.

So why were these figures for certain offences released in such a way? And why were the figures for rape and murder not broken down in a similar racial way? According to Assistant Commissioner Kelland, the decision was due to 'public opinion and pressure'. When asked how the police monitored public opinion, he replied: 'There is a demand for this information from the public and from the media on behalf of the public.' Kelland added that robbery and 'mugging' were 'beyond all doubt' producing the most concern and disquiet. Presumably murder and rape did not warrant this 'concern and disquiet'.

The fact that these crime figures were highly misleading and even plain wrong provoked little outcry in Fleet Street, except in the leading articles of a couple of serious papers. The only exception in Fleet Street was an article by the solicitor Gareth Peirce in the *Guardian* – 'Unleashing An Uncritical Press'.[23] Instead, it was left to the Lord Chief Justice, Lord Lane, to pass judgement on the figures in his maiden speech in the House of Lords on 24 March 1982: 'So far as the [crime] statistics are concerned, I propose to say nothing, except that they are mostly misleading and very largely unintelligible.' This damning indictment was given short shrift in the reporting of the figures the following year. The press repeated its image of London being racked by racial hatred, with black muggers waiting at every street corner to threaten innocent white shoppers.

On 22 March 1983, Patrick Mayhew, a junior Home Office minister, provided a parliamentary written answer for the rightwing Tory MP, Harvey Proctor, who wanted the total of recorded robbery and violent theft to be published with its racial breakdown. This was done in the same week that the government's Police and Criminal Evidence Bill, which extends police powers to stop-and-search, was showing signs of erosion after fierce political attacks in the Commons. Despite the fact that robbery comprises only 3 per cent and 'muggings' only 0.9 per cent of all recorded crime, the press reported them almost identically to the 1981 figures. 'Black Crime Shock', said the

Sun's front page. 'Blacks carried out twice as many muggings as whites in London last year. Of 19,258 street crimes in London, 10,960 were by blacks and 5,262 by whites'. On an inside page the paper's headline ran – 'Black Mugging Shocker'.[24] The *Mail* agreed – 'Black Crime: New Figures'.[25] The next day the *Daily Telegraph* gave prominence to Harvey Proctor's views about 'black and white vigilante groups "fighting it out" on London streets' – 'MP Predicts "White Backlash" on Crime'.[26] Only the *Mirror* took a different view – 'Fury At "Slur on Blacks"'.[27]

As in March 1982, the figures for street crimes incorporate offences which are *not* violent and so cannot be regarded as 'mugging'. Equally important, they included only those offences that are *reported* to the police. According to the British Crime Survey for 1982, only one in five violent crimes are reported to the police. In addition, little prominence was given to the fact that the victims of assaults, robberies and violent theft were black themselves – 18 per cent in London – while the black population of the capital is 13.8 per cent. But, as Martin Kettle wrote in the *Sunday Times*: 'The presentation of these figures tells us more about the people who released them and the people who wrote them up than about crime in Britain.'[28]

And yet, 18 months later, in September 1984, the Black = Crime headlines were reproduced again. On 26 September 1984, the Home Office published a bulletin on crime statistics for the Metropolitan Police Area. The report limited itself to a small proportion of recorded crimes in the London area – assault, robbery and violent theft. The bulletin said: 'It should not be assumed that those offences for which information is available are representative of crime as a whole'. More reliance, said the report, can be placed on ethnic statistics for arrests and court proceedings. However, since fewer than 20 per cent of recorded offences are cleared up by the Metropolitan Police, these figures have 'limited relevance'.

This is how the press reported their findings. 'Blacks Do 60 per cent Of London Muggings – Prime Target For Them Are Asians', said the *Sun*. 'Black muggers are responsible for almost 60 per cent of violent street crimes in London, a shock government report revealed yesterday.' The Press Council upheld a complaint against the *Sun*'s headline which was said to be 'too strident for an issue which called for sensitive handling'. The West Indian Standing Conference, which made the complaint, also objected to the attempt by the paper to link the weapons displayed in an adjacent picture – alleged to have been confiscated by a white person – as having been used by black people against white victims.

The *Daily Mail* took a similar line to the *Sun* – 'Most Muggers Are Still Black'. None of the national papers chose to emphasize the other findings in the Home Office document – that black people do not figure prominently in other forms of crime, that only a small percentage of robberies gets reported and that there is no assessment of the 'ethnic appearance' of the assailant in a high percentage of reported crimes.

Racial violence – from Deptford to Newham

The careful selectivity of the reporting of the crime figures was never more obvious than the absence of one simple fact in the overall coverage. It was this. That most racially motivated attacks are committed by whites, not by black people. According to a 1981 Home Office survey, an Asian is 50 times more likely than a white, and a West Indian 36 times more likely than a white person, to be the victim of a racist attack. In the survey's Introduction, the then Conservative Home Secretary William (now Lord) Whitelaw said: 'The study has shown quite clearly that the anxieties expressed about racial attacks are justified. Racially motivated attacks, particularly on Asians, are more common than we had supposed, and there are indications that they may be on the increase.'

Perhaps a major reason why Lord Whitelaw was surprised at the number of racial attacks on black people was quite simple. Most of Fleet Street has ignored them. For when the Home Office report was published on 17 November 1981, there was no coverage in the popular press at all except a short piece in the *Daily Mail*.

A good example of this under-reporting occurred earlier in 1981. On 18 January 13 young blacks were burned to death and 47 injured after a fire in a family home in New Cross Road, Deptford, southeast London. It happened during a party and in a fierce blaze the house was soon gutted. The New Cross area was renowned for arson attacks, notably on the nearby Moonshoot Club and Albany Theatre and the multiracial bookshop in Lewisham Way Centre in 1980. In addition, three days after the Deptford fire, five members of the British Movement were convicted in London of ten charges including possession of firearms and ammunition, arson and conspiracy to stir up racial hatred.

The press did report the Deptford fire story at the time. It made the front pages of the *Sun*, *Daily Telegraph* and the *Daily Express* (a picture caption). The papers also gave it reasonable space. The *Daily Mail* put in on page three, *Daily Express* on pages four and five, and the *Mirror* on page nine. However, Fleet Street then largely forgot about the story. They never accepted the possibility of a racial motive. This was despite the fact that the police were at the time treating it as arson, with a fire bomb being seen as the weapon. In contrast to the white victims of tragedies like the 1985 Bradford fire, there were few, if any, interviews with grieving relatives of the dead black teenagers. There was little independent investigation into the potential scandal.

This under-reporting angered the black community. As Russell Profitt, a local Lewisham Labour councillor, said:

I'm baffled by why the news media were silent about the event and its implications for black people. I would have expected follow-up interviews with the youngsters who had been at the party and with the families affected. Also articles trying to piece together evidence of what happened in the house. This was the greatest tragedy that has ever struck the black community in Britain. The only conclusion I can draw is that, to many white people, what happens to black people doesn't matter.[29]

Laurence Marks, the experienced *Observer* journalist, agreed with Profitt's analysis:

News coverage is not a simple measure of moral concern. It reflects a complex of half-intuitive judgements about public curiosity, timing, the practicality of digging out fresh evidence and the rival claims of subsequent disasters elsewhere. But when every qualification has been entered, the absence of comprehensive follow-up stories [about the Deptford fire] does seem to reflect an emotional and moral disassociation from the concerns of black citizens.[30]

Alastair Hetherington, the former editor of the *Guardian* and Professor of Media Studies at Stirling University, confirmed this newsdesk discrimination when he spent a day in the *Daily Mail*'s editorial offices. In his book, *News, Newspapers and Television*,[31] he wrote: 'If a reporter is sent to a big fire or emergency and finds out that the victims are working-class or black, newsdesk interest diminishes. If the victims or eyewitnesses are middle-class, newsdesk interest quickens.' Hetherington then added: 'This implies no racialism. The *Mail* has two highly competent black reporters and one specialist, all of whom are deployed on a wide range of assignments. It implies only a concentration on what are seen as the aspects of an event that will stir the greatest response among their readers.'

It's probably hardly surprising that the *Mail* doesn't have many black readers. For after the Deptford disaster the paper refused to give any credence to the possibility of a racial motive. This was despite the fact that the Home Secretry set up special police units to combat racial attacks within two weeks of the fire. But the *Mail* had other ideas. On 25 February 1981, the paper reported:

Police investigating the birthday party blaze that killed 13 West Indians in southeast London are hopeful of bringing a charge today ... One of the eight youths who volunteered to take part in the reconstruction has said that one boy sprinkled a bottle of wallpaper stripper on the floor and set light to it. All the youngsters involved are black. Initially, extremists claimed that the fire was started by whites. This has been dismissed by Yard evidence.

This was quite untrue. The police did not know either way. The next day Scotland Yard and south London police flatly denied the *Mail* story that a black had started the fire. 'No-one was helping with inquiries in the sense of being treated as a suspect,' said a Yard spokesman. 'No-one has been arrested and no-one likely to be charged in the near future.'

By the end of February, south London's black community were growing angry at what they saw as a lack of effort and interest by the police and the press to investigate the fire tragedy. And so on Monday 2 March 1981, an estimated 10,000 mainly black people marched through the streets of London to express their protest at the alleged cover-up. There was some trouble along Fleet Street and Blackfriars Road. Shop windows were broken and goods stolen and there were some violent clashes with the police. But this was due to a small group of youngsters who joined the march late and ignored stewards' instructions to remain with the body of the march. In addition, as John Radley, the Metropolitan Police's Deputy Assistant Commissioner, said later, most of the marchers 'who took part conducted themselves in a responsible manner'.

This police interpretation of the protest was ignored by the popular press. 'Rampage Of A Mob – Police Injured In Clash With Demo Blacks', said the *Express*. 'Violence erupted between police and black demonstrators in a march through London last night. 17 officers were injured – one a woman – six detained in hospital. There were 28 arrests.' The *Mail* took a similar line – '6,000 Blacks In Protest March – When The Black Tide Met The Thin Blue Line'. The report added: '6,000 demonstrators, most of them black, marched through London yesterday in a protest at a "police cover-up" which Scotland Yard deny has happened.' The *Daily Star* also concentrated on the violence angle – '17 Cops Hurt As Thugs Turn Blaze Protest Into A Terror Riot', although the paper did give space to black councillor

Russell Profitt the next day – 'Why The Blacks Took To The Streets'.[32]

The *Sun*'s coverage of the march managed to secure complaints to the Press Council from six organizations. 'Black Day At Blackfriars – Riots And Looting As Marchers Run Wild', said the paper's front page. The centre-page spread was then headed – 'Mob Fury Erupts As 5,000 Go On The March To Protest At Party Fire Massacre' and 'Day The Blacks Run Riot In London'. The main report began: 'Race fury erupted in the streets of London yesterday as Black Power militants turned a protest march into a riot. For seven hours a frenzied mob took part in an orgy of looting and destruction in the West End.'

Community, housing and council workers from Lewisham and Deptford complained to the Press Council that the *Sun*'s coverage was distorted, sensationalized, racist and inflammatory. Henry Douglas, the *Sun*'s legal manager, replied that the paper had reported objectively the events as observed by experienced and sympathetic reporters. He added that the *Sun* was proud of its reputation for honest, objective reporting and its reputation as the newspaper which had done more than any others to foster racial harmony in the past decade. The Press Council concluded that the paper's report was 'highly sensationalized, contained inaccuracies and gross exaggerations and lacked sensitivity'.

What was most noticeable about the coverage was the lack of analysis about the background to the march. As Lucy Hodges of the *Times* pointed out: 'The press coverage contrasted sharply with that on television. Both the BBC and independent TV made efforts to explain the reasons for the march and for the anger.'[33]

There was also the contrast with local press treatment. Later that week the *South East London Mercury* had a different tale to tell – 'Day Of Dignity' and 'A Plea For Justice'. The paper's editorial attacked the national papers for concentrating on the 'tiny minority of hotheads' who caused the trouble and ignoring the majority of marchers who 'demonstrated their anger with dignity and their frustration noisily but peacefully'.[34]

The Deptford fire was just one of many examples of deliberate under-reporting of racial attacks on blacks by Fleet Street. On 10 April 1981, a 17-year-old black youth, Malcolm Chambers, was murdered in Swindon by whites. The local press described the incident as a race riot. The national papers ignored the killing altogether.

But the most glaring incident of Fleet Street double standards happened in the first week of June 1981. On 31 May, Miam Aziz, a 50-year-old Asian, was found murdered in a park in Wandsworth, south

London. It was one of several racial attacks in that area. In fact, bus crews in Croydon had been planning three weeks earlier to refuse to operate late night services because of the number of racial attacks on black busmen. It was an open secret that fascist groups were active in the area of Wandsworth, Croydon and Thornton Heath. Indeed, until 1976 Croydon was the head office of the National Front.

So how did the national press report the murder of this Asian in that area? The *Daily Mail* gave it three paragraphs at the bottom of page 13 – 'Asian Man Killed In Park'. The *Express* ignored it completely. The *Sun* managed three sentences on page two, although it did mention that a racial motive could not be ruled out. The *Guardian* did little better – four sentences on page two. Only the *London Standard* produced anything remotely substantial – 130 words at the foot of page five under the headline 'Grudge Could Have Led To Park Murder', thus discounting the racial motive. Still, the *Standard* did give the reaction of the black community groups two days later on page nine – 'We Won't Be Turned Into Another Brixton'.[35] In the ensuing days there was also no attempt to find out whether Wandsworth was a district where racist attacks were frequent.

The day after Miam Azim was found battered to death, Terry May, a white teenager, was murdered in an equally brutal way by a black gang in nearby Thornton Heath. This racist attack was given rather different coverage by Fleet Street. The *Daily Mail* devoted most of its front page to the story: 'Race Murder In Suburbia – ''Terry Just Happened To Be A White Boy In The Wrong Place At The Wrong Time'' '. The paper reported how May ran 'straight into the path of a rampaging gang of black youths'. Their editorial added: 'Our fear is that the police determination to combat crime, especially violent crime in these areas of our inner cities where there are the greatest concentration of British citizens of West Indian origin, has been eroded.'[36] The *Sun* also gave the May murder front-page treatment – 'Innocent Terry May was torn from his motorbike by a rampaging mob of black youths – and met a horrific death'.[37] The story also made the *Express* front page – 'Loved Ones Who Weep For Race Hate Victim'. Inside two pages were devoted to the 'Innocent Victim Of Race Hate'. In the same edition the *Express* ran this story – 'Police had to take refuge in a store last night after a gang of black youngsters fought to free a coloured girl who had been arrested'.[38] The *London Standard* decided the May murder was important enough for the whole of its front page, together with detailed analysis.[39] The following day, 4 June, the story was still on the front pages of the *Mail* and the *Sun* with more personal and emotional reactions to the death.

The contrast in the coverage of the two murders is quite stunning. Many Asian groups in south London were furious at the under-reporting of racist attacks on black people. On 11 June 1981, at a meeting of Wandsworth Community Relations Council, an *Observer* journalist was asked to explain why the press had virtually ignored the murder of Azim. He replied that the papers depended on police sources for information on murders.[40] But the papers knew about the Azim murder and they had buried the story in the inside pages in two or three sentences. So what was the real reason? There can only be two explanations. Either Fleet Street's editorial management themselves believed that the murder of a black man was insignificant compared to that of a white person. Or that they assumed their readers also didn't put the life of an Asian in the same category as the life of a white person.

A more recent example of these discriminating newsdesk criteria occurred in July 1985. On Saturday 13 July, Shamira Kassan and her three young sons were burnt to death in their house in Ilford, Essex. The local police treated the case as arson and immediately launched a murder investigation. Three weeks earlier the Kassan family had been the target of another arson attack when petrol was poured through their letter box. In 1982, the previous owners of the same house, also an Asian family, had suffered an arson attack. In addition, Ilford is close to London's East End and that summer was one of the worst for racial attacks.

All the evidence, therefore, pointed to at least the possibility, if not probability, of a racial motive. But the only paper to explore this angle was the *Observer* in a story by Arlen Harris. The paper quoted case after case of racial assaults and arson on Asians and their families in east London, particularly in Newham. But the popular press preferred to adopt a different position. The *Mail on Sunday* found some 'distraught relatives' who thought it was all a case of 'mistaken identity'. The *Sunday Mirror* quoted the police who said the fire might have been meant for a previous occupant of the house. The *Sunday Express* declined to mention any motive, while the *News of the World* suggested: 'The motive for the blaze is not known. But one theory is race hate'.

Four days later, on 18 July, the papers reported the death of another woman: Mrs Jean Gidman had died when her house in Biddulph, Staffordshire, caught fire. Her husband, Brian Gidman, was a miner who had gone back to work halfway through the 1984-5 miners' strike. Police treated the fire as arson. All the popular press were quite sure about the motive in this case. 'Rebel Miner's Wife Dies In Arson

Attack', said the *Mirror*'s front page. All the other tabloid papers gave the story prominence, stressing the fact that Mrs Gidman's husband was a strike-breaking miner. And yet the following day Detective Chief Superintendent Peter Broomhill said: 'There is no evidence to suggest any connection with the mining dispute.'[41]

But 1985 was undoubtedly the year when the issue of racial violence came to the attention of at least some sections of the public. This was partly because of the sheer scale of the problem, but mainly because some Asians were so frustrated by the situation that they fought back physically. This happened in early April when seven Asians were involved in a fight with fascists in a pub in Newham.

On Saturday 27 April 1985, an estimated 2,000 anti-racist demonstrators marched through east London to protest about racial attacks on Asians and what they saw as a reluctance by the police to investigate these incidents. The march organizers had agreed with the police that they could stop outside Forest Gate police station to show their support to the 'Newham 7'. According to the stewards, the police broke this agreement and began arresting some demonstrators. That's when the trouble started, with some of the crowd throwing bottles and sticks at the police.

As usual the *Observer* presented the most balanced report. But only three papers – the *Sunday Telegraph*, *Sunday Times* and *Observer* – mentioned why the march had taken place. 'Mob Besiege Police', said the *Sunday Mirror*. '19 Held As Demo Mob Lay Siege To Police Station', reported the *Mail on Sunday*, while the *News of the World*'s story began: 'An angry mob of 1,000 howling demonstrators besieged a police station for four hours yesterday'. In fact, only a small section of the marchers was involved in any trouble. This was confirmed by a Scotland Yard spokesman who said that 'a small unruly element, unconnected with the main march organizers' had been involved in violence.

However, for the *Sun* columnist John Vincent, racial violence against black people was not a problem. Far from it, in fact. Instead, argued Vincent: 'It [the race relations industry] was founded on the assumption that there was a great problem over whites being intolerant to blacks. That hasn't happened. What nobody allowed for was blacks being frightening to whites. The race relations people ought to make it their top priority to get West Indian youths to throw away the knives that are so much part of their culture.'[42]

This 'argument' contrasts sharply with the well-documented evidence of various anti-racist organizations, like the Newham Monitoring Project. Their research shows that the problem of racial attacks on the Asian and Afro-Caribbean community is massive. So why has the issue been largely ignored by most of Fleet Street? It cannot be for professional reasons. The standard response from news editors is that they cannot cover these stories until the police take an interest. This argument is a non-starter. The police is only one source for such stories, particularly in the East End of London. And the nature of such stories ensures a 'human interest' angle for the tabloids. There has to be another reason. It is, I believe, that violence against black and Asian people is not seen as the same level of priority – either in moral or news terms – as an attack upon a white person.

The 1985 riots – plenty of blame, little explanation

Shortly after the riots in Handsworth, Brixton and Tottenham during the autumn of 1985, Stuart Hall, the radical black academic, was contacted by several journalists to discuss the possible causes of the violence. The premise of their questioning, according to Hall, was that unemployment and urban deprivation had already been cited as causes: 'There must be some other reasons,' they said.[43]

In some ways the journalists were right. Riots erupt for a whole range of reasons – from socioeconomic to emotional to criminal. They are a very complex phenomenon. But Hall's frustration with the press dismissal of the possible social factors did indicate the difference in approach from the 1981 riots. For during those disturbances a few papers at least, some as unlikely as the *Sunday Telegraph*, gave some credence to social and economic explanations. This time, four years later, such an analysis was given short thrift by most of Fleet Street, except the *Guardian*. This was partly because the 1985 riots were more violent with a number of deaths, including a policeman. But that was not the whole truth.

It was almost as though the publication by the Metropolitan Police of racially broken-down crime statistics in 1982 and 1983, plus a similar Home Office survey in 1984, had struck a nerve in the press. That between 1981 and 1985 these crime statistics, despite being grossly misleading and inaccurate, had been an opportunity to portray the black community as a largely criminal one. And that the 1985 riots now provided the 'proof' for Fleet Street to confirm this prejudice.

The first of the riots occurred on Monday 9 and Tuesday 10 September in Handsworth, an inner-city district of Birmingham. A wave of looting, burning and fighting hit the area and left two dead and dozens injured. On the Tuesday afternoon the Home Secretary,

Douglas Hurd, had to make a hasty retreat from the area after being stoned by a crowd.

The next day, 11 September, the press had no doubts about what happened. 'Let there be no doubt about one aspect of the bloody Handsworth riot,' said the *Express* leader. 'It was a criminal enterprise, planned and executed for loot and arson. It was racial only in the sense that successful, hard-working Asians were the victims of black mobs.' Much of the coverage took this argument a step further, suggesting that West Indians were inherently more likely to be the instigators and exponents of Britain's riots. The *Sun* provided a good example of this when it devoted a full page to an analysis of the 'flash-point cities' where riots could erupt – 'Where The Fear Of Mob War Grips The Streets'. Accompanied by a map of Britain, the article began: 'More than 2.2 million immigrants are now living in Britain – mainly in our big cities.'[44] This will come as news to black West Indians living in Handsworth, most of whom were born in Britain, although the *Sun* did acknowledge this later in the article. In the same issue, alongside a picture of a black rioter, their front-page news story began: 'A black thug stalks a Birmingham street with hate in his eyes and a petrol bomb in his hand. The prowling maniac was one of the West Indian hoodlums who brought race terror to the city's riot-torn Handsworth district.'[45]

Another major theme was that the Handsworth riot was due to inter-racial conflict and rivalry between the Afro-Caribbeans and Asians. The 'evidence' for this was that the two Asians had died after being beaten, tortured and left to burn by a gang of blacks. The *Sun* reported: 'Two Asian brothers screamed in agony as West Indian rioters beat them – and then left them to burn alive in their petrol-bombed sub-post office'. The *Express* also gave this story prominence – 'We're Innocent! Last Cry Of Beaten Brothers: Two Asian brothers were tortured and left to burn to death'. The story was based on an allegation by a Muslim community leader, Mohammed Zaman, who did not see what had happened but was in the next room and *overheard* screaming. He said: 'they must have been terribly beaten'.[46] This account was published, without checking, by the *Sun* and *Express*. In fact, a postmortem the next day revealed that the Asians had died from inhaling smoke. The torture theory was also wrong. 'There were no signs from weapons either blunt or sharp,' said Tom Meffen, West Midlands' Police Assistant Chief Constable. And few papers gave much space to the fact that the man initially arrested for the deaths was white. No wonder Geoffrey Dear, West Midlands Chief Constable, was moved to say after the riots: 'We are tending to lump all black faces together as criminals. That is patently unfair.'[47]

But the theme of black criminals attacking their Asian neighbours continued to be strongly promoted in the tabloids. On 12 September, the *Sun* devoted nearly a page to this explanation – 'Why The West Indians Hate Asians'. The article continued: 'The terrible events in Handsworth, murderous attacks on Indian shopkeepers and full-scale arson, must be seen against a background of anti-Asian murmurings among even the most respectable West Indians.' It was written by Roy Kerridge, a freelance writer who usually contributes to the rightwing *Spectator* magazine on racial issues. In his autobiography, *The Lone Conformist*, Kerridge describes himself as an 'imperialist of the 1882 variety', but when asked by *City Limits* what this meant he refused to comment.[48]

Kerridge's article infuriated many West Indians and particularly Asians. There were protests and pickets outside the *Sun*'s offices in London. Leaflets were handed out accusing the paper of pumping out 'race hatred propaganda'. A trading association was formed of 30 shop-owners in Lozells Road, Handsworth, whose properties had been burnt, and they issued a statement rejecting the allegations. Several Asian shop-owners also refuted the *Sun*'s claim of inter-racial jealousy. Astab Ali, who lost £15,000 of his stock in his dress shop, said: 'There was no rivalry between communities. They just wanted to steal what we had and it did not matter who owned the shop.' Mushtaq Rabbani, Chairman of the Handsworth and Aston Welfare Association, said: 'Rivalry between Asians and Afro-Caribbeans does not exist in this area. There is nothing wrong in this area.'[49]

If 'inherent' criminality and inter-racial envy was the press's explanation for the Handsworth riot, their analysis of the equally vicious unrest in Tottenham, north London, was a return to an old favourite – a Red plot planned by outside agitators. That was the alleged cause for the riot on Sunday 6 October which was sparked off by the death of local black resident, Cynthia Jarrett, during a police raid on her home the previous day. During the ensuing riot a policeman, PC Keith Blakelock, was hacked to death and over 250 people were injured. Both black and white people were involved.

The following morning, Monday 7 October, the Metropolitan Police held a press conference. The police's Chief Commissioner, Sir Kenneth Newman, told journalists that 'leftwing infiltrators' had provoked the riot. 'Activists are engaged in stirring up this kind of trouble,' he said. Newman was then asked if he had any evidence that 'political agitators' were responsible. He replied that the presence of 'anarchist and Trotskyist' activists had certainly 'been noted in areas of ethnic concentration' in London. In fact, Scotland Yard had used two paragraphs from a *Guardian* report which noted the presence of Class War, an anarchist group, and the Revolutionary Communist Party (RCP) in the Brixton disturbances the previous weekend. David Rose, who wrote the *Guardian* story, later said that he regretted the use of his account to spread 'the deeply ludicrous and mendacious theory that Class War or the RCP could cause the riot' in Tottenham. He added that their presence in Brixton was not only 'irrelevant but ineffective'.[50]

Later that day (Monday) a Scotland Yard press officer was asked by a *City Limits* journalist how he knew that outsiders from Brixton had arrived on the scene in Tottenham to stir up more trouble. 'How do you know they're not?' was the response.

That seemed to be enough evidence for most of Fleet Street, and there was little equivocation in their reporting. 'Plot Behind The Riot', said the *Standard*'s front-page headline later that afternoon. This was based on the police's allegations and also that 'Some witnesses claimed that at the height of the violence they heard a whistle being blown among the angry crowds as a signal'. The next morning, the *Daily Star* was more explicit. 'Red Butchers', ran their front-page banner headline. 'Leftwing infiltrators aim to spread race hatred,' the paper reported, 'and set black against white. Their object is to wreck and destroy. While buildings blaze and shops are looted, the agitators melt into the night.' Their leader added: 'Obviously sick-minded agitators with no regard for democracy – far less human decency – were at work in the background.'[51] The *Daily Telegraph* saw the sale of ultra-leftwing newspapers and leaflets, and the presence of 'white, bearded men in sandals, many accompanied by girls', as evidence of the sinister forces at work in the area. This is how their news story began: 'Trotskyites, socialist extremists, Revolutionary Communists, Marxists and black militants from as far away as Toxteth descended on Tottenham yesterday to take part in a protest meeting called because of Sunday's riot on the Broadwater Farm Estate.'[52]

But it was the *Daily Express* who was most convinced that the riot was a conspiracy orchestrated by secret Red agitators. Under the front-page headlines of 'Kill! Kill! Kill! – Red-Trained Hit Team Gave Orders As Riot Mob Hacked PC To Death', the paper reported:

> The thugs who murdered policeman Keith Blakelock in the Tottenham riots acted on orders of crazed leftwing extremists. Street-fighting experts trained in Moscow and Libya were behind Britain's worst violence. The chilling plot emerged last night as detectives hunted a hand-picked death squad believed to have been sent into

North London hellbent on bloodshed ... The killers' charge was orchestrated by sinister men with whistles and loud-hailers behind the main riot pack. Ringleaders with hailers were also seen in other streets guiding black and white petrol bombers to their targets. The same men could have sparked the Brixton and Handsworth terror ... Special Branch has drawn up a list of known activists who have been under observation for four years in London, Birmingham and Liverpool. Now police are trying to track them down. They include men and women from Commonwealth countries like Jamaica, Barbados and Nigeria, who have been trained in Russia and Libya in street revolutionary tactics. Some have been lying low under the umbrella of outwardly innocent racial pressure groups in London. Red Ken Livingstone's GLC and other leftwing councils have given thousands of pounds of ratepayers' cash to some of these groups, totally unaware that it was being filtered to activists.[53]

What was the evidence for such an extraordinary story? There was a quote from an anonymous police officer and another from an anonymous local resident, but neither of them mentioned the 'Moscow and Libya' connection. This lack of evidence was hardly surprising. The story was completely untrue. In fact, the *Express* had been the victim of a hoax by Rocky Ryan, who takes a delight in tricking certain Fleet Street newspapers into publishing false stories. But, as the *Observer*'s Peter Hillmore explained: 'His array of accents isn't what makes the hoaxing so easy. It's that Mr Ryan chooses stories newspapers not only want to believe, but are actually desperate to believe. This means they are not going to let a few facts stand in their way.'[54]

If final proof were needed that the outside agitator theory was a lie, it came from the police themselves a week after the Tottenham riot. 'No evidence of agitation before the riot by politically inspired groups has been found by the police,' reported the *Standard*. 'A Scotland Yard spokesman said: ''We don't believe outside agitators were responsible for what happened in Tottenham.'' '[55] Though most of the press were obsessed with nonexistent red plots during the 1985 riots, they were just as concerned with undermining the Scarman Report which had advocated community policing. Lord Scarman had also stressed that social and economic factors were a major reason for the 1981 Brixton riots. A unique insight into how Fleet Street was keen to portray the 1985 disturbances as purely and exclusively a criminal phenomenon is revealed by a transcript of an interview between a senior journalist and a local councillor in Haringey. On the morning of Wednesday 9 October 1985, Narendra Makanji, Labour councillor for Noel Park,

Tottenham, was interviewed by Anthony Doran, the *Daily Mail*'s home affairs correspondent. Here is an extract from their conversation:

Doran: I was at the Scarman press conference in 1982. I was also on the streets of Brixton. I saw the police move into Railton Road and I saw the waste. Files of wallets stolen, wallets and purses. I spoke to black people, decent law-abiding black people, who told me that they are frightened to go out, that they were mugged, their wives could not go out shopping and they could not go to work. Black youths were rampaging around Railton Road. They were being taught to mug, to rob and to take drugs by known criminals and where to look. Scarman did not mention the criminality involved. Do you think it should be mentioned?

Makanji: I don't know what this question has got to do with this topic.

Doran: You mentioned Scarman. I just replied to it. I have also been told on that estate [Broadwater Farm] by senior people...

Makanji: You are trying to put words into my mouth...

Doran: I was told by a senior person, not a policeman, but a Council employee who knows a lot about the estate, that there is a great deal of drug taking and drug pushing. Do you think Scarman should have mentioned criminality as one of the factors?

Makanji: Why don't you ask Scarman that? Why are you asking me that?

Doran: You raised Scarman, didn't you.

Makanji: The Scarman report is an authoritative political document.

Doran: (Inaudible abuse)

Makanji: Well, if you don't want to speak to me, there is one thing you can do. You don't have to carry on.

Doran: I would like you to answer the point about criminality, because it is a fact in the inner cities. I think so. I think you should answer the point... Is it a factor in the rioting that has been going on this area and in others?

Makanji: I am sure there are criminals all over London, in Tottenham and in the City of London. I am sure there are criminals all over the country and that has to be tackled. I oppose criminality wherever it takes place, including the people who tax-dodge and who fiddle their expenses like a lot of journalists do.

At this point Doran packed up his books and walked away. None of the interview was published in the *Daily Mail* the next day. Instead, Doran wrote a story headlined – 'Black Militants Face Backlash From

Workers'.[56] But it was his line of questioning that was revealing. Of course criminality was a factor in the 1985 riots, but it wasn't the only reason. Hundreds of black and white people didn't just suddenly take to the streets and attack the police because they felt like it or were all on drugs or were copying the blacks in South Africa. The explanations run far deeper. However, apart from the *Guardian* and a couple of serious papers, that complex analysis was sadly lacking.

Racism in Bouverie Street – proof at last

After the 1985 riots died down, the air was full of accusations of racism against the popular press. It has been a common enough complaint since the mid-1970s and the claim has been strongly denied by the papers' editorial management. However, for the purposes of this book, I have been given a copy of a 24-page diary which suggests otherwise. This document reveals direct evidence of racial prejudice among some senior editors and executives of the *Sun*, Britain's biggest-selling daily newspaper.

Between 13 June 1985 and 31 October 1985, Peter Court was employed on the art desk of the *Sun* as a casual worker. His desk was adjacent to the paper's chief subeditors' table and the 'back-bench' (night editors and executives) on the third floor of the Bouverie Street offices. Throughout that period Court kept a detailed record of comments and conversations among senior editorial management. At the office he would jot down remarks and decisions by editors on scraps of paper. Then, later that evening he would write up the day's incidents in a large book back at his north London home. The contents of this diary have been verified by another source at the *Sun*.

On the evening of Friday 2 August 1985, Dave Shapland, an assistant editor, was acting editor of the paper while Kelvin McKenzie was on holiday. It had been decided that the front page should have a photograph of some of the 36 people who had won the *Sun* bingo. A subeditor suggested a picture of an Asian man with his winnings stuffed into the folds of his turban. 'No, I'm not having pictures of darkies on the front page,' replied Shapland. 'That's the last thing our readers want,' agreed Roy Pittilla, a night editor. 'Pictures of blacks raking it in.' The next day, the *Sun*'s bingo winners on the front page were all white. The lone Asian winner out of 36 found himself pictured along with the others on page four

Two weeks later a major speech by South African Premier P.W. Botha provided an insight into editor Kelvin McKenzie's views of black people. On the evening of 15 August 1985 he commented on

Botha's speech which appeared to give the black majority a greater say in their country's affairs. McKenzie said: 'Well, Botha has said the days of white power are over in South Africa. What he doesn't say is what's going to happen when the darkies come down from the trees.'

Court's diary revealed similar attitudes during the Brixton riots. On the night of Friday 27 September, the *Sun* decided that their front-page story would be based on remarks by Tory MP Nicholas Fairbairn. The MP had apparently said that West Indians were lazy compared to the hard-working Asians. However, Kelvin McKenzie didn't like the original headline of the story – 'Fury Over Tory MP's "Racist Slur"'. He said: 'The readers should be allowed to make up their own minds whether it's a racist slur or not.' And so the headline was changed to 'Fury Over "Too Lazy" Blacks – Work Or Get Out, Says MP'.

Two nights later, on Sunday 29 September, amidst the heat of the unrest in Brixton, Court wrote in his diary: 'The *Sun*'s coverage of the riots was what one would have expected. The night editors only came to life when reports reached them of white women who had been raped. "This is it," said an executive. "Two white women raped by the mob. Or should we say by the yard"'. The next day the *Sun*'s headline ran – 'Two White Girls Raped By Blacks – Gang Horror During Riot'. The paper's editorial added: 'It is crucial that the leaders of the black groups take control and stop the madness of their young. If not, then the Afro-Caribbean section of British society will become the outcasts of our land.'

The following week Court recorded in vivid detail how the *Sun* reacted to the riots in Tottenham:

Sunday is usually a quiet day to work. Not this Sunday. The *Mirror* are going to print a story by Sarah Keays which was timed to coincide with the opening of the Tory Party conference. Not to be outdone the *Sun* planned to delay the printing of the third edition so they could pirate the story straight from the *Mirror*. It was going to be a big operation. Kelvin was coming in personally at 10.30 p.m. to supervise it. Almost from the time I started my shift things started to go wrong... At about 7 p.m. a story started to cause something of a panic amongst the editors. A rumour was doing the rounds that the *Mirror* was not going to print.

As it was the worries about the *Mirror* and Sarah Keays became unimportant. A small disturbance in north London had turned into a riot of epic proportions. A police raid on a household had resulted in the death of a black mother of five. It was a story. Then a *real story* appeared. The rioters were shooting at the police. The first time on the British mainland that such a thing had happened. Kelvin was slightly stunned when he discovered that.

'Three police shot,' said Kelvin McKenzie. 'What's happening. They didn't even let the miners do that. What's holding them back. If this was South Africa we'd be shooting back by now.'

Later, during that evening of Sunday 6 October 1985, Dave Naylor, a night editor, walked over to the art desk and said: 'We've got a quote from a policeman: ''The bastards are shooting at us now.'' Give us a trace of the headline (i.e. dummy version). You can put in the word ''black'' if you like.'

In fact, the quote from the policeman was left out of the story. The headline was left as – 'Gun Law In The Streets'. In the next issue, 8 October 1985, the paper gave prominence to rightwing Tory MP Harvey Proctor's call for repatriation of Britain's ethnic minorities – 'Give Blacks £7,000 To Go Home, Says Tory – Worried MP's Desperate Solution'.

The *Sun* then turned its attention to what they saw as the most pressing issue for Britain's inner cities – 'black racism'. On 24 October, the paper devoted a full-page editorial to 'The High Price Of Telling The Truth'. The leader said:

> Consider the disquieting, alarming case of one man in Britain in 1985 who spoke his mind. Jack Fuller is the principal of Waltham Forest College, London. Concerned about stealing at the college, he wrote a letter to the *Times* blaming the majority of thefts on West Indians. Immediately all manner of abuse and threats descended on Mr Fuller. He was branded a wicked racist . . . At no stage did anyone apparently ask whether what he said might be true. As it happens, there is good reason for believing it IS true . . . We have tyranny in Britain. We have intimidation. We have a sinister attempt first to curb and then destroy freedom of speech. We have racism too – and that is what is behind the plot. It is not white racism. It is black racism.

Later that day Lionel Morrison, a Commission for Racial Equality official, telephoned a friendly *Sun* reporter who was active in the NUJ chapel to ask for a right of reply. The journalist agreed and the idea was put to management and approved. An article by Peter Newsam, Chairman of the Commission for Racial Equality, was then sent over for publication. As the piece was being processed, McKenzie remarked: 'They shy away from saying what they actually believe. They actually believe Britain is a racist society. This is a real wet SDP argument.'

A week later, on 2 November 1985, the paper gave prominence to Enoch Powell's views. Under the headline of 'Big Danger Of Blacks, By Powell', the *Sun* reported: 'Rightwing MP Enoch Powell last night claimed that blacks and Asians pose the most dangerous threat to Britain since Hitler. And he warned Premier Margaret Thatcher that unless she acts now, Parliament will be overwhelmed by powerful black minority groups. He accused the Prime Minister of concealing the threat.'

Peter Court, a freelance layout artist since 1981, left the *Sun* in November 1985. A member of the NUJ, he was upset by what he saw as the racist attitudes of the *Sun*'s editorial management. And yet he acknowledges that the paper gets its message across by brilliant presentation. 'The *Sun* is absolutely clear and unequivocal about what it's doing,' said Court.

> They're very good at hitting the nerve. They know how to make the headlines have maximum impact, and the paper is written so it can be read in a few seconds . . . They know exactly how to stir up racial hatred and racism. They're very good at it, partly because of their professional experience but also because they're politically clear. And what's disturbing is that it does have an effect.

More black journalists – would it help?

It was late 1980. Rupert Murdoch was editing the *New York Post* for ten days while the executive editor, Roger Wood, a former *Daily Express* editor, was on holiday. At the time the *New York Times* and *Daily News* were involved in long, complex disputes with the Newspaper Guild over the employment of black journalists. In America newspapers are required by law to employ a certain number of blacks on the editorial staff. At one editorial conference, chaired by Murdoch, an executive suggested to his proprietor that he should hire some black reporters to avoid a similar dispute and fend off possible action by the Guild. Murdoch reluctantly agreed and commented: 'Do you think we can get any of those Vietnamese because they work so bloody hard.' Steve Dunleavy, the *Post*'s metropolitan editor, was then told by Murdoch to 'go out and find the whitest black you can find'. The unfortunate new recruit was Philip J. Holman Junior who was unaware that he had the dubious honour of only being hired by the *Post* because of the paleness of his complexion.

The pressure for more black journalists in the United States took many years. It began with the Kerner Commission which investigated the role of the press during the race riots in the late 1960s. Appointed by President Johnson, their report was a damning indictment: 'Along with the country as a whole, the press has too long basked in a white world, looked out of it, if at all, with white men's eyes and a white perspective . . . If the media are to comprehend and then to project the Negro community, they must have the help of the Negroes.'

Despite Murdoch's obvious resistance to more black journalists, the hiring of black staff appeared to have improved the coverage of ethnic minorities in America. Is this a solution for eradicating racism in sections of Fleet Street?

In 1985, of the 33,000-odd journalists working on British newspapers, magazines and in radio and television about 60 are black (less than 1 per cent). This compares with the country's black population of about 4 per cent, with 40 per cent of black youngsters being second generation.

Although the recruitment of black journalists has improved in recent years, some black reporters argue that the problem has been one of subtle discrimination and discouragement. Sam Uba, a former home subeditor at the *Times* recalls meeting an experienced, middle-aged English journalist working for a group with large publishing interests in Africa and the West Indies

> British newspapers, he said, more in sorrow than in condemnation, would never employ 'coloured' reporters, no matter how accomplished such reporters had been in their own countries . . . It was not a question of colour, he emphasized, it was just that nothing was going to convince British editors that 'coloured' journalists could do the job. Even if the editors were willing to give 'coloured' journalists a chance, they could not be sure how indigenous British people would react to 'coloured' reporters knocking on their doors or calling them on the phone for information. After recounting his many unsuccessful attempts to place black journalists on British newspapers, he tried to persuade me to take a job with the Post Office, British Rail or London Transport, and continue writing as a freelance. The same points were made to me over and over again by other British friends, journalists and non-journalists alike.[57]

That was in the middle 1970s but, apart from local papers and sections of broadcasting, there is little sign of a change in Fleet Street. According to Lionel Morrison, press officer for the Commission for Racial Equality and a former chairman of the NUJ, part of the problem is that black youngsters are strongly discouraged by school careers officers even to think about journalism as a profession. He also says that black parents show a similar lack of support because they see journalism as a white preserve.

But would a flood of black journalists into Fleet Street improve the way the black community in Britain is portrayed? Lionel Morrison is certain:

> There can be no doubt that the physical presence of black journalists in editorial offices would be a great psychological fillip to sane race relations reporting. Their presence would neutralize, at the least, rabid racialism in editorial offices, where it exists, and they could be on hand to provide the necessary background material, nuances and subtleties which make up the black scene. I am not saying that black journalists should be employed solely for reporting about blacks. No, what we should press for is the employment of black staff *per se*, not just to be employed in areas with large black populations, but even on papers operating in all-white areas.

Morrison believes that it is important to avoid the danger of hiring one or more token blacks and then effectively segregating them in an editorial ghetto of writing purely on 'black community affairs'.

Another problem, according to Hal Austin, editor of *Root* magazine, is that some editors believe that black reporters are too emotionally and morally close to stories on race:

> Black journalists working on race relations stories are not trusted by white colleagues – their 'objectivity' is brought into doubt. Of course, the 'inherent' impartiality of white journalists, like the impartiality of justice, is never questioned even when called upon to report matters internal to the black community, or matters of conflict between sections of the black and white communities. White journalists are, it appears, above suspicion. On the other hand, when a black reporter talks to members of the community (who might otherwise refuse to talk to the media) the final story is taken out of his hands by the in-built checks and balances in the system.[58]

Whatever the problems, the recruitment of more black reporters can surely be only a good thing for better coverage of Britain's ethnic minorities. One way of achieving this might be greater public pressure on the liberal papers who don't already have black journalists. According to Hal Austin, this worked with the *Guardian*. Following the election in 1978 of Trevor Phillips as the first black president of the National Union of Students, the *Guardian* published an editorial calling on employers to 'accentuate the positive'. A number of journalists then wrote a letter to the *Guardian*, said Austin, asking when they were going to hire a black staff reporter. The letter was not published, but the *Guardian* now has black journalists on its staff and its coverage of race is, along with the *Observer*, the fairest and most sympathetic in Fleet Street.

Racism – not a black and white issue

Perhaps more than any other issue, the reporting of race relations has a significant bearing on the state of race relations in both black and white communities. There are several reasons for this. Firstly, the intensity of commitment and strength of opinion that the issue of race arouses. This tends to make people look to the press for a confirmation or a rejection of their view. Secondly, the emotional heat that race generates can often influence government policies because of its intensity, and so the press has a special responsibility.

According to Hugo Young, former joint deputy editor and political editor of the *Sunday Times*, the role of the press is crucial because

> Race is hardly ever 'self-reporting'. Journalistic criteria alone offer few agreed guidelines. Any one specific collection of facts is susceptible to enormously different forms of treatment. Headlines, the length of the report, its position in the paper – all these variables of newspaper presentation vary more widely in racial than in stories concerned in many other issues. It is not enough for the news editor to say: 'Tell the story on its merits.' For that begs too many questions.[59]

Covering a race story is not like reporting the trade figures or the latest unemployment statistics where the facts are fairly clearcut. The information in a race report is rarely fixed, and is often open to disinformation and different interpretations. And so the journalist should be particularly meticulous in checking his or her facts.

But, in the interests of good race relations, the press should go further than this. As Hugo Young once told a conference of editors:

> If newspapers are concerned not to damage race relations then simple neutrality is inadequate. Neutrality, or 'judging the story on its journalistic merits', can all too easily become the ally of fear, delusion and unnecessary upheaval in the community...In the coverage of racial matters I suggest that the editor or reporter in search of objectivity would be positively assisted by the possession of a basic conviction or commitment. This is not a very large commitment. It does not involve any dilution of neutrality as

between black and white people . . . The desirable commitment is simply a commitment to good race relations – a *positive* acknowledgement that racial coverage can directly affect race relations, and a positive determination to avoid unnecessary damage.[60]

That analysis was delivered in March 1970. All the evidence suggests that most of Britain's national press have not just ignored such a proposition but have rejected it. Indeed, it seems almost as though some newspapers are not prepared to give a 'commitment to good race relations'. Perhaps the most frank admission of this in recent years came from Andrew Alexander, the *Daily Mail*'s former parliamentary correspondent and close friend and supporter of Enoch Powell,[61] when he wrote: 'The time has come to make a stand in favour of racialism.'[62] Unfortunately, judging by the coverage, much of Fleet Street has tended at least to give credence to, if not rally to, Alexander's stand.

5. The Battle for Bermondsey: A Fight for Labour's Soul

'The political coverage by the newspapers, by and large, was very fair. The press didn't hound Peter Tatchell.' Walter Terry, political editor of the *Sun* during the Bermondsey by-election campaign, *Open Space*, BBC2, 15 December 1983.

'Red Pete – otherwise known as extreme leftwinger Peter Tatchell – symbolizes everything that is appalling in the Labour Party today. A Marxist, who has been in the Labour Party only a few years, he has contempt for democracy,' observed the *Sun*, Britain's biggest-selling daily paper, on 5 December 1981.

There is little or no evidence to suggest that Tatchell was either a 'Marxist' or had 'contempt for democracy'. However, that *Sun* editorial did provide a clear insight into how Fleet Street perceived Labour's parliamentary candidate for Bermondsey and Southwark in southeast London. For between 1981 and 1983 Tatchell became an unwilling victim caught up in the fierce battle for the Party's political soul. Most of the national press stood on one side of the barricades, heavily partisan, while only a couple of papers stepped aside, aloof bystanders. In the propaganda war that followed, Tatchell was left defenceless.

Tatchell had been dragged into Labour's ideological civil war two days before the *Sun*'s analysis. His own party leader Michael Foot had stood up in the House of Commons and denounced him as 'not an endorsed candidate of the Labour Party and as far as I am concerned never will be'. It was not a spontaneous outburst. Earlier that week, Bob Mellish, the sitting Labour MP for Bermondsey and defeated by Tatchell in the reselection ballot, had met Foot in the House of Commons. Mellish said he would resign and force a by-election unless action was taken against the Left in Bermondsey.

Foot was unwilling to risk a by-election in early 1982 after poor Labour performances at Crosby and Croydon. Consequently, he used an article by Tatchell in an obscure leftwing journal, *London Labour Briefing*, as the public reason for his decision. Tatchell had called for extra-parliamentary protest against the government in the form of mass lobbies, marches and non-violent civil disobedience. It was construed by some Labour back-benchers as 'anti-Parliament' and a copy of the article was shown to Foot on the morning he condemned Tatchell.

While Foot's refusal to endorse Tatchell's candidature did not justify or legitimize the subsequent press campaign, it was the final signal that the Left were 'fair game'. And so Fleet Street set out to show that the Labour candidate personified 'everything that is appalling in the Labour Party today'.[1] By the end of the Bermondsey by-election, 14 months later, they had convinced the electorate.

Gay rights – out of the closet, into the fire

For the popular press, Peter Tatchell was a political deviant whose policies and ideas were dangerous and corrupt. But it was the Labour candidate's private life that came under much closer journalistic scrutiny. This was because Tatchell was a strong supporter of gay rights and reputed to be homosexual.

Within a week of being disowned by Foot in Parliament, the tabloid papers' Australian correspondents were at Tatchell's parents' house in Melbourne. One freelancer said he was from the *Melbourne Age* and tried to persuade Tatchell's mother to denounce her son as 'a queer Communist' and 'bastard child'. She angrily refused and showed him the door. A couple of days later, a Fleet Street reporter confronted Labour's candidate for Bermondsey outside his flat: 'Your mother's disowned you. What do you say about that?' 'It's not true,' Tatchell replied. 'I've just spoken to her on the phone. She would never say a thing like that.'

But it was the published material that undermined Labour's cause in Bermondsey. From the first press conference on 4 December 1981, Fleet Street was obsessed with Tatchell's appearance and sexuality. 'Has a habit of fingering the wide leather belt atop trendy cord jeans and two-tone wine and beige laced shoes, shows considerable irritation at personal questions,' observed the *Daily Telegraph*'s Gerald Bartlett the next day. Two days later, the *Daily Mail* took a similar line: 'Portrait of a New Working-Class Hero', describing Tatchell as having 'a male model's flair with clothes' and being 'a symphony in brown'.[2] The *Sunday Mirror* was less subtle that first weekend: 'The candidate bristles with self-importance . . . His pouting lower lip hardens if anyone dares to argue with him.'[3]

Meanwhile, the *Sun* had uncovered an old story about Tatchell's days as a gay activist. 'My Fight for the Gays – by Red Pete', ran the *Sun* headline on 5 December 1981, next to a retouched photograph of

Tatchell which made it look as though he was wearing make-up: 'In 1973 Mr Tatchell was involved in a violent scuffle in East Berlin when he raised a banner calling for solidarity with East German gays. Fellow members of his student delegation at a world youth rally ripped down the banner and attacked him, reducing him to tears.' Three days later the *Sun* repeated the same story – 'The Night He Hid Out With Gay Friends'. However, the paper added a few more details – 'Homosexual friends of Mr Tatchell protected him as violence flared' and 'the amazing trip was reported in the newspaper of the Socialist Labour League, now the Workers' Revolutionary Party (WRP)'. The implications in the two articles were clear – socialist gay men are cowardly ('protected him as violence flared'), whimpering ('in tears') and extremist ('WRP').

For Fleet Street, Tatchell's homosexuality, if not the issue of gay rights, was firmly on the agenda from early 1982. But the incessant probing went far beyond the odd questions at press conferences. Nor was it genuine investigative journalism. The perusal of Tatchell's private life went much further. One reporter made it quite clear: 'We're going to dig up everything you have ever said or done from the day you were born.' Tatchell was asked whether he visited gay brothels. Two national newspapers are said to have offered a £3,000 bounty 'for a good scandal story, preferably with photographs'. Other reporters visited several gay bars and clubs in London to find someone who would 'reveal all'. The *Daily Mail* was particularly diligent and compiled a list of 20 alleged former lovers which they touted around Bermondsey, hoping to get confirmation from local gay Liberals or Social Democrats.

Tatchell's flat on the Rockingham council estate was virtually under siege. Reporters sat in nearby cars taking photographs of everyone going in and out with telefoto lenses. The Labour candidate's neighbours were granted closer attention. They were continually pestered day and night with questions about Tatchell's private life.

Some of the residents refused point-blank to talk to the press, but were then occasionally met with a barrage of racist and obscene insults. One morning a Tatchell neighbour was confronted with reporters pretending to be Southwark Borough Council officers. They said they were 'investigating complaints that Mr Tatchell had been holding rowdy all-night, all-male parties'. They asked whether the tenants could give them any details. By that time the residents were familiar with these Fleet Street tactics and so they put the record straight.

The search for sexual scandal even stretched 12,000 miles away to Australia. Most of the popular papers dispatched reporters to his homeland and local correspondents (or 'stringers') were hired as full-time 'Tatchell hunters'. This involved a constant surveillance of his parents and close relatives. On one occasion, reporters waited until all the family except his stepfather had left the house to visit friends for the weekend. A young, female journalist then entered the house. She offered Tatchell's elderly, disabled stepfather two bottles of wine if he would talk about his stepson's private affairs. Eventually the whole family did talk to the press – but only after they were told that Tatchell had had a serious car accident.

Throughout 1982 reporters regularly asked leading questions about the Labour candidate's sexuality. Journalists were even asking local children as young as ten years old about Tatchell's private habits. The paedophilia angle was seriously considered by Fleet Street. He was falsely accused, more than once, of sexually assaulting young children. In June 1982 reporters from three tabloid newspapers visited Mr Michael Reid, headmaster of the Geoffrey Chaucer School, Bermondsey, where Tatchell was a governor. The journalists asked leading questions about the Labour candidate's personal relationship with the boys and his private life. 'Did he get on well with any one particular boy', one asked. Mr Reid refused to co-operate and declined to comment. Only later did he realize the obvious motives behind the questions.

Such conduct would not be defended even in the most amoral echelons of the popular press. However, for *Mirror* columnist, Paul Callan, 'It is vitally necessary – as a general principle – that the right to investigate the private lives of public figures be jealously guarded and maintained'.[4] Even the award-winning labour editor of the *Financial Times*, John Lloyd, is reluctant to attack some of the underhand methods: 'When does enthusiastic reporting end and harassment begin? There is no line – it is where the object of the reporting complains of being harassed and has the ability to stop it'.[5]

It is, of course, legitimate that individuals who put their names forward for public office should expect journalistic scrutiny of their personal background and actions. But the hounding of Tatchell and his family found no defender in Fleet Street. Walter Terry, political editor of the *Sun* during the Tatchell controversy, told me: 'I think it's relevant to discuss a candidate's behaviour, but I don't think it's legitimate to interfere with their family. That's deplorable.'

What was more significant about Bermondsey was that the press stories about Peter Tatchell and his sexuality were simply untrue. A case in point was when the *Daily Express* claimed during the 1982 TUC conference in Brighton that Tatchell 'could be seen slipping around the seafront hotels in immaculate suit, collar and tie'.[6] In fact, he had flown to California the week before for a three-week holiday with some close friends. He was not even in the country during the TUC conference.

When Tatchell returned from his vacation he was immediately confronted by three *Sun* reporters. They wanted him to 'confess' that he had attended the Gay Olympics in San Francisco while he was in the United States. Tatchell had never even heard of the Gay Olympics, but the *Sun* reporters persisted for the next three days. One afternoon they waited outside his workplace at the North Lambeth Day Centre for five hours in the pouring rain to question him about his holiday. Tatchell again strongly denied attending the event, but the *Sun* reporters were unperturbed and said they were going to publish regardless. When Tatchell threatened legal action over the story, one of the *Sun*'s journalists replied: 'Sue us. So what? What do we care? What's a few thousand pounds to us? This is a good story and we're going to use it.'

The next day, 25 September 1982, the story was published, two days before the Labour Party annual conference in Blackpool. Under the front-page headline of 'Red Pete ''Went to the Gay Olympics'' ', the *Sun* revealed:

> Leftwing Labour candidate Peter Tatchell has upset his tough dockland supporters who say he has been to the Gay Olympics. They claim the 30-year-old bachelor spent two weeks in the company of homosexuals at the bizarre sports event in San Francisco ... Philip Corr, chairman of the Young Socialists, said: 'Going to these Olympics is the last straw – he is not doing the image of the party any good at all. He should be spending his time in Bermondsey looking after the problems here – not swanning about at the Gay Olympics in California ... He only left Australia because he was called up into the army in the early 1970s to fight in Vietnam. Before that he was apparently a marathon runner in, would you believe it, Queensland.'

The *Sun* 'exclusive' was written by Phil Dampier. On 21 September he went to Bermondsey and approached Philip Corr, saying he was an enthusiastic Labour supporter and wanted to join the Party. The next day, posing as 'Phil Wilson', Dampier went out canvassing with local Young Socialists on the TUC Day of Action in support of the health workers. That evening he talked informally with other party activists where the allegations were supposed to have been made.

Tatchell's dockland supporters were only upset after they read the *Sun* story. Philip Corr told me: 'The whole story was fabricated from beginning to end. Number one, I didn't know whether Tatchell went to the Gay Olympics. Number two, I couldn't care less what Tatchell did in his private life. I never said any of those things and I didn't mention the Gay Olympics.' Corr also maintains that the final quote – 'he was apparently a marathon runner in, would you believe it, Queensland' – was also fabricated. In fact, Tatchell has never been to Queensland. However, Corr did say: 'he is not doing the image of the party any good at all', but this was nothing to do with the Gay Olympics – more of a general comment on Tatchell's candidature.

When asked about the story at his home in Beckenham, Kent, Phil Dampier refused to discuss it except to say: 'I don't want to talk about it. I've had so much trouble with this story with people ringing me up, but I stand by it.' Richard M. Parrack, the *Sun*'s editorial manager, was rather more keen to defend the article:

> We deny absolutely that the story was fabricated... The information that Peter Tatchell had attended the Gay Olympics in San Francisco came from Mr Phillip Corr, Chairman of the Young Socialists, who was quoted at length in the paper. The single quotation marks in the headline indicate that it was reported information. Our reporters put the matter to Mr Tatchell, and we also published his remarks, including his outright denial that he attended the Gay Olympics.[7]

Parrack's final point was correct. The *Sun* did print Tatchell's denial. It was near the end of the story – at the bottom righthand corner of page seven – under the headline of 'Gay Games Storm'.

The morning after the Gay Olympics article, 26 September, Tatchell woke up to find that the *Sun*'s sister paper, the *News of the World*, had repeated the story and also attacked his support for gay rights. Under the headline, 'Uproar As Labour Is Hit By Gay Row', Britain's biggest-selling newspaper reported: 'The far Left accused party leader Michael Foot of butchering a plan to sweep away restrictions on the activities of "gays". The row erupted as leftwing candidate Peter Tatchell was attacked by members of his Bermondsey party over allegations that he went to a bizarre Gay Olympics sports meeting in the US.'

The basis of this piece was a special supplement in *London Labour Briefing* including critical articles on 'Gays and the Labour Party', 'Discrimination in Housing' and 'Equal Opportunities for Gays'. The *News of the World* reported that these were 'outrageous and sometimes obscene articles by homosexuals, lesbians and a transvestite'.

The story was accompanied by a touched-up photograph of Tatchell which made him look as if he was wearing eye-liner and lipstick. Henry Douglas, legal manager of News Group newspapers, later admitted that the picture had been retouched in the paper's northern editions after it was wired from the London office: 'As not uncommonly happens in wiring, the colour tone and some of the features were somewhat bleached. In an attempt to compensate for this some retouching was done in Manchester. The retouching was not faultless, but I certainly do not agree that it has made Tatchell look more effeminate than the original.'[8]

The day after the *News of the World* piece, the *Daily Mail* devoted a full page to a meticulous profile of Tatchell's Australian background – 'What Makes Tatchell Tick'. This detailed account of Tatchell's youth included the suggestion that the Labour candidate's commitment to socialism resulted from the traumas of his parents' divorce! The *Mail* had spent tens of thousands of pounds tracking down old schoolmates and friends going back to 1964 in the remotest parts of Australia to find out about Tatchell's sex life.

When *Mail* journalist Wensley Clarkson interviewed him in London he assured Tatchell he would quote him fairly, but that he wasn't responsible for what the subeditors might do to the story. Tatchell refused to answer questions about his sex life which the *Mail* interpreted as 'routine protests about personalizing politics'. And so the paper used more underhand methods. One former friend was Robert Kroening who had once shared a flat with Tatchell. When the *Mail* traced him the paper's reporters tricked him into co-operating by claiming that Tatchell had asked for Kroening to provide information. This was untrue. Tatchell had not given permission for an interview.

On the evening after the *Mail* article was published, the Labour Campaign for Gay Rights (LCGR) held a fringe meeting at the Labour Party conference in Blackpool. Gay rights campaigners packed into the small basement room of the Cliffs Hotel. They were furious at the press coverage of the previous three days. Even before the meeting began some of the delegates demanded that journalists should sit on the floor. Then John Shiers stood up for his opening remarks as chair of the rally: 'The gutter press is continually trying to undermine our campaign with vicious attacks and personal innuendos,' he said. 'What we have decided is that there are three newspapers we wish to exclude from this meeting – the *Sun*, *Daily Mail* and *News of the World*. It's quite clear that these papers have no interest whatsoever in telling people the real issues of gay rights.' This was greeted with enthusiastic applause from the audience. However, the *News of the World* reporter refused to leave and only left after being surrounded by angry delegates. A fellow journalist then departed protesting that the expulsion was an act of discrimination. 'Now you know what it's like,' replied a member of the audience.[9]

But it was not until the day after the Bermondsey by-election that Fleet Street's attitude towards gay rights and homosexuality was really exposed. On Friday 25 February 1983, Max Hastings was named 'Journalist of the Year' by Granada Television, but it was his *Daily Express* column that day which was of interest to the gay community. Hastings had just taken his family out to dinner at a Knightsbridge restaurant. At the next table sat three men wearing make-up. 'How could I explain the spectacle to my son?' wrote the *Express* and *London Standard* columnist. He then moved on to the issue of gay rights:

> Where the whole equation has gone wrong, I think, is that a powerful and influential section of opinion makers in and out of the media has crossed the threshold from seeking just sympathy for homosexuals in their misfortune, and now seeks to persuade us that homosexuality and heterosexuality are to be treated as equally desirable states.
>
> In reality, of course, many adolescents go through a finely balanced phase during which they agonize greatly about which route to take. It seems essential that they should be given every encouragement to choose heterosexuality. This is not a matter of male chauvinism or machismo or intolerance. It is because it is obvious to any but the most absurd militant that the lives of many homosexuals are frustrated and tormented, not because of outside persecution, but because of the very nature of their predicament.

Hastings, now editor of the *Daily Telegraph*, concluded:

> When we lack the courage to declare this, when we allow ourselves to be intimidated by the threat of denunciation as 'reactionary', when we tolerate the granting of public money without protest to 'gay' groups in the sacred name of minority rights, then we shall have become not only a cowardly and hypocritical society, afraid to express the obvious, but also a truly decadent one.

More recently, former Fleet Street editor Derek Jameson was more direct in November 1985 when he said on BBC2's *Open Space*: 'I'll tell you quite straight. Fleet Street takes the view that homosexuality is abnormal, unnatural, a bit evil because it's wrong and so on. They [the editors] are not going to come out and say "Be gay, it's wonderful and isn't it great." They're going to say that gays are not normal natural people.'[10]

The dilemmas of 'coming out'

On 29 March 1982, Peter Tatchell was speaking on 'Gays and Social-ism' at a meeting at South London Polytechnic. After his opening speech, Gillian Hanscombe, a *Gay News* journalist, asked him: 'Are you a heterosexual supporter of gay rights or a gay supporter of gay rights?' Tatchell replied: 'I am a supporter of gay rights.' This response provoked half an hour of heated debate with the audience insisting, if not demanding, that Tatchell publicly declare his sexuality. But he was adamant that 'this whole issue has nothing to do with me as a person'.

Tatchell's stance on 'coming out' was consistent throughout the Bermondsey controversy. When Tatchell was first selected as the par-liamentary candidate for Bermondsey in November 1981, the constit-uency party had a number of informal discussions to decide whether he should openly declare his homosexuality. 'The majority, including myself, felt ideally that I should come out,' said Tatchell. 'But what convinced the majority that I should not discuss my sexuality was that gay rights would then become the predominant election issue ... Whilst gay rights was a very important issue, we also felt that jobs, dis-armament and the equality of other minorities should not be over-shadowed.'

This position was reaffirmed at all public meetings and press con-ferences, although Tatchell did 'come out' while canvassing on the doorstep during the by-election campaign. But his public response was, 'I support the civil rights of all minorities.' That provoked a storm of criticism from the gay rights movement and the gay press. Indeed, Gillian Hanscombe, a *Gay News* staff reporter, claims that Tatchell denied being homosexual at all. She says that just after being selected as Bermondsey's candidate, she rang Tatchell: 'He seemed very anxious but I do remember saying, ''Are you gay?'' and he replied ''No.'' I didn't know him at the time, so I didn't realize the significance of that statement because of him being active in gay politics in the early 1970s.' Tatchell denies this and maintains that the question was never put to him.

Hanscombe immediately told Andrew Lumsden, then news editor of *Gay News* and an experienced former Fleet Street journalist. He was very concerned and later telephoned Tatchell to discuss the situa-tion. During a long conversation, Lumsden urged the Labour candi-date to 'come out' for his own sake: 'If you don't take that step now, the innuendos that have already begun will become worse and worse once the Bermondsey writ is moved and will become extreme as the parties reach the climax of the campaign.' Lumsden added: 'I am *not* talking gay liberation. I am *not* saying what you ought to do according to the leading lights of the gay movement. I'm saying you have no ''cover'' any more, other than the libel laws, and that even though it may not work, honesty is your only hope of retrieving the situation.' But Tatchell stood his ground and reassured Lumsden that 'Once I'm in Parliament I will fight very hard for gay rights'.

Lumsden then discussed Tatchell's predicament with the *Gay News* staff. Hanscombe argued that they should print his 'denial' because Tatchell had already 'come out' in the early 1970s as a Gay Liberation Front delegate. But Lumsden believed that the Labour candidate had been under a lot of political and personal pressure. 'I tried not to pillory him in the eyes of gays at the very moment when he was being pilloried by straights,' recalls Lumsden. *Gay News* also had to abide by the unwritten code of not disclosing a person's sexuality without their consent.

Hence, Tatchell's sexuality remained under wraps for the duration of the public campaigning. But the gay movement's sharpest criticism of Tatchell was that he had 'climbed back into the closet'. David Dubow, an American freelance journalist, points out that Tatchell had a ten-year active history in gay politics. More important, he argues, he was active as an 'out-gay man'. This can be seen from back copies of *Gay News*. In April 1983, Tatchell was working on a sociological survey on gays – 'Social Survey of Gays, By a Gay'. Dubow and other gay journalists allege that Tatchell kept quiet about his homosexuality because he knew that the rampant homophobia in Bermondsey would keep him out of Parliament. Lumsden also believes a great political opportunity was lost: 'Tatchell's constituency party led him back into the closet in a London constituency at precisely the time when Livingstone's leadership of the GLC put a major world city behind the proposition that ''out'' lesbians and gay men require and deserve political backing.'

Even after his by-election defeat Tatchell was adamant that not discussing his sexuality publicly was the best policy. During a series of interviews with Tatchell in April 1983, David Dubow argued that it was unrealistic to expect Fleet Street not to discover his past record in gay politics. He also told Tatchell that by not 'coming out' at press conferences, he reinforced the idea that there was something shameful about being gay. 'Our decision was simply that I was not going to talk about my private life to the press,' replied Tatchell. 'But when the issue was raised on the doorstep, I would be honest and straightforward and say, 'Yes, I'm gay,' and argue the case for gay rights.'

Dubow also suggested that he should have told Fleet Street in January 1983 (a month before the by-election poll): 'Yes, I'm gay. It's an important issue. Now, let's get on with the business of the campaign.' But Tatchell strongly maintains that the press coverage would have been even more deplorable:

> Various Fleet Street journalists made it quite clear to me that once it was on public record that I was gay it was then, as an unwritten code, a matter of public interest. They would therefore be justified to pry into my private life and personal relationships. Frankly, neither myself nor my close friends were prepared to go through that ordeal at that particular stage.

When Dubow commented that the press coverage could not have been much worse, Tatchell was equally decisive:

> It could have been infinitely worse. The tabloid papers had sent people into every gay bar in London. Some papers had reams of notes and files of gossip from gay clubs. I met several people who had been approached by journalists for information about who I was seeing. At least two newspapers had bounties for good scandal stories with photographs. Many of the Fleet Street photographers did try to get into a number of gay clubs, but were caught and turned away by the owners. They had the material and it was ready to be used. I was told by journalists that if I came out, that would have been the signal. They would have found some non-libellous way of getting into print.

However, Andrew Lumsden, now news editor of the *New Statesman*, maintains that Tatchell's 'deception' about his sexuality was the problem:

> Labour knowingly set out to lie to the inhabitants of Bermondsey. It was hoped that he would be elected *as if* heterosexual. Doorstep honesty is a great credit to Tatchell's personal courage but the effort at deception remains . . . We all know that left-bashing was the motive behind the gutter pursuit of him, but as a journalist myself I know how the individual reporter's bloodlust is roused, however lamentable that may be, by evident hypocrisy.

Martin Linton, who covered the Bermondsey saga for the *Guardian* and is a former *Daily Mail* and *Daily Star* journalist, strongly disagrees:

> In electoral terms it would have made things much worse. But it

was not the factual knowledge of being homosexual that was the problem. It was the image associated with that of appearing effeminate and the degrading rumours which would have resulted in Bermondsey. The tabloid press would have exploited the situation much more if he had gone public.

Tatchell argues that the gay movement was remarkably naive if it believed that 'coming out' would have stopped all the press innuendos. He also makes the important point that the press attacks were based on political, not personal, factors. 'There was all the difference in the world between someone from the establishment declaring his or her homosexuality and someone who was opposed to the status quo,' said Tatchell. 'The crucial difference between myself and others in the public eye was that I was a leftwing socialist fighting a major by-election which the establishment and their friends in Fleet Street were determined that Labour should lose.'[11] According to Tatchell, there is a 'gentlemen's agreement' in the House of Commons between the political establishment and Fleet Street. This 'unwritten law' protects the dozens of gay MPs from unwarranted publicity, apart from the occasional indirect jibe, as long as they are discreet. Tatchell maintains that the press coverage of the controversy surrounding his candidature and the eventual by-election proves that the customary protection from Fleet Street was not forthcoming. This was due, not to his homosexuality, but to his politics.

The New Left and the old guard

During a BBC2 debate in December 1983 on press coverage of the Bermondsey by-election campaign, Walter Terry, a former political editor of the *Sun*, *Daily Mail* and *Daily Express*, was moved to say:

> The political coverage by the newspapers, by and large, was very fair. The press didn't hound Peter Tatchell . . . He says everyone else is to blame except himself. It can't be right. The thing that puzzles me is why homosexuality was an issue. It's bad politics. If you want to win an election you don't talk about homosexuality.[12]

But Sarah Benton, former deputy editor of the *New Statesman*, disagreed and struck at one of the prevailing roots of the problem: 'Walter Terry is looking through a political world where all journalists and MPs are all exactly the same kind of person – middle-aged, middle-class, white, heterosexual, happily married men. Anyone who doesn't fit that stereotype means the end of political dissent and discussion.'[13]

Peter Tatchell certainly didn't fit that stereotype and this, together with the Bermondsey Labour Party's radical policies, combined to incur the opposition of Fleet Street. The Labour candidate's name became synonymous from December 1981 with a number of political health warnings in the headlines and opening paragraphs of news reports. Readers were presented with 'disowned Australian Marxist' (*Daily Mail*[14]), 'extreme leftwinger' (*Daily Telegraph*[15]), 'freak', (*Sunday Mirror*[16]), 'Militant' (*Daily Mirror*[17]) and 'Red Pete' (*Sun*[18]). The *Sunday Express* preferred a more collective approach – 'hard-left, pro-gay, Australian, draft-dodger Mr Peter Tatchell'.[19]

The serious papers were not as guilty. The *Guardian* and the *Times* coverage was often impeccably fair and even the *Daily Telegraph* published Tatchell's accusations against Fleet Street in full. But many journalists were very uhappy at the press coverage of Labour's campaign in Bermondsey. This was revealed by Margaret van Hattam, the *Financial Times* political correspondent, on the day before the by-election: 'If defeated, Mr Tatchell will no doubt blame the media and many will think this justified . . . So virulent has been the anti-Tatchell reporting that some journalists have expressed disquiet at the by-election coverage in their own newspapers.'[20] Van Hattam now recalls: 'A lot of us were appalled by the reporting, particularly some of the Daily Mail journalists . . . The press clearly struck a chord with what Mellish and O'Grady were saying.'

Journalists on the popular press argue they are absolved from the ultimate responsibility. They say that as their copy is nearly always rewritten by subeditors and assistant editors (on the back-bench), they are not to blame for misleading political name-tags. One subeditor on the *Sun*, who is a Labour Party supporter, does not even accept there is political bias in the news:

> As far as I am concerned, I have never written a biased story and I don't believe that using words like 'Red' or 'hard left' implies support for extremists or a Soviet-type system . . . Part of the problem is that we have to fit a story into a limited number of words and there is simply no time to deliberate about its political meaning.

But the press coverage of the Bermondsey controversy was far more damaging than a few 'Red Pete' headlines. For the popular press, Tatchell in December 1981 represented the 'New Left' in the Labour Party. His selection the previous month came at a time when the radical Labour Left were very much to the fore. Tony Benn had only just narrowly lost the deputy leadership poll, Arthur Scargill was about to be elected President of the NUM with a massive majority and the

Labour-led GLC were implementing a whole range of radical new policies including support for gay people. And so when Michael Foot disowned Tatchell publicly, it was the green light for Fleet Street to attack what they saw as a new and dangerous political movement. However, instead of confronting the political issues, the coverage was consistently personalized. Philip Andrews, the *Sheffield Star*'s political correspondent, described it as 'a concerted media campaign of vilification in which political issues were largely ignored'.[21] ITN journalist Michael Crick agreed: 'An atrocious campaign of personal abuse directed against Tatchell by most of Fleet Street.'[22]

With most of the political news stories spiked, attention centred on the 'New Left' candidate's personality and background. For the tabloid press Tatchell didn't belong. He was not representative. 'There was a time when an extremist like Peter Tatchell would have belonged on Labour's lunatic fringe. Yet this week he is its standard bearer,' the *Sun* said just prior to the by-election.[23]

For most of the popular papers, Tatchell was also a personal symbol of the 'New Left' candidate – young, radical social worker with a background in one-issue politics like CND, gay rights and support for ethnic minorities. That symbol became a stereotype based on preconceptions. One of these was that Tatchell had lied to the working-class voters of Bermondsey about his own class background.

On 25 September 1982, in the same edition as the 'Gay Olympics' story, the *Sun* ran a 'Special Report' entitled: 'Middle-Class Past of Working-Class Hero – Tatchell Had An Easy Life in the Suburbs'. The feature accused the Labour candidate of 'talking bunkum' about his upbringing in Melbourne, Australia. The *Sun* said his stepfather, Edwin Nitschke, 'owned a taxi' and his mother 'worked as a bank clerk'. The article also claimed that 'Tatchell was not reared in a tough docklands area', but lived in a 'tree-lined street in Mount Waverley'. Also that he had been forced to leave school at the minimum age 'because of his stepfather's dislike of him'.

The facts paint a rather different picture of Tatchell's upbringing. His stepfather, Mr Nitschke, never 'owned a taxi' – he worked for a taxi company and his wages were below the national average. Tatchell's mother did work as a bank clerk – in 1942 for three months. Tatchell did leave school at the minimum age – but because his parents could not afford to keep him on, not because he 'did not get on well with his stepfather'. The *Sun*'s editorial manager, Richard Parrack, said on this final point: 'The circumstances of Tatchell's leaving school do not seem to differ substantially from what appeared in the *Sun*.'[24]

The discrepancies were hardly surprising. The *Sun* reporter,

Suzanne Chapple, did not speak to Tatchell's parents. They refused to see her. Instead, she interviewed one of his sisters by phone. Tatchell's neighbourhood was more contentious. Chapple maintains that Mount Waverley was 'an area settled in the early 1950s and 60s by the economically upwardly mobile'. She does not mention that Tatchell had spent many of his early years in the docklands area of Melbourne. Instead, Chapple states: 'At no stage did I learn from speaking to any of his distant or immediate relatives that he had been brought up in the docklands area.'[35] Tatchell is adamant: 'the streets were dirt roads and drainage flowed in open gutters in the streets. The family had an outside tin-can toilet.'

Parrack denied there were false statements in the article. However, when *New Statesman* journalist Patrick Wintour pressed him for more information, he replied: 'Look, I've got nothing to say about it. The answer is no comment, all right?'[26]

By the time of the by-election campaign in February 1983, Tatchell was beyond the pale for Fleet Street. The *Sunday Mirror* accompanied a photograph of him with the headline 'What A Freak',[27] while the *Mail on Sunday* preferred to compare Tatchell with Damien in the horror film *The Omen*.[28] But the *Daily Mail* was more interested in other aspects of Tatchell's character. Early one afternoon in February 1983 the Labour candidate was returning from lunch to continue canvassing. He was met by a *Daily Mail* journalist who asked him a series of questions before enquiring: 'And by the way is it true you are a vegetarian?' 'No, and if you don't believe me I've just been to Macdonald's for lunch,' Tatchell replied. 'Ah,' the *Mail* reporter asked in all seriousness, 'but did you eat a hamburger?'

Meanwhile, the other candidates were given rather different coverage. On 2 August 1982, Bob Mellish, the sitting Labour MP until losing the selection contest to Tatchell, resigned from the party. The *Daily Star*, at that time broadly pro-Labour, reported his decision as 'Mellish Mauls The Red Mafia' and then gave him a third of page four to explain 'Why I Had To Quit The Party'. The *Sun* lamented: 'What hope is there for any political body which spurns an old warrior like Bob Mellish and instead embraces an immigrant upstart who is most usually described as a "former activist for *Gay Rights*."' The *Daily Express* columnist Jean Rook was equally mournful: 'Bob's Cry Tugged At My Heart'.[29]

The *Express* and *Star*'s support for Mellish was more than editorial, according to *Private Eye*. The satirical magazine alleged that the election campaign of John O'Grady, the 'Real Labour' candidate supported by Mellish, was being financed by Sir Nigel Broakes, Chairman of the London Docklands Development Corporation (LDDC). O'Grady was a paid vice-chairman of LDDC as was Mellish. Sir Nigel was also head of Trafalgar House which had a 50 per cent holding in the *London Standard* and whose subsidiary, Fleet Holdings, owned the *Daily Star*, *Daily Express* and *Sunday Express*. Broakes strongly denied the allegations.

The militant who never was

Peter Tatchell's main reason for not publicly disclosing his homosexuality was simple but persuasive: 'Judging by the way in which the popular press reported all the other issues, there was no way that they were going to treat fairly and objectively my homosexuality without being derogatory and demeaning.' Tatchell's main source of evidence for this assertion was Fleet Street's repeated and relentless accusations that he was either a member, a supporter or a sympathizer of the Trotskyist Militant Tendency.

At his very first press conference, immediately after Foot's denunciation in the Commons, Tatchell continually emphasized he was not and never had been a supporter of Militant. The next morning the *Daily Mirror* headlined their story – 'Militant ''Won't Be A Candidate''' . The *Daily Express* described the Labour candidate as 'the young Marxist revolutionary'.[31] Foot hadn't referred to him as either 'Marxist' or 'revolutionary' in his statement. But the *Sun* had no doubts – Bermondsey Labour Party had been 'largely taken over by Trotskyites and other extremists'.[32]

Associating Tatchell and the constituency party with Militant was partly due to the political atmosphere of the time. In November 1981, the *Sun* and *Daily Star* had both conducted 'special investigations' into the power and influence of Militant within the Labour Party. On 7 December 1981, Labour's National Executive reaffirmed Foot's decision not to endorse Tatchell as the candidate. The next day the *Sun* published their report into Militant – 'The Red Guerrillas Destroying Labour'. The following afternoon, less than a week after Tatchell was disowned, the Labour leadership launched an inquiry into Militant. The Trotskyite faction was accused of acting contrary to the Party constitution and was to be under the threat of expulsion throughout 1982.

Two days before the Party inquiry began, the *Daily Mirror* linked Tatchell with 'leftwing extremists' Tariq Ali and Militant: 'The Battle For Bermondsey is Michael Foot's last-ditch stand against the takeover by the hard-line, intolerant Left'. Tatchell's alleged links with Militant could have been easily clarified by some simple professional political journalism – talking to Labour Party activists in Bermondsey who knew Tatchell's views. The day after the *Mirror*'s editorial, the *Guardian*'s Martin Linton performed such a task. He quoted a member of Tatchell's local party executive:

> Many of us are worried about his rhetoric which is sometimes open to misinterpretation, but in no way is he a supporter of the Far Left or Militant. There are people in the Labour Party like that. There are even one or two in Bermondsey. But if they think that Peter Tatchell is one of them, they have got the wrong man.[33]

The following Sunday Alan Watkins, the *Observer*'s political columnist, made a similar point:

> There has been a disposition in some quarters to lump the case of Mr Tatchell with the inquiry into the Militant endency which was announced last week. According to this view of events, Mr Tatchell and the Militants are much the same in terms of real politics . . . But the cases of Mr Tatchell and Militant are quite different and must be considered separately'.[34]

And yet the vast majority of Fleet Street continued to mutter Tatchell's name in the same breath as Militant. The *Daily Telegraph* described him as 'a militant-tending Labour candidate', and under the headline, 'Shadowy Group's Support', reported how he was allegedly backed by Militant.

By the autumn of 1982 it was clear on what basis the political correspondents were writing their stories. In August 1982, the *Daily Telegraph* reported: 'Both Sir Reginald [Goodwin] and Mr Mellish [now Lord Mellish] are angry at the domination of extreme leftwingers and members of the Militant Tendency in the Bermondsey party.' The paper then quoted Goodwin, a former leader of the GLC, as saying: 'In the Bermondsey party people who don't have Militant Tendency views are not allowed a voice. They are either not nominated or made so unwelcome that they cannot take part.'[35]

When Mellish resigned from the Labour Party on 2 August 1982, a late-night BBC1 news bulletin began: 'Peter Tatchell, the Militant Tendency candidate for Bermondsey . . . '. Local party members were furious and one activist immediately telephoned the BBC to complain about the inaccuracy. 'Well, it was all in the papers so there must be some truth in it,' replied a journalist on the BBC newsdesk.

The Militant accusation certainly was in the papers. The next morning the *Daily Star*'s leading article sympathized with Bob Mellish for having to contend with extremist subversives' and added: 'Mr Mellish has lit the blue torchpaper... and will retire immediately when the NEC endorses Mr Peter Tatchell, of the Militant Tendency, to fight his Bermondsey seat.'

The editorial was written by South African Rick McNeil, chief leader writer and former *Daily Express* night editor. He is described by one *Daily Star* journalist as having views 'well to the right of the Tory Party'. McNeil has now returned to South Africa. This is how he described the dispute between Tatchell and the national Labour leadership in that August editorial:

> His [Foot's] fight has been honest, out in the open and strictly in accordance with the rule book. The Left's fight has been secretive, behind closed doors and using every trick not in any rule book. But last week Mr Foot damagingly dropped his veto on Mr Tatchell. And the Militant Tendency chalked up their most damning victory yet over Foot.[36]

Tatchell immediately issued a writ for libel and started legal action against the *Daily Star*. The paper's defence was that, while the Labour candidate may not have been a member or public supporter of Militant, he was so leftwing that he was as good as in the Trotskyist organization. The *Daily Star*'s editor Lloyd Turner now tells me: 'I was upset at the takeover of the Labour Party at the time by people like Tatchell.' When told that Tatchell had nothing to do with the Trotskyist groups, particularly Militant, Turner replied: 'that was a matter of window-dressing'. However, one *Daily Star* journalist took a rather different view: 'That was a real cock-up and a bad mistake... I remember I did a similar thing in a news story about Tatchell linking him with Militant It was shoddy and careless, but I genuinely didn't know he had disassociated himself from Militant.'

Tatchell eventually withdrew the writ for libel and accepted an out-of-court payment, mainly because the urgency of setting the record straight was no longer there after the by-election.

Tatchell had continually denied being even associated with Militant since December 1981 – nine months before the *Daily Star* editorial So, was the Labour candidate conducting an elaborate cover-up? Was Militant the sinister ringmaster in Bermondsey Labour politics, pulling all the strings with Tatchell as their puppet?

The irony of the situation was that Militant actively opposed Tatchell – for strategic and ideological reasons. They did support his candidature in the first selection ballot in November 1981, but that was because Militant was even more hostile to Arthur Latham. The

Trotskyist group also had very little numerical strength. In December 1981 there were only four party activists, out of a total membership of over 800, who were Militant supporters. There were no Militants in Chaucer ward, Tatchell's branch, and they could only count on one ward secretary as a supporter.

In March 1982 Tatchell incurred the wrath of Militant when he abstained on a vote over who to nominate as candidates for Southwark Borough Council. Bermondsey's Militant activists, who now totalled nine, were furious and began a whispering campaign against Tatchell in Chaucer, branding him as 'a middle-class outsider'. One Militant supporter told Tatchell in October 1982 that 'there was no question of us automatically giving you support' in a future selection ballot. This became evident the following month when Mellish resigned his seat. The Trotskyist group seriously considered backing Sandy Macpherson from the Electricians Union, the EETPU, as the parliamentary candidate. Militant only eventually rallied around Tatchell when the non-Militant Left told them that they could not expect any support against expulsions if they backed Macpherson.

But Militant's hostility towards Tatchell's candidature was based on clear ideological differences. On many issues, the two were diametrically opposed. Broadly speaking, Tatchell belonged to the radical Left of the Labour Party which rallied round Tony Benn's banner during the 1981 deputy leadership campaign. According to Michael Crick's excellent book on Militant,[37] The 'Bennite Left' are often derided as 'petty bourgeois reformists' by Militant supporters. For Tatchell one of the major differences was on the structure of a socialist society:

> I see socialism as being essentially about the extension and enhancement of democracy, particularly in the economic realm. Militant have a very centralized vision of command socialism. Mine is more decentralized and concerned with empowerment. In other words, giving people the power to do things for themselves. Militant take a Leninist view based on a vanguard centre.

On specific policies, the discrepancies between Tatchell and Militant are also stark. For several years the Alternative Economic Strategy (AES) was Labour Party and TUC policy and Tatchell supported it fully. Import controls, one of the main proposals of the AES, was seen by Militant as 'nationalistic' and 'exporting unemployment'. Other policies on wealth tax, planning agreements and industrial democracy are rejected by Militant as not going far enough.

When it came to social issues, Tatchell and Militant may as well have been in different parties. Tatchell supports 'Troops Out' of Northern Ireland while Militant is against withdrawal. Positive action for women and ethnic minorities, backed by Tatchell, are seen as 'bourgeois diversions from the class struggle' by Militant. The issue of gay rights has only once been raised at the Labour Party Young Socialists conference since Militant took over Labour's youth section in 1970. According to Michael Crick, Militant supporters are often hostile to gay Party members.

By the time of the by-election in February 1983, Militant's active ranks in Bermondsey had risen to 12. In the final week of the campaign the Labour Party had approximately 350 canvassers – about 30 were Militant supporters. But three days before the final poll, the *Daily Mail* had a different story to tell.[38] 'Militant Grip On Tatchell', said the front-page lead headline and began: 'Members of the ultra-left Militant Tendency, whose leaders face expulsion from the Labour Party this week, have been at the forefront of Peter Tatchell's Bermondsey by-election campaign. Militant activists have been flocking to help his bid for Parliament.' The story was by-lined '*Daily Mail* reporter'. The paper's allegations were based on the fact that their anonymous journalist had met six Militant canvassers. 'A true Marxist government is what is needed. That is why Peter is our only chance,' one activist told the *Mail*. The other source of evidence was that 'Three of his [Tatchell's] active supporters have signed articles in the Militant newspaper.' In fact, Tatchell had no 'active supporters' in Militant. Indeed, many of the Militant canvassers spent much of their time trying to sell their newspaper rather than secure votes for Labour.

The *Mail*'s front-page story was accompanied by another piece on Militant on page two by Allan Hall. He spent two weeks in Bermondsey under false pretences. Hall first went to Chaucer ward where he told local party activists he was a Party member from Dagenham, Essex, and wanted to support Labour's campaign. After canvassing for a few days he moved to a different area as there were few Militant supporters in Chaucer. Hall wrote: 'I have been shocked and not a little frightened at the sheer intolerant fanaticism of many of the extremists canvassing on Peter Tatchell's behalf.' The *Financial Times* commented the next day: 'Labour claims that there has been a concerted hate campaign in the Tory press have been borne out daily by much of the by-election coverage, such as the extraordinary prominence given by the *Daily Mail* to allegations that Mr Tatchell was being controlled by the Militant Tendency.'

However, the *Mail* story was immediately picked up by the rest of Fleet Street. On the evening before the by-election, the *London*

Standard asserted: 'Mr Tatchell has never belonged to Militant but this Marxist group has consistently supported him before and during the byelection campaign.'[39] The following morning the *Sun* was more explicit: 'He is the standard bearer of the sinister, fanatical supporters of the Militant Tendency who would take politics into the streets and factories.'[40]

Some quite eminent public figures were taken in by these false allegations. The morning after his by-election defeat on 25 February 1983, Tatchell was interviewed by David Frost on ITV's breakfast show *TV-AM*. One of Frost's very first questions was: 'On reflection, don't you think it would have been better not to have associated yourself with the Militant Tendency?' Eight months later Tatchell again had to set the record straight. In November 1983 he travelled to Oxford to speak at a local Labour Party meeting. That evening he boarded the train back to London and found himself sharing a compartment with George Thomas, former Speaker of the House of Commons and now Viscount Tonypandy. After a brief exchange of views, the former Labour Cabinet minister asked Tatchell: 'Are you still associated with the Militant Tendency?' With an impatient sigh Tatchell had to explain that he had never been a supporter of Militant nor had sympathy with their views.

The candidate

About a week after Tatchell's by-election defeat in February 1983, Jim Innes, a former Labour press officer, received a phone call from Dave Fryer, the Party's agent in Bermondsey. Fryer wanted to talk confidentially about choosing a new parliamentary candidate for the forthcoming general election. Innes agreed and they met at the Queen's Head pub, off Walworth Road near the Labour Party's HQ. Tatchell was not invited and Fryer was anxious to talk about choosing what he called 'a more suitable' and 'less vulnerable' candidate. 'We want someone who is male, macho and married,' Fryer told Innes.

When the local party decided publicly to select a different candidate, Tatchell accepted but didn't agree with the decision: 'I think it was wrong,' he told David Dubow in April 1983,

> because it's effectively an admission that sections of the popular press can, through a sustained campaign of lies and exaggerations, dictate what candidates we choose – unless the candidate fits a very narrow stereotype ... If we start choosing Labour candidates on those criteria, then we're going to have no change in the House of

Commons at all. It's all going to be male, middle-aged, centre-moderate people. We can kiss goodbye to getting any working-class, women or black MPs. Certainly none who are openly gay. The next logical step is to let the press decide what policies we can speak up for. If we do that, then the Labour Party will just end up like the SDP.

However, many Fleet Street journalists, although sympathetic to Tatchell's plight at the hands of their own papers, argue that he *was* unsuitable for the Bermondsey constituency in a by-election. 'I know the area well,' said one *Mirror* executive, 'and he was the wrong choice for that seat.' Tatchell's press officer during the campaign, Monica Foot, agrees: 'The electors of Bermondsey were deprived of a candidate for whom they felt able to vote.'

Although strongly critical of the press coverage, she believes Tatchell himself was not entirely blameless in his handling of the press. This was backed up by an experienced by-election correspondent from a daily paper who told me: 'Tatchell did annoy some of the journalists, including myself, by not answering specific questions directly at press conferences. He seemed to take refuge in what appeared to be pre-prepared policy texts. He was not an adept candidate.'

Monica Foot also claims that Fleet Street's hostility towards Tatchell predated the by-election and Michael Foot's Commons statement: 'Michael Foot had been told about some 'Dave Spartish' press releases written by Peter [Tatchell] which were going the rounds of Fleet Street and causing some derision.'[41] Although these press releases contained Tatchell's name, they were in fact written by all the officers of Bermondsey Labour Party. Dating from May 1980, they now read as rather clichéd, but none more so than many press statements from leftwing constituency Labour Parties all over the country.

In addition, Jim Innes points to a biographical background paper written by Tatchell which the Labour candidate wanted to give to the press. Innes, who worked with Monica Foot in the final days of the by-election campaign, claims this document was evidence of his naivete. Apparently, Monica Foot squirmed with embarrassment when she read it and the paper was never released to the press. I have seen a copy of the document and it does over-romanticize Tatchell's working-class roots. But that hardly explains, let alone excuses, the treatment he received from Fleet Street. After all, he was hardly the first parliamentary candidate with alleged tactical weaknesses. And yet, because it was a by-election, the 'personality factor' has to be taken into account. For the press his liabilities were his political extremism, homosexuality, foreign birth, youth, inexperience and general 'outsider' image.

What are the facts? On politics, Tatchell's views are non-Marxist and closely aligned with the GLC's system of 'grassroots, community socialism'. Until June 1983, Keith Raffan was a political journalist on the *Daily Express* and is now Conservative MP for Delyn. This is what he said about Tatchell's politics as early as 7 December 1981: 'Tatchell is, after all, no more a member of the hard Left than numerous other Labour candidates all over the country. His views do not differ markedly from those of John Blackhouse, Labour's candidate who lost his deposit in the recent Crosby by-election.'

Tatchell wouldn't have been the first gay rights supporter in the House of Commons. It is no secret that there are at least 60 homosexual MPs in Parliament. Some MPs, like Chris Smith and Maureen Colquhoun, have been quite open about their homosexuality and haven't suffered the press attacks. The irony is that the winner of the Bermondsey by-election, Liberal Simon Hughes, was involved in the preparation of the Party's gay rights manifesto. It is believed that this new policy was delayed by Hughes' absence fighting the by-election. And according to Victor Williams in a letter to *Capital Gay*: 'Was it not an act of political expediency for the Liberal victor Simon Hughes to avoid declaring his sexuality? . . . I look foward to *Capital Gay* and the Gay Liberals hounding Simon Hughes, regarding his sexual preferences, as they've done to Peter Tatchell.'[42]

Tatchell was also hardly the first parliamentary candidate to be born in a different country. The late Russell Kerr, Labour MP for Feltham until 1983, was born in Australia. He never found it a handicap. It is true that Tatchell had only lived in his Bermondsey council flat for five years before the by-election. But Simon Hughes was born in Cheshire and only had his house-warming party in the constituency on New Year's Eve 1983 – just seven weeks before the poll. Bob Mellish hasn't lived in Bermondsey since 1963. He lives in west Lewisham and has a house in Lancing, a rural village in Sussex.

The Labour candidate's youth and inexperience were also said to be detrimental. This is a fair point. And yet both Simon Hughes and the Tory candidate, Robert Hughes, were the same age as Tatchell (31) and neither could claim more political experience.

Where Tatchell was vulnerable to a press campaign was that he was fighting a seat which was just a couple of miles across the Thames from Fleet Street itself. But more important was the character of Bermondsey and its people. This bleak inner-city district is a tough, traditional, working-class area of southeast London. It has a large number of old-age pensioners with 43 per cent of the 51,000 voters over 45 years of age, and many of the people have old-fashioned moral and social values. Clearly, Tatchell was prone to losing a number of votes in such a constituency. But it cannot really be argued that Tatchell's 'unsuitability' cost Labour 21,075 votes in a single by-election – nearly half the electorate.

In any case, as the *Guardian*'s Martin Linton remarked: 'In the House of Commons there are many homosexuals, there are several Australians and at least three dozen Labour MPs who are just as left-wing as Peter Tatchell.'

Reaction, regrets and remorse

During a BBC1 debate on the press on 18 October 1984, a *Daily Express* journalist suggested that the alleged distortions and personal attacks on Peter Tatchell occurred by mistake because of professional pressures. William Deedes, editor of the *Daily Telegraph* between 1975 and 1986 and a former Tory Cabinet minister, was then asked if he agreed. Deedes replied: 'I don't think it was done by mistake.'

Such a frank appraisal of Fleet Street's coverage was commonplace from journalists and editors after the by-election. Apart from the *Sun* who had no regrets, news editors and political editors were, if only in private, appalled at what happened. The Bermondsey campaign produced more soul-searching and self-criticism in Fleet Street than perhaps any other political event since the war. The reporters' own union, the National Union of Journalists, was openly ashamed of some of their members' conduct. The president of the NUJ in 1983, the late Jonathan Hammond, said:

> The NUJ has no political affiliation, so has no view on the result of the by-election. It does, however, have a very strong code of conduct and policy on unwarranted intrusions of privacy, both of which were consistently violated in Mr Tatchell's case. The personal abuse, vilification and lies to which he was subjected by several Fleet Street newspapers and journalists were appalling. I cannot remember any individual in recent times being subjected to such unfair and relentless pressures by the media. What was particularly disgraceful and unforgivable was the hounding of him and his colleagues at his place of work, so much so that he had to leave his job ... The fact that some of this provocation was provided by NUJ members is not something of which the NUJ can be proud.[44]

One political editor from a tabloid paper told me: 'I think Tatchell was the wrong candidate, but there is no way that a human being should have been treated like that.' However, few journalists were prepared to be critical in public. In November 1983, BBC2's *Open Space* invited 12 Fleet Street correspondents who had reported the by-election to take part in a debate about Bermondsey. Nearly all refused, mainly because their papers wouldn't allow them to.

The BBC2 debate did take place, with the *Guardian*'s Martin Linton admitting, 'There is no possible defence for some of the stories that appeared about Tatchell during the campaign. Some of them were quite unprofessional. Others were defamatory and should never have got past the lawyer. They were based mainly on innuendo. Overall, it was a character assassination of the worst kind.'[45]

Much of the criticism of Fleet Street came from Conservatives, Liberals and Social Democrats. Matthew Parris, then a rightwing Tory MP for Derbyshire West, was the first to speak out a week before polling day: 'Am I alone among non-Trotskyists in finding the vilification of Mr Peter Tatchell rather offensive?'[46] After the by-election Parris had not changed his mind: 'I felt that as the campaign progressed Peter Tatchell was increasingly hounded and victimized. All I want is that we shouldn't victimize people publicly. I'm saying that a man should be treated as a serious political candidate and be seen in that light.'[47]

Other MPs were equally concerned. On February 22, two days before polling day, 70 MPs from all parties signed a House of Commons motion expressing their

disgust at sections of the Press, TV and Radio in their treatment of the Southwark, Bermondsey by-election and their character assassination and smear tactics against candidates in that election; and calls upon the press and the rest of the media to deal with the real issues of unemployment, bad housing and poverty in the area.

Even a meeting of 40 Young Conservatives in Hornchurch on 22 September 1983 unanimously condemned the press treatment of Tatchell. A member of the Bermondsey Conservative Association, who had canvassed against Labour during the by-election and 'believed in the Tory Party 100 per cent', wrote to Tatchell: 'I absolutely deplore the shameful and sick campaign against you. Most of all I deplore the fabricated lies, untruths and deliberate war waged in many cases without foundation. I was embarrassed by the press. I believe you fought on the policies and so did I.'

Supporters of the Alliance were particularly anxious to condemn the press. After a SDP Scottish conference in March 1983 one of the organizers, who had left the Labour Party in 1965, wrote to Tatchell: 'At this meeting we discussed the dirty tricks and press coverage to which you have been subjected. There was unanimous revulsion at what happened.' Jonathan Fryer, Liberal parliamentary candidate for Chelsea in the 1983 general election and a Party member for 20 years, said: 'I know I speak for many Liberals when I say how much I deplored so much of the smear campaign being conducted against you. As a BBC journalist, I am yet again ashamed of my colleagues in the media.' The Liberal candidate added: 'In my view, it was politically motivated.'

Bermondsey – a fair trial?

Bermondsey had always been a safe Labour seat. At the 1979 general election Bob Mellish was returned with a majority of 11,756 votes. And so when the result of the 1983 by-election was announced in Southwark Town Hall even the Party's political opponents were astonished. Labour had lost the poll by 9,319 votes. The day after his defeat, Peter Tatchell had no doubts who was to blame: 'This press campaign was directly related to the hate campaign and irrational atmosphere of attacks and abuse. I am a victim of lies, lies, lies. It has been a non-stop smear campaign. You can't undo that with ten-minute chats on the doorstep.' Even Neil Kinnock, who had opposed Tatchell's candidature from the very beginning, agreed and accused the *Sun* of being the chief author of Labour's downfall in the by-election. The *Sun* replied in characteristic fashion: 'Rubbish, Mr Kinnock. No newspaper has that much power and influence. Judgements like that are an insult to the people of Bermondsey. It suggests they are gullible gooks without minds of their own.'[48]

Fleet Street's defenders also take the view that the press harassment, distortions and subsequent intimidation by local people was instigated by Tatchell's Labour opponents, Bob Mellish and John O'Grady. Walter Terry, the *Sun*'s political editor during the Bermondsey by-election, argues: 'It was the Labour Party who did it and caused the trouble. It was Bob Mellish stirring it up like mad. It wasn't the press. It stemmed from the House of Commons, the shadow Cabinet and Walworth Road.'[49]

Many senior journalists even argue that anti-Labour bias has no effect at all on the voters. As Peter Hitchens, the *Daily Express* political correspondent, told Tatchell during a by-election press conference: 'Do you really think that the public is so stupid that they cannot distinguish between what they read and what they can see for themselves?'[50] There is some substance in this argument. Many people do establish the truth and form their own opinion from a variety of sources, not least their own daily experience. Quite often, they don't need newspapers to tell them about unemployment, crime and bad housing – they can see it for themselves.

However, in Bermondsey the situation was very different. The issue was 'Peter Tatchell' and during the campaign only a third of the electorate would meet him or Labour canvassers. Even then a brief chat on the doorstep was hardly enough to dispel some of the sinister tales related by the tabloid press. The Militant story is a good example. How many local people were in a position to know whether or not the Trotskyist group had taken over the Bermondsey Labour Party? Very few. There can be little doubt that branding Tatchell as an extremist had an effect on the final vote. 'I've always voted Labour,' said a middle-aged man during the by-election, 'but I'm not going to vote for that Communist.' One elderly woman wrote to Tatchell after the by-election: 'I'm sorry, Mr Tatchell, I didn't vote for you. I don't know why. It's just that the papers and everyone else were against you. They all said you were bad. I guess I just got swept along with the tide. Like all the rest round here I voted for that Hughes chap.'[51]

Bermondsey Labour Party workers have no doubts about the decisive influence of the press. They point out how the abuse and threats towards Tatchell directly coincided with hostile press coverage, like the *Mail*'s 'Militant Grip On Tatchell' story. 'At the beginning we were getting a pretty good reaction,' said Doug White, a member of the local party's General Management Committee, 'but then the press stories started. When we went canvassing for a second time they suddenly started hurling abuse. The more the press attacked the worse it got.'[52]

The role of the press in Bermondsey was also intensified by the mere fact that it was a by-election. The power of the individual voter in by-elections contrasts sharply with general elections where the result in one specific constituency is normally insignificant in the context of the national political situation. In by-elections the ordinary voters are much more likely to see their vote as important because of the intensity of press coverage. As the media glare is constantly on their community, their votes are often cast in anticipation of the headlines rather than in line with normal political allegiances. This encourages startling voting fluctuations and partly explains the dramatic swing to the Liberals from Labour in the last week of the Bermondsey by-election.

This massive switch of support in the final few days before polling was due, according to the Labour camp, to an unprecedented atmosphere of fear and paranoia which gripped the constituency. And Tatchell holds the popular press directly responsible. One Bermondsey voter said after the poll: 'A lot of people got swept up in the atmosphere of hysteria. People have since told me that I got carried away because everyone and all the papers were saying he was bad and dangerous.'[53]

The hate campaign resulted in hundreds of examples of abuse and assaults, including 30 death threats. Tatchell regularly needed police protection after letters like this: 'You revolting sod. Get back to where you belong – down under, preferably six feet down under.' Others were more politically related: 'Dear Sir, I always understood that East Londoners loved city and country. For God's sake, why are they choosing that loud-mouthed little Commissar Tatchell ... He and Benn should be put in their soap boxes and sent back to Russia, or be shot.'

Less worrying was the verbal abuse. Tatchell was regularly met with insults like, 'Fuck off back to Australia, you Communist pooftah,' which were also written on local walls. In early October 1982, a car deliberately drove at Tatchell with the driver shouting: 'Get back to the Gay Olympics, you Communist cunt.' This was a clear reference to the fictitious *Sun* story the previous month about Tatchell allegedly going to the Gay Olympics.

These were not isolated incidents. When Tatchell went leafletting on Saturday mornings at the Elephant and Castle shopping centre, he was often assaulted and warned: 'If you don't get out of Bermondsey by midnight you'll be dead.' Bermondsey police have confirmed many of these incidents as did the manager of the 'Dun Cow' discotheque in the Old Kent Road. When it was announced that Tatchell would be appearing at the pub, the manager was inundated with threats to firebomb the place and kill Tatchell if he turned up.

An indication of the role of the press came in February 1984 during the Chesterfield by-election campaign. Tatchell travelled up to the small Derbyshire town to canvass for the Labour candidate, Tony Benn, who had supported him in Bermondsey. However, the assistant regional organizer, Janice Murar, told him he wasn't welcome and the *London Standard* picked up the story: 'Benn ... Courting the Kiss of Death. A spectre far more terrible than Tony Benn as their next MP was threatening the staid citizens of this attractive market town – an official visit by Peter Tatchell.' The news story then accused Tatchell of being 'threatening' and 'extremist'.[54]

Two days after the *Standard* story, on 16 February 1984, Tatchell was knocked off his bike on Abbey Road, Bermondsey, by a car whose driver shouted out: 'You Commie pooftah.' A similar insult was hurled at Tatchell the following day when a man stepped from a pavement on Tottenham Court Road, central London, to push him and his bike into a stream of traffic. These two incidents had been the first for some time.

It would be wrong and misleading to suggest that responsibility for *all* the cases of assault and intimidation against Tatchell can be directly laid at the door of Fleet Street. But clearly the *Sun*'s Gay Olympics story had a direct influence on a docklands constituency whose voters retained very old-fashioned, traditional views. And sadly the *Sun*'s coverage was not offset by any sympathetic reporting from the normally pro-Labour *Daily Mirror*. Their by-election report, by chief leader writer Joe Haines, was equivocal to say the least: 'Only a Labour man can win but which one ... John O'Grady of the Old Guard or Peter Tatchell of the Red Guard'. The article was accompanied by a cartoon of Tatchell having a fist-fight with the other candidates and wearing a 'Justice For Muggers' badge.

Clearly, the *Mirror* was caught between their traditional support for the Labour Party and their hostility to the Left. That dilemma did not face the rest of the popular press. Quite simply, most of the tabloid papers took out a contract on Tatchell. But, more important, he was convicted, sentenced and punished but never given a fair trial. The defendant's evidence was never heard.

Neither was there a right of appeal. Tatchell had no means of redress. He had no industrial muscle to secure a right of reply. Bermondsey Labour Party did submit eight complaints to the Press Council concerning articles in the *Sun*, *Daily Mail*, *News of the World*, *Private Eye*, *Daily Star* and *Daily Express*. Although they were received well before the by-election, the complaints were never heard mainly because of bureaucratic bungling by both sides, and the Press Council's unwillingness to conduct any business over the telephone.

Tatchell refrained from taking legal action for three reasons. Firstly, there is no legal aid for libel actions. Secondly, the papers warned the Labour candidate that their defence would be based on the notorious Vanessa Redgrave case. In other words, although the press stories about Tatchell may have been false, they were not defamatory because his 'extremist views' placed him in such low public esteem that he had no public reputation left to defame. There was also the fear that the papers would resort to a tactic employed by the *Daily Mail* against the Moonies. This was to demand an advance payment of £4,000 in court by way of security for costs. Thirdly, by the time the libel actions came to court their impact would have been greatly diminished because they would have been heard after the by-election.

Such a system clearly left the Labour Party candidate for Bermondsey vulnerable and without protection from a press clearly after political blood. With no imminent reform of the Press Council or the libel laws, it begs the question: how long before another Peter Tatchell is selected as a parliamentary candidate for an inner-city constituency? And, more importantly, how will Fleet Street react?

6. Peace Women at the Wire—
The Greenham Factor

'I told them (the newsdesk) that the majority of people out there were absolutely genuine, but they insisted on me filing the usual, loony lefty copy. They are sending someone else down to take over tomorrow who is more "politically reliable", I suppose.' John Passmore, *Daily Mail* reporter, at Greenham Common to a fellow journalist, Sunday 12 December 1982.

'In the past, men have left home to go to war. Now women are leaving home for peace.' Sarah van Veen, Greenham peace woman

In the summer of 1981, Ann Pettitt, a member of Women for Life on Earth, noticed a small item in *Peace News*, the feminist and pacifist fortnightly magazine. It gave details of a women-led march from Copenhagen to Paris in support of world peace. Pettitt immediately thought that a similar demonstration should take place in Britain to protest about the siting of 96 American cruise missiles at the USAF base at Greenham Common, an issue which had not been debated in Parliament.

And so on 26 August 1981, about 40 women, men and children set off from Cardiff for the 125-mile march to Greenham Common, near Newbury, Berkshire. When they arrived at the base ten days later, the marchers immediately demanded a live televised debate on cruise missiles between the women and a Defence Ministry representative. This was refused and so four women chained themselves to the perimeter fence at the main gate. Until then they had attracted virtually no media interst. But this suffragette-style action brought the photographers and reporters down to the peace camp, although it was soon apparent why they had made the short trip from London. As Helen John, one of the original marchers, later reflected: 'The photographers were more interested in taking bondage-type pictures than presenting a serious appraisal of the issue.' Initial questioning from reporters centred on the state of the marchers' blisters and 'how was your husband coping at home'.

In some ways, the initial response from Fleet Street was similar to their reaction to the women's liberation movement in the late 1960s and early 1970s. The peace women were not taken seriously and their action was seen as frivolous. Many freelance writers and journalists who went down to Greenham in the early months found it virtually impossible to get the mainstream national press to use their work. This was disastrous for the peace campaigners who desperately needed the publicity for their cause, mainly because of the isolation of their location. The press was crucial if any kind of public debate about cruise was to be stimulated.

By the early months of 1982, peace activists were becoming increasingly angry at the lack of coverage. Here's Dr. Richard Lawson writing to the *Guardian*: 'When 6,000 people turn up at Greenham Common for a peaceful demonstration against offensive weapons, we get a picture and caption in the *Times*, ten inches of reporting in the *Telegraph* and ten inches in the *Guardian*. What do we have to do to gain your attention? Tear down the fencing? Kick a few coppers' heads in?'[1] As it turned out, non-violent direct action was the only way to entice Fleet Street's news editors to send reporters.

How early sympathy turned sour

The Greenham peace women only really became national news in mid-November 1982. This was after a total of 23 women were found guilty of breaching the peace for occupying the security box inside the main gate of the base in August and for obstructing work on new sewer pipes in October. During the court cases in Newbury the defence lawyers gave evidence on behalf of the women, denouncing the use of nuclear weapons as immoral and unChristian. And when they were given 14-day prison sentences there were emotional scenes in the courtroom.

The press reacted with straight, factual reports. The *Express* even hinted a disdain for the law which had convicted the women. 'Eleven women campaigners against nuclear missiles went to jail yesterday – under a law dating back 621 years.'[2] There was more relatively sympathetic coverage when 11 of the women were released from East Sutton Park Prison. The papers' front pages included photographs full of smiling, defiant women. In fact, it was rather difficult to do otherwise. As Helen John said at the time: 'They [the press] didn't have any option. They haven't had any toeholds in any unpleasantness that they want to portray. They haven't been able to say that we're aggressive and violent because we're not, it's as simple as that . . . The press haven't been able to wheedle out aggression. They've looked for it. They've tried very hard to find it, but they've failed.'[3]

That judgement was a little premature, but in late 1982 the image of thousands of ordinary, defenceless women engaged in peaceful protest won the hearts if not the minds of some Fleet Street journalists. This was notably revealed on Sunday 12 December 1982, when at least 30,000 women arrived at Greenham to form a human chain around the whole of the base. As part of the protest photographs of children, baby clothes, toys and memorabilia were attached to the nine-mile fence. Some of the journalists were quite moved by this. 'These demos are usually so predictable, with the same old trade union and rent-a-mob contingents. But this is different,' said a Press Association reporter. 'It really gives you a lump in your throat.'[4] Alison Whyte, then CND's press officer, recalls meeting a 'hard-bitten *Sun* reporter staring at mile after mile of baby clothes, toys and family photographs, with tears streaming down his bearded face. He said he had never seen anything like it in his life.'[5] He was not the only journalist to express sympathy for the protest that day, according to the Greenham women.

However, back at the offices in Fleet Street, it was clear that management didn't see the demonstration in such a favourable light. As the *Daily Mail*'s John Passmore remarked to a colleague that Sunday afternoon: 'I told them [his newsdesk] that the majority of people out there were absolutely genuine, but they insisted on me filing the usual, loony lefty copy. They are sending someone else down to take over tomorrow who is more ''politically reliable'', I suppose'. The first few paragraphs of Passmore's report in the *Mail* the next day, 13 December, reflected his apparent fairmindedness towards the protest:

> It was a day of triumph for the women of protest. They forecast that 20,000 would be at the Greenham Common RAF base in Berkshire yesterday. In fact, about 30,000 turned up to form a nine-mile human chain around the base in protest against the siting of US cruise missiles there. They defied pouring rain and waded through ankle-deep mud to deliver their message.

But then the *Mail* saw fit to give prominence to the fact that there were Soviet journalists covering the demonstration. 'Their film will certainly make wonderful footage for the Kremlin in the propaganda war which surrounds the whole nuclear issue,' added the *Mail*.[6]

The *Daily Express* employed a similar tactic. Their reporter Ross Benson filed a fair and accurate report:

> They came in their thousands to Greenham Common, the old, young, socialist worker and high Tory, some on crutches, others in

fur, most in oilskins – from as far away as Scotland and Northern Ireland and as near as Newbury... Then they linked hands. Feminist-activist with suburban housewife, grey-haired grandmother and dishevelled student, to sing and chant and call for 'peace'.

Benson went on to say that the protest was 'a cause for deep embarrassment for the government,' and 'nor can it be dismissed as a protest by a radical minority'.

However, Benson's sympathetic report was buried by the *Express* subeditors in the main article and didn't start until the thirteenth paragraph. Instead, a rather different slant had been given to the overall report by management. 'The Peace War', said the main headline and 'Russian TV Cameras Roll As 30,000 Women Ring Missile Base In Anti-Nuclear Protest', ran the subheading. Under the anonymous by-line of '*Express* Staff Reporter', the story began:

> A Russian TV crew filmed the mass anti-nuclear protest by women at Greenham Common yesterday. Reporters from the Kremlin mouthpiece newspaper *Pravda* were also at the besieged American air base in Berkshire. As the Soviet cameras rolled, the 30,000 demonstrators milling in the mud appeared as unwitting dupes of a propaganda coup by Moscow.[7]

Not once in his long and detailed story did Benson mention the presence of Soviet journalists.

Interestingly, the Russian reporters and TV crews, who cover a wide range of news stories in Britain including the Conservative Party conference, were stopped by the Special Branch at a roadblock on their way to Greenham. Plainclothes officers took the names and details of their organizations. And their presence was seen as equally significant by the *Times* – 'Greenham Common Peace Protest Reported In Soviet Union'.[8] while the *Sunday Telegraph* was more explicit on the day of the demonstration itself. Under the headline of 'Soviet "Aid To Peace Groups"', the paper reported: 'Growing Russian involvement in the peace and anti-nuclear movements in Europe was attacked last night by Cecil Parkinson, the Conservative Party Chairman. He claimed that Moscow was giving large-scale funds to the peace movement and spoke of increasing Communist participation in CND.'[9] The papers also gave prominence to the claim by Defence Minister Peter Blaker that members of the peace movement 'were Communists under the direct influence of Moscow'.[10]

The day after the 'Embrace the Base', Monday 13 December,

hundreds of women took part in a non-violent blockade of the main gates to the base. Wyn Jones, Assistant Chief Constable of Thames Valley police who was in charge of operations that day, said of their actions: 'The women are not malicious. I am very conscious that these are ordinary, law-abiding women who believe passionately in their cause.'

There were no arrests at the blockade and yet some of the press managed to portray it as a violent demonstration. 'Ugly Face Of The Girls Of Peace', said the *Sun* together with their subheads – 'Mob Hurls Abuse' and 'Battle Of The Sexes'. The *Mail* reported that 'the fiercest scenes came when several women threw themselves in front of two coaches and an estate car', and the *Star* said that the peace women 'battled with hundreds of police'. The military metaphors were much in evidence – 'Militant feminists and burly lesbians were apparently the storm troops in the front line', claimed the *Sun*.

But the women's commitment to non-violent protest was barely mentioned. The *Guardian* quoted a peace camper saying 'we have been completely non-violent' and the *Times* said 'the women believed that they had succeeded in peacefully protesting', but that was it. According to the peace women, the press also played down alleged police brutality. Lucinda Broadbent said:

> Some of the police were careful and restrained, but one of the abiding images was of women lying passively before the gates, singing together, being grabbed, kicked and deliberately beaten by furious helmeted policemen. As women continued to sit down the police became more aggressive and violent and women were thrown into ditches, kicked, dragged away by their feet with their heads bumping along the ground.[11]

Few of these allegations were given prominence by Fleet Street. The *Times* and *Daily Star* did quote women who had been roughly handled, but the women's version of what happened was mostly reported as 'inevitable complaints'. The *Sun* said: 'Police, who played a softly-softly game, ... were accused by the screaming horde of nipple twisting, groping and strong-arm tactics'.[12] For the papers, the police 'tried to cool the situation' (*Express*[13]), 'tried to preserve a delicate balance' (*Guardian*[14]), were 'caught in the crush' (*Mirror*[15]) and 'tried desperately to maintain a good-humoured presence' (*Telegraph*[16]).

And yet, despite the under-reporting and the attempt to smear the peace women with the alleged 'Kremlin connection', there is little doubt that some individual journalists sympathized with their protest. There were even signs of respect in the leader columns – 'Moving But

Misguided', said the *Mail*,[17] 'impressive spectacle', admitted the *Sun*.[18] A more powerful weapon for the peace movement was the photographs and TV film of these ordinary women, many non-political from all kinds of background, demonstrating with such obvious courage and non-violent determination. And as 1982 drew to a close the opinion polls began to show a significant shift against cruise and Trident missiles. The Greenham women, together with CND, were winning the argument, and events were to show in the ensuing months that the government had noticed.

Enter Mr Heseltine and the news machine

In the early hours of New Year's Day 1983, 44 women climbed the perimeter fence of Greenham air base and ran the 300 yards towards the large, concrete silos which were being built to house the 96 cruise missiles. Watched by several photographers, journalists and television cameras, the peace women then held hands and danced in a circle on top of the 40-foot-high silo mound. For over an hour they waved banners and sang anti-nuclear songs, cheered on by their supporters back at the camp site. It was a remarkable sight and a stunning propaganda coup for the peace movement. For the incident was given prominence in the Sunday newspapers and on TV news bulletins.

The government was furious. In fact, the Conservative Party had been concerned for some time that the Greenham women and CND were winning over public opinion. And so an intense and prolonged news management strategy was co-ordinated by Tory Central Office, Downing Street and the Ministry of Defence.

It began in late 1982 with Whitehall briefings for a number of friendly editors and defence correspondents about the alleged Communist affiliations of some members of the peace movement and the need for cruise missiles. One target area was the young, Christian voters who had flocked to the CND cause. As one Defence Ministry official said at the time': 'We've got to get our message over, particularly to the young uncommitted people who can be won over by CND.'[19] And so journalists on the Christian weekly papers were called in for government briefings on nuclear weapons.

One of the key figures in this campaign to use the press against the Greenham women and CND was Tory MP Winston Churchill, the former *Times* war correspondent and member of the Institute for Journalists. He was appointed by Mrs Thatcher to mobilize the campaign and so he set up the Committee for Peace with Freedom, a loose co-ordinating group which met at his London flat. This was an umbrella organization for the Coalition for Peace through Security, based at Whitehall although it claimed to be an independent group, and the Campaign for Defence and Multilateral Disarmament (CDMD) which operated from Tory Central Office. Churchill was director of CDMD but its campaign co-ordinator was Harvey Thomas, now head of publicity for the Conservative Party. Another key figure in this strategy was Peter Blaker, Minister of State for Defence and the Armed Forces Minister. He had informal meetings with CDMD after being assigned a propaganda role by Sir John Nott, then Defence Secretary.

But it was the appointment of Michael Heseltine as Nott's successor, within a week of the Greenham women's protest on the cruise silos, that sparked off the propaganda war. From his first day as Defence Secretary, Monday 10 January 1983, the temperature rose. A new vocabulary was introduced into the nuclear debate. The word peace suddenly became 'peace' in inverted commas in a number of papers. One of the chief advocates of this new political language was *Daily Mail* columnist Paul Johnson. 'I believe we can fairly say that any organization sporting the word ''Peace'' in its title needs to have its supposedly non-political credentials examined very critically', he wrote.[20] Johnson also advised Cabinet ministers on other phrases to use. 'I said to Cecil Parkinson: ''Never refer to unilateralism. Tell all your fellows – ministers and everyone else – to refer to it as one-sided disarmament so people know what the hell you're talking about.'' I notice they are now doing so.'[21]

Within a week of Heseltine taking office, a number of editors and political correspondents of major newspapers in the West Country were invited to private lunches by Peter Blaker, the Junior Defence Minister. 'I hope to explain to you government thinking on nuclear policy,' wrote Blaker in his letter of invitation, 'and to seek your views on the state of the debate in your area . . . I hope that my lunch might go some way to redress the balance and be a useful means of testing the temperature locally on nuclear policy issues.'[22]

The West Country had been chosen because the peace movement was particularly strong in that area. However, Blaker's personal briefings were not a success. One editor refused to go to one of the lunches, on 17 January 1983 at the Mayflower Hotel, Plymouth, and another journalist staged a walkout. They were angry about the minister's decision to consult in private rather than debate in public.

Later in January Blaker was involved in meetings with the Central Office of Information and the advertising agency, J. Walter Thompson, for a £1 million-plus advertising campaign to put the case for cruise missiles. However, this plan generated so much political opposition that the idea had to be dropped in early February 1983.

Later that month, just after the advertising plan was scrapped, Michael Heseltine set up a special propaganda unit inside the Ministry of Defence, specifically designed to counter the growth of the peace movement, particularly CND. Known as Defence Secretariat 19 (DS19), the unit's tasks included dealing with the press on the nuclear issue and handling the publicity aspects of demonstrations mounted against Heseltine by CND. It was headed by John Ledlie, an Assistant Secretary and former Deputy Chief of Public Relations at the Defence Ministry. Ledlie, a career civil servant, admitted that he was no expert on nuclear weapons. 'I think perhaps it's a good thing. If you are too closely involved you sometimes cannot see the wood for the trees.' There was, he said, 'an information gap we shall try to fill'.[23] Ledlie is now head of information at the Defence Ministry.

It was soon clear that Greenham was a prime target for DS19. In one of the unit's first speeches written for Peter Blaker, the Junior Defence Minister said: 'Defence of the people will be decided by wise and cool judgement, not by the shouting of empty slogans on the streets or the carnival cavortings of woolly people in woolly hats'.[24] But DS19 had a more sinister role, according to ex-MI5 officer Cathy Massiter. She worked with the propaganda unit and said that intelligence information on leading figures in the peace movement were passed to DS19.[25] This was mainly about the so-called Soviet sympathies of some peace activists.

What was noticeable about the coverage of the peace movement in the spring of 1983 was how many of the articles concentrated on the political affiliations of their members. Take this remarkable story on the front page of the *Daily Star* on 2 April 1983, the day after 40,000 people turned up at Greenham for an Easter demonstration: 'Spies Alert Over Peace Army', ran the headline and continued:

Three Russian spies were kicked out of Britain as a warning to the Kremlin not to meddle in the peace movement. Intelligence chiefs believe Russian spymasters have tried to use CND as a way of embarrassing the government and piling on pressure to scrap cruise missiles. The peace link was revealed yesterday as 40,000 people formed a human chain between Greenham Common and a nuclear weapons factory. Senior officers in MI5 and MI6 believe that the Russians have close contacts with extreme leftwing elements in CND. It is feared that the good intentions of ordinary people who support the campaign against cruise should be exploited to sabotage the arms limitations talks between the USA and Russia. Some Tory MPs are even suggesting privately that the Russians want to use the peace movement to bring down the government at the next general election.

There was virtually no evidence for this extraordinary story except some groundless quotes from a couple of Tory MPs and 'officers in MI5 and MI6 believe'. But the *Star* was not the only paper to indulge in such reporting. A month later, on 4 May, Patrick Cosgrave, a free-lance journalist and former speech writer for Mrs Thatcher, wrote a feature in the *Daily Express* headlined – 'Moscow Link With Ban The Bomb Protesters: Exposed The Hard Left Behind CND'.This was merely a list of the senior CND members with their past and present political affiliations. It was similar to the information contained in a let-ter written by Heseltine ten days earlier on 23 April which was sent to all Tory MPs.

There can be little doubt that some of the information about the alleged Moscow Connection in the peace movement reached the fea-ture desks of many Fleet Street newspapers from DS19.

As well as DS19, Heseltine set up another public relations group in the spring of 1983 called Working Party On Public Opinion Of Nuc-lear Weapons. This was an ad hoc group chaired by Heseltine which included Bernard Ingham, the Prime Minister's press secretary, and some Foreign Office ministers. In addition, there was Women And Families For Defence which was launched a month after DS19 on 28 March 1983, to counter the popularity of the Greenham protest. This organization was headed by Lady Olga Maitland, the *Sunday Express* columnist and on the list of Conservative parliamentary candi-dates. She had the support of Churchill's Committee for Peace with Free-dom and also her own paper. 'The *Express* has been wonderful about Women for Defence,' said Maitland. 'I'd say my editor [Sir John Junor] is 100 per cent behind me.'[26] Many of her leaflets and booklets were published by the Ministry of Defence and the Foreign Office.

DS19 was officially disbanded on 1 September 1983. Part of its propaganda work was transferred to DS17, another Defence Ministry unit, known as the 'Holocaust Desk' in Whitehall because of its responsibility for nuclear policy. The rest of DS19's work was given to Heseltine's own PR department with its large staff. The Ministry of Defence has 350 press officers.

When the decision officially to close down DS19 was disclosed, a Ministry of Defence official said: 'There has been an extensive public debate on defence policy with nuclear weapons and the government believes that it has succeeded in explaining its defence policy.'[27] Whether there had been a public debate is highly questionable.

However, judging by the coverage of the Greenham Common peace women throughout 1983, the mandarins from DS19 will no doubt have felt quite pleased with their efforts.

A protest at Newbury Town Hall

One of DS19's specific functions was to handle the publicity aspects of demonstrations mounted against Heseltine by the peace movement. An interesting coincidence is that in the same month that DS19 was set up, February 1983, a major protest by the Greenham women took place against the Defence Secretary. And the press coverage of that demonstration proved to be the major turning point in Fleet Street's hostility towards the peace women.

In 1982, when still Environment Minister, Heseltine had been asked to address a private meeting of the West Berkshire Conservative Association by the Tory MP for Newbury, Michael McNair-Wilson. Normally, when a minister changes Cabinet jobs, he or she cancels such appointments, but clearly Heseltine saw this as an opportunity to confront the Greenham women. And so on the evening of Monday 7 February 1983, Heseltine arrived outside Newbury Town Hall faced with a large group of Greenham peace women, many of whom lay down in front of the main door. As Heseltine stepped out of his car, a group of six policemen formed a tight group around him. They then rushed him through the gauntlet of women. But, in their anxiety to get him into the hall, Heseltine tripped and stumbled to the ground. The incident lasted no more than 30 seconds on a cold, dark night in a confined, crowded space. Apart from the police and Heseltine himself, few people could testify as to what exactly happened.

However, on 8 February, seven of Britain's eight national papers had other ideas. 'Peace Camp Women Mob Heseltine', said the *Daily Telegraph*'s front page. 'Mr Heseltine, Defence Secretary, was dragged to the ground in a tussle with women anti-nuclear demonstrators at Newbury last night. Several women tried to punch and kick him ... Surrounded by constables, the Minister was propelled through the melée. Amid uproar, several women tried to punch and kick him.' The *Daily Mail* agreed – 'Women Knock Down Minister' and 'Ban-The-Bomb Mob Send Heseltine Crashing' said their headlines and the story added: 'Several women lay on the ground ... and as police tried to guide the minister over them, he was pulled to the ground.' The *Mirror* produced a similar story – 'Tarzan's War – Minister Felled By Peace Women. Defence Secretary Michael Heseltine was dragged to the ground last night by a crowd of peace women from Greenham Common.'

Other papers were more certain of the Greenham women's violent and hooligan tendencies. 'Jeering Peace Protesters Punch Minister', claimed the *Times* and added that he was 'punched and pushed by peace protesters'. The *Sun* agreed: 'Angry Peace Girls Rough Up Heseltine' and said in a leader:

> After his bruising encounter with the 'peace' demonstrators outside Greenham Common, Defence Minister Michael Heseltine must have concluded: 'If this is peace, give me war!' He is right to refuse to debate with these fiery, violent ladies ... Whatever idealism first inspired the anti-nuclear sit-in at Greenham Common, it is fast being overwhelmed by rancour, intolerance and, sadly, sheer bitchiness.

The *Daily Star* also saw sinister elements – 'Target Of The Mob – Heseltine Is Crushed By Angry Women', and said 'a mob of screaming, jeering women ambushed him'. There was an interesting discrepancy between the English and Scottish editions of the *Daily Express*. The London edition, under the by-line of Colin Pratt, reported that 'Heseltine was hissed and spat at by the women of Greenham Common. As police formed a chain around him, officers stumbled over some of the women protesters lying on the steps'. However, in the Scottish edition, under the same by-line, the paper reported that 'Heseltine *was brought to his knees* by a mob of howling, spitting women peace protesters'.

And so, according to Fleet Street, the Greenham women were a violent, spitting, intolerant, howling mob and had punched and kicked the Secretary of State for Defence. But was it true? Not according to Michael Heseltine. 'I went down,' said the Defence Secretary, 'because the policemen who were trying to get me inside were obstructed by women's bodies and stumbled over themselves. But I was not in any way hurt.'[38] All the papers except the *Guardian* carefully ignored this quote, although the *Daily Express* did include it in their third and final editions. Instead, the press merely quoted Heseltine as saying: 'I was pulled to the ground.'

A Ministry of Defence spokesperson also denied the Fleet Street version. The press officer said that Heseltine was 'certainly not pulled down' and added: 'The man is six-foot-three. It would take a fair bit of pulling'.[29] But more significant was the evidence from a senior policeman on the scene. Chief Inspector Brackin of Newbury police told CND activist Philip Braithwaite that Heseltine had not even tripped over, but merely 'leaned over' two policemen who had stumbled over some women demonstrators. Brackin added that the whole incident lasted 'only 30 seconds' and that he didn't 'know what all the fuss is about'.

Local journalists also provided eyewitness accounts. Elizabeth Cadell, who covered the story for the *Newbury Weekly News*, said: 'A police officer close to the Minister appeared to stumble as he tried to negotiate the demonstrators. The Minister was seen to trip although he immediately regained his balance with the help of other officers who were holding his arms.' She added that she did not see any of the demonstrators punch or spit at the minister.[30] A journalist from a Reading paper agreed: 'I wouldn't swear to it, but it certainly looked to me as if the police surrounding Mr Heseltine tripped and he stumbled ... Certainly I didn't see anyone trying to kick or spit at him. You would have to have been on the bottom of the pile to really see what happened.'[31] One such person was a local radio reporter who was knocked to the ground by police as Heseltine's car arrived. This is his account: 'As far as I could see he just stumbled, not because women were pushing but because of the speed the police were trying to go. There seemed to be no attempt on the part of the women to get at him at all. I wouldn't have thought that the women were trying to punch and kick Heseltine as has been reported. I didn't see anything like that'.[32] All this was backed up by the Greenham women who were at the demonstration. One said: 'We are here to stop cruise missiles, to stop violence and war. We can't use violence in our protest. It would be pure hypocrisy'.[33]

And so the overwhelming evidence suggested that the national press reports of the Newbury protest was at best exaggerated and at worst fabricated. Many supporters of the Greenham women tried to repair the damage of the coverage by setting the record straight. One such person was Daphne Francis who lives in Kirkpatrick Durham, Scotland. She complained to the Press Council about the reports in the *Sun*, the *Times*, *Scottish Daily Express* and *Daily Telegraph*. Her complaint against the *Sun* was refused a hearing by the Council, although they declined to give a reason. But the other three cases went ahead.

The *Daily Telegraph* case was an oral hearing in December 1983 at the Press Council office in Salisbury Square, central London. Francis complained that the *Telegraph*'s account 'inaccurately reported that women peace protesters tried to punch and kick the Minister and failed to correct this'. She added: 'I find it impossible to believe that a press reporter at three yards from Mr Heseltine could have seen a woman or women try to punch, kick and drag him to the ground, and that the police at closer range (and in larger numbers) failed to see this and did not charge the women/woman concerned.' Two Greenham women who were at the demonstration, Annie Butcher and Judy Harris, then gave their accounts of what happened which corroborated the police and Ministry of Defence versions.

Daphne Francis has provided me with a detailed five-page report of what was said at this Press Council hearing. Here is part of her account:

> All through the hearing, we found it very difficult to get things brought out into the open. We had naively assumed that the Press Council would do this. But when obvious differences came up, there was a noticeable silence from the Press Council. For a while, we didn't quite know what to do. We thought perhaps they would begin their probing questioning later. However, as time wore on we realized that we'd better seize the initiative ourselves and cross-question Mr Davies (the *Telegraph* reporter concerned) about the obvious inconsistencies in his story. However, we were interrupted by the Chairman for doing this or another member of the Press Council would divert the conversation on to a different track.

Hugh Davies, who wrote the *Telegraph* story, said that he had seen several women attempt to punch and kick the Minister as he got out of his car. He had not seen a policeman trip and thought the Minister had been pulled to the ground. Davies added that in general he had great sympathy for the women peace protesters. He was accompanied by his then editor William Deedes, the former Tory Cabinet minister, who provided videotapes of the news items shown by BBC and ITN as evidence for his paper's version of events. However, these films only showed Heseltine being surrounded by police and then stumbling. It was far from clear what happened from the films. Even the Press Council members agreed with this. 'Well, we can't make anything of that,' said one.

However, according to Francis, Deedes then tried to argue that the TV film had showed that in the confusion the women had in fact been the cause of Mr Heseltine falling by simply being there and refusing to get out of the way. He claimed that, although the peace women were trying to practice non-violence, lying down in front of Mr Heseltine had in fact caused the violence, albeit unintentionally. The two Greenham women objected strongly to this allegation. The Press Council members remained silent.

Daphne Francis then cross-examined Davies about some of the details of his story. She challenged his use of words like the phrase: 'Mr Heseltine seemed alarmed by the violence of the crowd but he soon regained his composure.' This, argued Francis, contrasted strongly with the use of the word 'mob'. Davies replied that this was mere quibbling about semantics. The Press Council remained silent.

Francis then asked him how he had known that the women were 'trying to kick and punch' Mr Heseltine. How could he assume their intention, she asked Davies. According to Francis, Davies replied that he had discussed what happened afterwards with the *Times* reporter who had said that he had seen someone punch Mr Heseltine. 'Ah,' responded Francis, 'that's odd,' and she delved into her file and produced a letter from the *Times'* deputy editor Colin Webb who said: 'If any of the participants had chosen to challenge the description (i.e. punched, kicked), we would probably allow that as the nearest we could get to an authoritative source unless, of course, there were any charges as a result.'[34] In other words, there was no corroborated version of what happened.

At this point Davies changed his mind and said: 'No, I didn't say I talked to the *Times* journalist.' Deedes backed him up: 'No, no, you must have misunderstood him. He was referring to something else.' There followed a short silence with no response from the Press Council panel. A Greenham woman then whispered: 'Well, this is pretty hopeless.' But later in the hearing a Press Council member did attempt to question Davies in detail. The panel member asked Davies: 'You have used the phrase ''Mr Heseltine was dragged to the ground'' and later on you say ''He fell to the ground''. Which was it?' Davies apparently 'froze' and couldn't answer the question. The Council member then got impatient and said: 'Come on, man, it must be one or the other.' Davies replied: 'Yes, yes, I mean he was dragged.'

On 14 December 1983, the Press Council produced their adjudication: 'It is not surprising that their accounts of the confused and confusing scene varied. It would have been impossible for any single observer to see everything that happened in the moments of turmoil when Mr Heseltine was moved through the crowd from his car ... The Council is not satisfied that it was inaccurate to report that some women peace protesters tried to punch and kick the Minister. The complaint against the *Daily Telegraph* is therefore not upheld.'

The Press Council produced similar verdicts regarding complaints against the *Times* and the *Scottish Daily Express*. The premise of their adjudication was: the situation was confused, therefore the stories cannot be seen as inaccurate. This was an astonishing decision by the Press Council. For it rejected the evidence of Michael Heseltine, the Ministry of Defence, a senior Newbury police officer, three local reporters and several Greenham women who were also at the demonstration.

Either Heseltine was dragged, kicked, punched and pushed to the ground or wasn't. It's as simple as that.

On the day the Press Council adjudications were published, 14 December 1983, the *Daily Express* produced what they called their 'Final Solution' for the Greenham peace women: 'Instead of a fence round Greenham Common they should dig a moat, and fill it with champagne, asses' milk, Chanel No. 5 and men with massive dorsals. They'd clear out all these awful women within half an hour.'

Other attempts to set the record straight on the Newbury protest met with equal frustration for Greenham supporters. Philip Braithwaite, a fomer Vice-Chairman of CND, pursued the *Times*, *Sun* and *Daily Mail* to find out if they had corrected their story, given Heseltine's admission that he was not attacked by the Greenham women. Colin Webb, the *Times* deputy editor replied: 'We have always accepted that this was a very confused situation, and the Press Council cannot say that we were inaccurate. Neither can we.'[35] Braithwaite responded: 'If there was a "very confused situation" . . . why did your front page the following morning claim that "Greenham protesters" had "punched" Mr Heseltine'.[36] The *Times* didn't reply.

Braithwaite also asked the *Sun* to justify their headline of 'Angry Peace Girls Rough Up Heseltine'. He got this response from William MacLelland, the paper's assistant editorial manager: 'Whether he [Heseltine] stumbled over a policeman is quite irrelevant. The incident would not have happened but for the angry demonstration by the women concerned.' He added: 'We had no reason to correct our report, and the subsequent Press Council hearing found that our report had been quite fair and accurate.'[37] This latter point was completely untrue. There was no hearing and no adjudication. Kenneth Morgan, the Press Council's director, confirmed this: 'The Council has made no declaration about the *Sun*'s coverage of the demonstration at Newbury'.[38] When Braithwaite pointed this out to the *Sun*, MacLelland told him: 'I would remind you of the laws of libel'.[39]

The *Daily Mail* produced an equally remarkable response to Braithwaite's inquiry as to whether they had corrected their original story, given Heseltine's denial of being 'knocked down' (*Mail*) by the peace women. The paper's managing editor, Gordon Cowan, said: 'We have since spoken to Mr Heseltine about the events of that night and, having done so, we see no reason to withdraw or correct our account of the incident'.[40] The Ministry of Defence's Deputy Chief of Public Relations, Martin Scicluna, twice would not either confirm or deny whether the *Daily Mail* had 'spoken to Mr Heseltine'. But Scicluna did confirm that Heseltine said that he had merely stumbled over policemen and not over the women.[41]

What is striking about Fleet Street's coverage of this whole affair is their complete refusal to accept for one moment any blame or even that they had made a mistake. Even when faced with a mountain of evidence – from the Secretary of State for Defence to ordinary Greenham peace women – editorial management from all the papers still refused to acknowledge any culpability. It was an extraordinary state of affairs.

But, perhaps more significant, the press coverage of the protest at Newbury almost certainly damaged the public's image of and support for the women of Greenham. As Philip Braithwaite reflected: 'What stimulated me most was the discovery that several local CND activists *did* accept the [press] accounts, and said to me: ''What a pity the Greenham women have turned violent.'' I have been told of other cases in other parts of the country.' There is plenty of evidence for this. The letter columns of national and local newspapers were full of people complaining about the 'violent' Greenham women. Here's one example in the *Times* from Mrs Vivienne Bridges from Sussex: 'Sir, ''Peace Women Punch Heseltine'' (headline, 8 February). Is there not something ironical in women dedicated to peace using kicks and blows to enforce their views?'[12] If only she knew . . .

Blockades, demos and 'Holding Hands With The IRA'

For the Greenham peace women the accusation of violence or aggressive tactics was by far the most damaging to their cause. It not only discredited them as legitimate protesters, it also undermined their whole strategy of non-violent direct action.

The allegations and stories of violence from Fleet Street only came into prominence during 1983 as the Greenham women began to win over public support. Take this *Daily Express* leader:

> Just who is 'chilled' by the thought of British troops on guard duty at a British base? The Greenham Common women are far more likely to revert to violence than the troops . . . The women are demonstrably the aggressors. Blockading the base. Ripping up fencing. Making a mess of the Common. Stirring bitter local resentment. The troops deserve our thanks. They are doing their best to contain this ragtag and bobtail of politically motivated harpies.[43]

The *Express* returned to this theme of 'blockading the base' the following month in a story which alleged that the Greenham women had a 'Red mole' inside the base. On 20 August 1983, the *Daily Express* front-page headline ran – 'Red Mole Shock At Greenham – Peace Women Were Tipped Off Over Top Secret Delivery'. Underneath appeared this story:

> Security chiefs are hunting a Red Mole buried deep inside the Greenham Common cruise base. The infiltrator is feeding secret information to the 'peace women' camped outside, it was revealed last night. There had been growing suspicions over the way the women seem to know what is going on in the base. Now the authorities have proof of the mole's existence. It emerged this week when the women were tipped off about an early morning lorry delivery of non-nuclear missile casings. Only six people inside the base were supposed to have known the date and timing of the top-secret delivery from a nearby arms factory. The civilian driver signed the Official Secrets Act forbidding him to talk about his load. But when he turned into the entrance at 8.30 a.m. he found his path blocked by a hostile human barricade. He was the only lorry the demonstrators tried to block this week. And from the insults they hurled at him and at police battling to get through, it was clear the women knew what the vehicle contained.

But did the blockade take place? Not according to the police, the Greenham women and the Ministry of Defence. The Chief Constable of Thames Valley police said: 'My records show that several incidents involving the demonstrators at Greenham Common did occur during the week referred to in the *Daily Express*, but there is *no record* of the specific incident referred to. The individual officers on duty have been spoken to and none can recollect any such incident'.[44] The Defence Ministry's denial was more categorical. Mr B.P. Neale, Heseltine's Private Secretary, said: 'The Ministry of Defence made inquiries of this kind shortly after the [*Express*] article was published, and found that we have no record of any of the incidents described. That remains the position'.[45] This was confirmed by six Greenham women who said in a joint statement: 'There was no blockade of the basic Greenham Common by the women at the camp in the week 13 to 20 August 1983...The main substance of the article is fictitious. The story about the lorry did not happen'.[46]

So, the evidence suggests that the blockade didn't even take place. How did the *Express* support their story? When asked by the Press Council to substantiate their report, Morris Bennett, personal assistant to the paper's editor Sir Larry Lamb, replied: 'The editor is satisfied that the story published was accurate. The numerous reports relating to proceedings against persons at the camp speak for them-selves. The editor has no wish to enter into a debate with the women concerned and thereby give them further publicity'.[47]

If the *Express* was unwilling or unable to provide any evidence for its story, then perhaps their real motive was contained in their editor-ial which accompanied the news report. 'Sweep Away This Tip', ran the headline and the leader added: 'The women of Greenham, with their mindless zealotry and tireless exhibitionism, have succeeded only in damaging their cause. They were at first appealing – until we all began to realize just how suspect their motives were. Then they became repulsive ... Their slatternly, disease-prone tip should be swept away and soon.' According to Henry Porter, the *Sunday Times* journalist:

> The most regrettable part of this editorial is the spirit of intolerance that it betrays. One is reminded of *Pravda*. People may put a point of view when the *Daily Express* judges it to be agreeable or harm-less, but as soon as an opinion acquires credibility and support and threatens to change things against the paper's wishes then the *Daily Express*, sometime champion of individual rights, calls for legislation to sweep away the 'slatternly tip'.[48]

The Press Council produced a devastating indictment of the *Express* story and editorial. Its ruling said that neither the delivery of the mis-sile casings nor the women's blockade had taken place. 'The com-plaint that the *Daily Express* account was inaccurate and prejudicial is upheld and the newspaper is censured. To the extent that it relied upon that account for its facts, the newspaper's editorial was unjusti-fied. It was also abusive.' On the day that the Council's adjudication was published, 16 March 1984, the *Express* replied to the accusations. The paper said it was 'quite satisfied that it [the story] was accurate ... The Press Council's failure to confirm what we had discovered does not entitle that body to accuse *Daily Express* reporters of telling lies.' But the *Express* was still unable to produce any evidence for their story. The paper refused to give the Greenham women a right of reply because such an article 'was designed solely to secure further publicity for their nefarious activities'.

Fleet Street provided rather different coverage when the Greenham women did stage blockades of the gates to the base. At 5 a.m. on Thursday 16 February 1984, a siren signalling a nuclear alert was sounded inside the base. This was the fourth nuclear alert and on each occasion the peace women responded with blockades of the gates. For this warning, the women blockaded the Main and Indigo gates during which one protester had her arm dislocated. An ambulance was called and she was taken to hospital. The next day the *Daily Mail* declined to mention this or the nuclear alert in their story. Instead, a different version was given:

> An ambulance on an emergency call was stopped twice yesterday by women protesters at Greenham Common air base. The women threw themselves in front of the vehicle as it tried to leave the base to attend to the wife of a serviceman who had collapsed in her home at the married quarters. Despite its flashing blue lights and clear red and white medical markings, the women refused to move away and police had to clear a path for it.

This was completely untrue, according to the women involved in the blockade. One peace camper, Veronica Balfour, said: 'We were block-ading Indigo gate when police warned us that an ambulance was coming out. We stopped blockading to let it pass.'[49]

However, it was the coverage of the Greenham demonstration on 11 December 1983 that confirmed how keen the press were to por-tray the peace women as violent, regardless of the supporting evi-dence. 30,000 women turned up at the base and at 3 p.m. they began to pull down the fence. They were met with strong and, according to the women, violent force from the police. The press reacted equally strongly. 'Storming of Greenham – Police Hurt In 'Peace' Women's Siege Fury', said the *Express* front page the next day. 'Thousands of women stormed Greenham Common air base yesterday and virtually tore the fence to the ground. The demonstrators who preach peace turned violent in a massive new protest against cruise missiles.' Above this story was a photograph of the protesters with the following caption: 'Faces of violence . . . 'peace' women batter at the fence as troops wait to repel them.' The *Sun* took a similar line. Under the headline of 'Women At War', the paper reported: 'The wild women of peace brought mayhem to Greenham Common missile base yester-day. Violence erupted as a massive 25,000 gathered to demonstrate against cruise.'

The press concentrated exclusively on the fact that some policemen were hurt. All the papers gave prominence to an injury sustained by Inspector Michael Page. He was knocked unconscious when a con-crete post fell on him. Despite the fact that Newbury police later said it was an accident, this was not pointed out by the papers. Nor did the press report that two women protesters who were nurses helped the injured policeman into the van after seeing he was being handled incorrectly. This was confirmed by Inspector Page himself who later thanked the two women.[50] Meanwhile, 29 women were taken to the same hospital as Page with equally serious injuries. These were caused by police and soldiers wrenching their hands from the fence and hitting the women with sticks as they held on to the wire. One woman lay in the intensive care unit with a back injury that rendered her unable to move one of her legs. Others were in the casualty unit with broken fingers.

Apart from a one-paragraph quote from the women's lawyers at the end of their stories, not one national newspaper reported the injuries sustained by the peace protesters. This was despite the fact that the information was freely available from the hospital and from the women themselves. The only journalist to make inquiries was Pat Healy from the *Times*. After she had filed her initial story on that Sunday afternoon she returned to Greenham and met a group of women who told her of a number of incidents of police violence and harassment. After visiting several gates at the camp and taking a photograph of one of the injured women, Healy drove back to the Chequers Hotel in Newbury where all the reporters were staying. She then telephoned Thames Valley police and the hospital to check out the allegations made by the women. Later that evening, Healy was sitting in the lobby of the hotel with two Press Association journalists and a freelancer when their telephone rang. One of the Press Association reporters took the call. Moments later, he returned to his colleagues and said: 'That was the police. They're worried we're going to file stories about police attacks on the Greenham women. They're saying a police horse was whipped by barbed wire.'

Neither Healy nor the Press Association journalists believed this story, but the rest of Fleet Street did. On the basis of the word of a police press officer, the press printed the story with no sign of scepticism. 'A police horse being ridden round the outside of the base was whipped by a woman wielding a length of barbed wire,' said the *Mirror*.[51] 'One woman whipped a police horse with barbed wire, leaving the distressed animal with wounds that had to be stitched by a vet,' said the *Express*.[52] Only the *Daily Star* and *Telegraph* even attributed the claim to 'a police spokesman'. The truth was rather different. The horse did get caught up in barbed wire. But a video of the demonstation showed that the police horse had stumbled backwards and caught its legs on the wire. The vet had in fact been called by the women. He said that the cuts 'were not conducive to inflicted injuries' and that it was an accident. This was a long way from 'whipped by a woman wielding a length of barbed wire' as claimed by the *Mirror*. More significantly, no woman was charged by the police for 'whipping the horse'. Still, the Thames Valley police press office must have been pleased with the coverage.

For there was no mention of the police attacks on the women which they had done so much to conceal. Ironically, though, there can be little doubt that, apart from Pat Healy of the *Times*, Fleet Street was just not interested in police violence against the women.

Within ten days of that December demonstration, the 'terrorist connection' was unleashed against the peace movement. On 20 December 1983, three days after the Harrods bombing the *Standard* produced this large front-page banner headline – 'CND ''Holding Hands With IRA'' '. The story continued: 'Police angrily criticized spontaneous CND demonstrators in London today for ''holding hands with the IRA bombers''. Judging by the headline and first paragraph, the implication was that CND and the peace movement either sympathized with or supported the nationalist terrorists. Only later in the article is the basis for the story revealed. An anonymous police inspector says: 'If another bomb goes off in central London these people can be held culpable. They are simply holding hands with the IRA.'

The *Standard* did point out it was a spontaneous demonstration with women from Greenham and from London CND groups, but the headline was hardly justified. Even the most fervent opponent of CND could not argue they supported terrorism. In addition, if the *Standard* had checked with CND's national office they would have discovered that Joan Ruddock, CND's chairperson, had personally checked that no demonstations were planned between the Harrods bombing and the New Year to ensure that police resources were not stretched. To emphasize this point, Ruddock phoned through a short statement at 12.30 p.m. on the day the *Standard* piece was published. Her four-paragraph statement was not published until the fourth and final edition at the end of the article on page two with the same headline.

It was difficult to find someone who would defend the *Standard*'s story, particularly the all-important headline. David Hoffman, who took the accompanying photograph for the story, said: 'I was furious and mortified. The headline was viciously misleading and the copy totally failed to justify it. There was nothing at all I could do about it'.[53] Bob Graham, who wrote the story, told a Campaign for Press and Broadcasting Freedom member: 'I didn't write the headline. I'm as upset as you are.' When asked about the editorial executive who wrote the headline, Graham replied: 'I'm afraid he won't talk to anyone.'[54] The *Standard*'s editor, Lou Kirby, former deputy editor of the *Daily Mail* under Sir David English, told me: 'Unquestionably, the headline was unfortunate, but I wouldn't put it any stronger than that.' Indeed, Kirby complained about the headline to his 'back-bench'. But then why wasn't the headline – 'CND ''Holding Hands With the IRA'' '

– changed in later editions? Kirby says: 'We were not able to change the headline because of production problems in the foundry.' However, this explanation rather conflicts with the evidence from his deputy editor, Roy Wright, who told the Press Council: the headline was 'an accurate summary of what the story was about'.

The *Standard*'s story produced no less than 13 complaints to the Press Council. One complainant, Peter Cormack from southeast London, said the implication that CND was in collusion with the IRA was a slander. The Press Council agreed. In a refreshingly quick adjudication, the Council ruled that the story

> was irresponsible in the extreme . . . Readers were likely to believe it meant that CND was in association or collusion with the IRA. The Press Council accepts the evidence that some readers did. The headline was unacceptably sensational. It was also misleading. The newspaper had ample opportunity throughout the day to revise it but, while reducing its size and prominence in later editions, continued to repeat the same words.

It is difficult not to notice that as December 1983 approached, the month when the cruise missiles were scheduled to be installed at Greenham, many papers were increasingly keen to portray the peace women as violent. Take this *Daily Express* leader: 'On Sunday, with thousands of equally dotty and demented friends, these 'peace' thugettes attempted to storm the air force base, tearing down a section of perimeter fence and injuring policemen'.[55] Or this from the *Sun*: 'In reality they are behaving like the female yobs they are . . . If they are going to behave like football hooligans, the time has come to draft in some police who won't stand any nonsense.'[56]

Inside stories – 'Disillusionment, Leaders and Manipulation'

The structure and nature of the Greenham peace camp – non-hierarchical, collectivized and independent – meant that the women depended greatly on two factors for their campaign: their own morale and, perhaps more importantly, public support.

As the women's protest mushroomed throughout 1983, there were a number of attempts by Fleet Street to undermine their morale and play down public allegiance and sympathy. A week after thousands of women had descended on Greenham for the 1983 Easter demonstration, the *Daily Star* published this front-page story – 'Pack Up And Belt Up – The Verdict Of Britain's Women On Greenham's Protesters'.[57] The paper, whose editor Lloyd Turner is strongly opposed to unilateral nuclear disarmament, added: 'Britain's women today give their verdict on the marathon peace vigil of the Greenham Common protesters. And after 18 months of headlines and public debate on the siting of cruise missiles in Britain their message is clear – pack up, go home and give us a break.'

The basis for this story was a MORI opinion poll, but there was little evidence that the vast majority of Britain's women were calling on the Greenham campers to 'pack up and go home'. Fifty-eight per cent of women in the sample did have an 'unfavourable' opinion about the protesters and 51 per cent of the men held a similar view. But this was hardly conclusive and in fact the poll showed that another 60 per cent said that Greenham had made no difference to their own opinions on the nuclear issue. The *Star*'s editorial added: 'What will hurt these militant feminists most of all – it is the women of Britain who are most contemptuous of their actions'.

When a *Daily Star* reporter went to Greenham to tell the women the results of the poll, he was asked to provide a list of the questions which were put to the public. He refused. This made some of the women highly suspicious of the report. As Jane Dennett said at the time: 'If people were asked if they approved of us breaking the law in the course of our protest, then I can understand that most people would say they did not approve.'

Another device which was prominent in the coverage throughout 1983 and early 1984 was to show how the peace camp had betrayed its origins and lost support because of the life style and behaviour of the women themselves. One notable example of this was a feature in the *Daily Mirror*, a paper which had previously given sympathetic coverage of the peace movement. On 11 July 1983, a double-page spread was entitled: 'Inside Greenham – Sad Truth That Shattered A Dream'. Written by freelance journalist Nicky Kirkwood, the report was illustrated by a woman with safety pins piercing her cheeks, lips, nose and ears. 'There are no more than three of four genuine pacifists living there on a regular basis,' wrote Kirkwood. 'The rest use Greenham and the worthy cause of peace for their own ends. This is why Greenham Common is losing public sympathy, losing support and the dedicated women behind the movement working from their London headquarters recognized that fact.' The *Mirror* provided no evidence for this assertion about 'losing public sympathy' or any attribution that the London office had 'recognized that fact'.

The *Mirror* feature also contained many of the prejudicial themes that characterized much of the coverage. The peace women were scroungers ('women went off to the pub to spend their social security benefits'), drug users ('a regular feature of camp life') and lesbians ('sadly, there's some truth in this, and for some, this is the very reason they came here and the reason they stay'). The rest of the article concentrated heavily on the unsanitary conditions at Greenham. However, she declined to mention some of the main causes of the squalor. Namely, that Newbury District Council had banned the use of tents and had also removed any self-made structures. In addition, that vigilante groups had cemented the water supply.

When asked by *Tribune* why these facts were not mentioned in her article, Kirkwood replied: 'That is common knowledge.'[58] She added: 'My piece did not knock the women of Greenham. They are knocking themselves. I was trying to see Greenham through the eyes of someone who was newly arrived there.' However, Andrew Wiard, a freelance photographer who regularly visits Greenham, said:

> There is no evidence that the reporter had ever strayed more than five yards from the main gate ... People like those she described have been there since the beginning. But the authorities would not have brought in the Thames Valley police, the Ministry of Defence, an RAF regiment with guard dogs and the Queen's Own Highlanders to protect the base [if it was] from a handful of women with pins through their noses.[59]

Six weeks later there was another attempt to undermine the spirit and morale of Greenham and discourage potential supporters. On 5 September 1983, the *Daily Mail* published this story by Stewart Payne – 'Women Who Have Turned Greenham Into A Squalid Mess'. The report ran: 'The Greenham Common Peace Camp was shunned by the women who founded it as it celebrated its second birthday in rain-soaked squalor yesterday ... It is the women-only environment with its hostility to men, the infiltration by leftist groups and the general squalor, that made the pioneers feel this is no longer their place.' Much of the article contained an interview with Ann Pettitt, who had organized the original march to Greenham. She made some criticisms about the conditions of the camp and the ban on men. However, what the *Daily Mail* failed to tell its readers was that Payne had not spoken to Pettitt. According to Pettitt:

> I did not give this interview to anyone representing the *Daily Mail*. About a week earlier I had given an interview over the telephone to a woman journalist who said she wrote for the *Mail on Sunday*. But this interview was not the basis for the quotes which appeared in the *Daily Mail* on the 5 September, and in fact has not been published to my knowledge.[60]

Pettitt also says that the source of the *Daily Mail*'s quotes was an article in the *Reading Evening Post* published two weeks earlier. But, even more importantly, she says: 'In that article [the Evening Post], my critical remarks about the Greenham Common Peace Camp are balanced by a number of important qualifying statements. I would never have agreed to that article being published in such an abbreviated form and have this balance destroyed.'[61] Pettitt alleges that the *Daily Mail* selected her critical remarks about Greenham and published them, while omitting her crucial qualifying comments which were more favourable about the peace women. 'What you have done is to extract word-for-word some of the statements made to the *Evening Post*,' she wrote to the *Mail*. 'The overall sense which results is a distortion of the original. My permission was never sought by you to do this, nor do you acknowledge the source of your quotes to be an interview given to another newspaper.'[62]

The evidence certainly supports Pettitt's very serious accusations. Her interview in the *Reading Evening Post* appeared on 18 August 1983, two and a half weeks before the *Daily Mail* article. I have compared the two, and the quotes attributed to Pettitt are virtually identically the same and in the same order. Here are some of the comments from Pettitt which the *Mail* chose to leave out: 'It's difficult to criticize when you know you are not prepared to make that sacrifice yourself. I am indebted to those who do ... I would try to ensure the peace message gets across and isn't obscured by the public's blind prejudice to the image of the women. We need people at the camp because the issue of cruise has not yet been resolved.'

What happened was that on Friday 2 September 1983 Pettitt received a phone call from a reporter who said he was from the *Newbury Weekly News*. 'He said he wanted to read an interview back to me to "check,"' said Pettitt. 'The interview which he read out was the one I had given to the *Reading Evening Post* ... I agreed that this was an accurate account of what I had said since the supposed *Newbury Weekly News* reporter stressed several times that the interview would be published in full.'[63] Pettitt later checked with the *Newbury Weekly News* who said that no reporter had telephoned her on Friday 2 September.

Three days after that telephone conversation, Monday 5 September, the *Mail* article was published. Pettitt was furious: 'I feel that the extracts published [in the *Mail*] are a distortion of the original sense of the interview, in which my critical remarks about the Greenham Common peace camp were balanced by a number of important qualifying remarks.' Gordon Cowan, the *Mail*'s managing editor, replied:

'We did not lift material from the *Reading Evening Post* or from any other newspaper.'[64]

Such attempts to demoralize Greenham's supporters with out-of-context criticisms were almost par for the course by the end of 1983. In fact, the peace campers had, to some extent, anticipated the press hostility. They knew that Fleet Street would come looking for leaders and personalize the campaign. And so a strategy was worked out which would, they hoped, preserve their independence and collectivity. Whenever a Greenham woman was interviewed by the press, she began by making it very clear that she was only speaking for herself and not as the 'spokesperson' or 'leader'. That she was only giving her personal view. Indeed, once a name had been mentioned several times in the papers, the woman concerned would then either refuse to be interviewed or ask the journalists to talk to the other women. Sometimes she would even leave the camp completely to avoid further publicity.

This desire to have no leaders is confirmed by this extract from some training notes drawn up for the blockade of the base at Greenham on 13 December 1982:

> Women organizing themselves into autonomous groups of about ten makes a large decentralized action far easier to co-ordinate and service. More important, forming small groups allows women to get to know one another well; provides a basis of trust and mutual support for the action; makes decisions easier to reach; and avoids the need for 'leaders'. It also makes it easier to absorb individuals into the action at the last minute.

This strategy worked relatively well for the first two years of the camp's existence. So much so that a reporter remarked in exasperation during one protest: 'It's all so damn decentralized'.[66] It was the perfect compliment for the women. They had set out to have no leaders and no hierarchy and it was working. As the *Financial Times* acknowledged:

> Their extreme diversity is what makes them infuriatingly impossible to classify by those who like their politics tidy. Male commentators in particular are baffled by them, and any attempt to shuffle them into a recognizable socioeconomic category or a common political or even peace party has had to be abandoned. The women are not attached to the Labour Party, CND or any other organization.[67]

However, it was also a high-risk strategy. The peace women had to rely on Fleet Street not to create 'leaders' and then bring in personalization and charges of manipulation of protests. Even if they didn't exist. And, as the time drew near for cruise to be installed, so the idea of 'no leaders' collapsed in the view of the press. This was revealed by an article in the *Mail on Sunday* on 20 November 1983. Entitled 'Sharp Tactics Behind Those Woolly Hats – The Shadowy Agit-Prop Operation Which Is Manipulating Greenham's Peace Women', the feature provided little evidence except for a quote from an anonymous police officer. Its premise was that the apparently mindless peace women were being manipulated by a trio of leaders based in London called the 'Inner Cabinet'. The paper doesn't say when, how or where this 'group' met except that 'it deliberately keeps a low profile and is difficult to penetrate'. In addition, that: 'Nothing happens there by chance. In short, the Greenham Common action is one of the most sophisticated agit-prop operations ever seen in Britain . . . Greenham Common is all about cynicism – cold, hard and calculating.'

Rather more specific allegations were made by the *Daily Express* in early 1984. Just one week after an *Express* story on Greenham had been censured by the Press Council as 'abusive and untrue', on 16 March 1984, Sarah Bond was despatched to the peace camp. Like many reporters, she went there undercover posing as 'Sarah Jennings'. Two weeks later, on 7 April, her series of articles was previewed by her paper thus: 'Read about the women behind the tent-dwellers. Shrewd, articulate manipulators who pull the power strings – and sleep in the comfort of their own homes.' Two days later, Bond reported: 'The frontline troops of Greenham's ''peace'' women are being used as pawns in an orchestrated campaign to destroy Britain's nuclear defences. I can reveal this today after sharing the squalor of their camps and penetrating the secrets of the cynical organization behind the Greenham phenomenon.' Her co-reporter, Tony Dawe, claimed: 'Exposed: Gang Of Four Who Pull The Strings'. He named four women – Helen John, Rebecca Johnson, Sarah Hipperson and Jane Dennett – who 'rule the roost at Greenham Common camp. But they are not seen there so often these days'. In fact, Johnson was at the camp throughout Bond's stay and lived at the camp for seven out of the 12 months in 1983. Dennett was also at the camp in March and April 1984. Sarah Hipperson was not at the camp because during November 1983 she had fasted for 30 days in Holloway prison and then lost two stone in weight. She was also in prison during Christmas week and so was unable to return to the camp. The paper didn't provide any evidence that these women were in fact 'leaders'. Interestingly, the *Express* 'leaders' were Johnson, Hipperson, John and Dennett while the *Mail on Sunday* named Lynne Jones, Jane Hickman and Helen John.

The *Express* also alleged: '£17,000 In Bank As Frontline Goes Hungry'. This was completely untrue. The bank statements for the women's joint account at Lloyds in Newbury clearly shows that between 9 March and 17 April 1984 their credit was never higher than £5,247.24p. On the day the article was published the credit was £4,287.24p. So what was Bond's evidence for £17,000? She says: 'I was told by one long-term resident there was £17,000 in the bank.'[68] Also that there was 'general talk about buying a house in Newbury or a mobile kitchen for the camps'. But she hadn't seen any bank statements.

There were hints of sympathy in Sarah Bond's articles for the Greenham women: 'It was sad to see. For at the heart of the camp was genuine dedication and a commitment to building a brave new nuclear-free world.'[69] But this was buried amidst accusations about 'leaders' and 'manipulators' with only circumstantial evidence. Still, the *Express* had had its revenge.

A non-male zone – including women, not excluding men

When the Greenham women voted unanimously not to allow men as residents at the peace camp, there were several reasons for their decision. The most obvious one at the time was that the men were shirking their domestic duties at the camp, behaving irresponsibly and dominating meetings. But there was a more fundamental reason. It was that Greenham was a unique opportunity to involve Britain's female population in the nuclear debate. The peace camp provided the potential conditions whereby ordinary women could directly participate in political action without being inhibited by orthodox political processes. In other words, the vote was designed not to exclude men, but to include women. As Dr Lynne Jones explains:

> It's not because the women are hostile to men, but because they feel the need for space to develop their own ways of working. They see more hope for the future in the political processes emphasized by the women's movement – shared decision-making, non-hierarchical, leaderless groups, co-operation and non-violence – than in the hierarchical and authoritarian systems that prevail in mixed groups.

The Greenham women also developed a feminist analysis of the nuclear debate. 'They saw the nuclear arms race at one end of the spectrum,' said Alison Whyte, 'at the other end of which was the violence of individual men towards individual women. They did not believe that the problem was Rambo's gun, but rather Rambo himself'.[71] It was the Greenham women's belief that there was a direct link between the militarism inside the base and male violence outside it that incurred the wrath of Fleet Street. Hence the *Daily Express* columnist Jean Rook:

> If the militant leaders of the 30,000 women surrounding Greenham Common with linked arms are about to take over the world they're claiming to save, I'd rather be blown sky-high than survive in the grip of the feminist ring-leaders. This is no Chain of Peace. This is war – Women v. Men ... It leaves me wondering why these militants are using the nuclear issue as a launching pad for their anti-male frustrations.[72]

Sections of Fleet Street hence used Greenham's feminist analysis as a way of undermining their cause. This was illustrated by a feature in the *Sun* entitled 'I Meet The Greenham Manhaters' which promoted the image that most of the peace protesters were not 'normal' women at all. The article concentrated almost totally on the fact that many of the women at Greenham were lesbians. The *Sun* assumed, without providing any evidence, that this meant they all hated men. 'The women of Greenham's lament,' wrote Jean Ritchie, 'is not for MAN-kind – they are manhaters, every one of them ... Cruise missiles may have been the reason the camp was established, but its reason for surviving and continuing is that it provides an open meeting place for the women to reinforce each other's hatred of men.'[73]

But there was also a more traditional male response from Fleet Street (still very much a male preserve at editorial management level) to the Greenham protest. This was that these women should not be involved in such serious matters. For the press, the women's moral and often emotional methods of protest only confirmed their prejudice. That they were not fit to have a role in such a sensitive matter as the nation's defences. This was the view of Peregrine Worsthorne, the *Sunday Telegraph*'s editor and a member of the pro-NATO Committee for the Free World, when he wrote:

> Disarmament negotiations, unless they are to prove disastrously destabilizing ... require cool nerves, clear heads, and an ability to calculate the exact consequences of every move down to that of the smallest pawn – a chess grandmaster's skill. Imagine, however, the effect on a chess grandmaster of having a crowd of women breathing down his neck while pondering the next move, all seeking to influence his judgement by reference to moral principle, even to the point of dangling their babies under his nose.[74]

This idea that women did not have a significant part to play in the political debate and their real place was back in the kitchen was promoted by the *Sun*. Hence this editorial: 'We accept that when the women began their siege of the nuclear base they did so because of genuine fears for the safety of humanity ... They ought now to recognize that they have a duty to the families they left behind and the children they took to share their hardship. In humanity's name, they must all go home. Now. This day.'[75]

Some women journalists argue that this failure to take women's political actions seriously was directly linked to editorial management's opposition to allowing women journalists a greater influence in their newspapers. According to Bel Mooney, the former *Daily Mirror* and *Sunday Times* columnist,

> There is an inescapable connection between the lack of proper opportunity for women within newspapers, and the scant respect shown to the women who read those newspapers, and the false stereotypes of women peddled by those whose advertisements give newspapers necessary income. It is the tabloid 'models 'n mums' packaging which refuses to acknowledge the independence, courage, resourcefulness and intelligence of half the population.
>
> Talk to the average deputy editor for ten minutes about the women's page content, and it soon becomes clear that his ideal reader is a bargain-basement Beatrice, ready to lead her man ever upwards in the question for a material 'Paradiso'.[76]

This 'scant respect' in the context of the coverage of Greenham was revealed in, of all places, the *Guardian*'s women page. Compared to the rest of Fleet Street, the *Guardian*'s women's section provides by far the most space for feminist views and issues, and the paper's general coverage of Greenham was often exemplary. However, between late 1981 and February 1984, according to the women page's secretary Pauline Willis, the Greenham women were not taken seriously by all the editors. Willis said this was mainly due to the page's editor Frances Cairncross, a financial journalist who later joined the *Economist*. According to Willis, who was secretary throughout that three-year period, Cairncross

> repeatedly refused to go to Greenham, even for an investigative trip. When, on 8 November 1983, Jill Tweedie wrote a stirring article concerning peace, and received hundreds of supportive letters, not one appeared on the page. And again on 20 December 1983, when Jill [Tweedie] wrote on Greenham, the next letters

page only contained three relevant letters – one requesting that men should be included, one condemning the 'violence' of the women and one which was vaguely supportive... In the case of politics, she [Cairncross] wrote in one of her pieces, 'women are either uninterested or too timid to express their views on paper'.[77]

'The editor gets upset when you talk about peace'

Despite the hostility that the Greenham protest provoked among Fleet Street's editorial management, there were a number of mainly women journalists who did try to report the peace camp in a fair-minded and sympathetic manner. On the Conservative tabloids any attempt to portray the positive aspects of Greenham, particularly in late 1983, was, of course, almost impossible. As one *Mail on Sunday* journalist told me: 'Greenham is a non-subject for the *Mail on Sunday*. If I wrote a story sympathetic to the peace women, it would be turned against them by the associate editors.' Given the paper's coverage, that should come as no surprise.

But what was more disturbing was that there was also pressure on journalists who reported Greenham for the reputedly liberal papers like the *Sunday Times*. Take the case of Suzanne Lowry, one of the most experienced women journalists and editors in Fleet Street. On Tuesday 4 October 1983, Andrew Neil spent his first day as editor of the *Sunday Times*. That afternoon he summoned Suzanne Lowry, editor of the 'Look' section (women's pages) since May 1981, to his office.

'I want to redeploy you,' Neil told her.

'Why is that?' asked Lowry.

'There's too much about Greenham Common,' said Neil.

'But there have been only two articles in the past two years', replied Lowry, 'and anyway, it's a major issue.'

'Yes, well, perhaps I mean there's too much of the Greenham spirit,' he said.

Neil told Lowry, former editor of the *Observer* and *Guardian* women's pages, that he was appointing a new editor for 'Look'. He offered her voluntary redundancy or a new role as a feature writer. Lowry decided to leave the paper and was replaced by Joyce Hopkirk, former editor of *Cosmopolitan* magazine.

What Neil meant by the 'Greenham spirit' later transpired in a letter he wrote to the then *Sunday Times* columnist Bel Mooney. Neil said:

My complaint, among several others, about 'Look' was not about the number of Greenham Common articles ... but about a Greenham Common spirit on the pages: a dour, humourless, militant feminism. That should not be taken as anti-feminist: since October [1983] I've hired more women than the *Sunday Times* employed, and intend to continue to place them in important positions on the paper.[78]

Neil maintains that his decision was based on professional not political factors: 'I did not like the heavy, drab nature of the 'Look' pages. I wanted a change of pace and there were too many Greenham Common-type articles in that section. I wanted to put them in the news pages ... I haven't ruled out Greenham as a feminist issue for 'Look'. It was simply a question of balance with the news pages.' However, the *Sunday Times* editor did acknowledge: 'I was fed up with reading every week in the news pages some concocted story about Greenham or nuclear waste. The *Sunday Times* is not frightened about taking on the nuclear industry, but I wanted to do it properly.'

The irony of Suzanne Lowry's departure was that there had been only two articles in two years in the 'Look' pages, and she had to fight to get even those published. From mid-1982, *Sunday Times* executives and management openly discouraged any attempt to publish features on Greenham. 'The paper is absolutely full of Greenham. Why do you want to do it,' Lowry was told by one executive. At one meeting of the heads of departments in late 1982, Lowry suggested a 'Review' front-page article on 'Peace and Feminism'. Her male colleagues looked aghast at such an idea and it was never taken up. They argued that there was already plenty of stories about Greenham in the news pages.

But Lowry did manage to slip in two articles on the peace camp in the 'Look' section. The first was published on 19 December 1982 – 'Greenham And The Web Of Life'. It was a sympathetic and committed piece by Leonie Caldecott who had just won the Catherine Pakenham Award for young women writers for an article on the peace women in Japan. Although it was published, the then *Sunday Times* editor Frank Giles commented after reading it: 'I don't like this emotional writing.'

The second feature almost never saw the light of editorial day. Lowry had asked Bel Mooney, a regular *Sunday Times* columnist at the time, to write an article on the involvement of women in the whole issue of the nuclear debate. 'I was not at all sympathetic to the separatism or the ''folkiness'' [of the Greenham women] and had written as much,' Mooney later noted. 'Yet after a long, cold day outside those gates I was impressed by those tenacious granddaughters of the suffragettes. I set out to write a piece that would (fairly) describe what I saw.'[79]

When Lowry took Mooney's feature to the editor Frank Giles, he disapproved and wanted to spike it. However, after two hours of spirited argument, Giles, a former Foreign Service diplomat and former member of the Military Services in the War Office, eventually agreed to publish. But only if Lowry conceded certain cuts and changes. Giles then proceeded to remove large chunks from Mooney's piece. One of the most significant acts of subediting involved Mooney's description of a meeting of Lady Olga Maitland's Women For Defence. In her original script Mooney wrote: 'Women cram the small room, in tens not thousands.' The published version ran: 'Women cram the small room, in tens not *yet* thousands.' It was a tiny but highly important change. Here's another one. The original: 'This group of women [Women for Defence] . . . wants to keep the bomb for insurance.' This became: 'This group of women . . . wants to keep the bomb for *reassurance*.'

A much more substantial change by Giles was the complete removal of the following passage:

> The astonishing fact is this: they [Women for Defence] and Winston Churchill, who is beaming in the front row, and indeed the whole government, are themselves frightened enough of the scruffy women at Greenham to counter them by all the power of wealth, organization and even by sombre and symbolic trips to the Berlin Wall.

Giles was absolutely adamant that Churchill, head of the Campaign For Defence And Multilateral Disarmament at Tory Central Office and a former *Sunday Times* journalist, should not be mentioned in the article.

After the feature was published, on 10 April 1983, the 'Look' section received a huge postbag with 70 per cent of the letters sympathetic to the Greenham women's stand. As for Giles, he later denied the charge of censorship: 'I am quite unaware of any concrete examples of this,' he said. 'As regards spiking stories, I am here to ensure that stuff that goes into the paper is not offensive not obscene and not objectionable in nature.'[80]

Giles's successor as editor of the *Sunday Times*, Andrew Neil, was equally hostile to the peace movement. In November 1983, a month after Suzanne Lowry's departure, he took a group of the paper's senior journalists to lunch at the 'Gay Hussar' restaurant in Greek Street, Soho. According to two reporters who were at the lunch, Neil said he was not in favour of taking the Greenham women seriously or covering the issue. 'The government are not concerned about the Greenham women,' he commented.

This had been evident within two weeks of Neil becoming editor. On 22 October 1983, the peace movement held their biggest-ever demonstration with up to 400,000 people marching through the streets of London. Ten days earlier, *Sunday Times* journalist Joan Smith was asked to write a general preview of the mass protest. Smith knew that management were well aware of her sympathies with the peace movement, so she was very careful to attribute her information and sources, particularly on the strength of CND. However, when Anthony Bambridge, managing editor (news), read her piece he frowned and said: 'We have to be very careful with these stories. This reads like a handout from CND. Couldn't we have a quote from the Ministry of Defence or Lady Olga Maitland?'

'But that's not the point of the story,' replied Smith. 'And anyway, who does Lady Olga Maitland represent? She has no constituency.'

Bambridge, a former *Economist* journalist, later told her: 'Look, it's not me. I just thought the deputy editor [Brian MacArthur] might complain.' Smith's article on the peace movement was not published as scheduled on 16 October 1983. Instead, the day after the mass CND march, on 23 October, the *Sunday Times* published this editorial:

> It [the demonstration] was the last great gasp of a campaign which has clearly failed, and whose outer fringes could now turn to increasingly desperate activities to stop by violence what could not be stopped by democratic means . . . The case for cruise is strong, and the imminent arrival of the missiles is a matter of some relief.

Two months later, 30,000 women descended on Greenham for a mass protest against cruise missiles. The day before, on Saturday 11 December 1983, Joan Smith phoned through her story from Newbury – a preview of the demonstration. She then drove back to the *Sunday Times* office in London later that evening and bought a first edition of the paper. However, when she got home and opened the paper she was appalled to see that an executive had put inverted commas around the word 'peace campaigners' in her report. Smith immediately rang the news editor Anthony Bambridge to complain that this had been done without her permission. He then agreed to remove her by-line for later editions, although her story didn't appear anyway because of reports of the TV debate on the nuclear war film *The Day After*.

Andrew Neil now admits that he may well have been the executive who inserted the inverted commas around 'peace'. 'I may have done it,' said the *Sunday Times* editor, 'but I honestly can't remember.' Neil added: 'I didn't believe that CND or unilateral nuclear disarmament would bring peace, so I started that [use of inverted commas for 'peace'] but it only lasted a couple of months . . . In retrospect, maybe it was a wrong decision, but I was strongly opposed to CND. It stood for everything I believed was wrong about the defence of this country.'

By early 1984 Smith, who was an expert on the nuclear issue and covered most of the stories on the Greenham peace women, was becoming increasingly frustrated. 'Stories that might damage the nuclear industry were no longer welcome at the *Sunday Times*,' she later reflected.[81]

Matters came to a head on 25 January 1984, when Smith was summoned by Bambridge for a general talk as part of a series of discussions with editorial staff. Early in their discussion, Bambridge commented: 'The editor gets upset when you talk about peace.' Then later he said: 'We live in difficult times. The editor feels you have got into a rut on nuclear matters. He would like to see you broaden your range. He would like to see you in the paper more often.' She then asked how often. Bambridge replied every week ideally. Smith then pointed out that she had 46 stories published in the past 44 weeks, many of which were non-nuclear and much more than the average *Sunday Times* journalist. Bambridge appeared uncomfortable at this: 'You are to be congratulated. I am having a terrible time. You are not the only one who is thinking of leaving.' Two months later, on 31 March 1984, Smith left the *Sunday Times*.

For many of the refugees from the *Sunday Times*, like Suzanne Lowry and Joan Smith, the issue of Greenham gave the paper's executives and editors a focus for their opposition to feminism. But it also illustrated that Fleet Street's editorial management, by and large, do not take women seriously as far as political and social issues are concerned. For the senior editors the Greenham women's protest had no substance. And, according to Bel Mooney, who also left the *Sunday Times*, there is a direct link with how women are treated inside newspaper offices. In other words, they are not taken seriously. She recalls how as a columnist for the *Daily Mirror*

Richard Stott [now editor, then features editor] warned me that I was 'too serious' . . . Mr Molloy [the editor] had promised me I could write anything tough-minded and controversial. I now found I had been deceived – my function was to chat about stars, slam television personalities and speculate on whether blondes are taken less seriously than brunettes. I was told, too, 'Mirror readers don't understand irony,' and 'Women readers aren't interested in politics,' and criticized and censored at every turn.[82]

Clearly, the experience of several women journalists who covered Greenham bears out this attitude of many male editors. It was almost as if peace and feminism were just too much to handle. And, as Suzanne Lowry found out to her cost, they were.

A different kind of pressure was exerted on Jean Stead, one of the most experienced journalists on the *Guardian*'s staff. She had been news editor from 1970 to 1979. In 1975 she was a leading candidate for the editorship of the paper after the retirement of Alastair Hetherington, but was unsuccessful and later became an assistant editor.

Stead was one of the first *Guardian* journalists to cover Greenham. Like many of the paper's women reporters, she was sympathetic to their protest. Along with some colleagues, she took part in the Embrace the Base protest in December 1982, and was a regular visitor. On Saturday 29 October, Stead paid one such visit while she was on holiday. When she arrived at the camp she was told by one of the women, Jane Dennett, that they were planning a big demonstration and had collected bolt-cutters to bring down the perimeter fence. Stead was also told that no-one from the *Guardian* was there to cover it. Unaware that her colleague Paul Brown was at another gate, she naturally decided to report the story from the main gate.

Later that day, hundreds of women surrounded the fence and then outmanoeuvred the police to bring down the fence. As Stead watched the women climb up the ladders she noticed a girl called Skeeta being arrested. Skeeta had just come back from Sicily where she had broken her arm in a peace protest but it had not mended. And so as she was dragged away by police, Skeeta screamed in agony because of the pain. Stead immediately took a photograph of the incident. But within seconds she was arrested, despite showing her Metropolitan police press card and identifying herself as a journalist. She was then put in a police van and driven into the base where she shared a small room with ten other peace women for about an hour. It was only when she caught the attention of a Ministry of Defence police commander and told him she was a reporter that she was released. He hastily apologized, although a police inspector still tried to confiscate her film. The MoD commander was clearly embarrassed and reproached the police officer. He then drove Stead back to Newbury, apologizing again along the way.

Such harassment revealed another side of the enemies of independent reporting. Clearly, it wasn't only the editors who became upset when journalists mentioned the dreaded word peace.

Greenham – the issue ignored

How many people thought about American cruise missiles being installed in Britain before the Greenham protest in September 1981? Certainly the women's mere presence and their level of support at demonstrations ensured media attention and the nuclear arms race subsequently came under much closer public scrutiny. But was the press coverage about the women themselves, or the nuclear weapons they were protesting about? Jean Stead of the *Guardian* has no doubts: 'If you can't face the facts of nuclear war then deny them. That seems to be the attitude of many journalists who either ignore or make fun of the peace movement . . . Many reporters tend to skirt away from the facts and reality of nuclear war.'[83]

The lack of investigation into the technical aspects of cruise was the glaring absence in the reporting of the Greenham protest. Perhaps this was because defence correspondents rarely covered Greenham. And there was also the problem of institutional secrecy in the Ministry of Defence. But that was only part of the truth. It doesn't explain the absence of articles on the role, power and effect of the 96 cruise missiles.

The reaction of the news editors to the Greenham women was that they were demonstrating for peace in only a broad, emotional context. And so they were treated as a news *event* rather than a political movement. The press came to the camp to find out about their life styles, sex lives, 'leaders' and organization. For most of Fleet Street the issue of cruise was of secondary importance. This was despite the fact that the women's protest was highly effective, which was acknowledged by no less a figure than General Charles L. Donnelly Junior, commander of the American air force in Europe. In a statement in the American magazine *Aviation Week*, he said that the demonstrations at Greenham had disrupted the deployment of cruise msisiles. Air force officials 'remained surprised' at their persistence, he added.[84]

The press perception of the Greenham women was focused on two levels. Firstly, that some of them (housewives, Christians, the 'ordinary' women) were sincere and well-meaning, but misguided and irresponsible. This was typified by an Ann Leslie feature in the *Daily Mail* entitled 'The Fantasy Of Greenham Common'. Ironically, the piece did try to focus on the key issue of the nuclear arms race, but it was also full of classic *Daily Mail* cynicism: 'How terribly sincere and loving they all are, their wind-roughed faces exuding that joyous right-eousness I've met over the years among so many cult followers, ranging from the Moonies to people who've smilingly assured me that the Martians have landed.'[85]

This comparison with the Moonies sums up perfectly much of the second level of perception, namely that the Greenham women were social misfits ('burly lesbians' – *Sun*[86]) and deluded militants ('the fruitcakes of Greenham, they seem to have lost all touch with real life' – *Daily Star*[87]). In addition, the *Daily Mail*'s analogy with the Moonies promoted the image that the Greenham women were unrepresentative, despite the fact that every opinion poll since 1983 has shown at least 55 per cent of British people oppose cruise missiles.

But, above all, the portrayal of the Greenham protesters was really an extension of how most of Fleet Street see women involved in political struggle generally – illogical, emotional, woolly-minded and sentimental. There were exceptions, of course. Probably the most fair-minded and tolerant article was by Anne Robinson, the *Daily Mirror* columnist and assistant editor, who wrote:

> I didn't find myself among a group of lesbian subversives. Most of the women I could just as likely have bumped into in a bus queue. Just a few were frighteningly tough, unforgiving and silently hostile because of the way they've been treated by the press. The conditions are foul. Not because of the dirt, but because of the cold, the wet, the icy winds and the lack of hot water or proper lavatories.

Robinson added: 'What the Greenham women suffer from more than anything else, I decided, is a distorted public image.'[88]

Precisely.

7. The 1983 General Election— a One-sided Affair

'I hope you have read the election programme of the Labour Party. It is the most fantastic and impractical programme ever put to the electors . . . This is not socialism. It is Bolshevism run mad.' Philip (later Lord) Snowden, election broadcast on behalf of the National Government, 17 October 1931.

'Pick up the Communist Manifesto and it might be Labour's. The two have chilling similarities.' *Daily Express*, 20 May 1983.

Press attacks on the Labour Party during general elections are not a new phenomenon in British politics. Ever since organized labour posed a threat to organized capital, the press barons have wheeled out their big battalions to blast away at Labour's large but ill-equipped ranks. During the 1923 general election campaign the *Daily Mail* was telling its readers that the Labour Party was 'a mere wing of the Bolshevist and Communist organizations on the continent'.[1] In June 1945, the *Daily Express* ran a headline – 'The National Socialists'[2] – which took its cue from Winston Churchill's remark that Labour would 'have to fall back on some form of Gestapo' if they were to implement their manifesto. Then in the 1979 general election it was the turn of the *Mail* with a front-page banner headline – 'Labour's Dirty Dozen – 12 Big Lies They Hope Will Save Them'.[3] That was a Conservative Central Office hand-out.

However, the difference in 1983 was that the Labour Party had precious little artillery with which to fire back. In past election campaigns they at least had papers like the *Daily Herald* and *News Chronicle* to prop up the *Mirror*'s traditional allegiance. And even papers like the *Times* and particularly the *Sunday Times* had a semblance of political independence, whereas now they are mere cheer leaders for the Conservative Party. But in 1983 the Tory government secured the editorial support of 74 per cent of Fleet Street's total daily circulation with only 44 per cent of the actual vote.

Such an imbalance was compounded by the radical nature of Labour's manifesto for the 1983 campaign. It was entitled *New Hope*

For Britain, not one national newspaper supported the major policy proposals. It was virtually an unprecedented situation. Even the *Daily Mirror* had to acknowledge: 'Labour is now taking a different road from the past'.[4]

Indeed it was. For in the past decade Labour had moved steadily to the left, especially after the defeat of the Callaghan government in May 1979. New radical policies were adopted on defence, the EEC and the economy. This was augmented by the establishment of an electoral college in January 1981, which widened the franchise for the election of the Party leadership. In addition, mandatory reselection of Labour MPs was set up to tighten the links between the parliamentary party and the constituency workers.

This shift to the left enraged Fleet Street. Mandatory reselection was reported by the *Daily Mail* as: 'The Fascists of the new Left, ruthless and intolerant, are out to grab decisive control of the party.'[5] Walter Terry, then political editor of the *Sun*, described it as 'the militants, Trotskyites, hidden Communists, loonies, nuts (there are an amazing number around) tugging the strings'.[6] The *Daily Express* preferred: 'Facing the Marxist Firing Squad'.[7]

And by the time of the 1983 election campaign, Fleet Street had not changed its tune. Labour, in their eyes, had been taken over by small groups of 'extremists' who had hijacked the party for their own revolutionary ends. That was the view of the large bulk of the press. In other words, Her Majesty's Opposition was not a legitimate political party. And, sadly, that was reflected in the papers' coverage of the 1983 campaign.

Manifestos, Nissan and the *Daily Mail* rebellion

On Tuesday 10 May 1983, the day after Mrs Thatcher announced the poll date, the *Daily Mail* published a news story which reported how the election would be between 'on the one hand a Thatcherite Tory government, on the other a revolutionary alternative'. In the paper's centre pages, under an anonymous by-line, Labour's programme was summed up as: 'Spend, spend, spend, is the motto of Labour's most leftwing programme ever. The Party is pledged to take Britain out of the Common Market and abolish the House of Lords. Mr Foot's men are pledged to one-sided disarmament.' In the *Sun* that morning the paper's 12.9 million readers were offered a clear choice: 'between building on the achievements of the past four years, bought at a high price in hardship and sacrifice, or moving into a new domain of doctrinaire socialism, red in tooth and claw.'

It was a taste of things to come, but not too surprising. Opposition MPs were more interested in the *Daily Mirror*'s editorial stance. The following day the paper gave them their answer on its front page. It was probably the most unconvincing endorsement the *Mirror* has ever given the Labour Party:

> Labour believes Britain should withdraw from the Common Market. The *Mirror* believes that would be reckless . . . Labour wants to scrap all of Britain's nuclear weapons and shut the American nuclear bases in Britain. The British weapons are irrelevant compared with the nuclear arsenals of the United States and the Soviet Union. They could be abandoned tomorrow without weakening our defences. But the bases could not. They are part of the NATO defence of the West.
>
> They were welcomed by past governments, Labour and Conservative, as keepers of the peace. They still fulfil that role. In a nuclear war, there would be no hiding place for neutrals . . . If Labour is to plan Britain's way out of the slump then a voluntary incomes policy is essential.

The paper added that they broadly agreed with the rest of the Party's programme on economic and social policy. The editorial concluded: 'Though Labour's decisions are sometimes wrong its instincts are usually right.'[8]

The *Mirror* had supported Labour – just. But it was hardly surprising that SDP MPs like Tom McNally were shaking their heads in bewilderment after reading such a paradoxical endorsement. After all, on defence, the EEC and a major section of economic policy, the paper had agreed with the SDP/Liberal Alliance.

By the time the Official Opposition party's manifesto was released the following Monday, 16 May, the campaign was hotting up. This was the *Times*'s reaction:

> The policies which the Labour Party has put forward are based on an illiberal sense of overweening officiousness which sits only too easily with the attitudes displayed at Labour Party conferences by the bullies of the block vote . . . The atmosphere created by an incoming Labour government would be xenophobic, illiberal, syndicalist and confiscatory.[9]

As far as reporting the contents of Labour's manifesto went, most of the popular press found this a rather difficult task. On 17 May, the *Daily Mail* employed its columnist Paul Johnson to do the job. Under the headline 'Britain In Bondage – The Truth Of Labour's Election

Plan: It Contains 80 New Curbs On Freedom', this was his analysis: 'Labour's astonishing election manifesto is the biggest and most comprehensive assault on our liberties ever proposed by a major British political party. It contains more than 80 new restrictions or legal obligations. It is a Magna Carta for the snoop, the inspector, the informant and the form-maniac.' The *Mail* had devoted two centre pages and 1,700 words to Labour's programme but hardly a reference to the Party's actual policies. Instead of allowing the paper's readers to make up their own minds, they were presented with sub-headlines like 'Power On Prices', 'No Hope For Britain' and 'Threat Over Wages'. An editorial added that it was 'the real juice of the fruit of extreme socialism'. And yet the *Sun* and *Daily Express* managed a factual, if very brief, summary of the main planks of Labour's policies.

Two days later, on 19 May, the Conservative manifesto was given a rather different reception. 'Up, Up And Away – The Tory Way' was the *Mail* 's headline over a centre-page report with the by-line of 'Daily Mail Election Team'. There were extensive quotations from the document, particularly on the 'economic recovery'. There were two paragraphs of criticism – one from Michael Foot, Labour's leader, and one from Ken Livingstone, the GLC leader. The *Sun* saw it as 'Maggie's Vision Of Great Days For Britain'. But for the *Daily Express* the Tory manifesto was not rightwing enough. Under the headline of 'Is Tebbit Too Timid?', the paper's leader continued: 'The Tories have rolled back union power a little. But only a little. Jim 'Pussyfoot' Prior tried the softly-softly approach . . . Norman Tebbit, the present Employment Secretary, is an altogether different animal. But does even Mr Tebbit go far enough? The manifesto does not make secret postal ballots obligatory for strike decisions.'

It was left to the pro-Conservative *Daily Telegraph* to take a more sagacious, independent stance. They devoted a lot of space to Labour's manifesto and the paper also criticized the Tory government on unemployment. On 20 May, for example, a *Telegraph* cartoon showed an imperious Mrs Thatcher rushing by in her campaign bus past a long queue of unemployed people at a bus stop. Some of the paper's more partisan readers wrote to complain. William Deedes, the editor and a former Tory Cabinet minister, replied: 'With respect, I disagree. Unemployment is a serious issue. We are an independent Conservative newspaper not, even during a general election, an organ of propaganda.'

On the news coverage of the campaign, the story that dominated the party press conferences in the first two days was a front-page *Daily Mail* report entitled – '35,000 Jobs Lost If Foot Wins: Japanese Would

Scrap Plan To Build Giant Car Plant Here'. Michael Kemp, the paper's motoring correspondent, reported:

> The Japanese car giant Nissan is to scrap plans for a £500 million British plant if Labour wins the general election. Up to 35,000 new jobs are at stake, many in areas of high unemployment which are Labour strongholds. It is Labour's commitment to pull Britain out of the Common Market that is scaring Nissan, makers of Datsun cars. The firm wants to be inside the EEC to benefit from European free trade without tariff barriers.[10]

The *Mail*'s evidence was a quote from a Nissan official: 'If Labour wins the election it is impossible to see how Nissan leaders in Japan can base a Common Market plant in Britain.' The paper's editorial, headlined 'Labour Scares The Japanese', said that the loss of these 35,000 new jobs would only be the tip of a very large iceberg if Labour were to win the election.

However, virtually everyone at Nissan strongly denied the story. Lord Marsh, the company's only UK employee, 'formally, officially and totally' denied that Nissan would refuse to locate a factory in Britain if Labour won the election. Marsh, a former British Rail Chairman, was a consultant to the company about a possible UK car-making plant. He said: 'I don't know where the story came from ... There is no Nissan office in Britain, and there are no Nissan executives in the UK who could have made such a statement ... I have spoken to Nissan by telex. I obviously want to know what the hell is going on and their reaction was one of total bewilderment.'[11] The *Daily Telegraph* reported that 'Nissan officials in Tokyo said the reports were ''utterly groundless'' but it is no secret that access to the tariff-free Common Market is one of the main attractions of investing in Britain.'[12] Brian Groves, Nissan's marketing director in Tokyo, told the *Observer* that the story 'came out of thin air, we have nothing to do with it. If you ask me it came out of Mr Kemp's head'.[13] Kemp says this quote was taken out of context: 'He [Groves] also said a lot of other things which the *Observer* didn't publish ... I replaced him as the *Mail*'s motoring correspondent. He has a dry sense of humour.'

Even the *Daily Mail* had to acknowledge another Nissan spokesman's denial: 'We think that if the Labour Party got to power it would not substantially affect our proposals. It is difficult to see Britain pulling out of the Common Market.' Undaunted, the *Mail* followed up the story on 17 May with another front-page story: 'Car Job Row Boils Over – Catastrophic If We Pull Out Of The Common Market, Warn

Industry Chiefs'. The denial from Nissan was buried inside on page two in the fifteenth paragraph.

Sir David English, the *Mail*'s editor, was asked about all these denials at the Press Council hearing. He replied that it was not unusual for stories to be denied if the truth was inconvenient. In this case, said English, Nissan had issued no official denial. I asked Michael Kemp about all the denials. He responded: 'They denied the story because they couldn't or wouldn't get involved in internal politics . . . It is a fact that no company or business is ever seen to involve itself in politics, particularly in foreign countries.'

Labour, of course, were horrified by the story as it undermined both the party's policy on the EEC and on its promises to create jobs. Jim Mortimer, Labour's General Secretary, wrote to the *Mail* on 27 May: 'It seems that the *Daily Mail* fabricated a story for the purposes of persuading readers not to vote Labour.' When asked about the allegation of fabrication, Kemp told me:

> I'm not being political, but the Labour Party had suddenly found themselves in an embarrassing situation which could have had a political backlash. They were in that situation because they had not thought through their policy that Britain should leave the Common Market. I'm not being political here, but it would make no sense at all for a foreign motor company to consider setting up a factory in Britain because, if having done so, they would have faced all the uncertainty about whether Britain would leave the EEC or not.

A more sustainable charge from Mortimer was that the news story contained unequivocal, unconditional assertions – 'Nissan *is* to scrap plans' and '35,000 new jobs *are* at stake' – without adequate evidence. In other words, the paper presented conjecture as facts. When asked about this distinction between an established fact and a report from a comment from a Nissan official, Kemp replied: 'That's splitting hairs. The headline is qualified by the story and I stick by the story . . . Mortimer shifted his ground at the Press Council hearing and moved on to the presentation issue. He originally tried to make out the story was a lie and then he changed his mind.' On why the *Mail* didn't give the Nissan denial more prominence, Kemp again said that was 'splitting hairs . . . You can always criticize a story but I know what I wrote was correct and I stick by it.'

On 3 June 1983, the Press Council ruled that the *Mail* did not make up the story, but that the report's headlines and presentation were not sufficiently qualified. Also that insufficient prominence was given to Nissan's denial.

The Nissan story was just one report which angered many *Daily Mail* journalists. One *Mail* subeditor described it as 'a transparent piece of propaganda'. The paper's coverage of the campaign's first ten days even worried some Tory voters on the staff. They said that the *Mail* had 'gone over the top' in its support for the government and that it would be counterproductive both in terms of the paper's credibility and circulation.

One of the main sources of discontent was the almost complete lack of coverage of Labour's policies and views. Here's a typical edition, Saturday 14 May. The front-page headline is – 'Maggie Comes Out Swinging', along with – ' ''We Aim To Banish The Divisive Cloud Of Marxist Socialism From Our Land'' '. Underneath, the news story began: 'Mrs Thatcher set the mood of the Tory election campaign in her opening speech last night by declaring herself an uncompromising freedom fighter. She called on the British people to join her in a crusade to sweep Marxist socialism away from the life of Britain for ever.' On to page two – 'Maggie Goes on to the Attack . . . And How'. Still no mention of Labour's policies. Turn a couple of pages and a news story about the Opposition. Entitled 'Labour's Department Of Dirty Tricks Case No. 1', the news report is headlined – 'Scare Tactics On Home Loans'. It continues: 'Shadow Environment Secretary Gerald Kaufman struck the first blow for Labour's dirty tricks department yesterday with a claim that the building societies had a secret plan to raise mortgage interest rates immediately after the election.' There was no by-line on the story.

That issue of the *Mail* sparked off the resentment among many of the journalists. One of these was Tully Potter, a subeditor on the paper since 1974. What was fuelling this discontent? 'There was no coverage of the Labour Party point of view,' he replied. 'Instead, there was constant vilification of Michael Foot.' The presence of Paul Johnson in the office was also resented. 'Many of us at the *Mail* don't consider Paul Johnson a journalist. He was brought in to do a propaganda job,' said Potter. 'We also felt that the articles on page six and the feature pages by Robin Oakley and Johnson were saying things that should have been in the leaders . . . What upsets me is that the same people who are the first to condemn *Pravda* or the *Morning Star* for propaganda, as I myself have done, are only too ready to do exactly the same for the Conservative Party.'

Potter felt so strongly about the issue that he proposed a resolution for an NUJ chapel meeting called to discuss a routine pay claim. And so on Monday 23 May 1983, Potter put the following motion to over 60 *Daily Mail* journalists:

This chapel feels that the *Daily Mail*'s general election coverage has so far been too one-sided in favour of the Conservative Party and is therefore losing readers. We request the Editor to give more space and a fair degree of prominence to unbiased factual reports and the positive proposals made by the other political parties.

The motion was seconded by John Ebblewhite, a financial journalist who is a Conservative Party supporter. And several Tory voters on the editorial staff spoke in favour of the motion, because of what they saw as the lack of political balance in the news reporting. The motion was passed by 57 votes to 7, and it also received almost unanimous support from the *Mail*'s NGA Imperial Committee. It was an unprecedented decision. A text of the NUJ's motion was then delivered by the then FoC Mike Edwards, the paper's industrial editor, to Sir David English, the editor since 1970. The chapel also agreed to reconvene before 1 June 1983, to consider the management's response. English's reply was swift and clear:

Dear Mike [Edwards], Thank you for your letter of 23 May. I have read it and I reject it for the following reason: it is unacceptable that the NUJ chapel – or anyone else – should attempt to interfere with or pressure the editor on the contents of the newspaper for which he, and he alone, is responsible. Incidentally, it is untrue that the *Daily Mail*'s election coverage is resulting in a fall in readership.

English was backed up by Christopher Ward, former editor of the *Daily Express*, who said: 'Newspapers are edited by editors, not shop-floor gatherings of disgruntled journalists, and the *Mail* editor, Sir David English, was right to stamp firmly and swiftly on the mini-revolt in the ranks.'[14] In addition, Tully Potter was approached after the chapel meeting by a *Daily Mail* executive who told him that the motion had done 'great harm' to the paper. 'I have a loyalty to the truth,' said the executive. 'The limitation is how we perceive the truth. How we see it with the facts before us.' What disturbed Potter about this remark was that it implied that his loyalty to the company was more important than his conscience. The *Mail*'s two leader writers, Russell Lewis and Christopher Nicholson, also didn't approve, although they did apparently acknowledge the feelings of the staff.

However, *Guardian* journalist Martin Linton, himself an ex-*Daily Mail* reporter, argued that both Ward and Sir David English had missed the point of the issue raised by the NUJ motion. 'The journalists were complaining for professional reasons,' said Linton, 'at the way they believe the *Mail* has been presenting opinion as fact, printing accusations without answers and failing to publish a straight account even of the Labour Party manifesto. They have no illusions that they can change the politics of the *Daily Mail*.'[15] Indeed. And even Peter Grover, Sir David English's deputy editor, admitted to Potter that their coverage of the election campaign had 'gone too far'.

Potter, who is now the paper's NUJ FoC, believes that the coverage improved after his chapel motion. That is debatable. But what it did achieve, perhaps for the first time, was at least to give editors and executives a nudge to their conscience. Grover's remarkable admission is testimony to that.

The economic recovery – all roads lead to Williamsburg

Most general elections are notable for the prominence given to a series of economic reports, assessments and statistics which can often swing the balance of power. The 1983 campaign was no exception. The government's record on the economy, particularly on unemployment, was clearly going to be the major issue for the Labour Party. And that was where they tried to target their attacks.

The first opportunity came on 17 May 1983, the day the Central Statistical Office published the monthly industrial production figures. These figures revealed that in April 1983, the index for industrial production had fallen by 0.9 per cent. Also that there was a decline of 5.6 per cent in manufacturing investment for the first three months of 1983. Some of the papers reported this correctly. 'Recovery Hopes Hit By 1% Fall In Output', said the *Times*. Even the *Sun* had to admit – 'Big Clash As Output Drops'. But the *Daily Telegraph* managed to tell a different story – 'Production Rises By 1.4%'. The *Daily Express* did the same with 'Tory Cheer As Output Takes Off'. The report continued: 'Good news came for the Prime Minister yesterday with heartening evidence that industry is pulling out of the doldrums. Figures from the Central Statistical Office showed that output in the year's first quarter was higher than at any time since 1980.'

What the *Express* and *Telegraph* had done was to massage the March figure and average it out with the results for January and February to get a quarterly instead of a monthly figure. And so the 1.4 per cent was the average of three months. The authoritative *Financial Times* rejected this approach. Under the headline of 'Recovery Hopes Are Dampened', the paper reported on 17 May: 'Hopes that Britain's industrial recovery might be gathering speed were dampened yesterday by official figures which showed a slight fall in production for

March ... The March figure will disappoint the government, as it underlines the relative weakness of the recovery.'

Three days later a secret economic report was either ignored or belittled by most of the press. Francis Beckett, an NUJ official working as a Labour press officer during the election campaign, had obtained a set of confidential minutes of a recent meeting of the National Economic Development Council (NEDC) from TUC sources. The document revealed that at a NEDC meeting on 2 March 1983 a paper on Britain's industrial performance was extremely pessimistic. Sir Campbell Fraser, President of the Confederation of British Industry, said that the paper was 'so gloomy that people reading it would want to get the first boat out of the country'. The CBI's Director-General, Sir Terence Beckett, believed that although the paper had been agreed at working level, 'publication would not be productive because there was not a single item of cheer in it'. But perhaps the real revelation was that Sir Geoffrey Howe, the Chancellor of the Exchequer, had decided to defer the report's publication for two months, despite the fact that it had been agreed at working level.

Beckett passed the document to Neil Kinnock and he used it as the main focus of his speech on the evening of Saturday 21 May 1983 in Manchester. He also handed copies of the minutes to the press, as well as his speech. Kinnock claimed that the NEDC report had been 'suppressed' by the government and that its gloomy predictions led to Mrs Thatcher calling an early election. That Saturday afternoon Conservative Central Office issued a denial to the Press Association.

This is how the press reported the story. The *Sunday Express* ignored it. The *Sunday Times* buried it within a general news story about the election. In the *News of the World* the NEDC report was a personal battle – 'Fury At Doom And Gloom Taunt ... A furious row broke out last night between Chancellor Sir Geoffrey Howe and Labour MP Neil Kinnock over a secret "gloom and doom" verdict on the economy'.[16] The *Mail on Sunday*'s report was headlined – 'Kinnock's Attack Backfires'. The paper added:

> There was Tory glee last night after Labour Education spokesman Neil Kinnock launched a campaign rocket against the government and it backfired. Mr Kinnock, speaking in Manchester, accused the government of suppressing an economic report which said that Britain's slump would worsen under present policies ... But the Chancellor Sir Geoffrey Howe pointed out that Mr Kinnock was confusing two separate reports. The first, discussed at the March NEDC meeting, dealt with inefficiency and lack of competitiveness

of British industry and was withheld from publication with TUC agreement. But the second report in April was very gloomy about short-term job prospects, and was published in the normal way.[17]

None of the Sunday papers except the *Observer* published the key comments of the CBI executives. Instead, Howe's interpretation was presumed to be the correct version of the truth. The next day (Monday), the coverage was more balanced, with the *Daily Telegraph* revealing the report's details. The NEDC paper concluded that Britain had had lower growth than any country except Switzerland, had lost 1.3 million jobs in manufacturing industry which was equal to the total loss in the previous 15 years and between 1979 and 1982 unemployment had increased twice as fast in Britain compared with other industrialized countries. At the Conservative Party's press conference that morning the NEDC report was not pursued by journalists except for two open-ended questions.

Later that day, Monday 23 May, another damaging and critical appraisal of Britain's economy was published. This was the quarterly analysis of the National Institute of Economic and Social Research (NIESR), an independent, forecasting body supported by several British companies and banks. NIESR is funded by grants from the Ford Foundation and the government. Their assessment of the economy contradicted the view of Patrick Jenkin, the Industry Minister, who said: 'The latest economic indicators all point upwards.' The Institute had a rather different interpretation of economic reality.

On industrial output, NIESR said: 'There is not much doubt that total output stopped falling around the middle of 1981 and that there has been some increase since. But it is not easy to say how large the increase has been ... There must in fact be some doubt as to whether the upturn in output during 1982 has been sufficiently clear and large enough to warrant description as a cyclical recovery at all.'

On unemployment: 'Registered unemployment currently outnumbers recorded vacancies by 25 to one, a relationship which has remained little changed over the past two years.' Inflation: 'The rate of inflation has continued to fall. The rate of increase in retail prices calculated on a year earlier, 12 per cent at the beginning of last year, was below 5 per cent in the first quarter.'

On economic growth: 'On unchanged policies, the rate of growth is forecast to slow to 1-1.5 per cent in 1984, when the contribution from stock changes is likely to be much smaller ... Taking the two years together (1983 and 1984), the rate of growth in prospect is not quite sufficient to halt the upward trend in unemployment.' The report concludes: 'At the present time there are strong arguments for more public investment . . . Per pound of budget deficit, public investment is a potent means of raising aggregate demand and reducing unemployment, much more so than income tax cuts for example.'

And so, apart from inflation, the NIESR was highly sceptical about the much-heralded economic recovery. The *Guardian* reported this accurately on 24 May – 'Economic Recovery "Will Fizzle Out Soon"'. But the same could not be said for most of Fleet Street. The *Daily Mail* saw the NIESR report as 'Britain Is On The Up and Up – More Cheerful News On The Economic Front'. The paper's news story led off with the increase in industrial output for 1983, which was correct, but ignored the 1984 figures. However, two paragraphs later, the *Mail* admitted: 'The Institute do not expect this year's predicted rate of growth to continue in 1984.'[18] Interestingly, the more the news story unfolded the more it was at variance with the headline of – 'Britain Is On The Up and Up'. The *Daily Express* took an only slightly dimmer view of the economy – 'The Bumpy Road Ahead To Recovery'. An anonymous *Express* journalist reported: 'Britain's economic recovery will gather pace this year but tail off again in 1984, a major economic report warned yesterday.'[19] The *Sun* ignored the report altogether.

Four days later, on Friday 27 May 1983, came far more dramatic news on the economic front. The Department of Trade revealed that Britain's current account trade deficit in April was £180 million. For the non-oil account the deficit was £834 million. Even more startling was the news that within the current account, Britain was importing more manufactured goods than exporting – for the first time since the Industrial Revolution. In other words, for the first time there was a manufacturing trade deficit.

Such devastating economic news would be enough to sink most governments. Indeed, it was widely believed that the balance of payments trade deficit of £31 million in June 1970 paved the way to Labour's defeat in that year's general election. The figure was announced on 15 June 1970, three days before the final poll. And the popular press gave it front-page treatment. The *Daily Mail* reported – 'Treasury Gloomsday – 18 Shillings For Your Pound in 1971'. The paper continued: 'The worst of all possible economic worlds, with stagnation and inflation. That is the picture of Britain's economic situation painted by the Treasury yesterday.' The *Daily Express* agreed – 'Trade Setback Dumps Gilts'. The *Times'* political editor, David Wood, who later worked for Conservative Central Office during the 1983 campaign, commented on 16 June 1970: 'Mr Heath and leading members of the Shadow Cabinet hope that the £31 million trade deficit will concentrate the electorate's mind in the last three days before the polls on the fundamental issues that face Britain.'

Three days later, on 18 June 1970, a Labour lead of 12 per cent, according to some opinion polls, had been wiped out and the Conservatives won the general election.

The 1983 trade figures, far worse than the 1970 deficit, were given a rather different reception from Fleet Street. Not one popular newspaper reported the story on its front page. Instead they were tucked away on inside pages balanced with a comment by the Conservative Trade Minister, Lord Cockfield, who said: 'Our export trade is doing well. Of course, the figures fluctuate from one month to another.'[20] This was the *Sun*'s reaction to the news that for the first time since the Industrial Revolution Britain had a manufacturing trade deficit: 'Shares Spree As Foreigners Back Maggie'. The news report added: 'Foreign investors went on a ''we're backing Maggie'' spending spree yesterday. They pumped millions of pounds into Britain as the opinion polls showed Mrs Thatcher heading back for No. 10. Even a dramatic plunge into the red of Britain's balance of payments did not dampen their enthusiasm.' The *Sun* then reported the export/import figures and added: 'But exporters described the figures as ''not too worrying'''. The story concluded with a quote from an anonymous stockbroker praising Thatcher and the comment by Lord Cockfield. This was described by Charles Wintour, the former *London Evening Standard* editor, as 'a contender for the most slanted story in the campaign'.[21]

On the day after those trade figures were released, Saturday 28 May, Mrs Thatcher flew to Williamsburg, the eighteenth-century colonial town in the United States, for a world economic summit. Accompanied by her media advisor Gordon Reece, the meeting of the world's most powerful leaders was turned into an international photo opportunity for the Prime Minister. That was a view widely shared, even by Mrs Thatcher's former Foreign Secretary Lord Carrington who said during that weekend: 'There is a temptation for leaders to attempt to make a bit of mileage out of these meetings. There is a temptation to go in front of the cameras and just say things.'[22]

It was a carefully stage-managed event with President Reagan breaking the summit ground rules to allow Mrs Thatcher a televised press conference on the Sunday afternoon before flying back to London. Apart from Reagan's endorsement, there was little direct evidence that the summit had supported the Tory government's economic policies unequivocally. Mrs Thatcher could only say at the press conference that there was general support for her view that there were 'no quick fixes' for the economy. But the *Daily Mail* headlined their story the next day – 'Maggie Wins All The Way – Summit Backs Britain's Road To Recovery'. The paper continued:

> Mrs Thatcher flew home from the Western Summit last night a winner all the way. Despite a last-minute attempt by the French to throw a spanner in the works, she got the six other nations to agree:
> ● that world recovery is on the way
> ● that Britain's sound money policies are the recipe for sustaining that recovery
> ● that they will all avoid protectionist trade barriers
> ● and that there is no quick fix solution for unemployment[23]

The *Express* whistled a similar tune – 'Maggie's Vision Of The Big Three – Leading World Role For Britain'.[24] So did the *Telegraph* – 'US Summit Boost For Tories'.[25]

The only evidence for such assertions came the following day with the summit's economic statement. Its contents, according to the *Financial Times*, were 'generally bland'.[26] The statement did give an undertaking to 'focus on achieving and maintaining low inflation', but it was a far from conclusive endorsement of Conservative Party policy. The press had other ideas. 'We'll Win Through The Thatcher Way', reported the *Daily Mail*. 'Maggie Leads On Road To Recovery', agreed the *Express*, although the paper also acknowledged: 'The detail of how these aims will be achieved was not spelled out. That suits Mrs Thatcher who gave the summit a new Saatchi and Saatchi-style slogan – "Quick cures for Quack Cures"'.

Clearly, Williamsburg was a useful filter for the press to pour through their notions of an economic recovery. This was despite the lack of real evidence of a sustained improvement. Even a Treasury Committee, under the chairmanship of prominent Tory MP Sir Edward Du Cann, cast doubt on such predictions. And this was the *Financial Times*, in a leader halfway through the campaign, on the alleged recovery: 'The economic outlook is still pretty bleak . . . the government has been lucky not to be more sharply attacked.'

The People's March for Jobs

Unemployment was always potentially going to be the most damaging thorn in the flesh of the Conservative government during the 1983 general election campaign. The number of people without a job had trebled to nearly 3.5 million since 1979. The issue was undoubtedly a vote winner for the Labour Party.

The event that did much to expose the government's record on unemployment during the 1983 election was the People's March for Jobs. Organized by the TUC, the jobless protesters set off from Glasgow on 23 April and were then joined by feeder marches before arriving in London for a rally on 5 June to be addressed by Labour leader Michael Foot. It was not long before the press dug their claws in. Here's a *Sun* leader on 26 April 1983:

> In rain and cold, 70 marchers set off from Glasgow for London . . . The idea began as a Trotskyite stunt. It will not create a single new job. Does anyone seriously imagine that there is some conspiracy by Mrs Thatcher to keep people on the dole at an estimated cost to the nation of £5,000 a head? Both Michael Foot and Len Murray originally opposed the march as a pointless waste. Why don't they tell the pathetic army to go back home.

The march continued to attract hostile comment and news coverage, particularly by the *Daily Express*. On 6 May 1983, the paper produced a news story by Peter Kent under the headline – 'Work Galore, But The Job Marchers Just Pass By'. The story ran:

> Hundreds of jobs were yesterday offered to 74 demonstrators marching on London to protest about unemployment. But the marchers turned down every one of the openings offered by the job centre manager. One protester raised his arm in a clenched fist salute and said: 'We are fed up with job centres and the cardboard cut-outs who work in them.' Then walking on he said: 'I'm sorry we have no time to talk.'
>
> The protesters, including punk rockers, several women and self-confessed Marxists, arrived in the market town of Carnforth, Lancashire, on the thirteenth day of the People's March for Jobs chanting, 'We want work . . . we want work.' But they were jeered by housewives on street corners. One group shouted, 'Bloody Trots, there's work if you want it.'
>
> And there was, offered by the Manpower Services Commission which forecasts that the Morecambe-Lancaster region around Carnforth will be 'a land of golden opportunity' within a year with thousands of jobs available. And a spokesman threw out this golden opportunity to the marchers. 'There are plenty of jobs available now. It is just a question of whether there are vacancies that match the jobs you are looking for. If you come in we'll give you a friendly, and hopefully, helpful response.'
>
> The Lancaster-Morecambe region which has jobs available has

an unemployment rate of 13.9 per cent compared with a national average of 13.5 per cent. The number of unemployed in the region is 6,610.

In fact, as the *Daily Express* itself later admitted, the jobs were *not* 'offered by job centre managers'. Neither were they 'offered by the Manpower Services Commission'. This could only have been the MSC office in Kendal as the next office is in Lancaster which the march only reached the next day. The Deputy Manager of the Kendal MSC office, Mr Harrison, unequivocally told James Milne, General Secretary of the Scottish TUC, that neither he nor the staff 'had any contact with the marchers during their stay in Kendal'.[27]

The alleged invitation by Jobcentre managers never happened. It was completely untrue. What had happened was that the *Express* reporter, Peter Kent, had visited the Jobcentre in Carnforth, gathered the number of vacancies and then approached the marchers himself with the figures. Kent later told the Press Council that he had included the phrase 'through the *Daily Express*' in his story to indicate how the figures were relayed, but that this was taken out by subeditors back at the office. However, the whole tone of the article, particularly the quoations by the MSC spokesman, indicated that the Jobcentre managers were talking directly to the unemployed marchers.

The *Daily Express* deputy editor, Leith McGrandle, admitted that 'the marchers were not approached by anyone at the Jobcentre in Carnforth'.[28] He agreed to publish a letter from Pat Smith, the People's March for Jobs National Press Officer. She immediately replied, stating: 'The *Daily Express* now acknowledges that their report was totally untrue... The report was a fabrication by your journalist, designed to discredit the marchers as not seriously seeking work, and to lend credence to the idea that the unemployed are shirkers and lay-abouts.'[29] McGrandle refused to publish the letter, saying it was 'both too long and covers much more than the one point of substance which I found in your complaint'.[30] Smith's letter was barely more than 300 words, but she agreed to shorten her reply: 'I have shortened my comments under the strongest protest. The space you are offering in no way constitutes an adequate right of reply.'[31] Once again the *Express* refused to publish her letter: 'We do not accept that "this story was quite untrue and was fabricated". We are not prepared to put up with simple abuse about "crude smears,"' replied McGrandle. Incredibly, the *Express*' deputy editor then wrote out a letter for Smith which 'we are prepared to consider for publication'.[32] She refused, accused the paper of censorship and decided to refer the matter to the Press Council.

In the *Daily Express'* Northern and Scottish editions, Kent had reported '400 Jobs But No Takers On The March'. The story asserted that there were more than 400 jobs in the Lancaster/Morecambe region. But, according to Scottish TUC General Secretary James Milne, 'I have confirmed with the Lancaster Jobcentre which covers Carnforth and Morecambe, that as of March 1983 they had 217 vacancies registered.'[33] In the same issue, 6 May 1983, the *Express* had included a leader on the jobs march. It repeated the untrue accusation about Jobcentre managers offering jobs, and added: 'The really significant thing about the People's March for Jobs is that it is so short of people. Fewer than 100 have reached Lancashire on their way to London from Glasgow . . . The March has all the hallmarks of a Leftie Road Show. No doubt it will swell to thousands when rent-a-mob drives out to join in at Potter's Bar for the last, short lap'.

The *Express* was censured by the Press Council for this leader and its news report: 'The newspaper published an inaccurate story and editorial . . . and its offer of a brief letter for publication did not fully correct this or give an adequate right of reply.' The *Express* published this Press Council adjudication on November 10 1983 – at the bottom of page 17.

There is evidence that the *Express* editorial was also guilty of misleading its readers. At the beginning of the march, the organizers had made it very clear to the press that there was never any intention to make it a mass demonstration. Each region had been told to keep its numbers below 50. This well-publicized upper limit was due to the cost of food, equipment, clothes, accommodation, full-time staff and literature. What happened was that 65 left from Glasgow, six joined them at Carlisle and they were later joined by five tributary marches.

But as the marchers approached London, the *Daily Express* again saw the spectre of the 'rent-a-mob' and 'clenched fists' in their midst. On 3 June 1983, two days before the big rally, the paper produced this editorial:

The march itself has been poorly supported though no doubt rent-a-mob will be out in force for the rally in London . . . Today's march is a cruel mockery of the jobless to exploit them for political ends. Unfortunately, the hard Left, which now controls the Labour Party, regards misfortune as a useful weapon against its opponents. Hence the March for Jobs. Taking to the streets is an extra-parliamentary activity at which Trotskyists excel . . . Labour's conferences for years have been near-Communist assemblies. These conferences wrote Labour's wrecking programme. Intimidated Labour MPs.

Drove out the moderates. The same kind of people, who rose with clenched fists to proclaim their triumph in Blackpool, are marching with clenched fists in London.

The reporting of the final rally on Sunday 5 June 1983 was notable for what is known as the 'numbers game'. At most unemployment marches, peace demonstrations and other protests, the press usually repeat the police assessment of the number of people involved. For the People's March for Jobs, however, there were some notable exceptions. The *Scotsman*, which firmly urged its readers to vote for the Alliance, reported – '150,000 Hail End Of Jobs March' – and noted how 'the three-mile-long column took two-and-a-half hours to snake its way across the city and into Hyde Park'. The *Daily Star*, another paper which rejected Labour, agreed on the figure of 150,000.

The police estimated between 15,000 and 20,000. They declined to include the marchers who were still entering the park an hour after the speeches had begun. Also that many spectators left to take cover because of the driving rain. The *Times* and *Guardian* agreed with the police and put it at between 15,000 and 20,000. The *Mail* also managed 'some 20,000 supporters' and reported: 'The People's March for Jobs ended yesterday amid claims of violence among the marchers caused by ideological clashes during the six-week trek.' The *Express* agreed: 'No more than 20,000'. Under the headline of 'Jobs Rally Flops As Thousands Fail To Turn Up', the paper added: 'Organizers of the People's March for Jobs put on a brave face yesterday when the final rally at London's Hyde Park won only meagre support.'

The *Daily Telegraph* put it at 'about 10,000' and claimed the march ended 'in chaos and confusion'. The *Sun*'s page two report managed even less. Under the headline 'Jobs March Fizzles Out In Rain', the paper reported: 'An embarrassed Michael Foot presided over the pathetic, rain-soaked end to the People's March for Jobs yesterday. The "magnificent 500" – as Labour supporters called them – straggled into Hyde Park in a downpour. And a crowd of little more than 5,000 was there to greet them.' The *Sun* also revealed Michael Foot '*looking* bewildered' and '*seemed* saddened by the flop'. Immediately above that story, another political rally was given rather different coverage: 'Superstar Maggie Is A Wow At Wembley', said the *Sun* and reported how the crowd cheered and roared. What the paper didn't mention was that the ecstatic 3,000 Young Conservatives were, in fact, carefully selected for the event.

But it was the *Daily Express* coverage, once again, that caused so much resentment among its own printworkers and the jobless marchers. In a final leader on the March the paper noted:

> The rain poured down yesterday on the March for Jobs rally in London. Most people will say: 'Serve them right.' For this was no honest outburst of anger from the unemployed. It was a political ploy – arranged by the extreme Left. And endorsed by the hapless leadership of the Labour Party and TUC. It was a dismal flop. Only a tenth of the numbers expected turned up to hear Mr Foot address the 'rent-a-mob'. The rally, like the march, was utterly false.

The printers were furious and particularly resented the first paragraph. The NGA demanded a right of reply. The *Express'* editor, Sir Larry Lamb, refused and so the first edition of the paper appeared but without the above editorial. Later editions carried the offending article.

It was an indication of how politically significant the issue of unemployment was during 1983 that so many newspapers went out of their way to discredit the March for Jobs. After all, two years earlier, an almost identical People's March for Jobs took place and was only sporadically attacked by Fleet Street. But then 1981 wasn't a general election year.

The red face of Labour

Ever since the Labour Party have been in a position to form a government – by themselves or in coalition – Britain's press have tried to portray them as being Communist wolves in sheep's clothing. In their polling day edition for the 1923 general election, the *Daily Mail* produced this headline: 'Moscow Funds For Rowdies – Labour Candidates Subsidized'. The paper alleged that Labour's parliamentary candidates 'received £300 apiece' from Bolshevik sources.[34] Two years later, on 25 October 1925, the *Daily Mail* produced – 'Civil War Plot By Socialist Masters – Moscow's Orders To Our Reds'. The basis for this story was a letter supposedly written by Zinoviev, president of the Third Communist International in Moscow, to the British Communist Party which the *Mail* described as 'the masters of Mr Ramsey MacDonald's [minority Labour] government'. Despite clear indications that the Zinoviev letter was a forgery, the story was given uncritical coverage by all the popular papers. Six years later, in 1931, MacDonald and his supporters deserted the Labour Party and formed a National Government with the Conservative Party.

Very little has changed. At almost every election various lists of Labour candidates with alleged Communist or Marxist sympathies are displayed with great prominence on the front pages of the popular papers. The 1983 campaign was no exception. In fact, Fleet Street tried harder than usual to show that the Labour Party was, as the *Sun* put it, 'penetrated at all levels by sinister Marxist forces'.[35]

On 16 May, the first day of real campaigning, the *Daily Express* produced this headline – 'Secret Reds ''On Way To Commons'''. The news report went on: 'Scores of Militants and Marxists will march into the House of Commons as Labour MPs after June 9, a former Labour MP warns today.' The allegation came from an SDP candidate, Neville Sandelson, who was publishing a book on the Militant Tendency. He didn't provide any names or figures except to say 'in considerable numbers'. An editorial added: 'With Mr Foot at No. 10, extremism would have its hands poised to clutch at the levers of power.' In the same edition, the *Express* headlined a story about the Labour leader's call for nuclear arms talks as 'Foot: Why I Trust the Kremlin'. The paper added: 'He [Foot] praised the Soviets for being ''sensible enough'' to reach an agreement. And although he denied being naive or the victim of a Soviet confidence trick, Mrs Thatcher is bound to exploit the opening and portray Labour as a soft touch for the Kremlin.'

Being a 'soft touch for the Kremlin' was exactly how the Conservative government wanted the Labour Party to be portrayed. Two days later, on 18 May, the *Express* provided a Tory Party Cabinet minister a platform with – 'Tebbit Slams Foot's Red Menace'. The paper continued: 'Labour was accused last night of bringing Communism into its policies for British industry. Employment Secretary Norman Tebbit claimed that no party except the Communists had ever planned such a massive attack on business and management.' The next day the *Sun* took this a stage further – 'Tebbit Lashes Out At Labour Communists'. This implied, of course, that there were Communists within Labour's ranks. Tebbit was, in fact, referring to an alleged similarity in policy.

That same day, 19 May, the Communist Party manifesto was published. The next morning, 'Red Shadows' headlined the *Daily Express* editorial:

> Pick up the Communist Manifesto and it might be Labour's. The two have chilling similarities. From unilateral nuclear disarmament to withdrawal from Europe, from economic controls to nationalization. The difference is that the Communists will not win a seat . . . The voters rumbled them long ago. That is why the clever Marxists have gone into the Labour Party. Mr Foot is no Communist.

> Doubtless he finds their support thoroughly distasteful. But his poli-
> cies have made him a tool of those who are foes of the democratic
> freedom he upholds.

This was not a sudden discovery by the *Express*. The paper produced
an *identical* response to the Labour and Communist manifestos in the
previous general election in 1979. 'The Red Face Of Labour – Communists Pick Same Policies', was the headline to a front-page news
report by John Warden on 11 April 1979: 'The Communist Manifesto made an astonishing appearance yesterday as the Red Face of
Labour. This ''carbon copy'' of policies is embarrassing for Mr Jim
Callaghan.'

The *Daily Mail* agreed with their rival's analysis on the alleged
Communist link in 1983 – 'You can hardly tell them apart'. The next
day, 21 May, the paper rammed home the message – 'A ''Marxist''
Manifesto From Labour'. The following morning a third national
newspaper, the *Sun* repeated the theme – 'Labour's Red Road – Labour
has moved so far to the Left that its manifesto bears an ''uncanny
resemblance'' to the Communist Party manifesto, SDP deputy leader
Dr David Owen claimed yesterday'.

But it was Douglas Eden, a member of the Council for Social Democracy, who was the chief instigator in using the press to paint the face of
Labour bright red. On 23 May, he wrote an article for the *Daily Telegraph* under the headline – 'Labour Radicals Consolidate Their
Power'. Eden continued: 'Labour's radical and revolutionary Socialists have consolidated their power in the party if its election manifesto
is anything to go by.' He then claimed that 55 Labour parliamentary
candidates had 'extreme left sympathies. These are men and women
whose attachment or attraction to Marxist-Leninism, or whose exceedingly sympathetic tolerance of this totalitarian philosophy in one or
more of its varieties is a matter of record'.

Ten days later, on 2 June, the *Daily Express* devoted a full page to
Eden's claims. By this time his list had been expanded to 70 Labour
candidates. Under the headline – 'Spot The Trots: Foot Bound To Be
Ruled By Reds', the paper's political editor John Warden named '70
Extremists Fighting Seats Labour Seems Set To Win'. These included
Neil Kinnock, Robin Cook, Stan Orme and Joan Lestor. The *Express*'
evidence for this assertion was a chart compiled by Eden. This revealed
that if you want to be a 'Labour extremist', all you have to do is write
articles for the *Morning Star*, *Marxism Today* or *Labour Monthly*,
to be involved with 'Soviet and Communist Party front organizations'
like the World Peace Council, oppose the expulsion of the Militant

Tendency and be 'associated with Mr Ken Livingstone's extreme left-wing political network'. The allegation of 'secret Reds' was not a tactic exclusive to the 1983 election. The *Express*, their political editor John Warden and Douglas Eden had done exactly the same in 1979. Their front-page headline during that election ran – 'Labour's Danger Men'. The basis for this story was a letter written by Eden with his friend Dr Stephen Haseler in which they named 43 'extremist candidates'.[36]

Accompanying the *Express*' 'Spot The Trots' feature in 1983 was this leading article

> Few of the people listed belong to the mainstream of Labour. Most of them represent the extreme Left of the party, cold doctrinaire advocates of the all-powerful, one-party state. They do not believe in democracy. Should they wield significant influence in the new Parliament we could be well on the way to becoming a carbon copy of an East European state. The men and women on the list tend to admire Karl Marx . . . In asking for your vote they are exploiting the traditional loyalty of Labour supporters. They do not deserve such loyalty. They ought not to get it.

One of the Labour candidates said by the *Express* to be one of the 'advocates of the all-powerful one-party state' was Robert Hughes, the leftwing Tribunite MP for Aberdeen North who is now in the shadow Cabinet. The 'evidence' for this was the fact that he had written articles for the *Morning Star*, *Marxism Today* and the pro-Soviet journals *Labour Monthly* and *Straight Left*. In addition, he was, according to the *Express*, involved in Soviet and Communist front organizations like the World Peace Council, British-Soviet Friendship Society and Friends of Afghanistan. In fact, Hughes had never been involved with any of the three 'front' organizations. The World Peace Council had simply made him a member without informing him or asking his permission. Hughes never even knew of his affiliation. The Labour MP had never heard of the other two bodies and made inquiries to find out if they existed. None of the people he spoke to knew anything about them either.

On the day the article was published, Hughes telephoned the *Express* office to point out he had never been involved in any of the three organizations. He mentioned that he also wrote for the *Aberdeen Press and Journal*, as well as the left press. The Labour MP's lawyers then wrote a letter of protest to the paper. Leith McGrandle, the deputy editor, replied that the *Express* saw no grounds for an apology, but would consider publishing a short letter saying that Hughes had renounced these affiliations. Hughes countered that he could hardly disown his affiliations to the British-Soviet Friendship Society and Friends of Afghanistan when they didn't exist! The *Express* then managed to produce two more 'front' organizations which had links with Hughes – Liberation and Voice of the Unions. This was correct. But there was little evidence, if any, that they were 'Communist front' bodies. The personal assistant of the *Express* editor, Morris Bennett, said that Liberation's leadership had *included* active members of the Communist Party.

In late February 1984, the case finally came before the Press Council. The *Express* said that they had accepted Eden's chart 'in good faith'. Hughes' solicitors then pointed out that the paper should have checked its information. The Press Council agreed. Its adjudication was that the *Express* 'published inaccurate information . . . a politically malicious and unjustified slur on Mr Hughes which should have been withdrawn'. The Council added: 'The newspaper failed to either substantiate or withdraw its allegation that most of the 70 Labour candidates it named were ''cold, doctrinaire advocates of the all-powerful, one-party state'' '.

Two days before the final poll of the 1983 election, on 7 June, the *Sun* produced a smaller list than the *Express* – and without the help of Douglas Eden. 'The Lefties Who Would Run Britain If Labour Won Power This Week', ran the headline across the paper's centre pages. 'Behind Foot are dedicated, ruthless men. Their reign will return this nation back to the days of Feudalism, Parliament will take a back seat and the men who take over will be the Barons who run the unions, the Red Knights who control the Party and the court jesters who'll turn farcical ideas into tragic reality', warned the *Sun*. Britain's biggest-selling daily paper then produced a series of mini-profiles of leading Labour politicians – 'The *Sun* gives the facts about Benn and Co. that every voter should know'. These included Tony Benn ('bent on the destruction of Britain as we know it'), Frances Morrell and Ken Livingstone among others.

On election day itself, Thursday 9 June, the *Times* evidently agreed with the *Sun*'s analysis. 'Don't Laugh Too Soon, The Fascist Left Is Just Biding Its Time', was their banner headline to a Bernard Levin piece attacking the Labour Party. And so it wasn't just the *Sun*, *Mail* and *Express* who were intent on linking Her Majesty's Official Opposition with sinister forces.

There is too much evidence to deny that these attempts to associate Labour with Communism and Marxism were anything but deliberate. Whether they had any real effect on the electorate is open to question.

The crude smears during the 1920s and 1930s elections coincided with Labour losing several polls. But then the Gestapo slur in 1945 appeared to have no influence on the voters. And yet 1983 was a bit special. For the first time, Labour was fighting on a truly radical, left-wing manifesto.

Why the *Daily Star* didn't support the Labour Party

By far the most eagerly awaited editorial decision in Fleet Street during the election campaign was whether the *Daily Star* would urge its 4½ million readers to vote for the Labour Party. Apart from the *Guardian*, *Sunday Times* and *Observer*, all the editorial pledges were known well in advance. And so it was the allegiance of the *Daily Star*, a popular tabloid with 82 per cent of its readers working-class, that the Labour Party were most keen to obtain in order to redress some of the political imbalance. This was because the paper had supported some of the party's policies and had attacked the Conservative government's record on unemployment. But there was a problem. The *Star* was owned by Fleet Holdings and had a proprietor called Lord Matthews. To understand why the *Daily Star* didn't support Labour, it is crucial to look at the paper's history.

The *Star* was launched in November 1978 to use up spare printing capacity and surplus editorial staff at the Express Group's office in Manchester. When Peter Grimsditch, a former *Sunday Mirror* executive, was appointed editor in August 1978, he went to see Lord Matthews and tried to persuade him to let the *Star* support the Labour Party. He argued that there was an obvious gap in the editorial market and pointed to what he saw as the decline of the *Daily Mirror*. Matthews listened patiently but refused. Grimsditch decided to ignore the issue of party political allegiance and instead the *Star* began to campaign on issues like rights for pensioners, social services and anti-racism – causes that wouldn't offend Matthews. The paper supported policies that were also backed by Labour, but the *Star* never actually came out for the party editorially.

But Grimsditch realized that the paper still lacked a political identity. And so in March 1979 he again visited Lord Matthews at his Trafalgar House office in Berkeley Street, central London. The general election was two months away and Grimsditch decided to take a chance. 'I want the *Star* to support the Labour Party in the election,' he told Lord Matthews. Once again his proprietor refused, but he did reveal the basic reason. 'I won't be able to justify it to the Board of Directors of Trafalgar House, having a newspaper that supported the

Labour Party,' said Matthews, no doubt mindful of the £40,000 his company gave to Tory Party funds for the 1979 general election campaign. But Grimsditch was unhappy: 'Well, I can't justify not supporting Labour, given the type of paper I'm producing.'

For the 1979 election Grimsditch and Matthews worked out a compromise. The *Star* wouldn't actually call on its readers to vote Labour but would back roughly the same social policies, like support for the National Health Service. Unfortunately, as Grimsditch now painfully admits, he was forced to write the most meaningless and politically innocuous editorials: 'Some of the leaders I wrote even I couldn't figure out. God knows what the readers made of them, particularly the leader for the 1979 election which to this day I can't understand.'

After the Conservative election victory in May 1979, which Matthews celebrated with a special lunch at the Ritz Hotel, Grimsditch was given a little more editorial licence. 'I don't mind you criticizing the Prime Minister providing it's fair,' Matthews told the *Star*'s editor.

However, this wasn't always the case. Every evening a copy of the *Star*'s leader was sent to the proprietor's office. Matthews rarely passed comment. But on Tuesday 12 June 1979, Grimsditch had written a leader attacking the Conservative government's first budget. 'Not everybody has a lot of income tax to save paying,' ran the editorial. 'So not everybody has that choice (of more money to meet extra VAT and mortgage payments). If you're in a mad scramble to snap up a colour TV before it goes up by six or seven pounds, spare a thought for the poor. Nobody else has.' At 8 p.m. the phone rang in Grimsditch's office. It was Matthews. 'There aren't any poor,' he told the *Star*'s editor. Grimsditch was too busy trying to get the paper out and wearily replied that he didn't have time to debate politics. But Matthews was insistent: 'You can just take my word for it. There are no poor in this country.' And so the phrase – 'spare a thought for the poor. Nobody else has' was changed by Matthews to 'spare a thought for those who can't afford one'.

But then the situation seemed to dramatically change during the 1979 Labour Party conference. At 7.50 p.m. on Wednesday 3 October 1979, Jocelyn Stevens, Deputy Chairman and Managing Director of Express Group papers, telephoned Grimsditch in his Manchester office and told him: 'You've got the go-ahead to support Labour.' Grimsditch was delighted and drove through the night down to Brighton for Labour's conference. There he met the *Star*'s political editor David Buchan who was also pleased that they could at last come off the political fence. Although Grimsditch was rather wary of

Stevens' decision, he felt confident enough to break the news to James Callaghan, then leader of the Labour Party, over lunch at the Grand Hotel.

Three days later, Grimsditch received another call from Jocelyn Stevens. The *Star*'s Managing Director had changed his mind! Stevens told Grimsditch that he could no longer support Labour because Lord Matthews had said he could not remain Chairman of the company with a pro-Labour newspaper. Stevens laughed off his earlier comment about the 'go-ahead'. Grimsditch now believes that that earlier decision was due to management having problems in negotiations with SOGAT, and so Stevens hoped to improve relations with the union's General Secretary Bill Keys.

In March 1980, Grimsditch was sacked, ostensibly because Derek Jameson had been appointed managing editor and the two weren't working well together. And there then followed a period of uncertainty although the paper remained broadly sympathetic to the labour movement.

It was the appointment of Lloyd Turner as editor of the *Star* in November 1980 that finally crystallized the paper's political stance. Turner, a former NUJ FoC at the *Daily Express*, agreed with Jocelyn Stevens that the *Star* should be left of centre and appeal to young industrial workers who were disenchanted with the *Mirror*. More important, with the aid of some market research, Lord Matthews was persuaded at last to let the paper move to the left.

And so began the campaigning period of the *Star*. They were the only national newspaper to support Michael Foot for the Labour Party leadership in late 1980. In the early months of 1981, the pro-Labour staff were delighted to see their own paper attack the Conservative government on the plight of the poor and jobless under the slogan of 'Thatcher's Britain'. Labour's leader was also impressed. 'Their coverage of unemployment was very good,' said Michael Foot, 'and some of their shock issues were, in my view, better than the *Mirror*'s, particularly on the pensioners'. So much so that Labour's leader would often come to lunch in the *Daily Star*'s boardroom with Turner.

Perhaps the first indication of discontent from the management of Express Group papers came in May 1981. Turner had written a leader calling on the *Star*'s readers to vote for the Labour Party in the local council elections. Lord Matthews was not too happy. 'You owe me one,' he half jokingly told Turner. Matthews was also complaining about the *Star*'s coverage of poverty and unemployment. 'Those stories are so miserable. They're upsetting people,' he once remarked to Turner. Mrs Thatcher, no less, was also unhappy about the *Star* and complained to Lord Matthews. According to Jocelyn Stevens, then Deputy Chairman and Managing Director of Express Group papers, this is what happened in the autumn of 1981: 'Matthews sent for me and told me that I was to instruct Turner that he must not attack Mrs Thatcher. I argued that this involved a fundamental change of policy. Matthews was not interested. Turner, when I told him, was incredulous. The *Daily Star* became another Tory tabloid.'[38]

It was not quite as simple as that, according to Turner. He says there were also commercial considerations, because the special issues on unemployment and pensioners were not attracting enough new readers, which was crucial for a popular paper. But Turner accepts the basic premise of Stevens' account: 'I knew the paper's policy was up for review ... There was some political pressure from the Conservative Party through Express Group newspapers, and I wasn't happy about it but there was no dramatic confrontation with Lord Matthews. He never directly ordered me to change direction.' But there was a change. Rick McNeil, a South African with strong rightwing opinions, was appointed by Turner as chief leader writer. The two had worked together on the night desk of the *Daily Express*. The *Star* also became very hostile to Labour's defence policy of unilateral nuclear disarmament.

The other determining factor was what Lloyd Turner saw as 'the leftwing takeover of the Labour Party'. By early March 1983, just after the Bermondsey by-election, Turner was disillusioned with the party: 'I was angry that the Labour Party was being taken over by default. I had private talks with some Labour MPs, but then I became upset because these MPs weren't doing the things in public that they were saying in private.' On two occasions, the *Star*'s editor contemplated writing front-page editorials calling on Foot to resign as Labour Party leader. And yet as late as 22 March 1983, deputy editor Ray Mills was telling Lancashire pensioner Joseph Lyons: 'I'm sorry you think we are turning Tory. I can assure you that the *Daily Star* would still like to see a Labour triumph in the next general election.'[39]

This attitude didn't last long among the editorial management. In fact, Turner had decided well before the election campaign that the *Star* wouldn't support the Labour Party. He even thought it might be *better* in the long run if Labour actually lost the general election. And so Turner called a meeting in early May with his deputy Ray Mills, chief leader writer Rick McNeil and executives Andrew Carson and Paul Burnell. They agreed not to support Labour and this news was related to Lord Matthews by Mills while Turner was on holiday. The rationale behind this decision was revealed in the *Star*'s first election editorial on 10 May: 'Can we trust Labour to resist the even more revolutionary elements who have infiltrated the party in the last few years?' Some of the staff journalists saw this as an excuse not to support Labour but, despite the fact that the majority of the staff are pro-Labour, they were not consulted.

Turner maintains that he wanted the *Star* to be an 'independent' paper. This was a forlorn hope on the editorial side, but their news coverage of the election campaign did give some substance to this claim. From the beginning the slogan was: 'The paper that gives it to you straight'. And, relatively speaking, it did. Their reporting of the inflation and unemployment figures was particularly fair and balanced with reactions from both sides. On the party manifestos, the *Star* provided a double-page table comparing the parties' proposals on the important issues.

But the litmus test of any national newspaper for a general election is always the final leading article. Although he had decided weeks before not to support Labour, Turner was unsure whether that meant championing the Conservative cause. David Buchan, his political editor, suggested that the *Star* should not come out for any party and have the slogan – 'Let the People Decide for Themselves'. This was rejected and Turner sat down to write the editorial. Two days before the final poll, Tuesday 7 June 1983, the front page of the *Daily Star* declared: 'Sorry Michael, We Can't Vote For You'. The editorial added:

> The *Daily Star* today declares that it can no longer support Michael Foot's 1983 Labour Party ... It is a decision which may be considered by some as a betrayal of our principles. But we have not changed. Our belief in the great principles of equality of opportunity, of justice for the working man remains rock solid. But the Labour Party HAS changed. And that is the main reason why we can no longer support it ... The militants with hard eyes and closed minds who want to put a stranglehold on the party and shackle its leaders to a manifesto which owes more to Marx than the facts of modern life.

In a long tortuous article, Turner continued:

> This newspaper believes in firm, clear leadership. And, like it or not, there is only one leader really in charge of a political party, a political philosophy in Britain today. That is Margaret Thatcher ... Britain's inflation is down by a tremendous amount – another example of Mrs Thatcher's determined leadership. But unemployment

is up. If Mrs Thatcher shows the same strength, determination and leadership in trying to solve unemployment and to get the economy firmly back on its feet, then we ARE in for better days.

On the evening before publication, Turner had showed Lord Matthews a copy of the editorial. He was well pleased. Turner claimed: 'We are not telling anyone how to vote ... The final decision is up to you not newspapers.' But this was not really true. By so firmly rejecting Labour and complimenting the government's leadership, the *Star* had done more than sit on the fence. In effect, taking into account the editorial's last sentence, the paper had supported the Conservative Party.

But perhaps the real issue is what would have happened if the *Star* had wanted to urge its readers unequivocally to vote for the Labour Party. Would Lord Matthews have allowed the paper to do so? 'I doubt it,' replied Turner. 'He really wanted Mrs Thatcher to win that election. If I had said to Lord Matthews that I wanted to support the Labour Party we would have discussed it. Then he would have said ''I don't agree'' and I would have had to resign.'

Foot, Thatcher and political leadership

It was Thursday 26 May 1983, during the Conservative Party's press conference at Central Office, Smith Square. After a statement and questions on rates and the environment, Ian Waller, the *Sunday Telegraph*'s political editor, stood up and asked Mrs Thatcher: 'Why is it that whereas you claim credit for curing inflation you say there's nothing you can do about unemployment?' The Prime Minister was stunned and glared back at him. She replied: 'I'm sorry, Mr Waller. You know you're totally and utterly wrong and, with due respect, you really have been doing some very selective listening during your presence at this press conference and very selective reading. Shall I give you some of my speeches and ask you to read them before you come and ask any more questions, if that is not too much of a burden?' But Waller stood his ground and repeated the substance of his previous question. Mrs Thatcher responded: 'Clearly, you have not been round with me or you know how to turn a deaf ear, because if you look back at my speeches you will find that one has said that repeatedly.'

Waller received a bundle of the Prime Minister's speeches within a couple of days but refused to be intimidated and returned to the theme of unemployment four days later on 30 May. But, clearly, the sheer ferocity of Mrs Thatcher's reply was due to her surprise at such hostile questioning from a member of the press corps. For, apart from the *Times'* Anthony Bevins, Waller was one of the few Fleet Street political correspondents to be critical of the Tory Party leadership over unemployment. This was despite the fact that the *Sunday Telegraph* is a staunchly Conservative newspaper.

It was an indication of the press's deference to the Prime Minister that such an obvious issue of 3.5 million jobless was not pursued with more vigour. Many of the reporters seemed almost awe-struck during the Tory press conferences. As Dave Rimmer commented in the *Listener* at the time: 'Criticize her bossy style as they might, none of her [Mrs Thatcher's] detractors in her own party can deny one essential fact: she has the press eating out of the palm of her hand. And what's more, they seem to love it.'[40] An example of this political deference came from Max Hastings, the *London Standard* columnist who is now editor of the *Daily Telegraph*, when he noted during an interview with Mrs Thatcher: 'I began to feel conscious of listening transfixed to the Prime Minister rather than steering the conversation very successfully towards the tough questions.'[41]

Such servility was clearly reflected in the stark contrast in the coverage accorded to Mrs Thatcher and Michael Foot during the campaign. The *Daily Express* was perhaps the most fawning to the Prime Minister. 'Maggie Swoops To Conquer – Foot Rocked By Snap Poll', the paper reported the election announcement.[42] The *Express* political columnist George Gale added: 'The Prime Minister remains the sun around which all other politicians orbit. They take their position from her. She might generally be regarded as lying on the Tory Right but, as far as present British politics are concerned, she is bang in the middle.'[43] In the same article the Labour leader was described as 'half socialist, half preacher, half politician, half ranter, half raver, half baked and half gone, this decent and intelligent man does not have about him the presence of our next Prime Minister.'

The *Express* provided even more evidence of political sycophancy in the shape of columnist Jean Rook. Her interview with the Prime Minister was headlined – 'Up, Up And Away With Wonderwoman'. Rook continued:

> Last time round the country she was only the brilliant blonde reaching for the sky and a dizzy place in history ... Surging down the runway at 145 miles an hour, I can feel Mrs Thatcher vibrating with crusading passion ... She's an astonishing bird. A plane in herself. Superwoman who could take off from Gatwick without her BAC 1-11 wings ... Mrs Big, Britain's Boss.[44]

Three days later, on 26 May, the *Express'* political correspondent Peter Hitchens, who until the spring of 1983 was a member of Michael Foot's Constituency Labour Party in Hampstead, reported – 'Michael In Dreamland'. He added: 'Michael Foot is living in two different worlds at once, wondering which is real and which is fantasy.'

Three days before Britain went to the polls, the *Sun* produced this profile of the Conservative Party leader: 'Soft Side Of An Iron Lady – It's The Little Things That Make Her So Special', ran the headline. Britain's biggest-selling daily paper added in a page-long feature: 'In public, she is Britain's toughest politician who never flinches from making a difficult decision. In private, she is caring, compassionate and concerned for the wellbeing of everyone.' The article managed to demonstrate 'her spontaneous generosity', 'her caring for her colleagues and opponents', 'her true compassion' and 'her devotion to her close staff'.[45]

This was the *Sun* on Michael Foot: 'Do You Seriously Want This Old Man To Run Britain?' asked the paper a week before polling:

> We see the vision of an amiable old buffer, his jacket buttoned too tight, his collar askew, his grey hair falling lankly... The party's leftwing wanted Michael Foot as a figurehead, a ventriloquist's dummy who would repeat whatever message was fed into his head. In him they found a willing dupe... Suspicion, if not hostility to the United States, is a permanent thread in his make-up. Nor should there be any doubt that Mr Foot is totally committed to the Trotskyite document which passes for Labour's election manifesto... In the name of sanity, would we entrust our destiny to him, would we hazard our fate as a nation on someone quite so alarming.[46]

Nor were these attacks on the Labour leader confined to the Conservative tabloids. Clive James used up one and a half pages of valuable space in the *Observer* to discuss the length of Foot's sentences and the colour of his suits, while referring to him as 'a floppy toy on benzedrine'.[47] The *Sunday Telegraph* described Foot as 'an elderly, ranting pamphleteer waving a stick in Hampstead'.[48]

If more evidence was needed that these personal attacks were based on political and not professional criteria, it came in the form of a written note obtained by Jill Craigie, Foot's wife. On Saturday 21 May, she picked up a piece of paper off the floor at St George's Hall, Liverpool, after a packed public meeting. Addressed to Merseyside's freelance photographers, it read: 'No pictures of Foot unless falling over, shot or talking to Militants. If Foot talks to any one of these drop a picture.' Alongside this message were the London phone numbers and names of the *Daily Mail*, *Daily Express* and *Sun* picture editors. Underneath were the following leading Liverpool Militants – Mulhearn, Hatton, Harrison, Fields, Dunlop and Taylor.

Some political journalists were privately dismayed at the way most of Fleet Street portrayed Mrs Thatcher as a flawless saint while presenting Michael Foot as an honest but dangerous and incompetent old fool. ' I think Foot was treated disgracefully by the press during the election campaign,' said a former *Sunday Times* journalist who attended most of the press conferences. 'And I thought he was remarkably well restrained afterwards. The contrast between the daily Labour and then Tory press conferences in the morning was very stark. At Labour's many of the journalists were aggressive and almost insulting, while at the Tory's the atmosphere was virtually sycophantic.' Robert Harris, a BBC *Newsnight* journalist and writer, agreed: 'Leaders of the Labour Party have seldom enjoyed a good press, but few have been treated with the contempt accorded to Foot.'[49]

Propaganda, Walworth Road and the power of the press

By the time Fleet Street had gone to the polls on Thursday 9 June 1983, their editorial allegiances made very revealing reading. They showed that they were way out of touch with public opinion. Of Britain's 17 national newspapers, nine endorsed the Conservative Party unambiguously, three had given qualified support and three urged their readers to reject the Tory government but vote tactically.[50] Only two newspapers – the *Daily Mirror* and *Sunday Mirror* – backed the Labour Party, and even that was a reluctant endorsement. In other words, the Conservative government had received 44 per cent of the vote and yet were the benefactors of 80 per cent of the total daily and Sunday circulation support from Fleet Street

In addition, not one national newspaper supported Labour on two of its most important manifesto commitments – withdrawal from the Common Market and a non-nuclear defence policy. Indeed, the real division in Fleet Street was between those papers campaigning unequivocally for a Conservative triumph and those who rejected the Tory government without endorsing Labour.

It was not necessarily inevitable that this would destroy any chance of a reasoned political debate and the free flow of information during the campaign. After all, some newspapers like the *Daily Telegraph* are heavily partisan editorially but will also be relatively fair and accurate in their news reporting of other parties' point of view. But in the four-week election campaign of 1983 the clear editorial imbalance was intensified by the invasion of comment into the news pages. And so, as the rightwing *Economist* magazine commented: 'Normal journalistic standards of news coverage have been abandoned for the campaign as the Tory tabloids turn themselves into propaganda sheets for Mrs Thatcher.'[51] Charles Wintour, former editor of the *London Evening Standard*, agreed: 'The Conservative popular papers have ruthlessly used their news and feature pages as adjuncts to Saatchi and Saatchi's advertising campaign.'[52] Of course, the *Daily Mirror* did much the same for the Labour Party. But that was *one* newspaper against three (*Mail, Express* and *Sun*), plus their Sunday sister papers, plus the *Times* and *Telegraph*.

This mixing up of news and comment reinforced the existing political bias of most of the papers and strengthened one side of the debate only. But it also failed to perform a more fundamental function during the election. About 8 million people, according to a *Sunday Times* MORI poll, were undecided about who to vote for. Given the partisan, partial reporting, who spoke for them? Why were they not allowed to make up their own minds, based on a balanced view of the important issues of the campaign?

Meanwhile, Labour had been screaming their message at the tops of their voices, but they weren't getting a hearing. For many senior Labour figures it was a fixed agenda. 'I was the chair of nearly every press conference,' said the party's General Secretary Jim Mortimer, 'and it was crystal clear that the press was not interested in reporting what Labour had to offer the electorate and what our policies were . . . They were purely interested in stories that would damage the Labour Party.' However, some of Labour's press officers working at Walworth Road during the campaign argue that while this was the case, it was not the whole story. They say that the party leadership was hyper-sensitive at press conferences, particularly on defence policy. They also argue that some Labour leaders held the naive view that the role of the journalists was to turn up at Transport House every morning at 9 a.m. during the campaign, take down their comments, return to the office and reproduce them for publication the next day. According to former Labour press officers Jim Innes and Francis Beckett, Labour's whole campaign strategy was hopelessly inept, particularly their dealings with the media. As Beckett bitingly remarked after the election: 'If a miracle had happened, and Fleet Street had suddenly come clamouring to Walworth Road for pro-Labour material, they would have been sent away with a copy of the manifesto each.'[53]

Obviously a more professional campaign and a coherent plan to combat Fleet Street, television and radio would improve Labour's chances at the next election. It might redress some of the political bias. But making Walworth Road run more efficiently can only be a stop-gap solution. It won't stop the papers distorting economic reports, or publishing spurious lists of 'secret Reds', or abuse jobless marchers or prevent the *Daily Star* (53 per cent of whose readers support Labour) from backing the Conservative Party. The solution embraces a far wider horizon.

Some Labour leaders now believe that Fleet Street should be bypassed and that the party should concentrate on television and radio. This ignores the fact that newspapers are still regarded by the electorate as a major source of information during the campaign. A BBC/IBA survey after the election revealed that 37 per cent of a national sample said they had learned 'a great deal' or 'a fair amount' about the political parties from the daily newspapers. The figure for television was not much higher at 43 per cent. Fleet Street also quite often sets the agenda for TV, as it did with the *Mail*'s Nissan story and the publication of leaked documents.

But how much power did the national press wield in the 1983 general election? It is always difficult to say, but one factor has emerged in recent years. That, apart from the *Daily Star*, most of Fleet Street's readership were well aware of their paper's political allegiances. For example, 64 per cent of the *Sun*'s readers perceived their own paper to be pro-Conservative during the 1983 election.[54] In addition, for the first time, about three in four Britons read a daily paper which campaigned for a Conservative victory. The figure for working-class readers is almost exactly the same at 74 per cent.[55] And so the sheer weight of numbers involved (one in four of the adult population read the *Sun*) must have had some effect on the final vote. To what degree will probably always be open to question.

8. The Miners' Strike: a Question of Censorship

'I cannot believe many newspapers would today carry an article by Arthur Scargill because he has discredited himself. His case is based upon a series of lies, which we could not assist with publicity.' Mac Keane, assistant managing editor of the *Daily Mail*, letter to Derek Hough, 27 July 1984.

Late one evening during the General Strike in May 1926, Aneurin Bevan, then a pit delegate for the South Wales Miners' Federation, led a solemn procession of protest to Waunpond, the mountain between Ebbw Vale and Tredegar. The *Western Mail*, Wales' national newspaper, had just published another vitriolic attack on Arthur James (A.J.) Cook, the leader of the striking miners. When they reached the mountain, dozens of copies of the *Mail* were burnt ceremoniously and then buried, with Bevan delivering a mock funeral oration.

Such a protest did not happen during the 1984-5 coal dispute. However, the striking miners were just as angry as their forefathers about the press coverage of their strike. Apart from the police, Fleet Street became the miners' public enemy no. 1. This was evident when miners marched down Fleet Street during the dispute. Their contempt was plain for all to see. On the picket lines copies of the *Sun* would be ostentatiously ripped up and there were angry exchanges between strikers and journalists at public meetings. Some reporters were forced to hide their notebooks and dress up in donkey jackets for fear of incurring the wrath of miners, furious at the hostile press coverage. One *Guardian* journalist described the situation as 'excruciating ... wherever you went you were told to fuck off and sometimes hit'.

But the miners' annoyance was due not so much to the daily editorial abuse from the popular press – 'Scum of the Earth' was how the *Sun*'s front page planned to portray them on 29 September 1984. They were more angry at what Fleet Street ignored and at the portrayal of 140,000 strikers and their families as unthinking cannon fodder being manipulated by one individual, Arthur Scargill. 'I have lost faith in the newspapers I once read,' said miner's wife Annette Holroyd from Blidworth, Nottinghamshire. 'The *Sun* and the *Daily Mirror* are banned from this house now. They are banned from most homes in this village. They have told lies, half truths and peddled propaganda.'[1] Margaret Holmes, a miner's wife from Deal, Kent, agreed: 'Either they don't respect our views, or they don't *want* to respect our views.'[2]

The editorial blindfold rendered invisible many important issues during the strike – police violence, the loss of civil liberties, the economic case for coal and Ian MacGregor's management style and his controversial American background. These were just some of the stories ignored by most of Fleet Street. But the elaborate cloak of censorship more than often fell on the unprotected shoulders of many industrial journalists themselves. During the dispute they were usually unable to shake it off.

Industrial correspondents have confirmed that during the strike articles were withdrawn just before publication; sections of stories cut between editions or submerged into other reports; paragraphs altered and reordered; whole stories removed after the first edition and paragraphs inserted – often without the knowledge of the journalist.

His Master's Voice – inside Maxwell House

In the early hours of Friday 13 July 1984, Robert Maxwell bought Mirror Group Newspapers for £113.4 million. That afternoon he held his first press conference in the *Mirror*'s staff restaurant at Holborn Circus. 'Under my management,' Maxwell promised,

> editors in the group will be free to produce their newspapers without interference with their journalistic skills and judgement. I shall place only two strictures on those who have editorial responsibility for newspapers that are members of the Mirror Group. One: the papers must retain their broadly sympathetic approach to the labour movement. Two: the papers must and will have a Britain-first policy.

Mike Molloy, then editor of the *Daily Mirror*, said he fully accepted Maxwell's guarantees that he would not interfere in editorial policy.

The first test of that formal undertaking proved to be the *Mirror*'s coverage of the miners' strike. One of Maxwell's first decisions was to restore the weekly column of Geoffrey Goodman, the paper's award-winning industrial editor. The *Mirror*'s new proprietor assured Goodman that he would have complete editorial independence. Less than two weeks later, on 27 July 1984, Goodman analyzed the role of Mrs Thatcher in the pit dispute in his resurrected column after she had attacked the miners as 'the enemy within'. In the paper's first edition, under the headline of 'Digging Into A Vendetta', Goodman revealed for the first time how Thatcher's hatred of the NUM stemmed from the 1974 Heath Cabinet. He showed how the Prime Minister had been opposed to an early election in 1974 and had preferred to 'take on the miners in a fight to the finish and win'. The *Mirror*'s industrial editor concluded that Thatcher was not interested in solving the 1984 strike but 'senses that she is on the brink of avenging that lost cause'.

Before the second edition, Maxwell removed ten paragraphs concerning the Prime Minister's role in the strike. He also changed the headline and inserted crossheads like 'Thugs' and 'The Pits'. At midnight, the night editor rang Goodman at his North London home to inform him about the cuts in his column. Goodman was furious but was told it was too late to remedy the situation. He then telephoned Mike Molloy, the editor, who implored his industrial editor not to do anything rash. The next morning, Goodman and Molloy visited their proprietor in his ninth floor office. Goodman threatened to resign and Maxwell immediately apologized. He said that he had merely wanted to 'brighten up the page and make it more lively'. Maxwell claimed he had not intended to act as a political censor and promised Goodman it wouldn't happen again.

Some *Mirror* journalists were rather sceptical about this explanation, given their proprietor's political views. 'I will never vote for Mrs Thatcher,' Maxwell told Channel 4 News, 'but she has done some good things for Britain and she should be supported.' The *Mirror* proprietor also believes in a measured dose of unemployment as a feasible economic policy. In a radio interview in Warsaw, Poland, Maxwell said: 'I suggested to the Prime Minister [General Jaruzelski] that in the interests of economic reform why doesn't he adopt a very small percentage of unemployment.'[3]

But it was Maxwell's desire to set the agenda for the miners' strike that made the *Mirror* so unpopular in the mining communities. The paper's proprietor was constantly in touch by phone with trade union leaders like Ray Buckton, General Secretary of the train drivers' ASLEF, and the late Terry Duffy, President of the engineering workers' AUEW. The *Mirror*'s industrial correspondents would then be summoned to Maxwell's office to discuss possible news reports. Maxwell often wanted certain stories to be published based on his informal conversations with Labour MPs and trade union leaders. The *Mirror*'s industrial journalists often stood their ground with their proprietor and persuaded him not to proceed with a story. Labour editor

Geoffrey Goodman was particularly resolute against Maxwell's activities since their initial row over his column.

However, that was not always the case. On more than one occasion during the strike, *Mirror* journalists were forced to remove their by-line from a news report because Maxwell had inserted paragraphs into the story. The paper's proprietor arranged for these sentences to be included through the 'back-bench' (the editor, night editor and assistant editors). One reporter told me that he took his name off because he knew Maxwell's information was inaccurate and it was also professionally damaging: 'It's very important for journalists to keep the trust of their sources. And so you should never write something that you don't believe in or know to be wrong. That's why I always take my name off in those situations ... It's not a completely satisfactory situation but it's the best compromise you can achieve.'

But Maxwell went even further with a story by the *Mirror*'s industrial correspondent, Terry Pattinson. On the evening of Sunday 9 September 1984, his forty-second birthday, Pattinson phoned through his copy from the first day of the NUM-Coal Board talks in Edinburgh. The next morning the *Mirror*'s front-page lead story contained his by-line but the published story – 'Scargill To Ballot Miners On Final Offer' – had nothing to do with him. Despite warnings by senior executives, Maxwell had in fact substituted this totally inaccurate story for Pattinson's straight report and had ordered the back-bench to insert the following information: 'The *Mirror* can exclusively reveal that whatever the outcome [of the talks], miners will be asked to vote on the Coal Board's final offer ... The union bosses have always resisted a ballot on the six-month old strike. But they are now ready to recommend a vote on the Coal Board's final terms.'

Without any evidence, the *Mirror* proprietor had also employed his ghost-writer, a senior journalist, to devote most of page two to give the Maxwell version of why the NUM leadership was ready 'to recommend a vote' in 'this astonishing development.' Under the by-line of 'A Special Correspondent', this article even attributed the story to the miners' executive – 'they will urge a ''No'' vote'. It was all completely untrue.

Unfortunately, none of the *Mirror*'s editorial management had told Pattinson on that Sunday night what Maxwell had done to his story. In the *Mirror*'s Scottish edition, Pattinson's name had been taken off Maxwell's 'ballot' story. And so he assumed the story was broadly correct. That Monday morning (10 September), much to his later embarrassment, Pattinson appeared on TV-AM and Radio 4's *Today* programme to defend his proprietor's front-page story. He simply could not believe that a story of such importance could be fabricated. And he only found out his name was on the inaccurate story for all the other editions when his wife rang him on that Monday evening. Pattinson was furious. But when he approached *Mirror* executives for an explanation, all he received was a resigned shrug. There was nothing they could do, they said.

Two months later, in November 1984, the *Mirror*'s coverage of the strike was again impeded by Maxwell. On Monday 5 November, Pattinson met his proprietor outside the conference centre in Sheffield where miners' delegates were holding a special meeting. Maxwell told him that the strike would definitely end on Wednesday 14 November. Pattinson, an experienced former *Daily Express* industrial correspondent, disagreed and cited his own sources on the NUM Executive. Maxwell then ended the conversation.

The next day, 6 November, Pattinson's story had been substantially changed in the London editions. For the northern edition he had reported that the dispute would be sustained through the winter – 'Pit Strike Could Last Through The Winter'. But in the London editions, Maxwell had ensured that the tone of his industrial correspondent's report had been changed to the mere fact that the strike would continue – 'We'll Battle On, Pledge The Miners'. The paper's proprietor had also authorized some extra material from Trevor Bell, the rightwing leader of the white-collar workers, who said: 'A resolution was passed at the end very hurriedly. But it is clear that there are a lot of blokes with itchy feet who want to go back to work.'

Maxwell has always publicly denied that he has interfered in the *Mirror*'s news columns. 'I have no intention of censoring the work of MGN journalists,' he said.[4] He also claims that the reporters would resist him: 'If I told my 600 journalists to toe the editorial line they would tell me to get stuffed.'[5]

However, the evidence paints a rather different picture of Maxwell's role regarding the *Mirror*'s coverage of the miners' strike. In August 1984, John Pilger, the paper's award-winning journalist, visited the picket line and mining village of Ollerton in Nottinghamshire. His report – 'Battleground: The Violence You Don't See On TV' – was highly critical of the police. On the evening of 28 August 1984, an editorial executive came into Pilger's office with a proof copy of his article and told him that Maxwell wanted certain changes. According to Pilger, these alterations would have changed the whole tone of the piece and so he went up to see Maxwell. There, in his ninth-floor office, Maxwell proceeded to edit the columnist's copy, word by word. Although a lawyer and an editorial executive were also present, Pilger had to negotiate directly with his proprietor. Maxwell was, in effect, editing the *Daily Mirror*.

The *Mirror*'s proprietor has also admitted being actively involved in the editorials during the miners' dispute. 'I certainly have a major say in the political line of the paper,' said Maxwell. 'I have a major say in the editorials which are compiled with the consent of the editor and our chief leader writer'.[6] When asked by the BBC's *Commercial Breaks* whether he wrote leaders himself, Maxwell replied: 'I occasionally write them myself, yes.' This was a reference to his articles under the pseudonym of Charles Wilberforce. However, Maxwell never actually wrote or dictated leaders himself. Neither does he attend the daily editorial conferences, although he is present at a weekly Tuesday lunch of senior *Mirror* executives and management. Instead, he would brief Joe Haines, the *Mirror*'s chief leader writer. Maxwell and Haines would decide on a topic and then discuss the contents of that day's editorial. A draft of the leader would then be shown to Maxwell who would occasionally make changes. But he would rarely, if ever, tell Haines, a former press secretary to Harold (now Lord) Wilson, what to write; mainly because their political views – right-wing Labour – happened to coincide.

Whatever the level of Maxwell's interference, there is little doubt that without his looming presence the *Mirror* would have given much more support to the miners. But Joe Haines rejects this view: 'Without Maxwell I would have taken exactly the same line that I did. I believe that from the very beginning Scargill's conduct of the strike was always inept and ultimately disastrous.'

As it happened, many striking miners and their families were very angry at the *Mirror*'s coverage of the dispute. When I visited the mining communities in South Yorkshire and South Wales while researching a book on the strike,[7] I was struck by the number of complaints about the *Mirror*.

The paper's senior journalists were confronted with this anger firsthand when some of them took part in the 'Tell-The-*Mirror*' tour of the country. On Monday 28 January 1984, the *Mirror* published a front-page leader entitled – 'Scargill: Coal Strike Lost'. The editorial ran:

> Arthur Scargill has lost the miners' strike. It is his defeat more than theirs. He has led the crack guards' regiment of the unions to disaster. No-one else is to blame. Not the men. Not the miners who struck. Not those who stayed at work. Not those forced by poverty to go back ... Mr Scargill's divisive and bullying tactics repelled

most ordinary trade unionists. They wouldn't go along with this undemocratic action. It was their sanity which decided the outcome. Not Mrs Thatcher's intransigence.

Three days later, on Thursday 31 January, the *Mirror*'s 'campaign train' arrived in Nottingham. At that meeting there was overwhelming criticism of the paper's coverage of the dispute. Several people condemned the *Mirror* to loud applause. Mike Molloy replied by claiming that 'millions of people' who supported the Labour Party would agree with his paper's line. A pensioner then stood up. She said that, having read that front-page editorial on Monday, she would never buy the *Daily Mirror* ever again.

The Peter Walker connection – sources close to the Energy Ministry

William Deedes, editor of the *Daily Telegraph* between 1975 and 1986 and former Conservative Minister for Information, once said that 'newspapers do not exist to please politicians – they should be apart and mistrustful of each other'. If similar advice had been offered to most Fleet Street editors and executives during the coal dispute, it would almost certainly have been ignored. For there is considerable evidence that senior editorial staff acquiesced to government requests to play down or suppress damaging information and news stories.

The chief architect of the government's news management policy was Peter Walker, Secretary of State for Energy throughout the year-long strike. He has long been regarded as the most adept public relations operator in the Conservative Party. His baptism in news management came in 1960 when, as Chairman of the Young Conservatives, he went to the United States to observe J.F. Kennedy's presidential campaign. Walker was particularly struck by how close some of the political correspondents were to Kennedy and how this benefited the Democratic campaign. In 1965 Walker masterminded Edward Heath's election campaign to become Tory Party leader, and soon became very friendly with selected lobby correspondents. But it was during the 1972 miners' strike that he learnt his real lesson. At the time, Heath's public relations strategy was in total disarray, despite his many supporters in Fleet Street, and the government's message was not conveyed with any clarity. Clearly, Walker, at the time Trade and Industry Minister, was mindful of Heath's PR failures when the 1984 miners' strike began. A former civil servant, who worked closely with Walker for many years, has no doubts: 'Absolutely, he is very sharp. I have no doubt he learnt the lessons of the early 1970s . . . He is a superb manipulator and communicator with the press. He can be very charming and is very good at persuading people round to his point of view.'

By the time of the 1984 miners' strike, it seems Walker had had only one skirmish with the press. That was in 1980 on the steps of the EEC chamber in Luxembourg. Walker, then the Agriculture Minister, was having difficult negotiations over the fisheries industry. Just before lunch he met a group of European correspondents. Margaret van Hattam of the *Financial Times* pursued a particularly tough line of questioning and Walker rounded on her: 'Why are you not taking the British point of view? You are a British citizen. You should be more sympathetic.' An angry van Hattam, now the paper's political correspondent, was furious: 'Why should I be partisan to the British point of view? I'm reporting this conference as an objective journalist.'

Unfortunately, during the coal dispute not all Fleet Street editors and executives were as independently minded as van Hattam. From the first weeks of the strike, the government used the non-attributable lobby system for political journalists to convey their message. Peter Walker was particularly adept at discreet individual briefings of his own for political correspondents (he didn't trust the industrial reporters). The Energy Secretary also arranged regular briefings for the editors of supportive Sunday and national daily newspapers. In addition, Walker was in regular contact by phone with Andrew Neil, editor of the *Sunday Times*, and the editors of several tabloid daily papers. Interestingly, Sir David English, editor of the *Daily Mail*, lives directly opposite Walker in Cowley Street, Westminster, near Conservative Central Office at Smith Square. Next door to Sir David English lives David Hunt, Walker's deputy and the minister for coal. Lord Hartwell, the *Daily* and *Sunday Telegraph*'s editor-in-chief, also lives in Cowley Street.

The government's line in the early weeks of the strike was that the dispute wouldn't last and briefed as such. And the papers obliged, as the information supplied at the private briefings was rarely challenged or scrutinized before publication. Four weeks into the year-long strike, on 3 April 1984, the *Daily Mail* reported: 'Miners Start "Slow Drift Back To Work"'. Later that week the *Sunday Express*' front page was rather more certain that the strike would collapse – 'Scargill On The Brink Of Defeat'. The news report added: 'Arthur Scargill faces crisis in the coal strike this week with his reputation and his job in the union at stake as he risks humiliating defeat.'

Although the dispute lasted another 11 months, the government ministers continued to brief friendly editors that the strike was in a state of imminent collapse. But a more important factor was that the end product of this close relationship between the government and

Fleet Street was that damaging news stories were kept out of the papers. This was revealed within three weeks of the start of the strike. On 25 March 1984, the first edition of the *Sunday Telegraph* published a front-page article about government plans to set up 'contingency measures which could mean the rationing of power supplied to domestic consumers and industry to conserve energy for a long battle with the miners'. Headlined 'Electricity Cut Plans Ready', the story compared the proposals with the situation in 1974. The report also exposed its code name ('Siege 84') and revealed that the contingency measures 'could allow for troops to be brought in' if power workers cut supplies of electricity.

The story never appeared in the second or later editions. Just before the printing of the paper's first edition at about 6 p.m., Walker telephoned the *Sunday Telegraph*'s editorial management and, according to one source, 'rubbished' the report. There was also a phone call from the press office at 10 Downing Street. The journalist concerned, industrial correspondent John Kesby, then checked back with his sources and stood by his story. But editorial executives decided to remove the story before the second edition. The *Sunday Telegraph*'s assistant editor (news), Derek Sumpter, would not deny or confirm Walker's involvement but would only say: 'It was removed from later editions as a result of a normal editorial decision based upon further information.'[8]

Less than seven weeks later, government ministers were again indulging in the art of news management. On Thursday 3 May 1984, Robert Porter, the *Daily Mail*'s political correspondent, and Graham Paterson of the *Daily Telegraph* had lunch with John Moore, the Treasury Minister responsible for privatization. Moore talked about how private capital could be injected into the coal industry and went into some detail about how a Cabinet subcommittee had agreed proposals to do so. Encouraged by Industry Minister Norman Tebbit's recent remarks on privatization of the pits, the two political correspondents began to check out the story. However, they were met with frantic denials from Whitehall, particularly by Bernard Ingham, the Prime Minister's press secretary. At the *Daily Mail*, the paper's editor Sir David English ran a check on the story and called Peter Walker, who was very angry. At least one senior minister then rang the *Mail* asking for the report to be spiked. Both the *Mail* and *Telegraph* stories were pulled out at the very last minute and were never published. One *Mail* assistant editor would not comment on Walker's involvement but said they removed the story because 'the information was inaccurate'.

Unfortunately for the government, details of the story had reached

Anthony Bevins, the *Times'* political correspondent. On Saturday 5 May, Bevins published a front-page story under the headline – 'Private Funds May Be Sought For NCB Expansion'. This provoked Walker into action. Later that day, the Energy Minister rang Andrew Neil, editor of the *Sunday Times*, to deny the report. Neil then wrote part of the paper's front-page story – 'Pits Will Not Go Private, Say Ministers'. This included a denial from John Moore who was said to be merely 'thinking out loud'. Neil confirmed that he spoke to Cabinet ministers that weekend but would not comment on Walker's role. However, he did say: 'The consensus view of the Cabinet at the time was that privatization was not realistic politically. We simply ran the story that it was not the government's intention to do so . . . Moore was speaking from a personal not a government point of view.' Since that incident, Moore has decided not to have lunch with lobby correspondents.

The close links between *Sunday Times* editor Andrew Neil and Walker had a strong bearing on that paper's coverage of the strike. The two have been close friends since the autumn of 1971 when Neil worked for Walker as his political assistant on the environment desk in the Tory Party research department during the Heath government. They parted ways in November 1972 when Walker was moved to the Trade and Industry Ministry, and the following year Neil joined the rightwing *Economist* magazine. But they kept in touch. They both share a passion for all things American, and Walker would often stay at Neil's flat in New York between 1979 and 1982 when Neil was the *Economist*'s US correspondent.

Neil and Walker also have similar political views. Liberal on social issues, on economic policy they are both keen advocates of the market economy and the deregulation of business. Although Neil is a firm supporter of privatization, he says he is 'left of centre' on the overall management of the economy.[9] Perhaps this is why he addressed a Tory Reform Group fringe meeting at the 1985 Conservative Party conference. Neil spoke alongside Tory MP Julian Critchley on the theme: 'Is It Policy Or Presentation?' Walker is, of course, president of the Tory Reform Group.

But when the 1984-5 miners' strike began Neil and Walker were of one view – the NUM must be beaten. Throughout the dispute, according to former *Sunday Times* political correspondent Robert Taylor, Walker telephoned Neil every Saturday morning with his current thoughts and fed him information about the government's strategy. Another former *Sunday Times* journalist said that 'these conversations certainly influenced the way the paper covered the strike'. Neil declined to comment about his personal links with the Energy Secretary. 'Any talks with Walker were off the record,' he said.

Walker's media strategy was to ignore the 140,000 miners who were on strike and their NUM representatives. Instead, the Energy Secretary relentlessly attacked Arthur Scargill, the union's president. As one senior civil servant in the Energy Ministry told me: 'The strategy was to isolate Scargill.' In virtually every speech and interview the message was the same. 'This strike has little to do with the future of the coal industry,' Walker told the 1984 Tory Party conference. 'It has everything to do with the Marxist challenge to the very roots of our parliamentary democracy.' He summed up the dispute as 'Scargill's Marxist crusade.'[10] This argument was clearly reflected in the *Sunday Times* coverage of the strike. 'Scargill's strike' was a regular description of the dispute in the paper's leader columns. Neil defends this by saying: 'There is no way the strike would have started without Scargill.'

This direct collusion between the government's stance and the *Sunday Times'* subsequent coverage of the dispute is also the view of Hugo Young. He was the paper's long-serving former joint deputy editor and political editor who resigned after Neil refused to consult the political staff over the writing of leaders. This is how Young described the *Sunday Times'* reporting of the dispute:

> Anyone depending on the *Sunday Times* alone for their picture of the dispute would have received a strange impression. This could be reduced to the following elements: that the strike was a Marxist plot, that it wasn't supported by the mass of miners, that it was prosecuted largely if not wholly by intimidation, that the miners were readily running out of steam, that coal stocks were almost permanently rising, that the strike was often just about to collapse, and that the whole operation had been planned by the government from the start with a view to defeating the NUM by tactics brilliantly masterminded in the offices of the Energy Secretary, Peter Walker . . .
>
> Against the background of this sort of unfailing support for the government and the Coal Board, the paper's more sober and objective inquiries lost some of their credibility. The longer the strike went on, the more did the paper's earlier predictions of its imminent end begin to look like a misconceived contribution to the government's propaganda battle.[11]

The evidence clearly supports Young's analysis. Hardly a week went by without some glowing reference to the Energy Secretary.

Here's a *Sunday Times* leader on 20 May 1984 echoing Walker's latest comments. Entitled 'Scargill's Strike', it ran: 'Consider the striking miner who coolly contemplates the consequences of Arthur Scargill's strike,' and added: 'Mr Walker's tone was firm but reasonable, and he offered the miners the prospect of big pay packets to come. The NCB should send the speech to every miner in the country and we should start to hear much more along these lines from the government and the Coal Board in the weeks ahead.' In an accompanying feature, the paper reported: 'Walker might be an outspoken critic of her economic policies but, in the words of one of his Cabinet colleagues, he has "acute political intelligence". She [Mrs Thatcher] wanted him to use his tactical abilities and his survivor skills to take on and beat the formidable Arthur Scargill'. This was followed up by a flattering, page-long profile of Walker on 8 July – 'Thatcher's Favourite Wet' – with the ironic analysis that 'even his critics concede his presentational prowess and media expertise'.

The *Sunday Times*, like many other papers, had also swallowed the government's line that the strike wouldn't last and didn't have any support. 'Government Scent Victory In Pit Battle' and 'Fear Is Keeping Miners Out', reported the paper on 8 April 1984 – 47 weeks before the end of the dispute. However, to be fair to Neil, he now acknowledges his paper was wrong in this aspect of the strike, although he says this was the only defect in the *Sunday Times'* coverage.

On 24 June 1984, the front page of the *Sunday Times* informed its readers about 'The Plan For Coal – The Truth' which continued on page two as 'NCB Stood By Plan For Coal' and exonerated the Coal Board's pit closure programme. The report was written by Ivan Fallon, appointed by Rupert Murdoch[12] as deputy editor. Fallon, former city editor of the *Sunday Telegraph* and close friend of Tiny Rowland[13] and Sir James Goldsmith, is a far from detached political observer. He is an active member and contributor to the Omega Project, an offshoot of the rightwing Adam Smith Institute, the influential Tory think-tank. Fallon was a joint author of the Omega Project report on energy policy in September 1984 which recommended full-scale privatization of the coal industry.

But the most serious allegation about the *Sunday Times* came from some of the paper's journalists themselves. They say that news reports and articles about the strike were regularly rewritten. So much so that the characteristic sound of a Tuesday morning in the *Sunday Times* office was of fair-minded journalists phoning their contacts and disowning what had appeared under their names the previous Sunday. Reporters who have since left the paper claim that stories and opinion polls were rewritten and paragraphs reordered to give greater prominence to the political iamge sought by editorial management. Donald Macintyre, the *Sunday Times'* former labour editor, said that during the strike 'the rewriting was done by Frank Barber (the splash subeditor) sometimes, but not always, under the direction of Andrew Neil'. On one occasion early in the dispute, information about higher electricity prices arising from the economic cost of the strike was removed from a story in the paper's first edition. It was only after protests from Macintyre that Andrew Neil restored the information in later editions. Neil admits there were changes to news copy: 'I had to do a lot of subbing.' However, he added: 'Everything that was done with the Labour staff's copy was always amended with the permission of the journalist concerned ... at no time did a journalist, to my knowledge, remove their name from a story. There were one or two complaints, but any copy that was changed was done with the consent of the journalist.'

Meanwhile, Peter Walker was so grateful to the *Sunday Times* for their coverage that he promised the paper's political staff an exclusive two-day briefing for their book on the strike. As it turned out, the Energy Secretary's seminar was a lunch and an afternoon briefing with Neil and Michael Jones, the political editor. But it was an indication of the close and, some *Sunday Times* journalists would say, politically insidious relationship that the Energy Secretary had with most of Fleet Street.

The propagandists – public relations or journalism?

During a conference between media editors and a large group of press officers, one of the highest officials in the government's public information department said: 'We are all journalists. We are here to give you the facts, to oil the wheels and give you the truth.' According to Ray Fitzwalter, editor of Granada TV's *World in Action*, even his own government colleagues laughed at this suggestion. Much more respect from the editors was given to the press officer who said: 'Frankly, I am a paid agent of my government. I have never knowingly lied but I am here to do a job and it is to represent the best interests of my ministry.'[14]

This conflict and disparity between public relations officials and journalists is an essential prerequisite for independent reporting of any major political and industrial event. However, one of the most bizarre aspects of the miners' strike was the role of some journalists who, it appeared, crossed that bridge into public relations in favour of the government and Coal Board.

The activities of David Hart were perhaps the most insidious. A *Times* columnist since June 1983, Hart was commissioned by the paper at the start of the dispute to tour the picket lines to talk to striking and working miners. After a visit to the divided village of Shirebrook in Derbyshire, he decided that the working miners held the key to winning the strike. And so he began writing features for the *Times* supporting the strikebreakers and attacking the NUM – 'Hit Scargill, Help Miners'.[15] Hart added: 'The battle has been joined. If it is to be won speedily, all who love freedom and believe in democracy should do what they can to help the working miners financially or in any other way.' He continued to pen similar pieces throughout the dispute promoting the cause of the working miners and their legal strategy against the union. 'Seeds Of A Union Revolution', was the headline above a piece on 13 September 1984, which gave scrupulous details of the National Working Miners' Committee's activities. Towards the end of the strike, Hart was unequivocal about the need to crush the NUM. After Ned Smith, the NCB's director-general of Industrial Relations, and Peter Heathfield, the NUM's General Secretary, very nearly negotiated a settlement on Monday 21 January 1985, Hart was furious and telephoned the *Times*' then editor, Charles Douglas-Home. Hart said that there should be no 'fudging'. Douglas-Home agreed and gave him space in the paper that Saturday under the headline – 'Nothing Short Of Victory'. Hart added: 'The time for negotiated settlements is past... There must be no equivocation.'[16]

Now, what readers of the *Times* were not told by the editorial management was that Hart was far more than a journalist with a touch of the political polemics. He was, in fact, Ian MacGregor's chief publicity advisor along with Tim Bell, the former Saatchi and Saatchi chairman, and Gordon Reece, Mrs Thatcher's top media advisor. At one stage, Hart phoned Peter Walker from his suite at Claridges Hotel and told him that MacGregor had asked him to be his PR advisor and could he offer the Energy Secretary any advice.[17] Hart also rang Peter McNestry, NACODS general secretary, said he was a *Times* reporter and asked for an interview. The *Times* columnist had virtually unlimited access to MacGregor, particularly as the Coal Board Chairman has been a close friend of the Hart family since 1975. Hart's influence was revealed on 22 August 1984 when he spent several hours with MacGregor, advising him about his Channel 4 News debate with Arthur Scargill that evening. During the debate Hart came into the studio and began holding up cue-cards and passing MacGregor pieces of paper with advice.[18] Three months later Geoffrey Kirk, the NCB's experienced Director of Public Relations, resigned and cited one of the reasons as Hart's unofficial role.

However, the *Times* columnist was even more active in setting up the National Working Miners' Committee. He attended the committee's first meeting and soon began to play an influential role. According to Bob Copping, the committee's secretary, Hart attended at least four meetings: 'In my opinion, Hart was not acting as advisor or journalist, he was running the show . . . He was introduced to me as the money-man and was handing over £300 in cash as floats.' Copping eventually resigned from the National Working Miners' Committee in protest at Hart's involvement.

Hart claims that he went to these committee meetings purely as a journalist. He says that he only arranged their location, simply to make it easier for him to meet the working miners in his role as a journalist.[19] Clearly, his editor, the late Charles Douglas-Home, must have known about Hart's political activities and his close links with MacGregor. But none of his articles indicated them. Presumably, the *Times* didn't see any conflict of interests between being the PR advisor of the Coal Board boss and at the same time writing features on the strike for their paper. Douglas-Home certainly didn't. The paper's then editor celebrated the end of the miners' strike with Hart over champagne at the Claridges Hotel along with Sir Ronald Millar, the former Hollywood screen writer and now Mrs Thatcher's chief speech writer.

The other journalist to be closely involved with the National Working Miners' Committee and not declare an interest was Graham Turner, the *Sunday Telegraph* feature writer. A former press officer for Shell and PR advisor to several car companies, Turner wrote several articles sympathetic to the working miners – 'The Rebel Miners Who Will Not Be Gagged'[20] and 'Men Who Brought Scargill To Book'.[21] He had met the leaders of the working miners in Nottinghamshire and it was Turner who arranged the very first meeting of the National Working Miners' Committee. He asked a close friend, Captain Edward Evans, a fellow member of the rightwing Christian revivalist group Moral Rearmament, if they could meet at his farm in Knightwick near Worcester. Evans agreed and on 12 August 1984 eight working miners assembled along with Turner and some Moral Rearmers from Birmingham.

At that meeting Turner helped draft a letter which was sent to all striking miners throughout the country. It was an appeal for funds to finance legal fees. Turner also designed and wrote advertisements which were later published in the *Daily Express*, *Sunday Times* and *Daily Mail*. That same day he also had a front-page exclusive interview with Ian MacGregor in the *Sunday Telegraph* entitled 'MacGregor:

End Of Strike In Sight'. Like Hart, it seems Turner also had close links with the Coal Board Chairman. After the strike he was to have two more exclusive front-page interviews with MacGregor.[22]

John Blessington, secretary of the National Working Miners' Committee after Bob Copping resigned, said that Turner was very useful to them: 'Graham was quite helpful with promotion and publicity, and attended a few of our meetings because we needed help in dealing with the press.' But Turner told me: 'I went there simply as a journalist. I thoroughly agreed with what they were fighting for but advised them to guard their honour and not take capitalist money.'

To be fair to Turner, he was quite open about attending those meetings, although he denies helping the Working Miners' Committee with publicity. The activities of freelance journalist Rodney Tyler were rather more secretive. He became notorious for a *Daily Express* feature he wrote on 3 April 1984 on the NUM president's advisors and aides. Headlined 'Scargill's Seven Shadows – When King Arthur Hears Voices, These Are The Voices He Hears', the article added: 'Every King needs a Court – a group of tried and trusted cronies to advise and guide him, flatter and applaud him. None more so in his present bitter battle than miners' leader Arthur Scargill.' Tyler went on to give titles to various NUM officials and friends – 'The Fixer' and 'The Worshipper'. He also revealed his knowledge about the strike. Tyler described it as a 'pay row'!

A month later, on May Day 1984, he secured an exclusive interview with Ian MacGregor for the *Sun* – 'Scargill Doesn't Scare Me'. This page-long interview portrayed the Coal Board Chairman thus: 'He is not Scargill's lurid bogeyman at all,' wrote Tyler. 'He is more like many of his miners than King Arthur himself. He has their toughness and sense of inner strength.' Apart from six introductory paragraphs, the interview was one long quote from MacGregor.

The day after this interview was published, Tom Condon, then the *Sun*'s industrial editor who now works for Eddie Shah's *Today*, telephoned Geoffrey Kirk, the Coal Board's Director of Publicity. Condon complained that his paper's industrial staff had not been consulted about the article. 'We didn't know about the interview either,' replied Kirk. In fact, Tyler had arranged the interview without the NCB's press office knowledge. Clearly, he had direct links with MacGregor. These were revealed after the strike when Tyler turned out to be the ghost writer of the Coal Board Chairman's book on the coal dispute.

But, perhaps more significantly, Tyler had closer ties with Downing Street. A close personal friend of the Thatcher family, Tyler's access to the Prime Minister can be traced back to the early 1970s during the Heath government. Tyler was the *Daily Mail*'s education correspondent while Mrs Thatcher was Secretary of State for Education and he also went out with her daughter Carol. He then joined the *News of the World* and became the paper's features editor. In 1982 Tyler became a freelance journalist and began to pen a series of long, favourable profiles and features on the Thatcher family. In February 1984, Mark Thatcher was in deep trouble after revelations by the *Observer* about his business activities in Oman. Tyler met Mark Thatcher at a hotel in New York. There followed a series of articles and front-page stories with pictures of the Prime Minister's son, particularly with his American girlfriend – 'Top Mark' ran a *Sun* headline on 20 February 1984. Five weeks later, on 1 April, Tyler published a double-page exclusive interview with Mark Thatcher in the *Mail on Sunday* – 'Mark Says I Am Sorry'.

On Sunday 13 May 1984, the *News of the World* published a front-page exclusive story – 'Our Love By Mark And His Girl'. Words and pictures by Rodney Tyler. Later that Sunday morning, Tyler arranged for Fleet Street photographers to be at Heathrow Airport when Mark Thatcher's girlfriend, Karen Fortson, flew in from Paris with her mother and twin brother. The freelance journalist then accompanied them to Chequers for Sunday lunch with the Prime Minister. Like David Hart, Tyler now writes features for the *Times*.

What has all this got to do with the miners' strike? The answer lies in the political significance of the dispute and the titanic nature of the struggle. Some newspapers clearly had no scruples about publishing articles by journalists who at the same time were actively involved in helping the working miners (Hart and Turner) in their public relations strategy. It seems to me a classic case of a conflict of interests. Obviously Fleet Street's editorial management didn't see it that way.

Back-to-work: drift, surge, drift, surge...

On 25 November 1984, the *Observer* published evidence, based on National Coal Board documents, which revealed how government ministers were 'grossly misleading about the drift back to work' during the strike. The article showed how Peter Walker, the Energy Secretary, had distorted the back-to-work figures when he told the Commons in July that there were over 60,000 miners working. NCB documents proved that this figure included 3,000 men providing safety cover with NUM permission, 5,500 members of the pit deputies' union NACODS and 8,700 members of the white-collar union APEX.

None of these workers had decided not to strike. In fact, the real figure at the time was just over 42,000 miners. The *Observer* had also revealed that the NCB had called in their own auditors on Monday 19 November 1984 to verify their figures and allay any public suspicion. But, much to the Coal Board's embarrassment, their auditors would only confirm that about 51,000 miners were working that day, whereas the Board had announced the figure to be nearly 60,000. In addition, a simple examination of the figures given out by the NCB's official newspaper, *Coal News*, showed a clear discrepancy with the number of working miners announced by the Prime Minister in the Commons.

However, neither the *Observer*'s evidence nor the discrepancies in the NCB's figures was followed up by any of the national newspapers. The report's analysis was simply ignored. There was no independent scrutiny of *both* the NUM and NCB's figures. Instead, the Coal Board's statstics were reproduced by most of Fleet Street with little scepticism.

It was a clear indication of how important any return to work was as a strategy for defeating the miners' strike. The daily reports of the back-to-work figures undoubtedly had an effect on the morale of the striking miners, although many of the NUM officials knew they were distorted. The miners' union said that there was little they could do. They argued that even when they were ready to provide regular figures, most of the national press didn't use them. Also that on a number of occasions Fleet Street used NCB statistics on working miners without indicating their source.

Some journalists counter that part of the problem was lack of access to the NUM's figures and information. Joe Quinn, a Press Association reporter based in Scotland, said: 'From our point of view, the Coal Board have got the machinery and the NUM haven't. It's as simple as that... So much of our work is reactive. We don't know what's happening on the ground. We rely on the Coal Board, the NUM or the police to keep us in touch. We receive very little information from the NUM.'[23]

However, a close analysis of the coverage of this issue provides a rather different picture. Throughout the strike the press reported that all the pits in Nottinghamshire were 'working normally'. This was untrue. In the early weeks of the dispute, there were up to 5,000 miners on strike and the pits were clearly not 'working normally'. At one Nottinghamshire colliery, Welbeck, half the workforce were on strike at one stage.

As early as April 1984, the *Daily Mail* was reporting the 'slow drift back to work'.[24] The next month, on 21 May, the *Sun* announced:

'Scargill Rocked In Back-To-Work Rebellion – Strike Is A "Futile Gesture" Say Fed-up Welsh Miners'. Despite the fact that the dispute would continue for another ten months, the early weeks' coverage was full of exaggerated return-to-work stories. Hence, the *Daily Express* on 1 June 1984: 'Back To Work Snub For Scargill'. The front-page story began: 'Arthur Scargill was dealt a devastating blow yesterday by pit men in his own coalfield.' This was based on a decision by Barnsley colliery winders who voted to go back to work. In fact, it later transpired that only two miners – Bob Copping and Tony Robson – crossed the picket line and returned to work.

An insight into how significant any miner returning to work was to Fleet Street can be seen in the case of Frank Branwell. On Tuesday 22 May 1984, the *Guardian*, *Sun*, *Daily Express*, *Times*, *London Standard* and the northern edition of the *Daily Telegraph* published a photograph of him with captions describing him as a lone Derbyshire strikebreaker at Markham Main colliery walking through a gauntlet of pickets. The *Guardian* said: 'Derbyshire miner defies pickets and goes into work at Markham Main colliery through a gate guarded by police.' The problem was that he wasn't crossing the picket line. He was joining in and remained there all day, as usual. The photograph came from a press agency and, to be fair, one can hardly blame the papers for the mistake, although they did give the picture prominence. But the photograph did cause a lot of despair and injury to the miner, Frank Branwell, who was a strong supporter of the strike. The least he deserved was an apology from the papers concerned. Did this happen?

When Branwell saw his picture splashed all over the papers, he immediately contacted the Campaign for Press and Broadcasting Freedom to try and secure a right of reply or an apology. At the *Guardian* Aidan White, the paper's NUJ FoC, wrote a memorandum to the newsdesk saying that Branwell deserved a right of reply. Eventually, after much lobbying, the paper published a retraction, but no apology, at the bottom of page two in the next day's edition: 'Frank Branwell, the miner pictured on the front page of yesterday's *Guardian* apparently going into work, has asked us to point out that he did not report for duty and did, in fact, join his workmates on the picket line.' When asked by a Kent miner, Terry Harrison, on Channel 4's *Union World* why the paper did not acknowledge any error, the *Guardian*'s editor, Peter Preston, would only say: 'That was clearly a wrong caption. It was supplied by the photographer, not a member of staff, who sent us the picture. In life there are always mistakes. It has been put right.'[25]

The *Sun* and *Daily Telegraph* printed small retractions nine days later, on 31 May 1984. The *Times* published a one-paragraph correction on 28 August 1984. The *Standard* and *Daily Express* didn't bother. David Flynn, the *Times*'s deputy executive editor, said that he would have sued if someone had taken away his good name (like Frank Branwell) without a correction for several months.[26]

But it was Fleet Street's reporting of the numbers of miners returning to work in the autumn of 1984 that provided evidence of partisanship. The months of August and September saw the most intense period of activity by the government, NCB and the working miners' committees to try to persuade miners to break the strike. It was the high point for the NUM who believed they were on the verge of victory. The government and the board were worried that the strike was still relatively solid. And so the Coal Board decided to target TUC Congress week for a mass return to work and marshalled their public relations office in preparation.

In the early hours of Monday morning, 3 September 1984, Jean Stead, the *Guardian*'s highly experienced Scottish corresopndent and former news editor, drove to the Bilston Glen colliery near Edinburgh. She decided to find out for herself what the real number of miners crossing the picket line was that morning, and not just rely on one set of figures. Stead stood on the picket line and observed the coaches of strikebreakers being escorted into the pit. She then visited the NUM strike committee centre in Dalkeith to record their figures which were written down in a logbook. Apart from the NCB-released figure, Stead also interviewed Harry Fettes, the leader of the Working Miners' Association at Bilston Glen and a Conservative Party candidate in a local council by-election. He was also a management trainee at the pit.

As it turned out, Fettes' estimate of the number of working miners at Bilston Glen was closer to the NUM figure, but Stead included all the different versions when she phoned through her 450-word story. This was part of her report:

> The NUM strike committee in Dalkeith said that only 50 men had reported for work and they were delighted that this total had dropped from attendances at the pit of about 90 non-striking miners every day last week. Later, the Scottish NCB HQ said that throughout the Scottish coalfield yesterday, the magic figure of 205 was, they said, the highest so far. They also claimed that 145 miners had reported for work at Bilston Glen...Mr Fettes himself said that between 85 and 90 workers, including safety workers, had reported for work at Bilston Glen yesterday.

The next day, 4 September, Jean Stead was stunned to read how the *Guardian* had used her copy for a lengthy page two report on the 'much-heralded mass return to work'. Virtually the whole of Stead's story had been spiked except for one piece of information – the Coal Board's back-to-work figure, plus two paragraphs about a different story. Instead of Stead's balanced reporting, the *Guardian* had merely included this paragraph: 'In Scotland, the number of miners at work passed 200 for the first time, with the NCB reporting that 205 crossed picket lines. Most were at Bilston Glen, near Edinburgh, where 145 are now working from a workforce of 1,500.'

What the paper had done was to ignore the NUM's figures and simply report the Coal Board's version as though it was the only legitimate source. Stead, a former news and assistant editor of the *Guardian*, was furious and confronted the paper's then news editor Peter Cole. 'We didn't have enough space,' he replied.

The next big push for a mass return to work by the Coal Board was also planned for a Monday. This was on 19 November 1984 after negotiations had broken down. At this stage, according to NCB Industrial Relations director-general Ned Smith, the government and Coal Board were intent on winning the strike by relying on a gradual return to work rather than a negotiated settlement. And so Monday the 19th was an important day for the Board.

Throughout that day the *Sun* had employed a group of reporters to ring all the different areas of the Coal Board and collect their figures for the total number of working miners. For the paper first edition, under the headline of 'The Flood Back To Work', the *Sun*'s total in their table came to 47,631. However, this was 12,369 *less* than the National Coal Board's figure of 60,000 working miners. The paper's editor, Kelvin McKenzie, was angry. What would happen if Arthur Scargill obtained these figures, he anxiously told his staff. And so when the *Sun*'s later editions were printed two hours later, the paper's figure of 47,631 had suddenly jumped to 62,631 working miners. Assistant editors on the back-bench had simply added 15,000 'ancillary workers' to the total. However, these ancillary workers were not even included in the NCB's figures. 'We have no separate group of ancillary workers in our accounting,' said a Coal Board spokesman.[27]

That same November week the *Times* was particularly vigilant in giving any back-to-work movement prominence in its news pages – 'Pit Strike Collapse By Christmas Predicted By NCB: The National Coal Board expects the return to work to bring about a virtual collapse of the miners' strike by Christmas'. That was a front page report in the *Times* on Saturday 17 November 1984. Two days later, on 19 November (the day before the *Sun*'s changing of the figures), the *Times* ran a similar front-page news story under the by-line of 'Our

Labour Editor'. Under the headline of 'NCB Ready For "Surge" Back To Pits', the *Times* reported: 'The strongest "surge back to work" yet seen in the coalfields is confidently expected today.'

Like its sister paper, the *Sunday Times*, journalists on the *Times*, particularly the labour staff, were put under political pressure from editorial management. According to an experienced senior *Times* journalist, stories were rewritten and amended by editorial executives to give more prominence to the working miners. 'Copy was changed to give certain stories a different slant, based on an executive not subeditor's decision,' said the *Times* journalist. This was confirmed by Barrie Clement, the former *Times* labour correspondent. As with the *Sunday Times*, the reporters concerned removed their by-line from the published story.

Violence – what the papers never said about the picket lines

In a critique of the NUM's alleged failure to use the media for their own benefit during the strike, Patrick Wintour, the *Guardian*'s labour correspondent, wrote: 'The NUM had no network or reporting centre to which miners could relay their stories of picket-line violence to the newspapers willing to print them'.[28] The key phrase here is 'willing to print them'. Was this true?

There is little evidence to suggest that the vast bulk of Fleet Street were 'willing to print' stories involving police harassment, the loss of civil liberties and overt violence against striking miners. That is also the view of Geoffrey Goodman, the *Mirror*'s industrial editor and winner of Granada TV's Gerald Barry Award for his coverage of the dispute. 'Of course, the miners' tactics invited a strong reaction, but not on the scale nor in the manner that became commonplace throughout the dispute,' wrote Goodman. 'What was equally condemnable was the failure of most of the press and TV, during the worst of these incidents, to question in any way the dangerous shadow that was thrown across the issue of civil liberties'.[29]

To be fair to Wintour, he was one of the very few journalists who did cover these issues. But his implication that the press would have readily reported police violence and harassment against strikers, if only the NUM had provided the information and facilities, has little foundation. One simple example. Throughout the dispute several *Daily Star* journalists collected money for the miners and their families in Armthorpe, a small pit village in south Yorkshire. Shortly after an alleged police riot on 22 August 1984, the *Star* journalists obtained several stories and eye-witness accounts plus photographs of police brutality in the village. 'We had some great stories and pictures about what happened. It was great stuff,' said a senior *Star* journalist. The material was never published. It had been spiked.

There are also some questions that need to be answered if Wintour's argument is to have any credibility. How was it that the *Mirror* columnist Paul Foot was able to report week after week during the strike incidents of police harassment against striking miners? How did the left press, with far less resources than Fleet Street, manage to publish stories about the loss of civil liberties in mining communities? How could this happen and Fleet Street not do the same? The answer, I believe, lies in the political significance of the dispute.

The omission and suppression of hostile news stories concerning the policing of the strike reached all parts of the labour movement. On 23 August 1984, Roy Hattersley, Labour's deputy leader, made a speech in Manchester condemning violence by both pickets and police. The *Sun*'s report was headlined 'Hattersley's Rap For Pit Thugs', but nowhere did Britain's biggest-selling daily paper print his remark that 'The police have been guilty of conduct which we would once have believed to be impossible in this country.' The *Guardian* included Hattersley's critique of the police, but the *Times* and *Daily Telegraph* carefully edited out this comment from their reports.

On a direct level there were dozens of examples of news stories and photographs involving intimidation of striking miners. Yet, in contrast to the almost blanket coverage of violence by pickets, the vast majority of allegations concerning police actions on the picket line were ignored. Perhaps the most notorious example was the photograph of a young woman, Lesley Boulton, being attacked by a truncheon-wielding mounted policeman at Orgreave coking plant on Monday 18 June 1984. She had been shouting at the police to 'get an ambulance' for a middle-aged injured miner. John Harris, a photographer with the International Freelance Library, managed to take two frames of film of the police attack and then ran off. Later that Monday afternoon his agency offered the pictures to the *Daily Mirror* who rejected them because they had 'got all they wanted'. Harris's photographs were freely available to Fleet Street later that week, but of Britain's 17 national newspapers only the *Observer* published the picture of Boulton the following Sunday. Instead, it was left to some European papers like *Stern* magazine to print it. However, the public display of the photograph at the 1984 Labour Party conference in Blackpool forced an interest from Fleet Street. Their response was to suggest that perhaps the camera angle or depth of field gave a misleading impression.

Detailed allegations of police harassment were also carefully documented. On 7 June 1984, a Nottinghamshire miner claimed he had recognized two plain-clothes policemen posing as pickets and inciting other miners to throw stones. But perhaps the most remarkable incident occurred on 15 June 1984 when two more plain-clothes policemen were caught red-handed posing as miners at the Cresswell Strike Centre in Derbyshire. The police officers, P.C. Stevens and Sergeant Monk, were even identified by local reporter Carmel O'Toole whose paper, the *Worksop Guardian*, carried the story on its front page. O'Toole then phoned through the story to the *Daily Mail* and *Daily Mirror*. They spiked the story. Names, addresses, telephone numbers and sworn statements concerning several alleged incidents were compiled by *Tribune* for any inquiring journalist or editor. Fleet Street turned a blind eye.

Discrimination by the press between violence against working and striking miners, particularly in the Midlands coalfields, was starkly exposed by the case of Derbyshire miner Pete Neelan. In January 1985 his car was set on fire, his garage burned down and the word 'Revenge' spray-painted on to his house. As soon as it was announced that he was a miner at Warsop Main, Derbyshire, several Fleet Street correspondents and an ITN team flocked to his house to record the details for publication. However, when Neelan told them he was on strike there was suddenly a loss of interest in the news story. 'Everyone seemed terribly disappointed,' said Neelan. The questions stopped and the journalists went home. The next day there was no sign of the story in the press.[30]

Rarely has there been a more lucid indictment that the selection and presentation of news involving an industrial dispute was based on political rather than professional judgements. After all, stories about police misconduct are by their very nature newsworthy and include plenty of human interest for the tabloid papers. Some labour correspondents do accept that police violence was ignored by Fleet Street. 'Yes, there is some truth in that,' said the *Guardian*'s labour editor Keith Harper, 'but it's difficult to cover these incidents because most reporters stand behind the police lines and tend to rely on police reports for their information.' This is partly correct. On several occasions, police have physically prevented journalists and photographers from witnessing picket-line violence, notably on 29 May 1984 and 18 June 1984 at Orgreave. However, other correspondents, like Jean Stead of the *Guardian* and many local reporters, have stood with the striking miners to obtain a first-hand view – rather than a printed handout from a police press officer.

To be fair, Patrick Wintour and David Hearst of the *Guardian*, did cover examples of police harassment and the role of the courts. A notable example was a feature by Hearst – 'The Day The Police Stormed Armthorpe'.[31] And the paper's agenda pages often included critical articles on the role of the law. That also begs the question, of course – why couldn't the other papers do the same?

One journalist who did acknowledge that there were two sides to picket line violence was Paul Routledge, then labour editor of the *Times*. In the January 1985 edition of *Red Tape*, the civil servants' union journal, he wrote: 'Without equivocation it ought to be stopped [picket-line violence]. All of it, the stone throwing by miners *and* the baton charging by policemen who actually seem to enjoy a week away from home for a pityard punch-up. And don't tell me they don't because I've seen them at it.'

Such honesty was rare. Instead, the British public was told that the assaults and brutality came from one side only – the striking miners. This image of the 140,000 strikers was being presented within 20 days of the beginning of the dispute. 'The threats, blows and insults of Arthur Scargill's storm-troopers', reported the *Mail on Sunday*.[32] On 4 April 1984, he *Daily Express* front page led with an attack on Arthur Scargill by the former railwaymen's union leader Sidney Weighell. 'Battling Sid' warned against 'those who would change society with the pickaxe handle'. The *Express* added that the pickets were 'extremists' and that 'wild men plan to use young pickets as Mao-style Red Guards to plunge the nation into chaos'. A week later, on 11 April, the *Express* front page was taken up by a photograph of 'specially sharpened' nail clusters which pickets had allegedly used to maim police horses.

But it was not until Thursday 19 April 1984 that the *Daily Express* hit their peak – the day of the NUM's special delegate conference in Sheffield. The paper's front-page headline ran – 'Scargill's Red Army Moves In'. And this is what their chief reporter Michael Brown wrote:

> The militant Red Guards responsible for most of the pit strike violence will attack again today when Arthur Scargill attempts to rewrite his union's rules. A rabble of political activists plan to invade the streets of Sheffield to browbeat any opposition to a delegates conference designed to reduce the majority needed for strike action ... It will be orchestrated by a '5th Column' of political activists who have taken over the running of the miners' strike. All are hand-picked men, some with university training who have Communist, Marxist or Trotskyist backgrounds. They run the flying pickets and handle funds for paying them.

Who were the 'Red Guards'? The *Express* didn't say. Who were the 'hand-picked men and 5th column of political activists'? Again the *Express* declined to name names except a Dave Douglass, who is in fact a miner from Hatfield Main, south Yorkshire. The paper's evidence was a quote from an anonymous police officer who commented that there were 'professional agitators' in Sheffield.

The *Mail on Sunday* was also intent on portraying miners as industrial gangsters – 'Say No To Mob Rule'.[33] On 15 July 1984, the paper reported that 'Scargill Backs The Bully Boys'. The story ran: 'Arthur Scargill plans to demand the reinstatement of 50 miners sacked by the NCB for committing criminal offences, including assault, during the pit strike.' What are the facts? Firstly, many of the sacked miners were *not* dismissed for criminal offences. A high proportion was for stealing coal and other industrial misconduct. Secondly, many, if not most, of the sacked miners were acquitted when they were tried in court.

But the picture of the striking miners was now firmly established in the public mind. They were 'rent-a-cheer supporters', 'cronies', 'bully boys', 'a rabble' and 'a mob', while the working miners were 'moderate', 'sensible', and 'honourable'. As the *Daily Express* commented: 'The mob rule of Mr Scargill's pickets must not be allowed to replace the rule of law.' Some angry Kent miners asked Stewart Steven, editor of the *Mail on Sunday*, to justify such coverage. Steven, who tells his staff privately that he is a 'moderate socialist' and a lifelong Labour supporter, replied:

> What we're saying is this. That through the emotion caused in an industrial situation of this kind, what happens is that people like you behave in a way which you would not normally behave. You employ physical measures to stop other fellow Englishmen from doing what they want to do. I think that is unacceptable ... You're only there [on the picket line] in vast numbers because you want to frighten. You don't want to persuade, you don't want to inform. Because once you start frightening people, once you start going out there and saying – 'Look, you do this or else', even if those people get that impression then you are subtly changing society and the forces of society in a way which I don't like. And once you start doing that then, I'm afraid, words like 'stormtroopers' and the memories of the 1930s start pouring in.[34]

By the time the return to work had been launched in the autumn, the issue of violence was even more prominent, because of the inevitable conflict between the strikers and the returning working miners. And so the *Sunday Express* reported – 'Scargill Army On Red Alert –

Terror Pickets Poised As ''Back To Work'' Revolt Grows'.[5] But it was the *Daily Express* front page on the first day of the TUC Congress that best summed up the press attitude. Under the headline of 'TUC In Alert Over Scargill's Secret Army – Police Seal Off Beach', the paper reported:

> Stormy Brighton shut part of its holiday beaches and braced itself for a tide of violence at today's opening of the TUC conference. A secret army of agitators is known to have infiltrated the resort with the aim of turning miners' demonstrations into a riot ... Officers were lining the pavements with their backs to the sea and facing the hall. The cordon was aimed at stopping troublemakers getting on to the pebble beach and picking up stones and rocks to hurl at delegates going in and out of the conference.[36]

What was the evidence for this news story? There was a quote from Brighton's mayor John Blackman who said: 'Force will be met with force'. But who were 'the secret army of agitators'? No names were mentioned and the information wasn't attributed to any source.

The image of violence was taken one step further in November 1984. That month Mrs Thatcher made a speech linking international terrorism and the IRA with the striking miners, Arthur Scargill and what she called 'the fascist Left'. This clearly struck a chord with most of the popular press. On 11 November 1984, Remembrance Sunday, the *Mail on Sunday* devoted most of its page two to 'Striking Miners In IRA Security Alert – Pickets Visit Dublin To Learn Paramilitary Tactics Against Police'. The report added: 'The Government has been warned about links between militant members of the National Union of Mineworkers and the IRA. In recent weeks there has been a constant traffic of miners or their representatives between the British mainland, Belfast and the Irish republic.' This was based on the claim that miners like Steve Green from Sutton Manor pit had spoken at meetings organized by Sinn Fein, the political wing of the IRA. This was strongly denied by Roy Jackson, the NUM's Branch Secretary at Sutton Manor, Merseyside, who said: 'Steve Green addressed three meetings of students and workers at five factories about the miners' strike. He spoke at *no* meetings called by Sinn Fein or any other political party.'[37]

But the *Mail on Sunday* had also published a more serious accusation. The paper reported: 'The Dublin Council of Trade Unions, which has strong links with Sinn Fein, the political wing of the IRA, has advised miners at closed meetings in the city how to use paramilitary tactics to combat police operations on the picket lines.' The paper's sole source for this allegation was John Jones, a 39-year-old miner from Point of Ayr pit at Prestatyn in North Wales. The *Mail on Sunday* said: 'He [Jones] claimed the Council of Trade Unions in Dublin has been advising miners how to handle "paramilitary tactics" being used by the British police.' This was reported by Sue Reid, one of three *Mail on Sunday* journalists who wrote the story. She visited Jones's house in Holywell, Clwyd, on Thursday 8 November 1984, seeking information about Steve Green. Jones mentioned that he had also visited the Republic of Ireland to raise money for his fellow striking miners and their families in North Wales. At no time, according to Jones, did he mention or say that miners were 'being advised how to handle paramilitary tactics'. And the Dublin Council of Trade Unions backs up his denial: 'We have no links with the IRA.' said Des Bonass. 'We are proud to have helped the families of striking miners in Britain but we have never given advice to miners on how to handle paramilitary tactics: neither would we know how to go about it.'[38] The Dublin Council of Trade Unions have since been advised by a solicitor that they have grounds for libel against the newspaper.

John Jones cannot afford to take out a libel action, but he is unequivocal about what happened. He says that Sue Reid fabricated the statement attributed to him and accused her of 'deliberately telling lies' for political purposes.[39] Two days after the article was published, on 13 November 1984, Jones wrote to Stewart Steven, the *Mail on Sunday*'s editor, and made the same accusation:

> I have never pursued or been involved in any meetings concerning Sinn Fein or instructions on paramilitary tactics to combat police operations on the picket line ... The role of the Dublin Council of Trade Unions has been to arrange and co-ordinate meetings between the NUM and Irish trade unions. They told us not to go to any fund-raising meetings organized by Sinn Fein for fear of the British press making political connotations. Their fears are well founded.

The letter was never published 'on the grounds of space', although NGA FoC John Warwicker believes this was the genuine reason.

Instead, Jones had to wait nearly eight months for an apology from the *Mail on Sunday*. It was published on 30 June 1985 – on the bottom right-hand corner of page 16. The retraction said: 'The remarks were not made by Mr Jones and we apologize. The mistake was rectified in later editions of the paper but not the one circulating in North Wales.' This was only partly correct. It was only removed from two of the five editions. And, perhaps more important, the substance of the claim remained in all five editions. This was that 'Sinn Fein, the political wing of the IRA in Dublin, has advised miners how to use paramilitary tactics to combat police operations on the picket line.'

Meanwhile, John Jones has been receiving hate mail from people all over the country. Here's a letter from a man in Sutton Coldfield, near Birmingham, who wrote three days after the *Mail on Sunday* article: 'After seeing the Remembrance Day ceremony and thinking of all the men who gave their lives so that this might be a country, I wonder if they thought their sacrifice was worthwhile if they could see the likes of you, now.' In addition, slogans like 'No More Food Parcels From the IRA' have been daubed on the underground roadways at the pit where Jones works. But perhaps the most bitter moment for Jones came in April 1984 when he spoke at a miners' meeting. Before he could start, a fellow miner shouted out: 'Get back to the IRA.'

Two days after the *Mail on Sunday* article on the 'links between the NUM and the IRA', the *Express* papers followed suit. 'Pit Pickets "Schooled in Terror" By The IRA', reported Harry Cooke of the *Daily Express*.

> Militant picket leaders have been schooled in IRA-style terror tactics, a member of the NUM executive claimed yesterday after a night of arson, looting and petrol bomb attacks on police. 'We have suspected for some time that a very sinister element has been brought into picket organization,' said the man, who insisted on remaining anonymous.[40]

Less than two weeks later came a fresh series of allegations of violence by striking miners. On 23 November 1984, Michael Fletcher, a working miner from Fryston Colliery, Yorkshire, was attacked and beaten up, sustaining severe injuries. The press immediately assumed miners were to blame. 'Shadow Of The Jackboot – Beaten-Up Miner Warns: Next Time They Could Kill Somebody', reported the *Daily Mail*. The *Sun* whistled a similar tune – 'Fury At Baseball Bat Mobsters'. However, on 23 October, 1985, Leeds Crown Court found four Yorkshire miners not guilty of all charges concerning the attacks on Fletcher.

The day after the attack on Fletcher, on 24 November, another Yorkshire working miner, Stuart Spencer, was being hailed as the victim of violence. His house had been burnt down. He immediately blamed striking miners. The press automatically believed him. 'Targets Of Terror – Pit Mob's Arson Attack', announced the front page of the *Mail on Sunday* the next day. The paper assumed it was part of 'a long list of terror outrages against men who have dared to disobey their union's diktat'. The *Sunday Mirror* agreed – 'Miner's Home Arson Horror – Working Stuart Vows: "Thugs Won't Stop Me"'. So did the *Sunday Express*: 'Victim of Hate – Arson Attack On Pit Rebel... The harrowing ordeal of back-to-work miner Stuart Spencer reached a terrifying peak yesterday when his bungalow was destroyed by fire. For five days, since his return to work last Monday, he had had to brave a howling mob of 100 strikers outside his home, death threats, obscene phone calls and hate mail.'

West Yorkshire police immediately launched a full investigation into the incident. In January 1985, the police published their report on the case. They concluded that the burning down of Spencer's home had 'nothing to do with striking miners or their supporters'.

Undaunted, most of the popular press continued to pursue the 'terror' line in the month before the Christmas of 1984. On 25 November 1984, the *Sunday Express* front page declared – 'Suitcases Of Cash Pay For Terror'. The paper reported: 'Moderates in the NUM are convinced the cash is being used to finance terror squads of militant youths and a group of intimidators selected to "persuade" working pitmen to join the strike.' The basis for this tale came from an allegation by an anonymous member of the National Working Miners' Committee who said: 'I am getting reports of 20 or 30 men walking into pubs and clubs. One or two always have wads of notes and call "drinks all round". No wonder they don't want to go back to work. Some of them seem to be better off on strike.' Based on this second-hand piece of information, the *Express* went on to describe them as 'free-spending intimidators'. Two weeks later, the *Sunday Express* had returned to portraying Britain's striking miners as industrial terrorists. 'Anger At IRA Link', said the front-page headline on 9 December 1984. The paper added:

> Arthur Scargill is facing demands for an investigation into links between the NUM and Sinn Fein, the IRA's political wing. At a meeting of the union executive on Thursday, moderate Trevor Bell is to raise a disturbing dossier of contacts and visits to Northern Ireland by striking miners. Reports have been reaching executive members for several months about fund-raising activities in Ulster and training for miners at Sinn Fein 'workshops' in Belfast... Many of the tactics used by strikers in attacks on working miners and police bear a strong resemblance to those used in Ulster.

Miners and their families – Scargill's cannon-fodder for the fascists of the left?

From the beginning of the strike government ministers, particularly Peter Walker, made a conscious decision to personalize the dispute around Arthur Scargill, the NUM's President. In every speech, interview and statement the message was the same – 'the real victims of Scargill's strike' and 'the cost of Scargill'.[41] Week after week this line was pumped out by ministers and MPs. It was as if the 140,000 striking miners and their families didn't exist. And when they were acknowledged they were, according to Walker, 'cannon fodder for Mr Scargill in the Marxist causes which he pursues'.[42] The strategy was clear – isolate the NUM President from his members.

All this was echoed by most of Fleet Street. The evidence was overwhelming. To such a degree, in fact, that even seasoned journalists like Simon Jenkins, political editor of the *Economist* and former editor of the *London Evening Standard*, admitted the coverage was 'ludicrously biased'. He added:

> Fleet Street obliges Scargill daily: its loathing for him is almost palpable. It searches for derogatory material, exaggerating every slip – the photograph comparing him with Hitler has become one of his most effective props. Wishful thinking showers down on him from headlines. First he was to fail for refusing a ballot, then through the drift back to work, splits in his executive, when power workers refused support, through the backlash against picket-line violence and now through the longevity of coal stocks ... A public kept in ignorance of the nature of his support, and told merely of his idiocy, grows ever more mystified at his survival.[43]

Jenkins' analysis is certainly borne out by the coverage. From day one of the dispute it was 'The Scargill Strike' (*Sunday Times*[44]). On 31 March, 1984, the *Daily Express* front page declared – 'Scargill's Cannon-Fodder ... Fuelled by an insensate hatred for the government and the "system", Scargill, McGahey and their camp followers have launched the miners on a Kamikaze campaign.' The *Daily Mail* agreed five days later – 'Scargill's War On Democracy', said their front-page headline. But did Scargill start the strike? In fact, the dispute began in Yorkshire when mass pithead meetings were held at every colliery to decide whether to support the fight to oppose the closure of Cortonwood. A Yorkshire NUM Area Council meeting was then arranged which took the decision to sanction all-out industrial action. Scargill didn't attend or speak at any of these meetings.

Nor does he have a vote on the miners' National Executive Committee.

And yet the press continued to portray the dispute as 'Scargill's obsession' (*Daily Express* [45]) and its effects on mining communities as 'The Price of Scargill's War'.[46] Such coverage infuriated the miners and their families who felt insulted at being portrayed as dupes of one individual. 'We are outraged at the way we are presented in the press,' Terry Harrison, NUM Branch Secretary of Betteshanger, Kent, told an NUJ meeting. 'Why does Fleet Street personalize the dispute, with Arthur Scargill as the bogeyman. We're not Scargill's cannon fodder. He is responding to decisions we have taken in our branches. We have got a leader who does what we tell him to.' Fellow Kent miner Morris Bryan agreed: 'Arthur Scargill is pursuing the policy of the union. It's not his policy, it's been formulated by the union,' he told *Mail on Sunday* editor Stewart Steven.[47]

Fleet Street's personalization was also rejected by Ned Smith, the Coal Board's Industrial Relations director-general, who said: 'I don't think Scargill has kept them out. That is nonsense. A lot of the areas have a great deal of autonomy. It's simply not true to say it's Scargill's strike'.[48] Former Conservative MP and Director of the Tory Party Political Centre, Lord Alport, also refutes the idea that it was 'Scargill's strike' (*Sunday Times* [49]). He said: 'The privation which half a million men, women and children have suffered during the past 12 months is not due to the charisma or eloquence of Mr Scargill'.[50]

However, the longer the dispute continued, the more the press blamed Scargill. Even falling share prices was his fault. 'Bogeyman Scargill Savages Market', reported the *London Standard* 'Arthur Scargill played the bogeyman in stock markets today as worries about the coal strike helped undermine share prices.'[51]

By the time of the 1984 Labour Party conference, the press had to report Scargill's speech which produced a thunderous standing ovation. This is how the *Sunday Telegraph*'s Edward Pearce managed it:

> Scargill gets his effects chiefly by embodying rage . . . With a claque working on the floor for him, he paralyses and enfeebles those who privately feel only disgust. He has a line in collective self-pity which he follows up with shouts and screams of ungovernable and delicate calculation. The claque cheers fervidly. The dimmer element in the audience is moved to ecstasy by this petrol and matches act.[52]

The *London Standard*'s front page reported: 'Hijacker Scargill . . . Arthur Scargill hijacked the Labour conference today to a cheering standing ovation from the hall and to the visible discomfort of Labour's leadership.'[53]

This kind of reporting was even rejected by John Torode, the *Guardian*'s leader writer on industrial affairs and a SDP parliamentary candidate, who commented the next week:

> It is nothing more than nonsense to suggeset, as most commentators have done, that Arthur Scargill has hijacked the Labour Party. Equally, it was nonsensical to suggest that King Arthur hijacked the TUC when union leaders met for their week beside the seaside at Brighton. What happened at both conferences was that the National Union of Mineworkers, accurately and effortlessly, reflected the militant and frustrated role of Labour activists.[54]

But Fleet Street was unrepentant. Here's a *Sunday Express* leader: 'There is only one butcher of the coal industry. It is Mr Scargill himself. He has split his own union beyond repair. He has dragged the reputation of miners into the gutter'.[55]

Nevertheless, it cannot be denied that Scargill did, to some extent, personalize the dispute himself by taking such a dominant, leading role in the daily running of the strike. More important, it was nearly always the NUM President and not Peter Heathfield, General Secretary, or Mick McGahey, the NUM's Vice President, who was interviewed on television or the radio. In addition, Scargill always chaired the press conferences. He even occasionally pre-empted the miners' union by announcing premature demands, like the 10p levy and the 24-hour general strike just prior to the TUC Congress. Now, this may well have been because Scargill was a better communicator. But the NUM President's constant TV appearances, in particular, did give the impression that Scargill was all-powerful.

But Fleet Street went much further than mere personalization. The *Sunday Times* described the dispute as a 'Marxist-inspired strike'.[56] This is how the paper's former joint deputy editor and political editor Hugo Young analysed such a claim and its implications:

> What exactly is the label Marxist meant to indicate? From its persistent use by the newspapers, which have seen their only role in the dispute as being to ally themselves with a government crusade, the answer is clear enough. Marxism conveys, first of all, illegitimacy. It carries powerful overtones of an alien force, which is not primarily interested in the miners at all. A Marxist strike is a political strike, for which industrial grievances merely serve as a pretext to be ruthlessly exploited. Marxism is Muscovite: an influence dedicated to manipulating innocent British citizens to take action against their best interests.

But the most important effect of 'Marxist', as used in this context, is the completeness of the explanation it appears to offer for what has been happening. Call Scargill a Marxist, and correctly identify members of the NUM executive as Communists, and you seem to have solved the entire analytical problem.[57]

But the *Sunday Times*, from which Hugo Young resigned in March 1984, also saw Scargill – 'a Marxist of Stalinist schooling' – in Orwellian terms. The paper commented – 'Hardly a day went past for most of the year without Scargill appearing on our telescreens' – and then quoted from page 16 of Orwell's novel *1984*:

What was strange was that although hated and despised by everybody, although every day a thousand times a day, on platforms, on the telescreen, in newspapers, in books, his theories were refuted, smashed, ridiculed, held up to the general gaze for the pitiful rubbish that they were – in spite of all this, his influence never seemed to grow less. Always there were fresh dupes, waiting to be seduced by him.[58]

This process of delegitimizing the miners' strike, as though it were purely a Marxist crusade and had little to do with the closure of pits and the loss of jobs, was taken one further step by Fleet Street. There was a serious attempt by some popular papers to associate Scargill with Adolf Hitler and striking miners with fascism. On 19 April 1984, the *Daily Express* ran their 'Scargill's Red Army Moves In' story. In the same edition was a feature article headlined – 'Scargill And The Fascists Of The Left – From The Man Who Witnessed The Rise Of Hitler: A Warning We Must Not Ignore'. The piece was by Professor Hans Eysenck, a psychiatrist, who argued that Scargill was using tactics employed by Hitler: 'Scargill is now building up his power along similar lines.' It was the same day as the NUM's special delegate conference and the *Express* also devoted a centre-page spread to the miners' strike. Their headline? 'Scargill's Cannon Fodder'.

The editor of the *Sunday Express*, Sir John Junor, also believed there were similarities with the dictator of Nazi Germany:

Mr Arthur Scargill has clearly been flicked in the raw by suggestions that he has been acting like Hitler. But isn't he? Hitler used his thugs to terrorize into submission people who disagreed with him. Isn't that precisely what is happening now at night in Nottinghamshire mining villages? Hitler had an utter contempt for the ballot box. By refusing the miners a right to vote, hasn't Mr Scargill again invited comparison? There the serious similarity ends. For although Mr Scargill may be a stupid man, I do not think he is an evil one.[59]

The *Sunday Telegraph*'s editor, Peregrine Worsthorne, preferred a more domestic comparison. Scargill and the miners were Sir Oswald Mosley and the British Union of Fascists – 1980s version. In one article Worsthorne referred to 'leftwing fascism' on no less than eight occasions.[60]

But it was the *Sun* who tried the hardest to portray the NUM President as a modern version of Adolf Hitler. 'Mods In Fury At ''Adolf'' Arthur', ran a headline on 2 May 1984. Two weeks later, on 15 May 1984, the paper planned to publish a front-page picture of Scargill with one arm raised and the banner headline – 'Mine Führer'. However, the *Sun*'s printworkers objected and the picture and headline were removed (see 'Right of Reply' for details). Later in the strike, the *Sun* tried again: 'Scargill Takes To The Bunker', headlined an editorial. It added: 'Arthur Scargill declares that he would ''rather go down fighting'' than surrender pits and jobs . . . This is Hitler in the bunker again – the Führer destroying himself and willing also to destroy all Germany.'[61]

The *Mail on Sunday* used the fascist analogy in their news columns. There were references to 'storm-troopers'.[62] On 1 April 1984, a news story was headlined – 'Coal Boss Hits Out At Union ''Nazis'''. When the paper's editor, Stewart Steven, was asked to justify such reporting, this was his reply:

> You see, I wrote a book about Poland. I then remember the disgust I felt when Scargill attacked the Solidarity movement, and attacked therefore, by definition, my friends in Poland. I felt his attack was to support a regime which I regard as a fascist regime. Now, what is it about the nature of this man that creates that kind of mood and impression? I believe it is within his politics. And I believe those politics to be of the extreme Left and, as history has shown, the extreme Left and the extreme Right do, I'm afraid, join in an unholy and deeply unpleasant union. And I think perhaps we are seeing that here.[63]

Right of reply – the printworkers strike back

During his concluding speech as the then Chairman of the Labour Party at their annual conference on 6 October 1972, Tony Benn told the delegates: 'I sometimes wish the trade unionists who work in the mass media, those who are writers, broadcasters, secretaries, printers and lift operators at Thomson House, would remember that they too are members of our working-class movement and have a responsibility to see what is said about us is true.' The speech was described as 'preaching industrial anarchy' by the *Daily Mirror* and 'dangerous nonsense' by the *Daily Express*. But it was a prophetic observation. For within 12 years, the consciences of newspaper production workers had been awakened by the coverage of the miners' strike.

It was the *Daily Express* coverage throughout April 1984 that set the scene for a number of battles between printworkers and editorial management. The striking miners had been portrayed as 'cannon fodder', a 'Red Army' and 'Fascists of the Left'. And so it was the last straw on the night of Tuesday 8 May 1984, when SOGAT '82 members in the *Express* machine room were presented with a three-page article entitled – 'The Truth That Scargill Dare Not Tell'. Under no by-line, this article was a fabricated, mock speech by Arthur Scargill. The *Express* claimed that the NUM President would have admitted to his members that the strike was pointless if he cared less about toppling a democratic government and more about the truth. The paper had Scargill saying:

> We have made no progess at all. Let me tell you frankly that this is the century's most senseless dispute. It won't bring down the wicked Thatcher and her government, as I had hoped. Nor will it protect your jobs and jobs for your children. It will destroy them. I want to say only this: 'I have lied. I have lied about the coal stocks at power stations. I have lied about the support we have had from other unions. . . . I confess that I have led you badly and I have caused you endless strife.'

The speech was, in fact, written by Geoffrey Levy, an *Express* feature writer, who was unhappy about his by-line being removed. He said he wanted his name on the article to ensure that readers could see that it was a mock speech.

However, the printworkers were far more angry. SOGAT members signed away the front-page section but scrawled across the proof – 'signed under protest'. They contacted their union's General Secretary, Bill Keys. He approached the then editor, Sir Larry Lamb, and Lord Matthews, the *Express* proprietor, and asked for a right to reply on page one – the same spot as the offending article. Matthews agreed, saying that the piece gave 'cause for concern'. But Lamb refused and offered his resignation. This was rejected by Matthews who still offered the NUM a right of reply. However, the next day, Thursday 10 May, the *Express* NUJ chapel passed, by 103 votes to 30 a motion proposed by Alex Hendry which 'condemned the irresponsible threats of Mr William Keys . . . to shut down the *Daily Express*'. The journalists voted not to handle the NUM's 2,000-word article, scheduled for that Saturday, until Keys 'withdrew his threat'.

Eventually the paper published the NUM's reply on Tuesday 15 May. But this was done only after editorial executives censored a section of the article. Lord Matthews described the introductory passage to Scargill's reply as a 'page of rhetorical abuse' and 'totally unacceptable'. Here is the first paragraph of the introduction:

> Wednesday's *Daily Express* carried on its front and centre pages a display which must have aroused horrified memories among those who can recall the propaganda techniques used by Dr Goebbels and his colleagues in Nazi Germany throughout the 1930s and 1940s. In its vicious and hysterical attack on Arthur Scargill and the NUM leadership, the *Daily Express* utterly abandoned all ethics and debased the standards of British journalism.

This struggle for the miners' voices to be heard was even more bitter inside the *Sun*'s offices at Bouverie Street. On 14 May 1984, John Smith, a staff photographer for the *Sheffield Star*, took a picture of Arthur Scargill with his arm raised high to greet a group of marching miners in Mansfield, Nottinghamshire. As is often the case the photograph was supplied to the national papers. The *Sun* decided to publish the picture on its front page under the banner headline, written by the editor Kelvin McKenzie, 'Mine Führer'.

The editor of the *Sheffield Star*, Michael Corner, described this decision as 'disgusting. To imply that Mr Scargill had made any kind of Nazi salute or gesture was taking the photograph completely out of context'.[64] The *Sun*'s printworkers agreed. After the headline was shown to process workers, all seven production chapels met and refused to handle it. The NGA Imperial Committee then sent a delegation of all the unions to see the management, who threatened workers in the NGA process and composing departments with the sack if they did not handle the picture and headline. However, without telling the NGA, McKenzie had already decided not to use it, and so the paper was published the next day with no front-page picture or headline. Instead, there was a brief statement from management.

During these negotiations the *Sun*'s NUJ chapel had supported management. Malcolm Withers, the NUJ FoC, said: 'Our chapel believes we should not interfere in editorial matters, and must remain neutral. It's up to the editors and the proprietor to do it.'

One of the few NUJ members to dissent was editorial layout artist

Oliver Duke. At a chapel meeting on 16 May to discuss their 23 per cent pay claim, he proposed a motion which condemned the (unused) headline and (published) story as 'a totally unjustified attack on the mineworkers' President and by implication the NUM itself'. The motion added full support for the production chapels for refusing to print the picture and headline and 'informs management that should such editorial excesses occur again it will refuse to produce them for the paper'. It was seconded reluctantly, not one chapel committee member supported it and when Ian Blunt, deputy FoC, proposed that the motion not be put to the meeting, he won by an overwhelming majority.

The journalists were again reticent when the paper's production workers lobbied for a statement in support of the miners to be published on 27 June 1984, the TUC Day of Action. The other 17 chapels agreed to press for a half-page statement or free advertisement, and three officials from SOGAT and the NGA went to see McKenzie and Bruce Matthews, Managing Director of the News Group papers.

When McKenzie was shown the statement he remarked, 'This propaganda is obviously written by a leftwing Marxist', and offered them space in the letters page or an advertisement – at the cost of £2,500. The unions refused and McKenzie said angrily: 'I can't understand why my paper is being hit.' The union officials replied they thought that was patently obvious. Matthews then said: 'I don't see why the *Sun* should print this when no-one at the Labour Party talks to our journalists and when Neil Kinnock came here he slipped in by the back door.'

McKenzie then proposed changes in the statement. He wanted references to a right of reply removed because it was 'a Marxist-inspired tactic', and the accusation that the government had lied about intervention because 'it was libellous'. And he was adamant that the unions would have to pay for the advertisement. The response from the usually placid production unions surprised the management. When the chapels met separately they were so angered by comments from labour relations executives about their 'plots' and 'disloyalty' that only the SOGAT machinists were prepared to stay at work. All the rest walked out on the night before publication (26 June) and, following a dispute on strike pay, the paper did not appear again until 30 June – three days later.

Three months later, on the night of Friday 28 September 1984, the *Sun*'s printworkers were again seeking some form of redress for the paper's reporting of the miners' dispute. 'Scum Of The Earth' was how the paper's front page planned to portray the striking miners the next day. The article was a leader, written by McKenzie, which attacked the miners as 'scum' for their involvement in violent confrontation with police near Silverwood colliery, south Yorkshire. I have obtained a copy of the offending editorial. Every paragraph enraged the printworkers:

> Miners were rightly once called the salt of the earth. No longer. Too many of them have become the scum of the earth. Not, of course, the brave pitmen who have worked on through seven months of intimidation. By scum we mean the mob who perpetrated the vicious ambush of police in South Yorkshire yesterday. This premeditated operation to trap, stone and beat up policemen was the behaviour, not of trade unionists, but of terrorists.
>
> At next week's Labour Party conference there will be nonsensical talk of police volence. It is a smoke screen to conceal the true brutality of the pickets. Scargill and Co. may choose to ignore the public revulsion because they believe their insane strategy will win them victory. But Scargill has totally misjudged the British people. The worse the violence gets, the greater the determination that there will be NO SURRENDER.

The reaction of the printworkers was of 'great horror'. At a meeting of 17 production chapels, only the FoC of the SOGAT machine assistants doubted whether he could deliver his members to support some form of right of reply. A print unions' delegation then met Paul Rochez, a senior News Group executive. They told him they didn't want to censor the paper. But they did want some redress – either a disclaimer, a paid advertisement or a statement in the letters page. 'We did not want to be censors,' said an NGA member. 'We just wanted to tell the *Sun*'s readers – "This is what the editor has written, but the people who work on the *Sun* and produce the paper don't agree with its contents."'

The paper's management rejected all three requests, although they had already decided to abandon production of the *Sun*. And John Brown, the NGA's deputy FoC, says he was roundly abused by one management official who approached him separately. Another NGA member was accused of being a 'shop-floor censor' by two *Sun* journalists whose union, the NUJ, had not supported the printworkers. On the Sunday afternoon, the 'Scum' editorial was to have been re-presented with additional criticism of the print unions involved in Friday night's stoppage. But the leader never materialized and wasn't published after a pay dispute.

A measure of the print unions' success in securing a right of reply for the miners was revealed in an incident on 15 January 1985. That morning the *Sun* had published a letter in their 'Have A Go' column. It was signed anonymously 'Fed-Up Miner's Wife, S. Wales' and complained about the NUM's alleged lack of action over the allocation of food and money:

> I am the wife of a striking miner who has been out for ten months and I would like to know what has happened to the £326,000 supposed to have been collected by the Labour Party and others. Each miner's family was promised a turkey and a present at Christmas for any child in the home. None was received in this area ... I think the people who sent the money should start asking questions.

Some NGA members were suspicious about this letter and alleged that it had been fabricated. This was angrily denied by the editor, Kelvin McKenzie, when John Brown, the NGA's FoC, went to see him to request a right of reply. Negotiations broke down, but then an astonishing thing happened. Within two hours of returning to his chapel office, Brown received a hand-delivered letter from McKenzie. The *Sun*'s editor was *offering* a right of reply: 'I am willing – in fact quite eager – for the *Sun* to publish a "Have A Go" from the South Wales NUM putting their side of the story.'

Clearly, the 58 million lost copies of the *Sun* in 1984 had been an influence on his decision, but it was an indication of the production workers' success in securing a right of reply for the miners.

The voice of the miners – arguments put but not heard

On 11 June 1984, three months into the strike, a group of industrial correspondents went up to Sheffield for a meeting with Peter Heathfield, the NUM's General Secretary, to discuss the union's hostile relationship with Fleet Street. The journalists complained that some of them were willing to report issues like the effects of pit closures on mining communities, loss of civil liberties and the role of coal in Britain's energy policy. But, they said, the NUM was not providing the facilities and information for them to do so, particularly as the NUM had only one national press officer compared to the Coal Board's battery of over 40 public relations officials. Little was done, mainly because of the deep mistrust between the two sides.

After the strike, Patrick Wintour, the *Guardian*'s labour correspondent, was more specific: 'The NCB had a strategy with the media. The NUM, by contrast, had none ... At the outset of the strike the NUM held no briefings or formal press conferences at which it could have presented its arguments for the retention of a large coal industry.'[65] Nell Myers, the NUM's press officer who doubles as Arthur Scargill's personal assistant, replied:

> When the strike began in March 1984, the NUM had already spent two years briefing industrial correspondents, supplying them with leaked government and Coal Board documents as well as our own monthly journal, and warning of the Board's pit closure plans and the consequential effects for Britain. However, we discovered a long time ago that no amount of 'access' for industrial correspondents from trade union officials stands a chance against similar briefings between respective employers.[66]

Wintour's argument presupposes that there were several newspapers willing to print the NUM's point of view, but were unable because of the union's inability to set the agenda. It is true, of course, that there was some balanced, independent and even sympathetic reporting from Fleet Street. The *Financial Times'* John Lloyd, the *Mirror*'s Geoffrey Goodman and the *Guardian*'s coverage were all notable, if rare, examples of this. And the odd local paper even produced editorial support. Here's a leader from the *East Kent Mercury* in March 1984:

> The 2,800 miners in Kent are on strike in an effort to safeguard the future of the Kent coalfield and because of that, whether we like it or not, they are striking for us. For if Mr Ian MacGregor did close the Kent coalfield this tiny area of southeast Kent would become a black spot overnight. There would be no alternative employment for the miners and the collapse of their spending power would result in further unemployment in the distributive trades and others.

However, the overwhelming factual evidence surely undermines Wintour's argument and supports Myers' analysis. Firstly, not one national newspaper supported the miners editorially. That in itself, although not necessarily in the serious papers, would discourage journalists from reporting the NUM's point of view. Secondly, and much more important, is the fact that news stories damaging to the NCB and the government were suppressed after interventions by proprietors, editors and ministers. One political correspondent from a serious daily newspaper told me that he even got to the stage where on certain stories he didn't call Whitehall for comment or information. This was, he said, because he knew Downing Street or ministers would be on the phone to his editor to 'rubbish' or suppress the story.

Here are yet two more examples of the use of the editorial blindfold for political purposes. In April 1984, Ros Franey, a freelance journalist, was hired by the *Sunday Times* as a researcher in the paper's political department. One of her major tasks was to research the *Sunday Times'* book on the miners' strike. And so she collected and logged material mainly on issues of the dispute which most of Fleet Street had largely ignored – the women's support groups, the role of the courts and the relationship between the police and the mining communities.

At Christmas 1984 her contract was suddenly terminated. When the book was finally published in September 1985, Franey read it with care. 'This was just as well,' she said. 'Most of the topics on which I'd worked for eight months were dismissed, between commas, in a single sentence.'[67] This was hardly surprising given the attitude of one of the book's authors, Michael Jones, the *Sunday Times'* political editor. On seeing Franey's material on the women's support groups on her desk one day, he dismissed their role as irrelevant.

A politically more damaging story was swiftly removed before it could be published in the *News of the World*. In the early days of January 1985 there were repeated reports of power cuts, particularly in London and the south-east area. On 13 January 1985 the *News of the World* planned to print a story on page four about the need for coal stocks to be moved. Written by the paper's political staff, it concluded: 'The CEGB is thought to have pressed the NCB for supplies to be directed to the London and south-east area, if power shortages are to be avoided in 1985, due to the uneven distribution of existing coal stocks'. The story was spiked. However, it was not long before its unpublished predictions turned out to be accurate. Within two days the NCB moved coal from one of its large collieries in the northeast for the first time in 10 months.

There is also some evidence, though far from conclusive, that Fleet Street's hostility was based on simple class hatred towards the miners and their families. Charles Moore is the editor of the *Spectator* but used to be a *Daily Telegraph* reporter and writer and still contributes to the paper regularly. Asked about the miners, he replied: 'I really hate those people, actually. This strike has brought out feelings I didn't know I had. It seems to me such a lie that these people represent or are the defenders of an oppressed class and so clear that Arthur Scargill is an oppressor, that it has finally brought out all my contempt for the Left.'[68] A perhaps more serious example came from the *Sunday Times* in August 1984. The paper commissioned a feature article by Professor Frank Musgrove of Manchester University. This is what he wrote:

In the past 30 years two social processes have siphoned off men of initiative and ability. Educational selection has left a residue of D and E stream secondary modern and comprehensive school pupils for pit work – there has been a massive haemorrhage of talent from mining communities. And earlier pit closure programmes have set up eddies of selective migration which have drained away the most enterprising men from the more northerly fields.

It is the diluted human residues that remain, especially in Yorkshire and Durham, that have been most effectively manipulated and mobilized by the tactics of the NUM. [my italics] They have been bounced into a strike without a ballot and have learned to repeat slogans ('No pit closures on economic grounds'. 'Cowards hide behind ballots') whose horrendous implications they do not begin to grasp.

We did not solve the educational problem by raising the school-leaving age to 15, still less to 16. *Five years in the E stream of a comprehensive school is an excellent training in sheer bloody-mindedness if not actual subversion* [my italics] ... This is not education. It is a species of trench warfare. It is anticipatory socialization for the mass picket line.[69]

The publication of such an article tells us more about the new *Sunday Times* than it does about Fleet Street as a whole. But it was an indication of some of the themes of the coverage of the 1984-5 miners' strike. Musgrove, in fact, touched on some of the recurrent attitudes that invaded the news pages of the popular press. That the 140,000 striking miners and their families were 'cannon fodder' (*Daily Express*[70]) for Arthur Scargill's political ambitions, that they were being brainwashed by the NUM President's propaganda and that they were being intimidated into supporting the strike against their will.

This argument didn't explain why, in the many pits where there was no intimidation whatsoever, the support for the strike was so solid. Nor did it explain why, if the miners were all unthinking dupes of Arthur Scargill, some miners stayed at work and others returned to their pits later in the dispute. The reality was that dispassionate, rational inquiry and investigation into the miners' strike was largely forsaken. Instead, prompted by editorial management and Cabinet ministers, many lines of inquiry which were damaging to the government and the Coal Board, were cut off. The miners' voices were not heard. But it would be wrong to blame the industrial journalists, many of whom were very unhappy with their own papers' coverage. They were, after all, under considerable pressure. One correspondent said that he received almost daily instructions from his editor about the news coverage of the strike. Another industrial reporter described how his editor had been summoned to No. 10 Downing Street for a meeting with Mrs Thatcher. The Prime Minister told his editor that she was concerned about the tone of some of the newspaper's reporting.[71]

It will be interesting to see if such pressure provides similar editorial dividends for the government in a future national miners' strike. Geoffrey Goodman, the *Daily Mirror*'s former assistant and industrial editor, believes: 'It is inconceivable that there would be the same media unanimity again – a press and TV coverage which, especially in the case of most newspapers, was the most one-sided and brazenly biased of any industrial dispute since the end of the Second World War. No government could expect to have that treatment repeated so quickly.'[72]

Indeed they couldn't.

9. Conclusion: What Is To Be Done?

'Knowledge will forever govern ignorance. And a people who mean to be their own governors must arm themselves with the power which knowledge gives.' James Madison, President of the United States, 1822.

'The press which claimed to be for so long is no longer the guardian of freedom in this country. The power of the press proprietors in this country has never been greater than it is today.' Edward Heath, former Conservative Prime Minister, House of Commons, 20 November 1985.

When he launched his pro-Empire crusade in 1930, Lord Beaverbrook, owner of the *Daily Express* and *London Evening Standard*, was regularly accused of suppressing his political opponents' speeches. Britain's most notorious press baron replied: 'I have been advised to open my columns to the opposition. My answer has been: "Go to the opposition papers." '[1]

It would be difficult for a contemporary Conservative press baron to make a similar suggestion to a disgruntled reader and look him or her straight in the eye at the same time. He would know that sending the reader to find the 'opposition papers' would be a forlorn journey. The search would be hazardous, to say the least. Along the way he or she might come across the *Daily Mirror* which during general elections and by-elections is certainly a pro-Labour paper but whose political substance is closer to the SDP/Liberal Alliance, particularly on defence policy. The reader might also pick up the *Guardian* or the *Observer*, two independent newspapers with fine liberal and social conscience traditions. But, although they could be deemed 'opposition papers', they are hardly staunch supporters of Her Majesty's Official Opposition in the shape of the Labour Party.

Instead, any reader visiting Fleet Street in 1986 would be faced with a rather different set of newspapers. He would find 12 of them, 10 unequivocally, supporting the Conservative government – out of a total of 18. Even the Tory Party's own supporters in Fleet Street acknowledge this, as *Daily Mail* columnist Paul Johnson said: 'Mrs Thatcher has had a square deal from Fleet Street; rather better than a square deal, I'd say. There are some editors and journalists who would almost go to the stake for her.'[2]

While this obvious editorial imbalance is highly disturbing, not least for the state of British democracy, it is not, in my view, the major problem. While the leader columns often set the tone for a newspaper, it is doubtful whether they have a major political impact on its readers. It is the news and features pages that really count and this is where the changes have been in recent years regarding coverage of the labour, trade union and peace movements.

The problem is not necessarily that the national papers are partisan or heavily anti-socialist and anti-union in their leader columns. It is only right and proper in a pluralist society that the press should be free to support or attack any political party or industrial movement in their editorials. What many journalists and readers resent is the invasion of their news and features pages with comment, innuendo dressed up as fact, allegations based on the flimsiest of evidence and, on occasions, even downright fabrication. That is the real issue. It is this failure to inform which has polluted Britain's democracy.

Some journalists argue that this is due to a decline in professional standards. They argue that today's reporters are lazy and will regurgitate anything which is fed to them on a plate. It is said that the reasons for the distortions, bias and untruths are mainly due to enormous pressures on journalists because of the circulation war. In addition, that the reason labour, trade union and peace movements suffer more than most is mainly due to their own inadequate public relations and lack of organization.

It seems to me that it is no coincidence that 'standards have declined' at the same time as the power of the proprietors has increased and the concentration of ownership in Fleet Street has contracted and intensified. The explanation for poor reporting in terms of 'the circulation war' is rather spurious. There has *always* been a circulation war in Fleet Street, except perhaps during wartime.

The belief that journalists have suddenly become lazy or incompetent does not stand up. The reality is that as the labour, trade union and peace movements have become increasingly radical and militant, so the press attacks have intensified and increased. There *are* increased pressures on journalists but it has little to do with the alleged circulation war. It is political. Editors and executives are not directly ordering reporters to write certain stories or telling them to leave out certain facts which would embarrass the government. The system is more indirect. As one *London Standard* journalist said: 'The pressure on journalists is much more subtle than people think. What happens is that you know what type of story will get in the paper. If you start writing stories that are sympathetic to the Left you won't get ordered to stop. After a while, your stuff simply won't get published.' In other words, it is self-censorship.

The subsequent coverage of the groups of protesters, workers, individuals and political parties as examined in this book has produced one persistent theme which has coloured the judgement of Fleet Street's editors, executives and subeditors. It is that people who take a highly critical view of the capitalist economy and propose radical alternatives, or who challenge the decision to install cruise missiles in Britain, or who believe that racial and sexual discrimination needs to be met with positive, vigorous action, are not politically legitimate. For the press, these views are somehow outside the orthodox arena for debate. It is as if these radical views have intruded into a private dinner party where the hosts and guests have already arranged the terms of their discussion and anything that might threaten that presupposed agenda is 'unrepresentative'. Hence any gate-crashers are deemed 'loony' or 'extreme' or 'power-mad'. And the result is that they are marginalized as 'outsiders' whose views are a threat to the 'national interest', thereby implying treachery. This was revealed by a front-page *Daily Express* editorial on 29 August 1983, entitled: 'The Enemy Within – ''Scargill and Livingstone, Hate-Makers of Britain'''. The article attacked Scargill for his criticism of Britain and America's policy on nuclear weapons which he said was a threat to world peace. The *Express* launched into Livingstone because he compared Britain's treatment of the Irish people over hundreds of years with Hitler's massacre of the Jews in the Second World War. The paper told its 6 million readers that morning:

Arthur Scargill and Ken Livingstone have exhausted their credit at the bank of tolerance. *They have deliberately set out to wound their own country* ... Yet Scargill and Livingstone should realize that there is a limit even to the British people's unbelievable patience. For years we have treated these two with the humorous contempt normally reserved for amiable eccentrics. Their championship of grotesque causes has been greeted as a joke ... Not any more. The joke has turned sour. By their despicable speeches, Scargill and Livingstone have put themselves beyond the pale ... Arthur Scargill and Ken Livingstone have become the hate-makers of Britain. They must not be surprised if they reap as they have sown.

That article clearly summed up most of Fleet Street's attitude towards this country's radical socialists, trade union leaders and peace protesters. Once labelled as 'the enemy within', then the usual rules for balanced and fair-minded reporting can be, and are, discarded. Judging by the coverage, it is almost as though they have a different set of editorial criteria. That these people are so 'beyond the pale' that it doesn't really matter what headlines or political health warnings are inserted before their names. They are fair game.

There are exceptions, of course, and it would be dishonest to pretend that all newspapers and journalists are guilty and indulge in the same editorial practices. On the whole, the *Guardian* and *Observer* are prepared to give space in their feature pages to people with radical and socialist explanations of political life. Although neither the *Guardian* nor *Observer* supports the Labour Party editorially and both are also anti-union, they are prepared most of the time in their news pages to accept that socialists and peace activists are serious and sincere in their views. Indeed, the *Guardian*'s agenda, features and letters pages are the only forum for radical thought in Fleet Street. Meanwhile, the *Observer* has, in David Leigh, Paul Lashmar and Nick Davies, the best and only investigative journalists, apart from the *Mirror*'s Paul Foot, to publish information embarrassing to the rich and powerful. In addition, there are political correspondents, like the *Times*' Anthony Bevins and the *Daily Telegraph*'s Nicholas Comfort, who are even-handed in their approach and are prepared to write stories that run against the editorial grain of their own papers – a true test of independence. And the *Guardian* columnist Hugo Young is by far and away the only political commentator with a capacity for unprejudiced, detached analysis.

But these journalists and newspapers have become an increasingly dwindling and beleaguered community in recent years as proprietor power has expanded. A good example of this deterioration is the decline of the *Sunday Times*. Under the editorship of Harold Evans, and before it was bought by Rupert Murdoch, the paper conducted campaigns and operated from the premise that governments, companies, trade unions and any agent of power always needed constant vigilance and scrutiny. Together with its non-party stance, except during general elections, the old *Sunday Times* also published stories which were often out of line with the leader columns. However, since Murdoch bought the paper, it has moved steadily to the right and stayed there. This has manifested itself not only in the leader columns where the editor Andrew Neil has a virtual monopoly, but also in the news pages when during the miners' strike and Chesterfield by-election copy was rewritten for political purposes. The *Sunday Times*, like its sister paper, the *Times*, is now virtually a cheerleader for the Conservative government's privatization, industrial and nuclear policies.

And so what can be done to reform Fleet Street? Some argue that newspapers should be more objective and neutral. That is a rather naive view. After all, they are not a mirror of society. Newspapers do not coldly reflect and report events in a dispassionate manner. They select which facts to stress, whose speeches to report, which stories to spike, the size of the headline and its position and prominence in the paper. And so newspapers are hardly mere neutral looking glasses. That's not really possible. Instead, a first step should be a return to the old maxim – facts are sacred. As Brit Hume, the American investigative journalist, said in 1972: 'They [political journalists] shouldn't try to be objective, they should try to be honest. Their so-called objectivity is just a guise for superficiality . . . They never get around to finding out if the guy is telling the truth. What they pass off for objectivity is just a mindless kind of neutrality.'

Of course, balanced reporting of political events, debates and elections is crucially important, particularly as a matter of public record and service. But surely political journalism should go further than that. It should not merely reproduce the latest speech from a Labour MP or the thoughts of the Prime Minister as relayed to lobby correspondents by Downing Street's press secretary Bernard Ingham. The press should, as Harold Evans says, monitor power – whichever party is in government. That is the crucial test of editorial independence. As Anthony Bevins, the *Times*' political correspondent, said, 'My job as a political correspondent is to be even-handed but get in there and ask tough questions. It is to nick away at the stitches of the political parties and reflect the truth as I see it.'

Right of reply

When Frank Allaun, then Labour MP for Salford East, presented his Right of Reply private member's bill in February 1983, most of Fleet Street's reaction was that the mechanisms already existed for redress. As the *Daily Mail* commented: 'There are letter columns where complaints may be published. Corrections may be printed. Those who fail to get satisfaction may appeal to the Press Council. Those who consider themselves libelled can go to the courts.'[3]

However, let's consider a closer analysis of these methods of redress. Firstly, the courts. This is probably the least rewarding form of satisfaction. There is no legal aid for libel actions, so that rules out a large segment of the population. In any case, the results are unpredictable and involve high risk. Secondly, the Press Council. This book has examined in some detail how that body works. The main problem is that the Press Council has no power or legal sanction. It regularly produces a damning indictment of a popular paper, but sometimes the offending paper won't even publish details of the adjudication. After being censured by the Press Council for an untrue story about the Greenham women, the *Daily Express* published the decision and then printed another article on the same page attacking the Press Council! Even when the adjudications are published they end up at the bottom of page 27, or similar position in the paper. Another problem is that their committees of investigation are not vigorous enough in their scrutiny of the offending newspapers, particularly during oral hearings. In addition, its decisions over the years have been baffling and they seem over-deferential to the newspapers. That is almost certainly due to the fact that the Press Council itself is funded by the Fleet Street proprietors.

The third form of redress is the letters page. However, it is well known that many newspapers often refuse to publish letters correcting distortions and misrepresentation. The Press Council even initiates official complaints that papers haven't published letters of correction. Some papers will only print critical letters after they've been vetted or rewritten. As was seen in the chapter on the 1983 general election, the *Daily Express* even wrote out a draft letter for Pat Smith, the press officer for the People's March for Jobs, to authorize. And this was when she was suppose to be writing to them!

This refusal to publish letters of correction, particularly those that are critical of the newspaper, can be seen from the following examples – one from the *Times* and another from the *Sun*. On 6 November 1982, the *Times* published this report from a parliamentary debate based on remarks by the then SDP MP Shirley Williams: 'We are seeing (she said) a system of outdoor relief for Labour councillors, based upon public expenditure, which cannot be justified. The GLC has co-opted to its body two gentlemen who are very active in Labour politics. One was once a Labour MP, Arthur Latham, and the other the leader of Lambeth Council, Ted Knight.'

Latham, Chairman of London Labour Party, was angry at what he saw as 'a slur' because of the implication that he received money for his work on the GLC policy committee. He wrote to the *Times* complaining that the report was untrue as he only received travel expenses: 'We receive no fee, attendance allowance or ''wage'' for our endeavours. It is offensive that the charge should have been made without first checking the facts.'[4] The *Times* refused to publish the letter. Latham replied, again asking for the record to be set straight. Once again the *Times* refused: 'We would point out, with respect, that Mrs Williams' remarks about you and Mr Knight were made in the House of Commons and included in our parliamentary report . . . We cannot make ourselves responsible, any more than the editor of Hansard can do, for the truth of everything that is said in the House. Your quarrel is with Mrs Williams, not with us.'[5] It took another two letters from Latham for the *Times* to publish a 35-word letter on 2 December 1982 – nearly a month after the original story was printed.

Former Labour MP and journalist Frank Allaun had even less luck with the *Times'* sister paper, the *Sun*. At the 1982 Labour Party conference, he called for a right of reply to be introduced by the next Labour government. In its news report of Allaun's speech, the *Sun* said: 'New curbs on the freedom of the press were demanded at the Labour Party conference yesterday – amid an astonishing attack on the *Sun'*. The paper's editorial added:

> Frank Allaun, MP, whose whining and whingeing has been such an unedifying feature of the Labour Party for many years, had his big moment yesterday. He is the leader of a campaign orchestrated by Labour's backwoodsmen to shackle this country's free press. Yesterday, putting forward his lunatic plans to force newspapers to allow what he grandly calls a 'right of reply' to aggrieved people, he let all the pent-up venom of his years as a political nonentity flood out.[6]

Allaun immediately telephoned through a 140-word letter in response to this attack. An hour later, he received a call back from the *Sun*. They told him that his letter would only be published if he omitted certain paragraphs – almost half the letter. Allaun wouldn't co-operate. Here are the paragraphs the *Sun* refused to print:

> That Rupert Murdoch, the proprietor (of the *Sun*), brought down the Australian Labour government by his sensational attacks. That he owns chains of newspapers, television and radio stations throughout the world. That when the Argentinian cruiser was sunk with 300 human lives, outside the 200-mile zone, the sickening headline placed by your executives on the story was 'GOTCHA'. I might add that Mr Murdoch has only one vote – but he owns media influencing the minds of millions.

The letter wasn't published.

And so the existing forms of redress are simply not strong enough, mainly because Britain's national papers find it extremely difficult to admit they have made a mistake.

Many people, including some Conservatives, now believe the answer lies in a statutory right of reply. On 18 February 1983, Frank Allaun proposed such a bill and it failed by only three votes to secure a second reading in Parliament. Ninety-seven MPs voted for it, including Tory MPs like Sir Derek Walker-Smith and Sir Nigel Fisher. The bill would allow *any* individual or organization a legal right of reply to distorted and misrepresentative attacks in the press, television and radio. These replies would have to appear within three days, or 24 hours during a general election campaign. In addition, it would have to be printed free of charge, be of equal length to and in the same position as the offending article or item. The complaint would be considered by a committee, consisting of members of the public and headed by a judge. This panel would have the power to impose fines of up to £40,000 for failure to grant a reply in cases where it was deemed necessary.

Most of Fleet Street oppose such a right of reply law. The *Daily Mail* said: 'Consider for a moment what it could do to clog up newspapers with pages of turgid self-justification. It would be a gift to those who seek to neuter and neutralize the press. It would inhibit editorial freedom.'[7] This argument ignores the fact that the bill caters only for inaccurate or distorted *facts*. It is not designed to impose a right of reply for opinions in editorials or features.

The opponents of a right of reply should also address themselves to the fact that such a law already exists in France, Austria, Denmark, Sweden, West Germany and Canada. In West Germany, for example, the basic right of reply originated from a law introduced by Bismarck in 1871! Their system ensures that a reply has to be published within three months and on the same page as the offending article. It is legally enforceable through the courts, although the dispute is usually settled by lawyers representing the complainant and the newspaper.

In Britain the pressure for a right of reply is growing. Printworkers' action, particularly at the *Sun*, during the 1984-5 miners' strike, secured numerous rights of replies. The Campaign for Press and Broadcasting Freedom has set up a right of reply unit which helps ordinary people with no political and industrial muscle to seek a redress. Fleet Street has reacted bitterly, particularly to action taken by their own production workers. On 20 July 1982, the *Times* accused printworkers of abusing their position. Two weeks later, John Jennings, then Secretary of the Campaign for Press and Broadcasting Freedom, provided this convincing argument: 'Do you seriously suggest that people must continue to believe that the printworkers' action was arbitrary, intimidating and partisan, while at the same time accepting the activities of editors and proprietors as unbiased, impartial and objective?'[8]

But as the press currently operates, regarding its coverage of the labour, trade union and peace movements, it will find it very difficult to avoid a form of right of reply. Even rightwing journalists like Paul Johnson have acknowledged this:

> It is my belief that some kind of statute dealing with the media is now inevitable. Ministers and Tory MPs must recognize that the Left's campaign to censor the press is fed by genuine grievances. The press in Britain is much hated and with reason. The Press Council is useless, especially now it has chosen to wallow in the gutter itself. Broadcasting complaints bodies are equally ineffective. Members of the public ought to have a statutory right of reply.[9]

However, the existence of a right of reply can only be a partial and limited solution. The essential problem remains the lack of editorial diversity and unbalanced political reporting. The main reason that a right of reply has worked in many European countries is that they already have a relatively balanced press. As the General Secretary of the Norwegian Journalists Union said: 'One of the reasons why we have not had much trouble with the question of a right of reply in Norway might be that we have so many newspapers with different political ideological orientations. The differentiated daily press makes it possible for most people to have their views presented somewhere.'[10]

Nevertheless, a right of reply would undoubtedly be an important check on abuses of journalistic power. It would only inhibit or shackle reporters and editors who produce factually distorted and inaccurate articles. As long as that basic creed is adhered to, Fleet Street would have nothing to fear from the right to reply. However, it would be wrong, in my view, to extend the right of reply to comment and editorials. Adjudicating on opinion would be far too subjective, as long as the comment was not based on incorrect information.

Breaking up the monopolies

'Free enterprise is a prerequisite of a free press,' declared the first Royal Commission on the Press in 1949. The premise behind this view was that a free market economy would produce a wide range of newspapers which would represent all political views and hence reflect public opinion. In addition, that if most of those newspapers published opinions and reports that lent or were biased towards a certain political ideology, then they were merely accurately reflecting society and public opinion.

This image of today's press as an impartial democratic pressure group safeguarding the public interest has shown itself to be quite incorrect. The Labour Party's public support is considerably under-represented in Fleet Street. Even more so is the fact that no one national newspaper is in line with the British people's views on their opposition to Trident and cruise missiles. There are many other examples, notably during major strikes.

And so, clearly, the open market economy has not delivered the goods. The plurality of competing views has simply not happened. In fact, the reality is that as the range of editorial diversity has contracted so the concentration of ownership of Fleet Street has increased. Three proprietors (Maxwell, Murdoch and David Stevens) now control two out of three national newspapers bought in Britain. These three, together with Tiny Rowland and Lord Rothermere, control 84 per cent of the daily circulation. In addition, the *Guardian* is the only remaining newspaper whose owner doesn't have outside, non-newspaper commercial interests.

In view of the growing concentration of ownership, the 1973 Fair Trading Act gave the Secretary of State for Trade the power to with-hold consent to, or impose conditions on, any newspaper sale after a Monopolies Commission investigation. Among the terms of such an investigation are the consequences for 'accurate presentation of news and free expression of opinion' in the advent of a takeover.

However, these are serious defects in the Fair Trading Act. Firstly, it can only refer acquisitions to the Monopolies Commission if the company already has substantial holdings in other newspapers. This enabled Robert Maxwell's Pergamon Press to take over the Mirror Group, despite the fact that Maxwell has constantly interfered in the editorial independence of his papers. As Geoffrey Robertson, a barrister and an expert in media law, said of the *Mirror* acquisition: 'A Monopolies Commission investigation would almost certainly have led to the imposition of guarantees of editorial independence of the kind which has been so important at the *Observer* (the row between editor Trelford and owner Rowland).[11]

Another major problem is that the Trade Secretary can decline to refer a sale to the Monopolies Commission when the newspaper 'was not economic as a going concern'. This is what happened in1981 when Rupert Murdoch made a bid for Times Newspapers. John Biffen, the then Conservative Trade Secretary, ruled that the takeover should not be referred to the Monopolies Commission because the *Times* and *Sunday Times* were loss-makers. In his book *Good Times, Bad Times*, the former *Sunday Times* editor Harold Evans claimed that Biffen and the Trade Ministry declined to include revenue from various activities which would have made the *Sunday Times* a 'going concern'. Evans said that this amounted to a total of £4.6 million. This figure included receipts and syndication worth £187,000, contracts to print the *Guardian* for £1,439,000, and direct mail business, including the *Sunday Times* Wine Club, for £3,056,000. Evans said that if these amounts were included in the accounts, the *Sunday Times* would have made a profit of £700,000.

Biffen replied: 'All these items were left out of account as not being relevant to the test I had to consider under the Fair Trading Act which was whether each newspaper was economic as a going concern and as a separate newspaper. The determination of non-newspaper business was inevitably a matter of judgement.'[12] Evans said these items of revenue were relevant. More important, he alleges, the final figures were adjusted to make it easier for Murdoch to buy Times Newspapers. 'It was Mrs Thatcher's will which prevailed in the government discussions on the take-over in 1981,' said Evans.

> I heard on 22 January 1981 that she had insisted there would be no monopolies inquiry. Murdoch had stood by her in the dark days and she was going to stand by him. The new Secretary of State for Trade, John Biffen, put it differently when he rose in the Commons five days later, but it added up to approval for Murdoch on condition that he gave various undertakings of editorial independence, which he readily did.[13]

The very fact that the government can make such a decision against referral based on contentious sources of income is in itself a defect in the current Fair Trading legislation regarding newspapers. It was this almost subjective criterion which reveals another loophole in the Act. Even when a sale is referred to the Monopolies Commission, the subsequent investigation must consider 'whether the transfer in question may be expected to operate against the public interest'. The problem here is that opponents of the transfer must prove that it is 'against the public interest'. And as the 1977 Royal Commission on the Press pointed out: 'In individual cases it is almost impossible to establish this to the [Monopolies] Commission's satisfaction and in none of the cases so far referred has it been established.'

So, what can be done to break up the monopolies and multinational companies that control and dominate Fleet Street? Once again, other countries are streets ahead of Britain. New Zealand, France and Italy all have a law preventing foreigners from holding a majority stake in a newspaper company. Where no law exists, as in West Germany, there are strict rules against monopoly cartels. Britain could also introduce some safeguards. For example, when a sale is referred to the Monopolies Commission, it should be up to the newspaper conglomerate to prove that their acquisition of new titles is in the public interest – and not for its opponents to show otherwise. In addition, there could be legislation to simply ration the number of newspapers in which proprietors have a controlling interest.

However, to make anti-monopoly legislation effective and open up the opportunity for true reform and greater editorial diversity, more radical proposals are needed. James Curran, the distinguished media academic and writer, has produced perhaps the most coherent plan so far. He argues:

> The key to making new anti-monopoly measures work is to set up a public funding agency which would finance alternative ownership of divested media. A Media Enterprise Board should be established along the lines of the successful and independent Greater London Enterprise Board, with the difference that it would be subject to parliamentary scrutiny. It could enable, through low-interest loans, new and innovatory forms of ownership that would extend the diversity of the media ... The board should also provide start-up loan capital for new launches across the full spectrum of the media. Otherwise there is a danger that it could become a rest-home for lame ducks. The board could be funded directly by the Exchequer but its establishment could be accompanied by a new tax on all media advertising. Even at only 1 per cent, it would yield a gross annual income of over £35 million.[14]

Critics of such a plan claim that public subsidies would interfere with editorial independence and that any government role is an infringement of the freedom of the press. However, the taxpayer is already indirectly subsidizing parts of Fleet Street, because the proprietors are able to set their newspaper losses against tax. In any case, some papers like the *Times* are already subsidized by the more profitable sectors of Murdoch's corporation. Newspapers are also exempt from VAT.

However, whether any anti-monopoly legislation and radical initiative is feasible depends largely on political will. It is difficult to see how the current Conservative administration would enact such proposals, given the fact that 75 per cent of the current national newspapers are cheering their every move. It would be political suicide. For the Labour Party, reforming the media is rather like their attitude to the Official Secrets Act and freedom of information. While in opposition,

Labour makes a lot of noise and says all the right things, but once in office such issues are either ignored or relegated down the list of priorities. However, in the Party's 1983 manifesto there was a commitment to 'breaking up major concentrations of press censorship'. And the intensity of the press attacks on the labour movement in recent years has made many Labour MPs see the reform of Fleet Street as an important issue. Certainly shadow Cabinet members like Michael Meacher believe it should be given a much higher priority.

A more obvious solution to the lack of political diversity is to simply start up new papers. But, as the 1977 Royal Commission put it: 'Anyone is free to start a daily national newspaper, but few can afford even to contemplate the prospect.' Even the new cost-cutting *Today*, published by Eddie Shah with his new technology system, is not a cheap venture. The paper's combined start-up and run-in costs, including initial trading losses, were £22 million.

However, there is no doubt that the use of new technology, whereby journalists type in their stories through a direct-input terminal and avoid having the copy reset in hot metal by printers, would reduce production costs substantially. It would certainly help, but it's only a partial solution. After all, according to the 1977 Royal Commission, the total production wages account for only 21 per cent of national newspaper costs.

The labour movement does desperately need to finance more papers rather than try to reform the existing ones. But the costs are still huge. An official Labour daily newspaper, financed say by the trade unions, would also create editorial problems. As with proprietors, it seems almost inevitable that some trade union leaders would want some form of editorial input in the paper. The last Labour paper was the *Daily Herald*, which closed in 1964 mainly due to a lack of advertising revenue rather than lack of readers, as some suggest. Apparently, Percy Cudlipp, one of the editors, would often complain that Ernest Bevin, a Labour Cabinet minister and union leader, was on the phone to him day and night during the 1945-51 Labour government telling him what to put in and leave out of the paper. No doubt a similar problem would arise with an official Labour paper in the late 1980s.

Blaming the thermometer for the fever?

'On the whole, the British don't believe what they read in the tabloids,' wrote Neal Ascherson in his *Observer* column in September 1985.[15] He argued that the average reader of the *Sun* or *Star* has a healthy scepticism of his daily newspaper. Derek Jameson, former editor of the *News of the World* and *Daily Star*, goes further than that: 'The vast majority of our readers regard their papers as rubbish and don't take them seriously.'

This may or may not be correct (it is extremely difficult to prove one way or the other whether a newspaper can influence its readers' political views). But it is true that, apart from the *Daily Star*, most readers' political allegiances are in line with their paper's editorial line.[16] This was backed up by a survey by Patrick Dunleavy and the London School of Economics' Election Studies Unit just after the 1983 election. Dunleavy concluded:

> Our findings suggest that media influences are very closely and precisely associated with the ways in which people vote. Even if we allow for some tendency for people to choose a paper which fits their political leanings, the correlation between press readership and voting is so great that it dwarfs most of the influences on political attitudes to which liberal political science directs our attention.[17]

The counter-argument is that television is now the primary source for political news rather than newspapers. But while circulation has fallen, television has not made the inroads into newspaper consumption that many commentators predicted. Apart from Sweden, the British people read more newspapers proportionately than any European country. A staggering 35.3 million, or 69 per cent of the population, read a popular daily paper, according to official newspaper industry estimates. In addition, the LSE survey found that 88 per cent of their sample included TV news and 73 per cent included the press in their top two sources of political information.

However, I do not subscribe to the view, held by some sections of the Labour Left, that the British newspaper-reading public are being systematically brainwashed by Fleet Street. Some proprietors and editors try very hard, but there are too many different sources of information for that to happen. Equally, it cannot be seriously argued that press coverage has no effect at all. Even on a subconscious level, the press must have some influence.

What is true, however, is that newspapers can and do determine what their readers *think about*. This is simply because of the selection of news, features, letters and the prominence they receive in the paper. By including certain stories and excluding others, the press inevitably sets the range of political debate in their papers. For example, the deliberate exclusion of material about police violation of civil liberties during the miners' strike unquestionably set the terms of argument, particularly in the south of England, about the issue of violence.

And yet, even if the power of the press to influence public opinion were completely nonexistent, that would be no excuse for what has been happening in Fleet Street in recent years. Individuals, groups of workers and political parties have been vilified personally and their views derided without so much as a hearing in a quite extraordinary manner which has even disturbed many journalists. Fleet Street's response is that if the readers found such coverage offensive, they wouldn't buy the paper. There are a number of holes in this argument. Firstly, as *Sunday Times* journalist Henry Porter explained: 'Since newspapers do not publicize their deceptions, their readers are hardly in a position to decide whether or not to take their custom elsewhere.'[18] Secondly, the reality is that there is so little choice and such a lack of political diversity that there is nowhere else to go. Consider, for example, a *Daily Mirror* reader who supports the Labour Party but is a strong advocate of unilateral nuclear disarmament and was a keen backer of the striking miners in the 1984-5 dispute. Given the fact that the *Mirror* didn't support the NUM and opposes a non-nuclear defence policy, where is that reader to go? None of the other papers comes even close to reflecting his views. Even the *Morning Star* can hardly be seen as a national paper, because of its high price (35p for six pages) and an uneven distribution system throughout the country. And so, having discarded the *Mirror*, the reader wanders into his local newsagent the next day and surveys the alternative Fleet Street papers on display. No doubt he or she would then frown with frustration and walk straight out.

The British people deserve a lot better.

Appendix 1: Ownership and Commercial Interests of Britain's National Press

'I don't think that a newspaper should own outside interests ... By owning something outside journalism you lay yourself open to attack. And newspapers should be above that.' Rupert Murdoch, *More* magazine, November 1977.

Associated Newspaper Holdings

The company's interests are as follows:

Newspapers

Daily Mail
Mail on Sunday
London Standard
Bristol Evening Post plc (has a 23.8 per cent holding and a direct interest of 25.1 per cent in that company's subsidiary, Bristol United Press Ltd)
Cheltenham Newspaper Company Ltd
Cornish Guardian Ltd
Cornishman Newspaper Company Ltd (93.7% holding)
Derby Daily Telegraph Ltd
Essex Chronicle Series Ltd
F. Hewitt and Son Ltd
Gloucestershire Newspapers Ltd
Hull and Grimsby Newspapers Ltd
James Heap (Hanley 1925) Ltd
Courier Printing and Publishing Company Ltd
Lincolnshire Publishing Company Ltd
North Devon Journal Herald Ltd
Staffordshire Sentinel Newspapers Ltd
Swansea Press Ltd
West Briton Newspaper Company Ltd
Western Morning News Company Ltd

Western Times Company Ltd
Woodham and Wickford Ltd

Magazines

The Field
Weekend
'Girl About Town' Ltd (92 per cent holding)
'13-30' Group Inc. (USA). Publishes advertising information (80 per cent holding). The 13-30 Group is also a major investor in *Esquire* magazine
AM-Law Publishing Corporation (USA). Publishes *American Lawyer* (75 per cent holding)
Euromoney Publications (90 per cent holding). Provides financial information for the international capital markets. Publishes *Euromoney*, *International Financial Law Review*, *Euromoney Currency Report*, *Trade Finance Report*, *Euromoney Syndication Guide*, *Euromoney Bank Report* and *Euromoney Corporate Finance*

Reuters

The company made £16 million profit from the flotation of Reuters Holdings in June 1984. However, the company retains a substantial interest comprising 'A' shares which it holds as a newspaper proprietor, and approximately 6.3 per cent of the listed 'B' shares. On 30 September 1984, the market value of these shares amounted to £54.7 million

Television and Radio

Has a 50 per cent holding in Independent Radio Sales, a radio advertising representative company.
Several minority interests in local independent radio stations
Has a 17 per cent holding in Limehouse Studios, the independent TV studio complex.
Has interests in cable television through Greenwich Cable Communications (15 per cent holding)
Southern TV Ltd (37.6 per cent holding)

Energy interests

The company's energy interests are channelled through its subsidiary, Blackfriars Oil Co. Ltd. Blackfriars has a 12.5 per cent participation in the Argyll and Duncan oilfields and has a stake in the Innes oilfields.

Blackfriars also negotiated a £44 million loan to develop the Esmond, Forbes and Gordon gas fields.

Other commercial interests

National Opinion Polls Ltd
N.O.P. Market Research Ltd
Purfleet Deep Wharf and Storage Company Ltd
London Cab Company Ltd
London Service Stations Ltd
Consolidated-Bathurst Inc (Canada). Has a 17.8 per cent holding through its subsidiary, Les Investissements Bouverie. Consolidated-Bathurst is a major forest products and packaging group.

Directors

Chairman	Viscount Rothermere
Managing Director	R.M.P. Shields
Directors	P.J. Saunders
	Sir David English
	E.J. Winnington-Ingram
	A.A. Robinson
	S.M. Gray
	I.G. Park
	Major-General P. Blunt

* *Source*: Annual Reports and Accounts for 1984.

The Guardian

The *Guardian* is owned by the Scott Trust, through its parent company (The Guardian and Manchester Evening News Ltd) and the trustees are the ultimate authority. The trustees appoint the company directors and, jointly with the Board of Directors, appoint the editor of the *Guardian* and *Manchester Evening News*.

The Scott family trust was set up in 1936 after the death of the paper's founder and editor C.P. Scott, a former Liberal MP. The Scott family transferred to the Trust the whole of their ordinary shareholding in the company and divested themselves of all beneficial interest in the shares. The trust deed also prevents the return of any shareholding to them.

The terms of the Scott Trust deed leave the trustees almost total discretion as to how they conduct their affairs and apply their funds. The main requirement is to run the papers 'on the same lines and in the same spirit as before'.

There is little doubt that the editor of the *Guardian* has more freedom than any other editor in Fleet Street. 'I can never recall', said the current editor, Peter Preston, 'a moment over the last ten years when the Trust has expressed any view on [editorial/political] matters. That has been left to the editorial team here.' With no proprietor hovering above Preston, the *Guardian* is certainly an exception in Fleet Street.

There is a potential for ten company directors and ten trustees. In general most trustees tend to be members of the Scott and Montague families – descendants of C.P. Scott. However, in recent years the trustees have come from wider backgrounds. At time of writing, there were eight trustees:

Alastair Hetherington	Chairman (editor of the *Guardian* 1956-75)
Peter Gibbings	(Chairman of the G. and M.E. News Ltd)
Peter Preston	(editor of the paper since 1975)
Louis Blom-Cooper QC	(former member of editorial staff)
Peter Newsam	(Chairman of Commission for Racial Equality)
Gerry Taylor	(former Managing Director of the *Guardian*)
Charles Scott	(member of Scott family)
Victor Keegan	(financial columnist of the paper)

Apart from the *Manchester Evening News*, the Trust also owns between 45 and 50 local newspapers in the Manchester area and the south of England. The company also has a 21.6 per cent holding in Anglia TV and 15 per cent of Manchester Piccadilly Radio.

Mirror Group Newspapers

The Mirror Group newspapers (*Daily Mirror*, *Sunday People*, *Sunday Mirror*, *Daily Record* and *Sunday Mail*) are ostensibly owned by Pergamon Press Ltd, whose Chief Executive and Chairman is Robert Maxwell. However, the precise details of the ownership of Pergamon Press, a privately quoted publishing company, have never been properly disclosed.

What is known is that Pergamon Press Ltd is owned by the Pergamon Holding Corporation (PHC). Until 1982 PHC's equity was held entirely by a French lawyer called Geouffre de la Pradelle. PHC was then taken over by the Pergamon Holding Foundation (PHF).

PHF is registered at 5 Aeulestrasse in Vaduz, the capital city of the tiny Duchy of Liechtenstein in central Europe. Under Liechtenstein law, PHF has neither members, participants nor shareholders. It seems the closest the Mirror Group papers have to a proprietor is PHF's resident director Dr Walter Keicher, because PHF is the ultimate holding company of the *Daily Mirror*.

But who actually owns PHF? Dr Keicher told the *Financial Times* on 6 December 1984 that details about his foundation were not accessible by any legal or diplomatic proceedings: 'I regret not being able to tell you more.' When Maxwell bought the Mirror papers in July 1984, it was widely assumed that he owned PHF and hence Pergamon Press and the *Mirror*. Indeed, he told a meeting of all the *Mirror* union officials the day after his acquisition: 'I am the proprietor, 100 per cent, and I want that to be understood very clearly. There can only be one boss and that's me.' But by December 1984, he was only the publisher and refusing to discuss who owned PHF (the *Mirror*'s holding company). 'That is not a matter for me to disclose,' Maxwell told the *Financial Times*. 'It is a perfectly proper and legal matter. But I am not in the business of disclosing other people's business.'

Although foundations like PHF are often based in Liechtenstein by corporate proprietors seeking anonymous and conspicuous tax advantages, Maxwell strongly denies that his family will benefit financially from the elaborate structure of Pergamon's ownership: 'Neither I nor my family nor my wife will inherit one penny of all the wealth that I have managed to create.'

Someone who does know the owners of PHF, and hence the Mirror papers, is Lindsay Smith, a director of merchant bankers Henry Ansbacher, which has advised Maxwell on his corporate affairs for 30 years. But he's not telling. 'It would be wrong to assume that Mr

Maxwell controls PHF,' Smith said. 'We do know who the owners are and we, as his merchant bank, are satisfied.'

So just who owns Mirror Group newspapers is shrouded in mystery. Despite several telephone calls and letters to Maxwell's private office in Holborn Circus during the research for this book, I was not given any annual accounts, reports, prospectus or general information regarding the ownership of the papers. Clearly, his advisors and aides don't know either!

However, it is well known that Pergamon Press publishes a wide variety of books, mainly scientific and academic. The company also has extensive commercial interests in broadcasting and cable television. This includes large holdings in Central Television (13.8 per cent shareholding and Maxwell is a director), Rediffusion Cablevision, Selectvision and Mirrorvision (Maxwell is the major shareholder).

In addition, Pergamon has a controlling 61 per cent holding in the British Printing and Communications Corporation, whose Chief Executive and Chairman is also Robert Maxwell. BPCC's interests are as follows:

BPCC Communication and Information Corporation Ltd

Hazell Watson and Viney Ltd
Waterlow Ltd
Purnell and Sons (Book Production) Ltd
BPCC Graphics Ltd
BPCC Design and Print Ltd
BPCC Laser Print Ltd
BPCC Information Services Ltd
Dorstel Press Ltd
Waterlow Security Printers Ltd
Waterlow Petty Business Forms Ltd
BPCC Direct Mail Ltd

BPCC Prepress Corporation Ltd

Nickeloid Ltd
Carlisle Type-Setting Services Ltd
M1 Studios Ltd
Nickeloid Computer Graphics Ltd
Clarke and Sherwell Ltd
Clarke and Sherwell (Corby) Ltd
T&T Gill Ltd

BPCC Video Graphics Ltd
London Typesetting Centre Ltd

British Catalogue and Magazine Printing Corporation Ltd

Odhams-Sun Printers Ltd
Purnell and Sons Ltd
Waterlow and Sons (1984) Ltd
H.G. Bentley Ltd
Chromoworks Ltd
Petty and Sons Ltd
Carlisle Webb Offset

BPCC Packaging and Labelling Corporation Ltd

Jas Broadley Ltd
E. Hannibal and Co. Ltd
Numeric Arts Ltd
B. Taylor and Co. (Manchester) Ltd
Taylowe Ltd

BPCC Publishing Corporation Ltd

Waterlow Publishers Ltd
Purnell Publishers Ltd
Caxton and English Educational Programmes International Ltd
MacDonald and Co. (Publishers) Ltd
Financial Weekly Ltd

Overseas publishing companies

Cedibra Editora (Brazil)
Delphin Verlag GmbH (West Germany) – 99 per cent owned
International Learning Systems (Japan) Ltd – 65 per cent owned
International Learning Systems Ltd (Zimbabwe)
Jetcat Ltd (Jersey) – 50.1 per cent owned
K.G. Bertmarks Forlag AB (Sweden)
IPA Produktion Forlag (Denmark)
IPA Distribusjon (Norway)
MacDonald Futura Australia Pty Ltd
MacDonald Middle East sarl (Lebanon – 51 per cent owned)
MacDonald Purnell (Proprietary) Ltd (South Africa)
Marketing Services (1974) Ltd (New Zealand)
Purnell Inc (USA)

Systems Publishing (Portugal) Editores Lda
Verlag Das persöniche Geburtstagsbuch GmbH (Germany) – 66 per
  cent owned

Service and holding companies

Birn Brothers Ltd
Bishopsgate Trust plc
BPC do Brasil Comercio E. Participacoes Lda (Brazil)
BPC Finance (Guarantees) Ltd
BPCC Financial Services Ltd
BPCC Group Services Ltd
BPC Investments Ltd
British Printing and Communication Company (New Zealand) Ltd
BPC Sales Ltd
Camberry Ltd
British Printing and Communication Corporation (Australia) Pty
  Ltd
Houses and Estates Ltd
Paulton Holdings Ltd
Thomson Printers Ltd (holding company for Dorstel Press Ltd – 60
  per cent owned by BPCC and 40 per cent owned by Pergamon
  Press)
Source: Annual Reports and Accounts for 1984

News International

The company's interests are as follows:

Newspapers
London
Times
Sunday Times
Sun
News of the World
Times Literary Supplement
Times Educational Supplement
Times Higher Educational Supplement
USA
Boston Herald
Star (New York)
New York Post
Chicago Sun-Times
Houston community papers
San Antonio Express
News (San Antonio, Texas)
Sunday Express-News
Australia
The Australian
Daily Mirror (Sydney)
Daily Telegraph (Sydney)
Sunday Telegraph (Sydney)
News (Adelaide)
Sunday Mail (Adelaide)
Daily Sun (Brisbane)
Sunday Sun (Brisbane)
Sunday Times (Perth)
Cumberland (New South Wales)
Northern Territory News (Darwin)
Northern Daily Leader (Tamworth)
Wimmera Mail Times (Victoria)
New Zealand
Independent Newspapers (22 per cent holding)

Magazines
Australia
Business and Commercial Aviation

New Idea
New Woman
Elle
TV Week (50 per cent holding)
USA
New York
UK
Sun Day Publications Ltd (publishes *Sun Day* magazine)
Ziff-Davis (14 business titles)

Book Publishing

Australia
Bay Books
Angus & Robertson
UK
William Collins and Sons (42 per cent of the ordinary shares and
   10 per cent of the non-voting shares)
Times Books
USA
News America Publishing Incorporated (50 per cent holding)
Holland
Newscorp Netherlands Antilles N.V

Broadcasting

Channel Ten-10
Channel ATV-10
Satellite Television (75.5 per cent holding)
Sky Channel (Cable TV)
20th Century Fox
Associated R and R films (50 per cent holding)
Festival Records
News Group Productions

Other commercial interests

Computer Power Software
Progress Press
Ansett Transport Industries (includes Ansett Airlines) – 50 per
   cent holding
Santos (natural gas – 15 per cent held by Ansett)
Shell Consortium (offshore oil and gas – 20 per cent holding)
News-Eagle (offshore oil and gas – 50 per cent holding)

F.S. Falkiner and Sons (ranching) (Australia)
Eric Bemrose Ltd (printers)
C. Townsend Hook and Co. Ltd (newsprint and paper manufac-
    turers)
Convoys Ltd (warehousing and transport) (UK)

Directors

Chairman	Rupert Murdoch
Managing Director	Bruce Matthews
Directors	S.C.F. Allen
	Lord Catto (from Murdoch's bankers – Morgan Grenfell)
	P.R. Ekberg
	P.B. Hamlyn
	Brian Horton
	Donald Kummerfield
	Mervyn Rich
	R.A. Sarazen
	Richard Searby, QC
	Peter Stehrenberger

Source: Annual Reports and Accounts for 1984

The Observer

The *Observer* is owned by George Outram and Co., a subsidiary of Lonrho International whose Chief Executive and Managing Director is Tiny Rowland. Lonrho has the controlling shareholding (80 per cent) of the *Observer*. The paper's former owners, the oil multi-national Atlantic Richfield, retain a 20 per cent holding. Tiny Rowland is Chairman of the *Observer* Board of Directors. Robert Anderson, head of Atlantic Richfield, is Deputy Chairman.

Lonrho's commercial interests are as follows

Newspapers

Observer

Glasgow Herald

Glasgow Evening Times

Scottish and Universal Newspapers Ltd (publishes 22 provincial papers)

Kenya Standard (Lonrho has a 52 per cent holding in Consolidated Holdings Ltd which prints and publishes the *Standard* and also manufactures paper)

Commercial interests in Zimbabwe

Lonrho Zimbabwe Ltd (investment holding and finance – 100 per cent holding)

The Wattle Company Ltd (wattle growing and processing – 100 per cent holding)

Construction Associates (pvt) Ltd (civil engineers and building contractors – 60 per cent stake)

David Whitehead Textiles Ltd (manufacturers of textile products – 66 per cent holding)

W. Dahmer and Co. Ltd (vehicle manufacturers and coach-builders – 60 per cent holding)

Zambesi Coachworks Ltd (coach-builders – 100 per cent holding)

Corsyn Consolidated Mines Ltd (gold and copper mining – 100 per cent holding

Independence Mining (pvt) Ltd (gold mining – 100 per cent holding)

Zimoco Ltd (distribution of Mercedes cars and heavy commercial vehicles – 100 per cent stake)

Crittall-Hope Ltd (steel windows and doors for construction products)

Lonrho also has ranching operations with over 58,000 cattle reared mainly for export.

Financial services

UK

Balfour, Williamson and Co. Ltd (export confirming)

F.E. Wright (UK) Ltd (insurance brokers)

John Holt Group Ltd (export confirming)

L.A. Rix and John Holt Ltd (insurance brokers)

London City and International Ltd (property ownership)

London City and Westcliff Properties Ltd (ownership and development of residential and commercial property)

Lonrho Exports Ltd (export confirming) and Lonrho Finance plc (finance)

Scottish and Universal Investments Ltd (investment holding)

Foreign

Cominière S.A (investment holding and property in Belgium and Zaire – 54 per cent holding)

JHI Ltd (associate) (investment and property holding in Nigeria – 48 per cent holding)

Lonrho International Finance (N.V) (finance in Netherlands – 100 per cent holding)

Lonrho South Africa Ltd (investment holding – 100 per cent holding)

General trade

UK

Baumann, Hinde and Co. Ltd (cotton merchants)

Peter Hopkinson Ltd (plumbing and electrical appliance factors)

Kuehne and Nagel (UK) Ltd (freight forwarding and warehousing – 50 per cent holding)

Southern Watch and Clock Supplies Ltd (suppliers to the horological trade)

Tradewinds Airways Ltd (cargo airline operators)

Foreign

African Commercial Holdings Ltd (distributors of electrical goods and batteries, Coca-Cola bottles and manufacturers and distributors of paint – 100 per cent holding in Zambia)

Kühne and Nagel (AG and Co.) (freight forwarding and warehousing in West Germany – 50 per cent holding)

Kuehne and Nagel Holding Inc. (freight forwarding and warehousing in USA – 50 per cent holding)

Kühne and Nagel International AG (freight forwarding and warehousing in Switzerland – 50 per cent holding)

Lonrho Industrial Corporation Ltd (wholesale hardware and steel merchants in South Africa – 100 per cent holding)

National Airways and Finance Corporation Ltd (retailers and lessors of Beechcraft aircraft in South Africa – 100 per cent holding)

Teal Record Co. (Zambia) Ltd (distribution of records and tapes – 100 per cent holding)

Turnpan Zambia Ltd (importers and distributors of Bucyrus Erie, Wagner, Wabco)

Goodman and Robbins (mining machinery and spare parts – 100 per cent holding)

Leisure, wine and spirits

UK

Birmingham Metropole Hotels Ltd (proprietors of the Birmingham Metropole and Warwick Hotels)

Brighton Metropole and Bedford Hotels

London Metropole Hotel

Metropole Casinos (Holdings) Ltd

Pembroke Hotel in London

Whyte and MacKay Distillers Ltd (whiskey distillers, blenders and brokers)

Foreign

Chibuku Products Ltd (Malawi) (70 per cent holding)

Heinrich's Syndicate Ltd (proprietors of the Edinburgh and Lusaka hotels in Zambia with a 90 per cent holding)

Louis Eschenauer S.A. (wine shippers, owners and blenders of vineyards in France – 100 per cent holding)

Merville Ltd (proprietors of the Merville Hotel in Mauritius with 55 per cent holding)

National Breweries Ltd in Zambia – 49 per cent holding

Princess Properties International Ltd (proprietors of hotels in the Bahamas, Bermuda and Mexico, and casino operators in the Bahamas – 100 per cent holding)

Manufacturing

UK

Church and Bramhall (Stockholders) Ltd (steel stockholders)

Coated Strip Ltd (manufacturers of precoated aluminium and steel strip)

David Whitehead and Sons Ltd (manufacturers of domestic textiles)

Fassnidge Son and Norris Ltd (contract builders)

Firsteel Ltd (manufacturers of cold-rolled steel strip)

Firsteel Metal Products Ltd (manufacturers of cold-formed sections)

Greenaway Harrison Ltd (security printers)

Harrison and Sons (High Wycombe) Ltd (security printers and paper processes)

Holmes McDougall Ltd (printers, publishers and booksellers)

Lightfoot Refrigeration Co. Ltd (manufacturers of commercial refrigeration equipment)

Lonrho Textiles Ltd (manufacturers and distributors of polyester and cotton products)

Newell Dunford Ltd (designers and suppliers of processed plant systems and equipment)

Nicol and Andrew (London) Ltd (specialist engineers)

Page Bros (Norwich) Ltd (printers of periodicals, directories and books)

Pland Stainless Ltd (manufacturers of filing cabinets and office equipment)

Sportworks Ltd (sportsground and civil engineering contractors)

Foreign

David Whitehead and Sons Ltd (manufacturers of textile products in Malawi with 50 per cent holding)

Delkins Ltd (civil engineers and building contractors in Zambia – 100 per cent holding)

John Holt (associate) (manufacturers of cosmetics, confectionery, boats, assembly and distribution of motor cycles and generators; distribution of motor vehicles, agricultural equipment and pharmaceuticals in Nigeria – 40 per cent holding)

John Holt Agricultural Engineers Ltd (manufacturers of ploughs and other agricultural equipment in Nigeria with 60 per cent holding)

Nicol and Andrew (Far East) Pte (marine engineers in Singapore – 100 per cent holding)

Stainless Steel Products Ltd (manufacturers of stainless steel sinks in Malta – 100 per cent holding)

The Blantyre Netting Company Ltd (manufacturers of polypropylene products in Malawi with 52 per cent holding)

Motor and equipment distribution

UK

Dovercourt Motor Co. Ltd (retailers of Volkswagen and Audi motor cars)

Dutton-Forshaw Facilities Ltd (contract hirers of motor vehicles – 25 per cent holding)

Jack Barclay Ltd (retailers of Rolls Royce and Bentley cars)

MAN-VW Truck and Bus Ltd (importers and distribution of MAN and Volkswagen trucks and buses – 80 per cent holding)

Saville Tractors (Belfast) Ltd
Saville Tractors Ltd
Dutton Forshaw Motor Group Ltd (retailers of British Leyland motor cars)
V.A.G. (United Kingdom) Ltd (importers and distributors of Volkswagen and Audi motor cars)
Watveare Overseas Ltd (importers and distributors of Deutz-Fahr tractors and machinery)
Western Machinery and Equipment Co. Ltd (agricultural equipment)
Foreign
Lonrho (Malawi) Ltd (importers and distributors of BL, General Motors and Daihatsu)
Lonrho Motor Holdings Ltd (distribution of General Motors and Mercedes in South Africa)
Lonrho Zambia Ltd (importers and distributors of Toyota, Fiat, BL, Mercedes and Peugeot)
Matermaco S.A. (retail agents for engineering and industrial equipment in Belgium – 88 per cent holding)
Motor Mart and Exchange Ltd (distribution of cars and spares in Kenya – 79 per cent holding)
Power Equipment Ltd (importers and distribution of Massey Ferguson in Zambia – 75 per cent holding)
Star Commercial Ltd (importers and distributors of commercial vehicles in Zambia – 100 per cent holding)
Wankel International S.A. (joint owners of patents to Wankel rotary engine – 72 per cent holding)
Westlands Motor Ltd (agents for Toyota vehicles and spares in Kenya – 100 per cent holding)

Agriculture

Dwangwa Sugar Corporation Ltd (sugar growing and processing in Malawi – 32 per cent holding)
East African Tanning Extract Co. Ltd (crop and livestock farming in Kenya – 100 per cent holding)
Kalangwa Estates Ltd (mixed livestock and crop farming in Zambia – 80 per cent holding)
Lonrho Sugar Corporation Ltd (sugar growing and processing in Malawi, Mauritius, South Africa and Swaziland – 99 per cent holding)
P.S. Mandrides and Co. Ltd (associates) (oilseed merchants in Nigeria – 38 per cent holding)

Makandi Estates Ltd (ownership of tea estates and tobacco plantations in Malawi – 100 per cent holding)

Mining and refining

Ashanti Goldfields Corporation (Ghana) Ltd (associate) (goldmining with 45 per cent stake)

Duiker Consolidated Mines Ltd (anthracite, coal and goldmining. Also shareholding in Eastern Gold Holdings Ltd in South Africa)

Lonrho Refinery Ltd (platinum refining in South Africa – 100 per cent stake)

Directors

President	Lord Duncan Sandys
Chairman	Sir Edward du Cann
Deputy Chairman	A.H. Ball
Managing Director and Chief Executive	R.W. ('Tiny') Rowland
Directors	R.F. Dunlop
	N. Kruger (Zimbabwe)
	M.J.J.R. Leclezio (Mauritius)
	R.A. Lee
	T.J. Robinson
	Paul Spicer
	P.M. Tarsh
	R.E. Whitten
	Sir Peter W. Youens

Source: Annual Reports and Accounts for 1984

Pearson

The company.'s interests are as follows:

Newspapers
Financial Times Group Ltd
Westminster Press Ltd
The Economist Newspaper Ltd (50 per cent holding)

Publishing
Penguin Publishing Co. Ltd
Longman Holdings Ltd

Oil and oil services
Camco Inc (USA) (64.7 per cent holding)
Lignum Oil Co. (USA)
Whitehall Petroleum Ltd
Compressor Systems Inc (USA) (35 per cent holding)
Hillin Oil Co. (USA) (38.9 per cent)

Other commercial interests
Madame Tussauds Ltd
Royal Doulton Ltd (fine china)
Fairey Holdings Ltd (engineering)
Societé Civile du Vignoble de Château Latour (France) (53.6 per cent)
West Thurrock Estate
Longman Nigeria Ltd (40 per cent holding)
Goldcrest Films and Television (Holdings) Ltd (41.2 per cent holding)
Yorkshire Television Holdings plc (25 per cent holding)
Cedar Fair (USA) (37.5 per cent)
Lazard Brothers and Co. Ltd (merchant bankers – 50 per cent of ordinary shares)
Lazard Frères and Co. (USA) (merchant bankers – 10 per cent of profits)
Lazard Frères et Compagnie (France) and Maison Lazard et Compagnie (France) (10 per cent stake)
Blackwell Land Co. Inc (USA) (36.9 per cent holding)

Directors
President   Viscount Cowdray
Chairman   Viscount Blackenham

Managing Director	J.H. Hale
Directors	M.W. Burrell
	M. David-Weill
	I.J. Fraser
	Lord Gibson
	P.G. Gyllenhammar
	S.M. Hornby
	J.A.B. Joll
	D.M. Veit
	A.A. Whitaker

Political donations

Conservative Party	£15,000
Social Democratic Party	£5,000
Liberal Party	£5,000
Centre for Policy Studies	£1,000

Source: Annual Reports and Accounts for 1984.

The Telegraph Group

After 57 years of being controlled by the Hartwell/Berry family trust, the *Daily Telegraph* and *Sunday Telegraph* are now under the ownership of Conrad Black, the Canadian multimillionaire business tycoon. Black has a 57 per cent controlling stake in the Telegraph Group which he took over in December 1985.

The papers are now owned by Hollinger Argus Ltd, a Toronto-based mining firm which is a subsidiary of the Argus Corporation – a private holding company controlled by Black. Of the £20 million share capital which paid for the controlling holding in the *Telegraph*, £14.4 million came from Hollinger. The remaining £5.6 million was raised by a rights issue to outside shareholders which was underwritten by Hollinger.

Hollinger also has a 37.8 per cent stake in Norcen Energy Resources, based in West Canada, which owns 28 per cent of Hanna Mining Co. in Ontario.

Another of Black's private holding companies is the Ravelston Corporation of which he is Chairman. This company owns several Canadian newspapers as well as Ravelsub which controls 100 per cent of Western Dominion Investment Company.

Apart from newspapers, Black has interests from mining to stores. His Hollinger company, for example, owns 100 per cent of Dominion Stores, once the largest food supermarket chain in Canada. He also has a holding in London Weekend Television.

Black is also a Director of the following companies: Canadian Imperial Bank of Commerce (the second biggest chartered bank in Canada), Carling O'Keefe (a brewing group), Confederation Life Insurance Co., Eaton of Canada (the country's largest chainstore), Iron Ore Company of Canada and, of course, Hollinger Argus.

At the time of writing, it was unclear whether the *Telegraph*, traditional supporters of the Conservative Party, would take a rightward direction under Black who is known to be a keen advocate of monetarism. According to his friend Rupert Hambro, Chairman of Hambro's Bank and a member of the *Telegraph* board, Black 'is a great Anglophile and a supporter of President Reagan,' Hambro told the *Guardian* 'He's very non-interventionist. He likes to put in place the people he has confidence in and let them get on with it.' This appeared to be borne out when it was announced that Lord Hartwell would remain Chairman and editor-in-chief of the *Daily* and *Sunday Telegraph*. However, in February 1986, Max Hastings was appointed editor of the *Daily Telegraph* and Peregrine Worsthorne became editor of the *Sunday*

Telegraph – both of whom have political views to the right of their predecessors.

Directors

Chairman	Lord Hartwell (Michael Berry)
Deputy Chairman	Viscount Camrose (John Berry)
Directors	Conrad Black
	Adrian Berry (Lord Hartwell's son)
	Lord Rawlinson of Ewell
	David Montagu
	Rupert Hambro
	Nicholas Berry (Lord Hartwell's son)

United Newspapers plc

Newspapers

Daily Express
Daily Star
Sunday Express
South Wales Argus Ltd
Scottish Express Newspapers Ltd
Express Newspapers Western Ltd
West Lancashire Evening Gazette
Yorkshire Post
Northampton Chronicle and Echo
Yorkshire Evening Post
Lancashire Evening Post
Sheffield Morning Telegraph
Sheffield Star
And 42 other local newspapers in Britain

Magazines

UK
Exchange and Mart
Industrial Exchange and Mart
Opportunities
Punch
Countryman
Geographical Magazine
Arable Farming
Dairy Farmer
Pig Farming
Northampton and County Independent
Broadcast Systems Engineering
Camping and Trailer
Caravan Magazine
Car and Car Conversions
Communicate
Custom Car
Do It Yourself
Glass Age
Hi-Fi News and Record Review
Kit Cars and Specials
Mobile and Holiday Homes

Off-Road and 4-Wheel Driver
Prediction
Sporting Cars
Stamp Magazine
Studio Sound
Superbike
Morgan Grampian plc
Morgan Grampian (Publishers) Ltd
Morgan Grampian (Professional Press) Ltd
Morgan Grampian (Construction Press) Ltd
Morgan Grampian (Process Press) Ltd
Travel Trade Gazette Ltd
Daltons Weekly
Spotlight Publications Ltd
Spotlight Magazine Distribution Ltd
Yellow Advertiser Newspaper Group Ltd (31.8 per cent holding)
Merseyside and Lancashire Publications Ltd (50 per cent holding)
US
Morgan Grampian Inc. (USA)
Gralla Publications (publishes 17 American magazines)
Miller Freeman Publications (publishes seven American magazines)

Broadcasting

TV-AM Ltd (at time of writing, United is the largest shareholder with a 31.8 per cent holding, although this stake is likely to be sold off with a substantial profit)
Britannic Film and Television Ltd (40 per cent holding)
PR Newswire Association Inc (USA)
Canada News-Wire Ltd (24.5 per cent holding)
Yorkshire Television Holdings plc (10 per cent holding)
Radio Hallam Ltd (13 per cent holding)
Two Counties Radio Ltd (10.5 per cent holding)
Also has minority holdings in Capital Radio Ltd, Radio Clyde plc, Cardiff Broadcasting Co., plc and Gwent Area Broadcasting Ltd

Other commercial enterprises

Ludgate Properties Ltd
Ludgate Leasing Ltd
Link House Books Ltd
United News Shops Ltd

George Pulman and Sons Ltd (printing)
Fleet Group Investments Ltd
J.H. Lake and Co. Ltd
David McKay Co. Ltd
Joseph Batchelor Ltd (50 per cent holding)
M.G. Insurance Brokers Ltd (50 per cent holding)
Sir Joseph Causton and Sons plc (21.6 per cent holding)
Marine Management Systems Inc. (information systems for shipping
  – 27.5 per cent holding)

Directors

Chairman	David Stevens
Chief Executive of Express Group Newspapers	Roger Bowes
Directors	Brian Rowbotham
	Graham Wilson
	A.F. Ford
	Sir John Junor
	Gordon Linacre

Political donations

£3,000 was donated to local Conservative Party associations in York-shire during 1984.
Source: Annual Reports and Accounts for 1984.

Appendix 2: Circulation Figures of National Papers

ABC figures for July-December 1985

Daily papers:

Sun	4,125,480
Daily Mirror	3,033,271
Daily Express	1,902,425
Daily Mail	1,815,056
Daily Star	1,454,727
Daily Telegraph	1,202,290
Guardian	487,080
Times	478,174
Financial Times	233,604

Sunday papers

News of the World	5,103,164
Sunday Mirror	3,009,397
Sunday People	2,961,982
Sunday Express	2,449,246
Mail on Sunday	1,630,886
Sunday Times	1,251,442
Observer	735,745
Sunday Telegraph	686,298

The actual readership of a national newspaper is roughly three times the circulation figure.

Appendix 3: Fleet Street Editors

Sun	Kelvin McKenzie
Daily Mirror	Richard Stott
Daily Express	Nicholas Lloyd
Daily Mail	Sir David English
Daily Star	Lloyd Turner
Daily Telegraph	Max Hastings
Guardian	Peter Preston
Times	Charles Wilson
Financial Times	Geoffrey Owen
Today	Brian MacArthur
News of the World	David Montgomery
Sunday Mirror	Mike Molloy
Sunday People	Ernie Burrington
Sunday Express	Sir John Junor
Mail on Sunday	Stewart Steven
Sunday Times	Andrew Neil
Observer	Donald Trelford
Sunday Telegraph	Peregrine Worsthorne

Appendix 4: NUJ Code of Professional Conduct

1.   A journalist has a duty to maintain the highest professional and ethical standards.

2.   A journalist shall at all times defend the principle of the freedom of the Press and other media in relation to the collection of information and the expression of comment and criticism. He/she shall strive to eliminate distortion, news suppression and censorship.

3.   A journalist shall strive to ensure that the information he/she disseminates is fair and accurate, avoid the expression of comment and conjecture as established fact and falsification by distortion, selection or misrepresentation.

4.   A journalist shall rectify promptly any harmful inaccuracies, ensure that correction and apologies receive due prominence and afford the right of reply to persons criticized when the issue is of sufficient importance.

5.   A journalist shall obtain information, photographs and illustrations only by straightforward means. The use of other means can be justified only by over-riding considerations of the public interest. The journalist is entitled to exercise a personal conscientious objection to the use of such means.

6.   Subject to justification by over-riding considerations of the public interest, a journalist shall do nothing which entails intrusion into private grief and distress.

7.   A journalist shall protect confidential sources of information.

8.   A journalist shall not accept bribes nor shall he/she allow other inducements to influence the performance of his/her professional duties.

9.   A journalist shall not lend himself/herself to the distortion or suppression of the truth because of advertising or other considerations.

10.   A journalist shall neither originate nor process material which encourages discrimination on grounds of race, colour, creed, gender or sexual orientation.

11.   A journalist shall not take private advantage of information gained in the course of his/her duties, before the information is public knowledge.

12.   A journalist shall not by way of statement, voice or appearance endorse by advertisement any commercial product or service save for the promotion of his/her own work or of the medium by which he/she is employed.

Bibliography

Aubrey, Crispin (ed.), *Nukespeak – The Media And The Bomb* London: Comedia, 1982.

Baistow, Tom, 'Fourth Rate Estate – An Anatomy of Fleet Street', London: Comedia, 1985.

Benn, Tony, *Speeches*, London: Spokesman Books, 1974.

Benyon, John (ed.), *Scarman And After*, Pergamon Press, 1984.

Black, Sydney, and Reddaway, Peter, *Soviet Psychiatric Abuse*, London: Victor Gollancz, 1984.

Browne, Alfred, *Tony Benn: The Making of a Politician*, London: W.H. Allen, 1983.

Butler, David, *The 1983 Election*, London: Macmillan, 1984.

Carvel, John, *Citizen Ken*, London: Chatto & Windus, 1984.

Chibnall, Steve, *Law-and-Order-News*, London: Tavistock Publications, 1976.

Cohen, Phil, and Gardner, Carl (eds.), *It Ain't Half Racist, Mum*, London: Comedia, 1982.

Cook, Alice, and Kirk, Gwyn, *Greenham Women Everywhere*, London: Pluto Press, 1983.

Crick, Michael, *Militant*, London: Faber & Faber, 1984.

Crick, Michael, *Scargill and the Miners*, London: Penguin, 1985.

Curran, James, and Seaton, Jean, *Power Without Responsibility – The Press and Broadcasting in Britain*, London: Methuen, 1985.

Curtis, Liz, *The Propaganda War*, London: Pluto Press, 1983.

Evans, Harold, *Good Times, Bad Times*, London: Weidenfeld & Nicholson, 1983.

Evans, Harold, *The Practice Of Journalism*, London: Heinemann, 1963.

Fallon, Ivan, and Srodes, James, *DeLorean*, London: Hamish Hamilton, 1983.

Foot, Michael, *Another Heart and Other Pulses – The Alternative to the Thatcher Society*, London: Collins, 1984.

Foot, Michael, *Debts Of Honour*, London: Davis Poynter, 1980.

Goodman, Geoffrey, *The Miners' Strike*, London: Pluto Press, 1985.

Harris, Robert, *The Making of Neil Kinnock*, London: Faber & Faber, 1984.

Hennessy, Peter, Cockerill, Michael, and Walker, David, *Sources Close to the Prime Minister*, London: Macmillan, 1984.

Hetherington, Alastair, *News, Newspapers and Television*, London: Macmillan, 1985.

Higgins, Sydney, *The Benn Inheritance*, London: Weidenfeld & Nicholson, 1984.

Jones, Dr Lynne, *Keeping the Peace*, London: Women's Press 1983.

Kettle, Martin, and Hodges, Lucy, *Uprising – the Police, the People and the Riots in Britain's Cities*, London: Pan, 1982.

Kitzinger, Uwe, *Diplomacy and Persuasion: How Britain Joined the Common Market*, London: Thames & Hudson, 1973.

Leapman, Michael, *Barefaced Cheek – The Apotheosis of Rupert Murdoch*, London: Hodder & Stoughton, 1983.

Leigh, David, *The Frontiers Of Secrecy*, London: Junction Books, 1980.

MacShane, Denis, *Using the Media*, London: Pluto Press, 1980.

Margach, James, *The Abuse Of Power*, London: W.H. Allen, 1978.

Matheson, Nigel and Pearse, Peter Gerard, *Ken Livingstone or the End of Civilization As We Know It*, London: Proteus Books, 1982.

Mooney, Bel, *Differences Of Opinion*, London: Robson Books, 1984.

Porter, Henry, *Lies, Damned Lies and Some Exclusives*, London: Chatto & Windus, 1984.

Somerfield, Stafford, *Banner Headlines*, Shoreham Scan Books, 1979.

Sunday Times Insight Team, *358 Days that Shook the World – Thatcher, Scargill and the Miners*, London: André Deutsch/Coronet Books, 1985.

Tatchell, Peter, *The Battle For Bermondsey*, London: Heretic Books, 1983.

Taylor, A.J.P., *Beaverbrook*, London: Hamish Hamilton, 1972.

Watkins, Alan, *Brief Lives*, London: Hamish Hamilton, 1982.

Wilson, Harold, *Final Term: The Labour Government 1974-76*, London: Weidenfeld & Nicholson, 1979.

Recommended articles

'In Defence of Wedgie', Keith Waterhouse, *Daily Mirror*, 5 August 1974.

'Strange Case of the Anti-Benns', Paul Johnson, *Daily Telegraph*, 4 January 1975.

'The Values of a Misrepresented Man', Simon Hoggart, *Guardian*, 29 August 1980.

'Unleashing an Uncritical Press', Gareth Peirce, *Guardian*, 15 March 1982.

'The Press We Don't Deserve', Hugo Young, *Sunday Times*, 18 March 1984.

'Rupert Murdoch and the *Sunday Times*: A Lamp Goes Out', Hugo Young, *Political Quarterly*, Winter 1984.

'The Marxist Myth that Made the Tories Misread Arthur', Hugo Young, *Guardian*, 7 January 1985.

'Coals In The Bath, Sun On The Brain', Neal Ascherson, *Observer*, 15 September 1985.

'Not Fit to Print', Paul Charman, *Time Out*, 14-20 November 1985.

'A Peace Woman Scorned', Alison Whyte, *Sanity*, November 1985.

Notes and references

1. Fleet Street – the Pursuit of Power

1. *Daily Express*, 20 December 1973.
2. *Daily Mail*, 2 March 1974.
3. *Daily Express*, 20 December 1983.
4. *Daily Mail*, 2 March 1974.
5. *Sunday Times*, 18 March 1974.
6. Sydney Black and Peter Reddaway, *Soviet Psychiatric Abuse*, London: Victor Gollancz, 1984.
7. *London Review of Books*, 21 February 1985.
8. *Guardian* 15 November 1983.
9. Letter to Sir Samuel Hoare, quoted in A.J.P. Taylor, *Beaverbrook*, London: Hamish Hamilton, 1972.
10. Alan Watkins, *Brief Lives*, London: Hamish Hamilton, 1982.
11. *Observer*, 8 January 1984.
12. Harold Evans, *The Practice of Journalism*, London: Heinemann, 1963.
13. Denis MacShane, *Using The Media*, London: Pluto Press, 1980.
14. *More* magazine, November 1977.
15. Michael Leapman, *Barefaced Cheek – The Apotheosis of Rupert Murdoch*, London: Hodder & Stoughton, 1983.
16. *The Press Barons*, BBC World Service, 23 December 1984.
17. *Time Out*, 20 November 1985.
18. *New Statesman*, 4 October 1974.
19. Monopolies and Mergers Commission: The Observer and George Outram Company Ltd, a subsidiary of Scottish and Universal Investments, whose parent company is Lonrho Ltd, HMSO, 1981.
20. *Guardian*, 18 April 1984.
21. *Guardian*, 18 October 1983.
22. *Observer*, 22 April 1984.
23. *Guardian*, 18 April 1984.

24. *Observer*, 22 April 1984.
25. *Observer*'s five independent directors were Sir Derek Mitchell (former Treasury civil servant and now senior advisor to Lehman Brothers), Lord Windlesham (former Conservative minister and now Chairman of the Parole Board), Dame Rosemary Murry (ex-Vice-Chancellor of Cambridge University), William Clark (former diplomatic correspondent of the *Observer* and former advisor to Sir Anthony Eden) and Sir Geoffrey Cox (founder of Independent Television News).
26. *Observer*, 22 April 1984.
27. *New Statesman*, 14 June 1985.
28. *UK Press Gazette*, 21 November 1985.
29. *Listener*, 21 November 1985.
30. *New Statesman*, 14 June 1985.
31. 'Labour Daily? – Ins and Outs of a New Labour Daily and Other Media Alternatives', pamphlet published by the Campaign for Press and Broadcasting Freedom, 1984.
32. *Press Barons*, BBC World Service, 23 December 1984.
33. *Ibid*.
34. James Curran and Jean Seaton, *Power Without Responsibility – The Press and Broadcasting in Britain*, London: Methuen, 1985.
35. Harold Evans, *Good Times, Bad Times*, London: Weidenfeld & Nicholson, 1983.
36. *Media Week*, 8 February 1985.
37. Stafford Somerfield, *Banner Headlines*, Shoreham Scan Books, 1979.
38. *Bad Times At The Times*, Channel 4, 30 October 1983.
39. Ivan Fallon and James Srodes, *DeLorean*, London: Hamish Hamilton, 1983.
40. *Ibid*.
41. *World in Action*, Granada TV, 14 March 1983.
42. *Press Barons*, BBC World Service, 23 December 1984.
43. *The Greatest Paper In The World – The Times*, Thames TV, December 1984.
44. Harold Evans, *Good Times, Bad Times*, Weidenfeld & Nicholson, 1983.
45. *Ibid*.
46. *Ibid*.
47. *Time Out*, 20 November 1985.

48. *Time Out*, 20 November 1985.
49. *Guardian*, 27 April 1984.
50. *Press Barons*, BBC1, 23 December 1984.
51. James Curran and Jean Seaton, *op. cit*.
52. *Press Barons*, BBC World Service, 23 December 1984.
53. *Ibid*.
54. *Ibid*.
55. *Ibid*.
56. *Free Press*, Journal of the Campaign for Press and Broadcasting Freedom, November/December 1984.
57. Harold Evans, *op. cit*.
58. Michael Leapman, *op. cit*.
59. *The Journalist*, February 1981.
60. *Observer*, June 1985.
61. *Free Press*, May/June 1982.
62. Letter to *Socialist Worker*, 12 May 1984.
63. David Leigh, *The Frontiers of Secrecy*, London: Junction Books, 1980.
64. James Margach, *The Abuse of Power*, London: W.H. Allen, 1978.
65. *Platform One*, BBC1, 15 November 1979.
66. *UK Press Gazette*, 28 October 1985.
67. *Times*, 14 May 1985.
68. *Daily Telegraph*, 25 March 1985.
69. *Daily Mail*, 26 April 1979.
70. *Daily Express*, 29 March 1979.
71. *Daily Express*, 11 April 1979.
72. The other guests at the lunch were Jacob de Rothschild, Lord and Lady Hartwell, Lord Delfont, David Montagu, Gianni Agnelli, Roland Cramer, Gerald Oldham, Jack Durlacher, Sir Charles Forte, Sir Barrie Heath, Sir Michael Milne-Watson, Sir John King, Angus and James Ogilvy, Leonard Sainer, Mark Weinburg, Gerry Akroyd, Marquis of Tavistock, John Sainsbury, Sir David Napley, Peter Gibbings, Sir John Spencer Wills, Kingman Brewster, Jeremy Bullmore, Garry Weston, Sir Eric Penn, Lt. Colonel Blair Stewart-Wilson, Geoffrey Knight, Charles Tidbury, Peter Bennett, David Somerset, Howard Thomas, Geoffrey Kent and Raymond Seymour.
73. The Kenneth Allsop Memorial Lecture, Edinburgh University, 14 November 1985.

74. *Ibid*.
75. David Leigh, *op. cit*.
76. *Guardian*, 8 October 1985

2. Benn – the Socialist Threat

1. *Guardian*, 9 October 1980.
2. *Daily Express*, 1 February 1975.
3. *Sun*, 28 May 1981.
4. *Daily Express*, 28 May 1981.
5. *Daily Mail*, 1 February 1975.
6. *Sunday Mirror*, 11 November 1979.
7. *Daily Mail*, 26 May 1981.
8. *Sun*, 26 September 1981.
9. Tony Benn, *Speeches*, London: Spokesman Books, 1974.
10. *Daily Mirror*, 4 June 1970.
11. *London Evening Standard*, 7 October 1969.
12. *Sunday Times*, 12 October 1969.
13. *Observer*, 12 October 1969.
14. *Daily Mirror*, 15 June 1971.
15. *Sunday Times*, 7 November 1971.
16. *Tony Benn, op. cit*.
17. *Daily Telegraph*, 1 June 1973.
18. *Daily Express*, 11 May 1973.
19. *Sun*, 3 October 1973.
20. *Sunday Telegraph*, 13 May 1973.
21. *Daily Express*, 3 October 1973.
22. *The Editors*, BBC1, 10 June 1973.
23. *News of the World*, 30 October 1973.
24. *Daily Mail*, 22 April 1974.
25. *Sun*, 8 May 1975.
26. *Daily Mail*, 1 August 1974.
27. *Daily Mail*, 16 January 1975.
28. *Guardian*, 22 February 1974.
29. *Sun*, 12 June 1974.
30. *Daily Telegraph*, 31 July 1974.
31. *Daily Mail*, 17 May 1975.
32. *Daily Mail*, 11 June 1974.
33. *Daily Express*, 26 June 1974.
34. *Daily Mail*, 22 April 1974.

35. Anthony Shrimsley, who died in November 1985, wrote a favourable account of the 1964 Labour government entitled *Harold's First 100 Days*. He was also a former political editor of the *Sunday Mirror* and the *Sun*, and editor of *Now* magazine which was launched by Sir James Goldsmith but closed under a mountain of debt.

36. *World in Action*, Granada Television, 5 March 1984.

37. *Daily Mail*, 2 August 1974.

38. *Sunday Times*, 18 August 1974.

39. *Sun*, 14 June 1974.

40. *Guardian*, 25 March 1980.

41. *Daily Mail*, 1 February 1975.

42. *Times*, 16 May 1975.

43. Kenneth Tynan, *More Words*, London: BBC Publications 1975.

44. *Daily Express*, 14 March 1975.

45. *Daily Express*, 24 April 1975.

46. *Sun*, 24 April 1975.

47. *Daily Telegraph*, 26 April 1975.

48. Harold Wilson, *Final Term: The Labour Government 1974-76*, London: Weidenfeld & Nicholson, 1979.

49. Peter Hennessy, Michael Cockerill and David Walker, *Sources Close To The Prime Minister*, London: Macmillan, 1984.

50. Uwe Kitzinger, *Diplomacy and Persuasion: How Britain Joined The Common Market*, London: Thames & Hudson, 1973.

51. David Butler and Uwe Kitzinger, *The 1975 Referendum*, London: Macmillan, 1976.

52. *London Evening News*, 28 April 1975.

53. *London Evening News*, 14 May 1975.

54. *World in Action*, Granada Television, 5 March 1984.

55. *Sunday Express*, 11 May 1975.

56. *Sun*, 21 May 1975.

57. *Times*, 16 May 1975.

58. David Butler and Uwe Kitzinger, *op. cit*.

59. *Times*, 19 May 1975.

60. *Sun*, 20 May 1975.

61. *Daily Mirror*, 20 May 1975.

62. *Daily Mirror*, 29 May 1975.

63. *Daily Mirror*, 26 May 1975.

64. *Sun*, 28 May 1975.

65. On 20 March 1981, Mrs Thatcher wrote to Sir John Junor: 'The things that stuck in your gullet were the things that stuck in mine too... We must have a talk again soon. Yours ever, Margaret'. This was published instead of a preface to Junor's book, *The Best of J.J* (London: Sidgwick & Jackson, 1981). Sir John Junor was knighted later that year in the New Year's Honours List.
66. *Sunday Express*, 1 June 1975.
67. *Sun*, 3 June 1975.
68. Alfred Browne, *Tony Benn: The Making of a Politician*, London: W.H. Allen, 1983.
69. Letter from Ernest Wistrich to *Labour Weekly*, 31 October 1977.
70. *The Editors*, BBC1, 26 June 1977.
71. *Sun*, 11 May 1979.
72. Letter from Sir Larry Lamb to Tony Benn, 14 May 1979.
73. *Daily Mail*, 27 October 1979.
74. *Daily Express*, 5 July 1979.
75. *Daily Mail*, 11 July 1980.
76. *Sun*, 11 July 1980.
77. *Daily Star*, 30 September 1980.
78. *Daily Express*, 30 September 1980.
79. *Times*, 30 September 1980.
80. *Daily Mirror*, 1 October 1980.
81. *Daily Express*, 1 October 1980.
82. *Daily Mail*, 1 October 1980.
83. *Daily Express*, 24 September 1979.
84. *Sun*, 4 October 1980.
85. *Sun*, 4 June 1981.
86. *Daily Express*, 22 May 1981.
87. *Times*, 3 April 1981.
88. *Daily Star*, 7 April 1981.
89. *Sun*, 3 April 1981.
90. *Daily Mirror*, 3 April 1981.
91. *Guardian*, 3 April 1981.
92. *Guardian*, 28 May 1981.
93. *Daily Mail*, 8 April 1981.
94. Undated letter to the Press Council.
95. Letter to the Press Council, 27 June 1981.
96. Statement to the Press Council, 25 October 1981.

97. *Daily Mail*, 11 May 1981.
98. *The World This Weekend*, BBC Radio 4, 20 September 1981.
99. *Daily Express*, 1 June 1981.
100. Michael Foot, *Debts of Honour*, London: Davis Poynter, 1980.
101. *Sun*, 18 September 1981.
102. *Sun*, 26 September 1981.
103. *News of the World*, 13 September 1981.
104. *Sun*, 7 September 1981.
105. *Daily Mirror*, 10 September 1981.
106. *London Standard*, 25 September 1981.
107. *New Statesman*, 25 September 1981.
108. *Times*, 22 September 1981.
109. *New Statesman*, 25 September 1981.
110. *Guardian*, 22 September 1981.
111. *Sun*, 22 September 1981.
112. Letter from the Head Office of the Bank of Bermuda to Mr H.J. Witheridge, their London representative, 6 November 1981.
113. *Tribune*, 27 October 1981.
114. *Observer*, 17 May 1981.
115. *Tribune*, 27 October 1981.
116. Letter from Harold Evans to Tony Benn, 25 September 1981.
117. Letter from Tony Benn to Harold Evans, 23 October 1981.
118. Letter to the author, 24 July 1984.
119. Research study by Steve Taylor for the Labour Party in October 1981. The poll was conducted in a marginal Midlands constituency where 500 potential voters were interviewed.
120. *Sun*, 16 January 1984.
121. *Daily Mail*, 16 January 1984.
122. *New Statesman*, 17 February 1984.
123. *World in Action*, Granada TV, 5 March 1984.
124. *Daily Express*, 7 March 1984.
125. *Daily Telegraph*, 1 March 1984.
126. *Derbyshire Times*, 24 February 1984.
127. *Ibid*.
128. *Observer*, 26 February 1984.
129. *World in Action*, Granada TV, 5 March 1984.
130. *Daily Express*, 28 February 1984.

131. *Sunday Express*, 26 February 1984.
132. *World in Action*, Granada TV, 5 March 1984.
133. *Ibid*.
134. *Sun*, 1 March 1984.
135. Letter to Tony Banks, Labour MP for Newham Northwest, 3 April 1984.
136. *Daily Mail*, 13 August 1980.
137. *Guardian*, 29 August 1980.
138. *Daily Telegraph*, 4 January 1975.
139. *World in Action*, Granada TV, 5 March 1984.
140. Peter Hennessy, Michael Cockerill and David Walker, *op. cit*.
141. Alan Freeman, *The Benn Heresy*, London: Pluto Press, 1982.

3. Ken Livingstone and the GLC

1. Quoted in Nigel Matheson and Peter Gerard Pearse, *Ken Livingstone or the End of Civilization as We Know It*, London: Proteus Books, 1982.
2. *Guardian*, 21 December 1981.
3. *Guardian*, 21 December 1981.
4. John Carvel, *Citizen Ken*, London: Chatto & Windus, 1984.
5. Nigel Matheson and Peter Gerard Pearse, *op. cit*.
6. *Daily Mail*, 9 May 1981.
7. *Sun*, 9 May 1981.
8. *Standard*, 12 May 1981.
9. *Daily Telegraph*, 31 August 1981.
10. *New Society*, 16 February 1984.
11. Nigel Matheson and Peter Gerard Pearse, *op. cit*.
12. Letter to Sir David English, 9 October 1981.
13. Letter from Colin Newman, Scientific and Professional Secretary, British Psychological Society, to Press Council, 23 June 1982.
14. Undated letter to the Press Council.
15. Letter to Professor Blackman, 14 September 1981.
16. Press Council evidence, submitted on 4 May 1982.
17. Letter to Professor Blackman, 28 October 1981.
18. Letter to the Press Council, 26 October 1981.
19. Press Council evidence, submitted on 4 May 1982.

20. Letter to Mr C. Moshenska and Mr R. Salkie, of Hove, Sussex, 27 October 1981.
21. *Sunday Express*, 27 September 1981.
22. *Sunday Express*, 15 November 1981.
23. *Sun*, 9 February 1983.
24. John Carvel, *op. cit.*
25. Letter to the *Standard*, 10 September 1981.
26. Interview with *East End News*.
27. *Daily Express*, 23 February 1983.
28. *Daily Mail*, 16 February 1983.
29. *Sun*, 19 August 1981.
30. *Daily Express*, 19 August 1981.
31. *News of the World*, 21 February 1982.
32. Letter to the *Times*, 14 October 1981.
33. John Carvel, *op. cit.*
34. *Sun*, 13 October 1981.
35. *Times*, 13 October 1981.
36. *Daily Express*, 13 October 1981.
37. *Daily Mail*, 13 October 1981.
38. *City Limits*, 23 October 1981.
39. *Sun*, 9 August 1982.
40. This was pointed out in *Propaganda War* by Liz Curtis, London: Pluto Press, 1983.
41. *Daily Express*, 6 December 1982.
42. *Daily Star*, 7 December 1982.
43. Press Council evidence, submitted on 16 March 1983.
44. *Sun*, 8 December 1982.
45. *City Limits*, 17 December 1982.
46. *Daily Star*, 8 December 1982.
47. *Sun*, 6 December 1982.
48. *Sun*, 27 August 1982.
49. *Daily Express*, 29 August 1983.
50. *Standard*, 24 November 1982.
51. *Sun*, 11 November 1981.
52. *Standard*, 28 October 1981.
53. *Sun*, 29 October 1981.
54. *Daily Mail*, 11 November 1981.
55. *Daily Express*, 11 November 1981.
56. *Sun*, 11 November 1981.
57. *Sun*, 9 March 1982.

58. Speech to the Greater London Labour Party conference, 6 March 1982.
59. Nigel Matheson and Peter Gerard Pearse, *op. cit*.
60. *Sun*, 26 March 1982.
61. *Daily Express*, 26 March 1982.
62. *Daily Express*, 27 December 1982.
63. After joining the *Mail on Sunday*, Holliday turned his attention to other Labour councils. On 13 February 1983, he wrote a feature entitled, 'The Mad, Mad, Mad, World of Islington'.
64. *Daily Mail*, 20 April 1983.
65. *Guardian*, 20 January 1984.
66. *Daily Express*, 30 April 1984.
67. *Financial Times*, 14 September 1984.
68. *Standard*, 6 August 1984.
69. *Daily Express*, 30 August 1984.
70. *Daily Mail*, 20 September 1984.
71. *Observer*, 26 May 1985.
72. *Daily Mail*, 30 May 1981.
73. *Sun*, 28 January 1984.
74. *Sunday Times*, 1 July 1984.
75. John Carvel, *op. cit*.
76. John Carvel, *op. cit*.

4. Racism in Fleet Street

1. Martin Kettle and Lucy Hodges, *Uprising – the Police, the People and the Riots in Britain's Cities*, London: Pan, 1982.
2. *Guardian*, 27 November 1985.
3. *Sunday Telegraph*, 29 November 1981.
4. *Times*, 2 July 1981.
5. *Sunday Express*, 19 April 1981.
6. John Benyon (ed.), *Scarman and After*, Pergamon Press, 1984.
7. Scarman Report, 3.108 to 3.110.
8. Scarman Report 3.101 to 3.103.
9. *Observer*, 12 April 1981.
10. *Sunday Telegraph*, 12 April 1981.
11. *Standard*, 13 April 1981.
12. *Times*, 7 September 1981.
13. Harold Evans, *Good Times, Bad Times*, London: Weidenfeld & Nicholson, 1983.

14. *Standard*, 10 July 1981.
15. *Daily Mail*, 10 July 1981.
16. *Daily Mail*, 10 July 1981.
17. Martin Kettle and Lucy Hodges *op. cit.*
18. *Times*, 10 July 1981.
19. *Daily Mirror*, 8 July 1981.
20. *Daily Telegraph*, 24 March 1982. Taken from *The Old People Of Lambeth* by Charles Moore, published by the Salisbury Group, 1982.
21. Steve Chibnall, *Law-and-Order News*, London: Tavistock Publications, 1976.
22. *Daily Mail*, 5 March 1981.
23. *Guardian*, 15 March 1982.
24. *Sun*, 23 March 1983.
25. *Daily Mail*, 23 March 1983.
26. *Daily Telegraph*, 24 March 1983.
27. *Daily Mirror*, 24 March 1983.
28. *Sunday Times*, 27 March 1983.
29. *Observer*, 8 March 1981.
30. *Ibid.*
31. Alastair Hetherington, *News, Newspapers and Television*, London: Macmillan, 1985.
32. *Daily Star*, 4 March 1981.
33. *Times*, 4 March 1981.
34. *South East London Mercury*, 6 March 1981.
35. *Standard*, 3 June 1981.
36. *Daily Mail*, 2 June 1981.
37. *Sun*, 2 June 1981.
38. *Daily Express*, 2 June 1981.
39. *Standard*, 3 June 1981.
40. *Searchlight*, July 1981.
41. *Guardian*, 19 July 1985.
42. *Sun*, 6 September 1984.
43. *New Socialist*, November 1985.
44. *Sun*, 11 September 1985.
45. *Sun*, 11 September 1985.
46. *Daily Express*, 11 September 1985.
47. *Observer*, 19 November 1985.
48. *City Limits*, 4 October 1985.
49. *Guardian*, 12 September 1985.

50. *City Limits*, 11 October 1985.
51. *Daily Star*, 8 October 1985.
52. *Daily Telegraph*, 8 October 1985.
53. *Daily Express*, 8 October 1985.
54. *Observer*, 13 October 1985.
55. *Standard*, 17 October 1985.
56. *Daily Mail*, 10 October 1985.
57. Seminar on 'Race and the Media', Kenilworth Hotel, London, 17 October 1975. Organized by the Community Relations Commission and the National Union of Journalists.
58. *Root*, October 1981.
59. Part of a paper for the Runnymede Trust and presented to a conference of editors in Birmingham, March 1970.
60. *Ibid*.
61. *Daily Mirror*, 19 May 1985.
62. *Daily Mail*, 9 November 1981

5. The Battle for Bermondsey

 1. *Sun*, 5 December 1981.
 2. *Daily Mail*, 7 December 1981.
 3. *Sunday Mirror*, 6 December 1981.
 4. Letter to the *New Statesman*, 8 August 1975.
 5. *New Statesman*, 21 September 1984.
 6. *Daily Express*, 9 September 1982.
 7. Letter to Peter Robinson, Press Officer for Bermondsey Labour Party, 29 November 1982.
 8. *New Statesman*, 14 January 1983.
 9. *Gay News*, 13 October 1982.
10. *Open Space*, BBC2, 4 November 1985.
11. *Capital Gay*, 18 March 1983.
12. *Open Space*, BBC2, 15 December 1983.
13. *Open Space*, BBC2, 15 December 1983.
14. *Daily Mail*, 4 December 1981.
15. *Daily Telegraph*, 4 December 1981.
16. *Sunday Mirror*, 27 February 1983.
17. *Daily Mirror*, 4 December 1981.
18. *Sun*, 5 December 1981.
19. *Sunday Express*, 6 December 1981.
20. *Financial Times*, 23 February 1983.

21.   *Sheffield Star*, 20 January 1984.
22. ` Michael Crick, *Militant*, London: Faber & Faber, 1984.
23.   *Sun*, 13 February 1983.
24.   Letter to Peter Robinson, 30 December 1982.
25.   *Ibid*.
26.   *New Statesman*, 14 January 1983.
27.   *Sunday Mirror*, 27 February 1983.
28.   *Mail on Sunday*, 13 February 1983.
29.   *Daily Express*, 4 August 1982.
30.   *Daily Mirror*, 4 December 1981.
31.   *Daily Express*, 4 December 1981.
32.   *Sun*, 4 December 1981.
33.   *Guardian*, 8 December 1981.
34.   *Observer*, 13 December 1981.
35.   *Daily Telegraph*, 4 August 1982.
36.   *Daily Star*, 3 August 1982.
37.   Michael Crick, *op. cit*.
38.   *Daily Mail*, 21 February 1983.
39.   *Standard*, 23 February 1983.
40.   *Sun*, 24 February 1983.
41.   *Journalist*, November/December 1983.
42.   Letter to *Capital Gay*, 25 March 1983.
43.   *Open Space*, BBC2, 15 December 1983.
44.   Letter to the *Guardian*, 8 March 1983.
45.   *Open Space*, BBC2, 15 December 1983.
46.   *Times*, 19 February 1983.
47.   *Open Space*, BBC2, 15 December 1983.
48.   *Sun*, 26 February 1983.
49.   *Open Space*, BBC2, 15 December 1983.
50.   *The Friday Alternative*, Channel 4, 25 February 1983.
51.   Peter Tatchell, *The Battle for Bermondsey*, London: Heretic Books, 1983.
52.   *Open Space*, BBC2, 15 December 1983.
53.   Interview during a film made by first-year students for a B.A. film course at the London College of Printing in November 1983.
54.   *Standard*, 14 February 1984.

6.   Peace Women at the Wire

 1.   *Guardian*, 25 March 1982.

2. *Daily Express*, 16 November 1982.
3. *Marxism Today*, February 1983.
4. *Time Out*, 17 December 1982.
5. *Sanity*, November 1985.
6. *Daily Mail*, 13 December 1982.
7. *Ibid*.
8. *Times*, 14 December 1982.
9. *Sunday Telegraph*, 12 December 1982.
10. *The World This Weekend*, Radio 4, 12 December 1982.
11. *Peace News*, 21 January 1983.
12. *Sun*, 14 December 1982.
13. *Daily Express*, 14 December 1982.
14. *Guardian*, 14 December 1982.
15. *Daily Mirror*, 14 December 1982.
16. *Daily Telegraph*, 14 December 1982.
17. *Daily Mail*, 13 December 1982.
18. *Sun*, 13 December 1982.
19. *Observer*, 30 January 1983.
20. *Daily Mail*, 20 January 1983.
21. Peter Hennessy, Michael Cockerill and David Walker, *Sources Close to the Prime Minister*, London: Macmillan, 1984.
22. *New Statesman*, 21 January 1983.
23. *Times*, 3 March 1983.
24. *Guardian*, 3 March 1983.
25. *Observer*, 3 March 1985.
26. *Sunday Times*, 16 October 1983.
27. *Daily Telegraph*, 6 August 1983.
28. Mr Heseltine later confirmed this view in a statement to the Press Council.
29. *Ms London* magazine, 14 February 1983.
30. Letter from Brian McDonald, of the *Newbury Weekly News*, to Daphne Francis, 10 October 1983.
31. *Ms London*, 14 February 1983.
32. *Ibid*.
33. Leaflet produced by Philip Braithwaite for Birmingham CND.
34. Letter to Daphne Francis, 5 July 1983.
35. Letter to Philip Braithwaite, 23 March 1984.
36. Letter to Colin Webb, 28 March 1984.
37. Letter to Philip Braithwaite, 22 March 1984.
38. Letter to Philip Braithwaite, 17 April 1984.

39. Letter to Philip Braithwaite, 4 May 1984.
40. Letter to Philip Braithwaite, 11 April 1984.
41. Letter to Philip Braithwaite, 19 April 1984.
42. *Times*, 10 February 1983.
43. *Daily Express*, 12 July 1983.
44. Letter to the Press Council, 9 January 1984.
45. Letter to the Press Council, 19 December 1983.
46. Statement from the following Greenham Peace women: Sarah Green, Beatrice Kindred, Amanda Bush, Katrina Howse, Sue Popper and Arlene Trudeau.
47. Letter to the Press Council, 9 November 1983.
48. Henry Porter, *Lies, Damn Lies and Some Exclusives*, London: Chatto & Windus, 1984.
49. *City Limits*, 23 February 1984.
50. Letter to the *Guardian*, 24 January 1984.
51. *Daily Mirror*, 12 December 1983.
52. *Daily Express*, 12 December 1983.
53. *Free Press*, journal of the Campaign for Press and Broadcasting Freedom, November/December 1985.
54. *Free Press*, January/February 1984.
55. *Daily Express*, 13 December 1983.
56. *Sun*, 30 December 1983.
57. *Daily Star*, 11 April 1983.
58. *Tribune*, 16 July 1983.
59. *Ibid*.
60. Letter to the *Daily Mail*, 15 September 1983.
61. Letter to the *Daily Mail*, 15 September 1983.
62. *Ibid*.
63. Letter to the Press Council, 15 September 1983.
64. *Ibid*.
65. Letter to Ann Pettitt, 10 October 1983.
66. Alice Cook and Gwyn Kirk, *Greenham Women Everywhere*, London: Pluto Press, 1983.
67. *Financial Times*, 18 December 1982.
68. Submission to the Press Council, 18 February 1985.
69. *Daily Express*, 9 April 1984.
70. Dr Lynne Jones (ed.), *Keeping the Peace*, London: Women's Press, 1983.
71. *Sanity*, November 1985.
72. *Daily Express*, 15 December 1982.

73. *Sun*, 7 November 1983.
74. *Sunday Telegraph*, 12 December 1982.
75. *Sun*, 26 August 1983.
76. Bel Mooney, *Differences of Opinion*, London: Robson Books, 1984.
77. *Spare Rib*, February 1984.
78. Letter to Bel Mooney, 19 April 1984.
79. Bel Mooney, *op. cit*.
80. *Guardian*, 28 May 1983.
81. *Guardian*, 30 October 1985.
82. *Listener*, 17 October 1985.
83. Joint CND/Campaign for Press and Broadcasting Freedom meeting, 12 October 1984.
84. *Guardian*, 30 August 1985.
85. *Daily Mail*, 13 January 1983.
86. *Sun*, 14 December 1982.
87. *Daily Star*, 4 November 1983.
88. *Daily Mirror*, 23 November 1983.

7. The 1983 General Election

1. *Daily Mail*, 20 November 1923.
2. *Daily Express*, 5 June 1945.
3. *Daily Mail*, 26 April 1979.
4. *Daily Mirror*, 11 May 1983.
5. *Daily Mail*, 21 October 1980.
6. *Sun*, 1 October 1979.
7. *Daily Express*, 4 October 1979.
8. *Daily Mirror*, 11 May 1983.
9. *Times*, 17 May 1983.
10. *Daily Mail*, 16 May 1983.
11. *Sunday Times Business News*, 22 May 1983.
12. *Daily Telegraph*, 17 May 1983.
13. *Observer*, 22 May 1983.
14. *Times*, 27 May 1983.
15. *Guardian*, 25 May 1983.
16. *News of the World*, 22 May 1983.
17. *Mail on Sunday*, 22 May 1983.
18. *Daily Mail*, 24 May 1983.

19. *Daily Express*, 24 May 1983.
20. *Daily Mail*, 28 May 1983.
21. *Observer*, 5 June 1983.
22. *The World This Weekend*, BBC Radio 4, 29 May 1983.
23. *Daily Mail*, 30 May 1983.
24. *Daily Express*, 30 May 1983.
25. *Daily Telegraph*, 30 May 1983.
26. *Financial Times*, 31 May 1983.
27. Letter from James Milne to the *Scottish Daily Express*, 6 May 1983.
28. Letter to Pat Smith, National Press Officer for the People's March for Jobs, 18 May 1983.
29. Letter to Leith McGrandle, 20 May 1983.
30. Letter to Pat Smith, 23 May 1983.
31. Letter to Leith McGrandle, 25 May 1983.
32. Pat Smith, 25 May 1983.
33. Letter to the *Scottish Daily Express*, 6 May 1983.
34. *Daily Mail*, 6 December 1923.
35. *Sun*, 10 May 1983.
36. *Daily Express*, 9 April 1979.
37. *Daily Express*, 2 June 1983.
38. *UK Press Gazette*, 28 October 1985.
39. *Daily Mirror*, 23 June 1983.
40. *Listener*, 2 June 1983.
41. *Standard*, 2 June 1983.
42. *Daily Express*, 10 May 1983.
43. *Daily Express*, 10 May 1983.
44. *Daily Express*, 23 May 1983.
45. *Sun*, 6 June 1983.
46. *Sun*, 2 June 1983.
47. *Observer*, 22 May 1983.
48. *Sunday Telegraph*, 22 May 1983.
49. Robert Harris, *The Making of Neil Kinnock*, London: Faber & Faber, 1984.
50. The following newspapers endorsed the Conservative Party unequivocally: *Daily Mail*, *Sun*, *Daily Express*, *Mail on Sunday*, *Times*, *Daily Telegraph*, *Sunday Express*, *News of the World* and *Sunday Telegraph*. These papers gave the Tory government a qualified endorsement: *Daily Star*, *Sunday Times* and *Financial Times*. Finally, the *Guardian*, *Observer* and *Sunday People*

opposed the Thatcher government but urged its readers to vote either for the SDP/Liberal Alliance or tactically in their constituencies in order to keep the Conservative candidate out.

51. *Economist*, 28 May 1983.
52. *Observer*, 5 June 1983.
53. *Guardian*, 15 June 1984.
54. David Butler, *The 1983 Election*, London: Macmillan, 1984.
55. *Ibid*.

8. The Miners' Strike

1. *Times*, 4 March 1985.
2. *Union World*, Channel 4, 8 July 1984.
3. Radio Poland, English-language radio interview, 31 May 1985. Maxwell had just visited General Jaruzelski for an interview for a book which was published by his company Pergamon Press *Selected Speeches of General Jaruzelski*.
4. Letter to the *Times*, 23 June 1985.
5. Radio Poland, 31 May 1985.
6. *Commercial Breaks*, BBC2, 12 July 1985.
7. Geoffrey Goodman, *The Miners' Strike*, London: Pluto Press, 1985.
8. Letter to the author, 13 December 1984.
9. *Media Week*, 8 February 1985.
10. *Guardian*, 10 October 1984.
11. *Political Quarterly*, Winter 1985.
12. *Standard*, 29 February 1984. Fallon said: 'It [the *Sunday Times*] has got to go back and down a generation. That's obviously what Murdoch feels appointing an editor [Andrew Neil] at 34 and me at 39.'
13. Department of Trade Investigation into House of Fraser and Lonhro, conducted by John Griffiths, QC, and published by HMSO, 1984.
14. Debate on investigative journalism, Edinburgh TV Festival, August 1984.
15. *Times*, 3 August 1984.
16. *Times*, 26 January 1985.
17. The *Sunday Times* Insight Team, *358 Days That Shook The World – Thatcher, Scargill and the Miners*, London: Andre Deutsch/Coronet Books, 1985.

18. Michael Crick, *Scargill and the Miners*, Penguin Special, 1985.
19. *Ibid*.
20. *Sunday Telegraph*, 22 July 1984.
21. *Sunday Telegraph*, 9 December 1984.
22. *Sunday Telegraph*, 10 March 1985 and 28 July 1985.
23. *New Statesman*, 25 January 1985.
24. *Daily Mail*, 3 April 1984.
25. *Union World*, Channel 4, 7 July 1984.
26. Letter to Dave Shepherd, member of the Campaign for Press and Broadcasting Freedom National Committee, 20 June 1984.
27. *Daily Mirror*, 22 November 1984.
28. *Guardian*, 17 May 1985.
29. Geoffrey Goodman, *op. cit*.
30. Paul Foot column, *Daily Mirror*, 17 January 1985.
31. *Guardian*, 3 December 1984.
32. *Mail on Sunday*, 25 March 1984.
33. *Mail on Sunday*, 5 August 1984.
34. *Union World*, Channel 4, 7 July 1984.
35. *Sunday Express*, 30 September 1984.
36. *Daily Express*, 3 September 1984.
37. Letter to the *Mail on Sunday*, 18 November 1984.
38. Letter to the *Mail on Sunday*, 18 November 1984.
39. Letter to the General Secretary of the National Union of Journalists, 18 March 1985.
40. *Daily Express*, 13 November 1984.
41. *Observer*, 1 July 1984.
42. *Guardian*, 9 October 1985.
43. *Times*, 5 November 1984.
44. *Sunday Times*, 18 November 1984.
45. *Daily Express*, 14 April 1984.
46. *Daily Express*, 28 February 1985.
47. *Union World*, Channel 4, 7 July 1984.
48. BBC1 News, 7 March 1985.
49. *Sunday Times*, 20 May 1984.
50. *Daily Telegraph*, 25 March 1985.
51. *Standard*, 16 April 1984.
52. *Sunday Telegraph*, 7 October 1984.
53. *Standard*, 1 October 1984.
54. *Guardian*, 10 October 1984.
55. *Sunday Express*, 19 August 1984.

56. *Sunday Times*, 20 May 1984.
57. *Guardian*, 7 January 1985.
58. *Sunday Times* magazine, 23 December 1984.
59. *Sunday Express*, 20 May 1984.
60. *Sunday Telegraph*, 2 December 1984.
61. *Sun*, 22 January 1985.
62. *Mail on Sunday*, 25 March 1984.
63. *Union World*, Channel 4, 7 July 1984.
64. Letter to to Caroline Rees, 14 August 1984.
65. *Guardian*, 17 May 1985.
66. *Guardian*, 3 June 1985.
67. Letter to the *New Statesman*, 25 October 1985.
68. *Media Week*, 15 February 1985.
69. *Sunday Times*, 12 August 1984.
70. *Daily Express*, 19 April 1984.
71. Nicholas Jones, *Strikes and the Media*, Oxford: Basil Blackwell, 1986.
72. Geoffrey Goodman, *op. cit*

9. Conclusion: What Is To Be Done?

1. A.J.P. Taylor, *Beaverbrook*, London: Hamish Hamilton, 1972.
2. *Spectator*, 26 January 1985.
3. *Daily Mail*, 17 February 1983.
4. Letter to the *Times*, 12 November 1982.
5. Letter to Arthur Latham, 24 November 1982.
6. *Sun*, 2 October 1982.
7. *Daily Mail*, 17 February 1983.
8. *Times*, 4 August 1982.
9. *Spectator*, 15 September 1984.
10. 'The Right Of Reply In Europe', paper prepared by Denis MacShane, 6 March 1982.
11. *Guardian*, 30 July 1984.
12. *Guardian*, 1 November 1983.
13. Harold Evans, *Good Times, Bad Times*, London: Weidenfeld & Nicholson, 1983.
14. *Guardian*, 10 June 1985.
15. *Observer*, 15 September 1985.
16. David Butler, *The 1983 General Election*, London: Macmillan 1984.

17. *New Socialist*, January 1985.
18. Henry Porter, *Lies, Damned Lies and Some Exclusives*, London: Chatto & Windus, 1984.

Index